TEACHER'S EDITION

Vocabulary for Achievement

SIXTH COURSE

Margaret Ann Richek

Arlin T. McRae

Susan K. Weiler

GREAT SOURCE
WILMINGTON, MA

AUTHORS

Margaret Ann Richek
Professor of Education, Northeastern Illinois University; consultant in reading and vocabulary study; author of The World of Words *(Houghton Mifflin)*

Arlin T. McRae
Supervisor of English, Evansville-Vanderburgh School Corporation, Evansville, Indiana; Adjunct Instructor in English, University of Evansville

Susan K. Weiler
Instructor of Art History at John Carroll University in Cleveland, Ohio; former teacher of Latin, Beaumont School for Girls, Cleveland Heights, Ohio

CONSULTANT

Larry S. Krieger
Social Studies Supervisor, Montgomery Township Public Schools, New Jersey; author of World History *and* U.S. History *(D.C. Heath), co-author of* Mastering the Verbal SAT 1/PSAT *(Great Source)*

CLASSROOM CONSULTANTS

Jack Pelletier
Teacher of English, Mira Loma High School, Sacramento, California

Valerie M. Webster
Teacher of English, Walnut Hill School, Natick, Massachusetts

ACKNOWLEDGMENTS

Definitions for the three hundred words taught in the textbook are based on Houghton Mifflin dictionaries—in particular, the *Houghton Mifflin College Dictionary,* copyright © 1986, and *The American Heritage Dictionary of the English Language, Third Edition,* copyright © 1992. The dictionary passages in the skill lesson on pages 19–20 are adapted from the latter, as is the pronunciation key on the inside front cover. Also on pages 19–20 are passages from *Roget's International Thesaurus,* 4th edition revised by Robert L. Chapman (Thomas Y. Crowell), as follows: entries 630.9 (p. 485), 691.9 (p. 544), and 893.21 (p. 698), as well as index entry for *improve* (p. 1018). Copyright © 1977 by Harper & Row, Publishers, Inc. Reprinted by permission of Harper & Row, Publishers, Inc. The reading passage on pages 39–40 is from Robert F. Biehler and Lynne Hudson, *Developmental Psychology,* Third Edition, copyright © 1986 by Houghton Mifflin Company. Reprinted by permission of Houghton Mifflin Company.

(Acknowledgments are continued on the bottom of page iv.)

CREDITS

Production: PC&F, Inc.
Illustrations: Nanette Biers: pages 37, 65, 97, 111, 145; Sylvia Giblin: pages 85, 131, 137, 165; Norman Nicholson: pages 25, 45, 51, 71, 77; Phyllis Rockne: pages 17, 57, 171

Printed in the United States of America

International Standard Book Number: 0-669-46491-0

1 2 3 4 5 6 7 8 9 10 HS 04 03 02 01 00 99 98

CONTENTS

(Acknowledgments, continued)

The reading passage on pages 79–80 is from *The Journals of Lewis and Clark* by Bernard de Voto. Copyright 1953 by Bernard de Voto. Copyright © renewed 1981 by Avis de Voto. Reprinted by permission of Houghton Mifflin Company. The reading passage on page T11 is abridged from *Comparative Economic Systems,* Second Edition, by Paul R. Gregory and Robert C. Stuart. Copyright © 1985 by Houghton Mifflin Company. Reprinted by permission of Houghton Mifflin Company. The reading passage on pages T11–T12 is abridged and adapted from *Patterns on the Earth: An Introduction to Geography* by Rhoads Murphey. Copyright © 1978 by Houghton Mifflin Company. Reprinted by permission of Houghton Mifflin Company. The passage on page T25 is abridged from *Introduction to Law and the Legal System,* Third Edition, by Harold J. Grilliot. Copyright © 1983 by Houghton Mifflin Company. Reprinted by permission of Houghton Mifflin Company. The passage on page T26 is abridged from *Film: Forum and Function* by George Wead and George Lellis. Copyright © 1981 by Houghton Mifflin Company. Reprinted by permission of Houghton Mifflin Company. The sample SAT questions were written by the authors and are not actual SAT questions were written by the authors and are not actual SAT questions. The directions and boxed examples were reprinted by permission of Educational Testing Service, the copyright owner. SAT and Scholastic Assessment Test are registered trademarks of the College Entrance Examination Board.

ABOUT *VOCABULARY FOR ACHIEVEMENT*

Why Study Vocabulary Systematically?

Teachers generally agree on the importance of vocabulary development in the refining of language skills. The greater the store of words we have at our disposal, the better equipped we are to comprehend what we read and to express what we think.

A systematic approach to vocabulary building helps students

- understand and use words effectively
- recognize, retain, and apply new words
- unlock meanings of new words
- learn independently for lifelong vocabulary acquisition
- improve reading comprehension across the curriculum
- improve performance on standardized tests
- select and use words forcefully in speaking and writing
- continually assimilate new words into their vocabularies

A systematic program ensures the development of the large storehouse of words that is important to achievement, both in and out of the classroom.

How Were the Vocabulary Words Selected?

The criteria for vocabulary word selection for *Vocabulary for Achievement* were three.

— The principle source for the word lists was recent Scholastic Assessment Tests (SATs), published by the College Entrance Examination Board.

— The authors and editors also consulted numerous scholarly works, including the American Heritage *Word Frequency Book*, *The Living Word Vocabulary*, and many standard thesauruses.

— Most importantly, the words were chosen for their usefulness, appropriateness to grade level, and applicability to the lesson themes or topics.

Over 80% of the *Vocabulary for Achievement* words are on a so-called "hit parade" of SAT words. The "hit parade" is a group of words representative of the difficulty level of words frequently used in analogy and sentence-completion test items in the verbal section of the SAT. Further, almost one quarter of these "hit parade" words is taught in *Vocabulary for Achievement's* Fourth Course or earlier, providing students with ample time to incorporate them into their vocabularies before encountering them on the SAT.

Vocabulary for Achievement ensures success, not only on the SAT but in lifelong vocabulary acquisition, by offering students early help with challenging new vocabulary.

A Tour of the Program

Vocabulary for Achievement is a systematic program of vocabulary development that provides comprehensive instruction and practice. In devising the seven-book program for grades 6 through 12, the authors have followed four major principles:

— Structured lessons teach best.

— Application aids retention.

— Special vocabulary-acquisition skills promote independent learning.

— Vocabulary materials must be readily accessible and easily adaptable to classroom needs.

These four principles are reflected throughout the program, which provides the structure necessary for students to learn new words; apply them in a variety of practice formats to ensure ownership; and to use dictionary, test-taking, and reading strategies to build and incorporate their growing pool of words independently. The authors' guiding principles also make the structure of the program teacher- and student-friendly.

Teacher-Friendly Elements

The consistent structure of *Vocabulary for Achievement* makes it ideal for classroom instruction or for independent use, allowing you to direct a sound and successful vocabulary program.

- **Lessons**: provide complete presentation, abundant practice (with answers), numerous examples of context, and opportunities for application.
- **Skill Features**: furnish practical strategies for ongoing vocabulary acquisition.
- **Flash Cards (in student book only)**: include all vocabulary words, with the word on one side, phonetic spelling and definition on the other. An effective tool for learning and review.

- **Tests**: 10 reproducible multiple-choice tests (with answers), each covering 3 consecutive lessons.
- **Bonuses**: 7–15 reproducible bonus activities (with answers), each covering 2–5 consecutive lessons, offer students "lighter" opportunities for reinforcement and enrichment in the forms of crossword puzzles, word searches, scrambled words, etc.
- **Teaching Suggestions**: provide concrete ideas to help you adapt the materials for special classroom needs and to extend their range and usefulness.

The Lessons

- 30 six-page lessons per level
- 10 words per lesson, theme- or root-centered
- pronunciations, part-of-speech labels, multiple definitions, etymologies, related words, usage notes, and example sentences provided dictionary-style from Houghton Mifflin dictionaries
- 4 follow-up exercises for practice in identifying definitions, using words correctly, choosing the best word, and using different forms of a word
- a reading comprehension passage, incorporating the 10 words in context, followed by a comprehension exercise. The reading passages cover all areas of the curriculum, from history, science and nature, and the arts, to myths and legends, technology, and careers.
- a writing assignment related to the theme or topic, in which students apply their newly acquired words in an effective piece of writing
- analogy exercises for practice in identifying vocabulary words in the context of word relationships
- vocabulary enrichment and activity for interesting and unusual word histories, helpful in unlocking meanings of unfamiliar words

The Anatomy of a Lesson

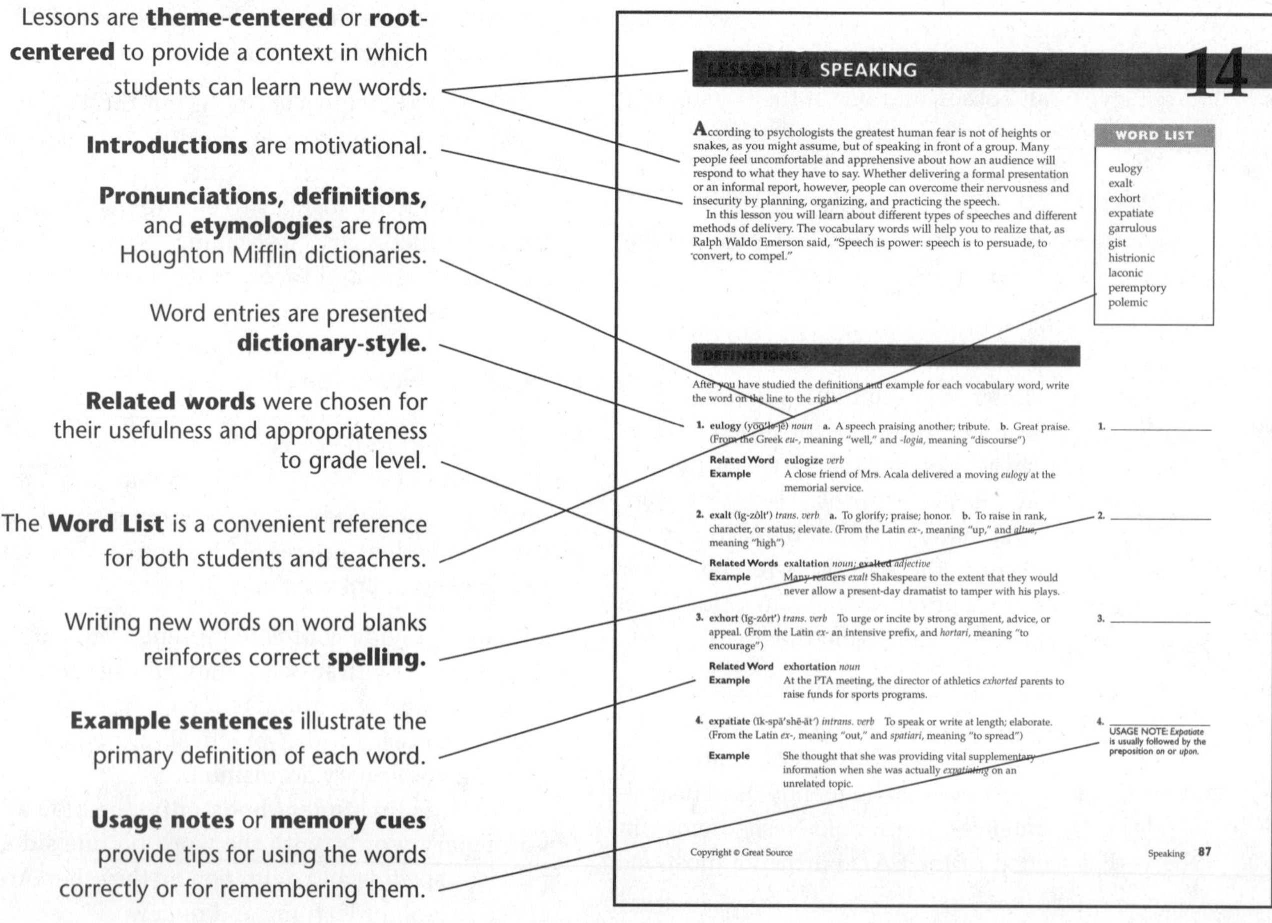

LESSON 14 SPEAKING 14

According to psychologists the greatest human fear is not of heights or snakes, as you might assume, but of speaking in front of a group. Many people feel uncomfortable and apprehensive about how an audience will respond to what they have to say. Whether delivering a formal presentation or an informal report, however, people can overcome their nervousness and insecurity by planning, organizing, and practicing the speech.

In this lesson you will learn about different types of speeches and different methods of delivery. The vocabulary words will help you to realize that, as Ralph Waldo Emerson said, "Speech is power: speech is to persuade, to convert, to compel."

WORD LIST

eulogy
exalt
exhort
expatiate
garrulous
gist
histrionic
laconic
peremptory
polemic

DEFINITIONS

After you have studied the definitions and example for each vocabulary word, write the word on the line to the right.

1. **eulogy** (yo͞o'lə-jē) *noun* **a.** A speech praising another; tribute. **b.** Great praise. (From the Greek *eu-*, meaning "well," and *-logia*, meaning "discourse") 1. ____________

Related Word **eulogize** *verb*
Example A close friend of Mrs. Acala delivered a moving *eulogy* at the memorial service.

2. **exalt** (ĭg-zôlt') *trans. verb* **a.** To glorify; praise; honor. **b.** To raise in rank, character, or status; elevate. (From the Latin *ex-*, meaning "up," and *altus*, meaning "high") 2. ____________

Related Words **exaltation** *noun*; **exalted** *adjective*
Example Many readers *exalt* Shakespeare to the extent that they would never allow a present-day dramatist to tamper with his plays.

3. **exhort** (ĭg-zôrt') *trans. verb* To urge or incite by strong argument, advice, or appeal. (From the Latin *ex-* an intensive prefix, and *hortari*, meaning "to encourage") 3. ____________

Related Word **exhortation** *noun*
Example At the PTA meeting, the director of athletics *exhorted* parents to raise funds for sports programs.

4. **expatiate** (ĭk-spā'shē-āt') *intrans. verb* To speak or write at length; elaborate. (From the Latin *ex-*, meaning "out," and *spatiari*, meaning "to spread") 4. ____________

USAGE NOTE: *Expatiate* is usually followed by the preposition *on* or *upon.*

Example She thought that she was providing vital supplementary information when she was actually *expatiating* on an unrelated topic.

Copyright © Great Source

Speaking 87

A variety of **exercise formats** provides practice and aids in **recognition, recall,** and **application** of the words.

NAME ________________ DATE ________

EXERCISE 1 MATCHING WORDS AND DEFINITIONS

Match the definition in Column B with the word in Column A. Write the letter of the correct definition on the answer line.

Column A	Column B	
1. garrulous	a. using or marked by the use of few words; terse	1. h
2. peremptory	b. a speech praising another; tribute; great praise	2. g
3. eulogy	c. to speak or write at length; elaborate	3. b
4. histrionic	d. to glorify; raise in rank, character, or status	4. f
5. exhort	e. a controversy or argument, especially one that is an attack on the opinions of another	5. i
6. polemic	f. excessively dramatic or emotional; pertaining to actors or acting	6. e
7. laconic	g. not allowing contradiction or refusal; having the nature of expressing a command	7. a
8. expatiate	h. habitually and excessively talkative	8. c
9. gist	i. to urge or incite by strong argument, advice, or appeal	9. j
10. exalt	j. the central idea of a matter; essence	10. d

EXERCISE 2 USING WORDS CORRECTLY

Each of the following statements contains an italicized vocabulary word. Decide whether the sentence is true or false, and write *True* or *False* on the answer line.

1. A shy student is usually the most *garrulous* one in the class. 1. False
2. If someone *exhorts* you to do something, he or she is offering you a casual suggestion. 2. False
3. A *eulogy* is the opening address at a large gathering, such as a political convention. 3. False
4. An aggressive rebuttal to the argument of another is a *polemic*. 4. True
5. Employees would not be likely to offer their bosses *peremptory* suggestions on how to improve the office environment. 5. True
6. If you *expatiate* on a particular subject, you deliberately fail to bring it up. 6. False
7. When you grasp the *gist* of a topic, you understand the central idea. 7. True
8. A *histrionic* individual is overly dramatic. 8. True
9. A *laconic* speaker tends to be verbose and repetitive. 9. False
10. A newspaper article that *exalts* a person's achievements praises that individual. 10. True

EXERCISE 3 CHOOSING THE BEST DEFINITION

For each italicized vocabulary word in the following sentences, write the letter of the best definition on the answer line.

1. Maxwell often quotes *laconic* proverbs to emphasize his point. 1. b
   a. subtle b. terse c. colorful d. striking

 Speaking **89**

Reading passages incorporating the vocabulary words reinforce the important link between vocabulary and reading comprehension.

NAME ________________ DATE ________

READING COMPREHENSION

Each numbered sentence in the following passage contains an italicized vocabulary word or related form. After you read the passage, you will complete an exercise.

STYLES OF PUBLIC SPEAKING

The difference between a good speech and a great one is how well a speaker accomplishes the purpose. Whether delivered to inform, inspire, entertain, or persuade, a speech must be instantly intelligible to the audience, appropriate for the occasion, and expressive. Although stylistic conventions in public speaking have differed throughout history, the most memorable speeches share the characteristic of having influenced people's thoughts and feelings.

Whatever public speakers wish to express or in what manner, they must have a definite purpose in mind. In ancient Greece citizens learned to devise and arrange plausible arguments that would persuade judges to grant them rights to confiscated property. (1) In making a serious ***polemic*** for or against declaring war, such famous speakers as Patrick Henry, Winston Churchill, and Franklin Delano Roosevelt emphasized their points through the logical organization of ideas and forceful language. (2) These men were successful in ***exhorting*** their listeners to think about, to believe in, and to act for a specific cause. (3) Audiences expect to hear somber speeches for serious occasions; lighter, informal presentations for social events; or ***peremptory*** remarks in a debate or political speech. (4) An audience prepared for a ***eulogy,*** for example, would undoubtedly be confused and disturbed by negative, sarcastic comments.

Another key ingredient in effective public speaking is the speaker's choice of words and his or her style. (5) When Franklin D. Roosevelt substituted the sentence "We are going to make a country in which no one is left out" for the more ***exalted*** language of "We are trying to construct a more inclusive society," he chose a more direct, conversational style to influence his listeners. (6) If John F. Kennedy had ***expatiated*** on the virtues of patriotism rather than stating "Ask not what your country can do for you—ask what you can do for your country," his eloquent message might have been forgotten. The best speakers balance the grace and elegance of language with its precision and clarity. As the Arabian proverb suggests, good speakers "make [others] see with their ears."

Successful public speakers develop a style that best suits them and the purpose of their speeches. (7) Early Roman orators believed in the power of the address and were masters of physical gesture and ***histrionic*** displays. (8) Other speakers, such as the American statesman Daniel Webster, adopted a ***garrulous*** approach. Convinced that words speak louder than silence, Webster chose a lengthy, ornate mode of presentation. (9) Still others were subdued and ***laconic,*** such as President Lincoln, who delivered his Gettysburg Address in three minutes. A speaking style may be elaborately formal, such as that of William Jennings Bryan, or simple but dignified, as was that of Chief Joseph of the Nez Percé tribe. Regardless of the style, a speaker's ease, confidence, and authority of delivery continue to be factors in how listeners respond and how the purpose is achieved.

(10) Although all speakers intend to communicate the ***gist*** of their topic, the greatest speechmakers are able to accomplish more. Providing lasting inspiration, they change opinions, excite emotions, draw out deep feelings, and stir listeners to action. Using mere words, Patrick Henry stirred the colonists to revolt, Winston Churchill bolstered the spirits of the British during World War II, and Martin Luther King, Jr., demanded equality for all.

 Speaking **91**

A **follow-up exercise** on the passage tests student understanding of the vocabulary words in context.

A **Writing Assignment,** related to the lesson theme or passage topic, lets students apply new words. Assignments are designed to stimulate interest, enthusiasm, and creativity.

Vocabulary Enrichment provides interesting and unusual word histories.

The **Activity** encourages students to investigate the origins of several related words.

READING COMPREHENSION EXERCISE

Each of the following statements corresponds to a numbered sentence in the passage. Each statement contains a blank and is followed by four answer choices. Decide which choice fits best in the blank. The word or phrase that you choose must express roughly the same meaning as the italicized word in the passage. Write the letter of your choice on the answer line.

1. Famous speakers used forceful language when they made a(n) _____ for or against declaring war. — 1. c
   a. supplication b. effort c. argument d. excuse
2. These speakers succeeded in _____ their listeners to think and to act. — 2. a
   a. urging b. begging c. forcing d. permitting
3. Audiences expect to hear _____ remarks in a debate. — 3. b
   a. trite b. commanding c. hesitant d. exaggerated
4. An audience prepared for a _____ would be confused by negative comments. — 4. c
   a. resolution b. sacrifice c. tribute d. justification
5. Franklin D. Roosevelt substituted a direct statement for more _____ language. — 5. d
   a. vague b. commonplace c. repetitive d. elevated
6. If John F. Kennedy had _____ patriotism, his eloquent message might have been forgotten. — 6. b
   a. lectured about b. elaborated on c. ignored d. restored
7. Early Roman orators were masters of _____ displays. — 7. a
   a. dramatic b. opinionated c. tactful d. timid
8. Other speakers adopted a(n) _____ approach. — 8. a
   a. excessively talkative b. plainly superior c. sarcastic d. antagonistic
9. Still others were subdued and _____. — 9. d
   a. weak b. honest c. obscure d. terse
10. All speakers intend to communicate the _____ of their topic. — 10. b
    a. emotion b. central idea c. tone d. nature

WRITING ASSIGNMENT

"Speech is the mirror of the soul; as a man speaks, so he is." (Publilius Syrus, Latin writer of the first century B.C.)

Using at least five of the words from this lesson, explain in a composition why and how this quotation is or is not true to human experience. Underline each vocabulary word that you use.

VOCABULARY ENRICHMENT

The word *polemic* comes from the Greek word *polemos,* meaning "war." During the seventeenth century, the meaning of the word gradually shifted from the aggressiveness of physical combat to the controversial nature of discussion or argument between opposing sides.

Activity Many other English words have etymologies that are closely connected with the idea of war. Look up the following words in a dictionary and write their origins and definitions. Then write a sentence in which you use each word.

1. Armageddon 2. bellicose 3. blitz 4. martial 5. pugnacious

92 Speaking — Copyright © Great Source

A **Practice with Analogies** exercise helps students use the vocabulary words in a different context. Students learn various ways to complete analogies, to identify the different types of analogies, and to understand relationships between words.

READING COMPREHENSION EXERCISE

Each of the following statements corresponds to a number sentence in the passage. Each statement contains a blank and is followed by four answer choices. Decide which choice fits best in the blank. The word or phrase that you choose must express roughly the same meaning as the italicized word in the passage. Write the letter of your choice on the answer line.

1. People contrived various methods for weaving vines and _____ them from trees in order to cross a river or gorge. — 1. a
   a. hanging b. cutting c. lowering d. ejecting
2. A suspension bridge is a long roadway hung from wire cables that are attached to _____ towers. — 2. c
   a. concrete b. massive c. vertical d. concentric
3. A suspension bridge resembles a clothesline except for a heavy deck that is _____ the cables. — 3. b
   a. outlined by b. attached to c. behind d. transformed by
4. In fact, the _____ of public opinion held that suspension bridges were unsuitable for long spans. — 4. a
   a. great amount b. minimum c. pandemonium d. assault
5. Ten years passed _____ approval of Roebling's proposal. — 5. d
   a. after b. since c. during d. while awaiting
6. Approval of the plan was some _____ for Roebling's efforts. — 6. b
   a. hope b. repayment c. excuse d. support
7. Further trouble _____ when Washington Roebling took over his father's project. — 7. c
   a. was anticipated b. ended c. threatened d. was avoided
8. The bridge was completed after the _____ of eighteen million dollars. — 8. b
   a. initial fee b. outlay c. commission d. gamble
9. Washington Roebling _____ iron and used steel instead. — 9. d
   a. considered b. refurbished c. experimented with d. did away with
10. John Roebling's design has been retained, except for certain _____ elements. — 10. a
    a. unnecessary b. ridiculous c. expensive d. obsolete

PRACTICE WITH ANALOGIES

See pages 32 and 66 for some other strategies to use with analogies.

Strategy Watch out for reversed elements in analogies.

Incorrect ship : hull :: wing : airplane
Correct ship : hull :: airplane : wing

Directions On the answer line, write the letter of the phrase that best completes the analogy. Some of the items use the strategy explained above.

1. REPREHENSIBLE : BLAME :: (A) historical : approval (B) virtuous : censure (C) concise : praise (D) questionable : ignorance (E) notable : attention — 1. E
2. PENITENT : CONTRITE :: (A) visionary : practical (B) conformist : original (C) hypocrite : sincerity (D) bigot : biased (E) miser : generosity — 2. D
3. ATROPHY : MUSCLE :: (A) narrow : mind (B) amplify : sound (C) nibble : food (D) stretch : fiber (E) wither : leaf — 3. E
4. DEBILITATE : STRENGTH :: (A) deplore : misbehavior (B) depreciate : value (C) restore : confidence (D) organize : victory (E) depict : event — 4. B
5. LIVID : ANGER :: (A) juvenile : maturity (B) astonish : surprise (C) delicate : texture (D) agile : stiffness (E) despondent : hope — 5. B

86 The Roots *-pend-*, *-pens-*, and *-pond-* — Copyright © Great Source

Skill Features

A skill feature on dictionary use, on test taking, or on reading appears after each group of three vocabulary lessons.

- 10 special features provide students with techniques for building and using their pool of words independently.
- Clear explanation includes examples, tables of information, strategies and procedures for learning and using new words effectively.
- Accompanying exercises allow students to practice each skill.

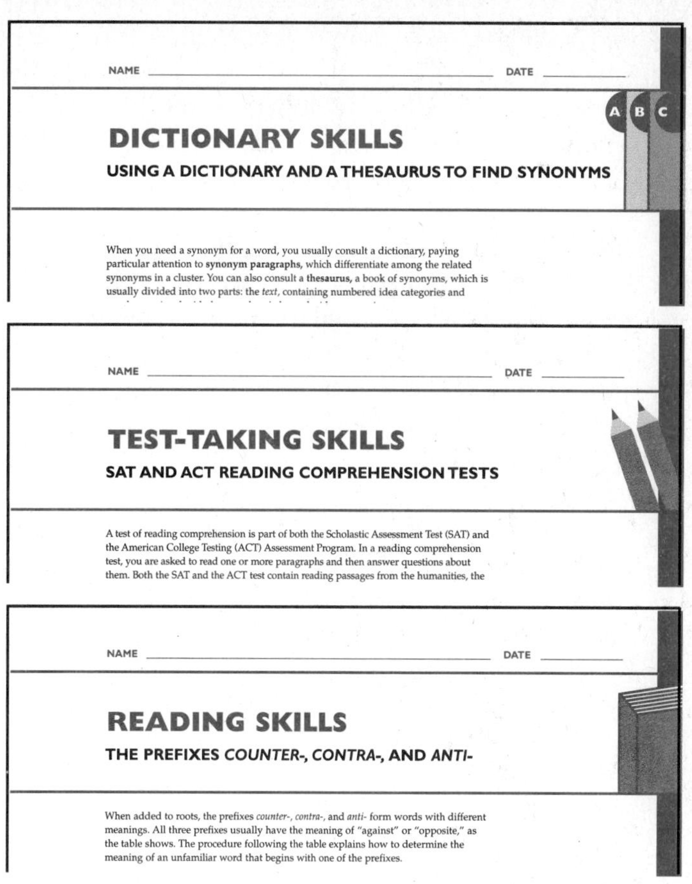

Dictionary Skills

- Emphasis in lessons is grade-level appropriate.
- Skills range from finding the right definition, understanding parts of speech, and utilizing etymological information, to reading usage notes, differentiating among synonyms, and using a thesaurus.
- Follow-up exercises give students an opportunity to practice their new skills by using dictionary extracts and writing original sentences.

Test-Taking Skills

- Students are given pointers for successfully completing different types of tests—sentence-completion, analogy, antonym, and reading comprehension—often found on standardized tests such as the SAT and ACT English Test.
- Examples are provided so students can understand the thought processes required to eliminate inappropriate answer choices and to select the correct answer.
- Accompanying exercises give students the opportunity to put the strategies into practice by becoming alert to misleading choices, sentence clues, and shades of meaning.

Reading Skills

These features address two separate areas of vocabulary proficiency: using context clues and analyzing word parts.

- Students learn to use context clues to determine the meanings of unfamiliar words.
- Methods of reasoning are illustrated so students can see how information in a sentence can be utilized.
- Students check their understanding by comparing their "working" definitions against those in a dictionary.
- Students are acquainted with a method of determining the meanings of unfamiliar words by analyzing word parts.
- Word-attack strategies focus on learning prefixes, suffixes, and roots.

Teacher's Edition

- **Teaching Suggestions:** The activities on pages x–xiii will help you to incorporate vocabulary study into every area of the English curriculum. Ideas for exercises, assignments, and discussion topics have been provided for vocabulary review, spelling, reading, word histories, grammar and usage, literature, composition, and college-entrance examination preparation.
- **Tests:** 10 reproducible multiple-choice tests, each covering 3 consecutive lessons, are found at the back of the Teacher's Edition. Each test is divided into 2 parts. Part A tests recognition and recall of definitions; Part B emphasizes placing

words within the context of sentences or discriminating among a choice of antonyms. Answers to the tests are located on the front sides of the reproducible masters.

- **Bonuses:** 7–15 Bonus activities, each covering 2–5 consecutive lessons, give students a "lighter" form of vocabulary study. In crossword puzzles, word searches, sentence completions, scrambled words, and other word games, students review their knowledge of vocabulary words and their definitions, synonyms, antonyms, and etymologies. Answers to the Bonuses are located on the front sides of the reproducible masters.
- **Verbal Aptitude Tests (4th–6th Courses):** 2 Verbal Aptitude Tests provide practice for students taking college-entrance examinations. Each 4-page reproducible test covers antonyms, sentence completions, analogies, and reading comprehension. Answers to the tests appear on the front sides of the reproducible masters found at the back of the Teacher's Edition.

Teaching Suggestions

Review and Retention

Frequent review helps students retain the meanings of new words. Use any or all of the following practices to help students learn and apply new words.

1. Have students use the **Flash Cards,** located on pages 201–220 of the student books, for individual drill or game-style classroom practice.
2. Assign the **Bonuses** (see page 201) as follow-up activities for the vocabulary lessons.
3. Have students conduct a weekly search of newspapers and magazines to locate vocabulary words. Award a set amount of extra-credit points for each word found and for the student finding the most occurrences of the same word, the most occurrences of all the words, and so forth.

Vocabulary and Spelling

Vocabulary study and spelling are complementary. Students cannot completely understand a word until they can say and write it as well as cite its definition. Make use of the numerous opportunities provided in *Vocabulary for Achievement* in order to reinforce spelling skills.

1. Once students have studied the definitions and examples for each vocabulary word, have them write the word in the blank provided for this purpose. Writing the word reinforces the visual-graphic patterns of letters, aids in sight recognition, and helps students to apply the word.
2. Encourage students to pay close attention to the listing of related forms and the use of these, along with the inflected forms of words, throughout the exercises. Point out to them how different endings can change the spelling of a word.
3. Have students pay special heed to lessons based on word roots, since these show how similar word elements contribute to the similarity of meaning and spelling. In the same way, have them study the **Skill Features** treating prefixes and suffixes.

Vocabulary and Reading

1. To help students improve their ability to make inferences, provide them with practice in drawing conclusions and predicting outcomes. Have students read the opening paragraphs of a short story or novel. Ask them questions about the sequence of events and the details that establish the personalities of the characters. Based on the facts and details the author provides, coupled with their own understanding of the author's vocabulary, students should be able to make predictions about what will result. Have students explain and support their predictions, pointing out specific words or phrases that set up expectations in their reading of the text.
2. To help students realize how they naturally make inferences about what they see, hear, or read, provide several photographs or cartoons. Ask them to summarize the main idea of the picture in a single sentence. Then ask them a series of questions that help them to focus on the details, such as the ages of the people depicted, the time of day, the weather, the location, the circumstances, and so forth. Assure students that you are more concerned with their logical thinking process than you are with right and wrong answers. Point out that their statements of the main idea may include few, if any, of the answers to your specific questions. Hints from the cartoon or photograph coupled with their own experience and the use of logic will allow them to make judgments, reject extremes, and make inferences.
3. Another way to help students master the interpretive level of comprehension, or inference-making, is to provide them with newspaper or magazine editorials. Ask them questions like the following.

EXAMPLES What is the issue presented in the editorial?
What side of the issue is represented?
What specific evidence is given to support that side?
What evidence supports another point of view?
How does the writer show a bias? What particular words or expressions accomplish this? What are synonyms for these words or expressions? Explain why the writer chose the word that appears rather than one of the synonyms. Which synonyms weaken the tone? Which strengthen it? Are there any synonyms that strengthen the tone too much?

Vocabulary and Word Analogies

1. To give students practice identifying word relationships, provide them with the first half of several analogies and have them work together to determine the types of analogy. You may want to draw from the following types of analogy:

degree	characteristic of
type of	antonym
part/whole	definition
relative size	part of
is used to	expression of
place where	

2. Challenge students to write visual analogies. Their analogies should be written entirely with pictures or symbols instead of words. Invite pairs of students to solve their partners' analogies.
3. To help students practice their analogy-solving strategies, give them several word pairs and ask them to restate the relationship between the words in a simple sentence. For example, in the word pair "scrap/paper," a restated simple sentence could be "A scrap is a small piece of paper."

Vocabulary and Word Histories

To help students appreciate language as dynamic, use the following as discussion or assignment topics.

Words that have undergone changes in meaning: *clerk* (member of the clergy), *deer* (wild animal), *engine* (skill), *naughty* (nothing), *officious* (duty), *outlandish* (of foreign origin), *passion* (to suffer), *quaint* (to learn), and so forth.

Shortened forms of words: *metro/metropolitan, vet/veteran, perk/perquisite, hype/hyperbole, hi-fi/high fidelity, a co-op/a cooperative, cinema/ cinematograph,* and so forth.

Doublets, or two or more words derived by different routes from the same source: *guardian/warden, tavern/tabernacle, human/humane, reward/regard, dungeon/dominion, clench/clinch, feeble/foible,* and so form. Have students use the dictionary to compare the present meanings and the common origins of the words.

Compound words: *hit-and-miss, ne'er-do-well, off-the-record, standby, turboprop, backlash, wiretap, monorail, wingspan,* and so forth.

Special interest words, such as those from computer science, that have been adopted for more general use: *input, output, throughout, cursor, scroll, on-line, data base, byte, user-friendly,* and so forth.

Portmanteau words, in which the sounds and meanings of two or more words are merged to form a new word: *medicaid* (medical + aid), *twissors* (tweezers + scissors), *arcology* (architecture + ecology), *quasar* (quasi + stellar), *albeit* (although + it + be), *agribusiness* (agriculture + business), *aquaculture* (aqua + agriculture), and so forth.

Acronyms, or words formed from the initial letters of words or phrases: *RAM* (random access memory), *BASIC* (Beginner's All-Purpose Symbolic Instruction Code), *COBOL* (Common Business Oriented Language), *cyborg* (cybernetic organism), *ASCAP* (American Society of Composers, Authors, and Publishers), and so forth.

Words borrowed directly from other languages, such as Dutch: *yacht, cruise, buoy, schooner, skipper, smuggle, dock, stove, skate, landscape,* and so forth.

Vocabulary, Grammar, and Usage

1. Remind students that a word may be used as several parts of speech. Then have them examine the multiple meanings of such words as *use, transport, transfer, torment, subject, separate, retail, stunt,* and so forth. Have students write groups of sentences like the following that illustrate the different meanings.
   EXAMPLE As an out-of-state visitor, Manuel is *subject* to the chaperone's approval if he wants to attend our dance. *(adjective)*
   EXAMPLE Gillian knew little about the *subject,* but she enjoyed listening to the conversation about coral reefs. *(noun)*
   EXAMPLE Children gain immunity to infection when they are *subjected* to a variety of childhood diseases. *(verb)*

2. When discussing usage problems, have the students examine the likelihood of confusion between pairs of homophones like the following: *breech/breach, alter/altar, compliment/complement, straight/strait, council/counsel, cede/seed, pour/pore,* and so forth. Then have them look up the definitions of each word and write a sentence for each illustrating its use.

   As an alternative, have students examine the likelihood of confusion between pairs of homographs (words spelled the same but which differ in meaning and possibly in pronunciation): *row, sow, tear, present, bar, shed, fair,* and so forth.

Vocabulary and Literature

1. In discussing literature selections, reinforce vocabulary study by pointing out authors' literary techniques. Ask students questions like the following.
   EXAMPLE Which words or phrases contribute to the mood and tone of the story?
   EXAMPLE How does the author create humor?

2. To help students understand the rich nature of idioms, explore with them the literal and figurative meanings of expressions used in short stories and novels.
   EXAMPLES *apple of one's eye, bark up the wrong tree, beat a dead horse, beat around the bush, bite off more than one can chew, bone of contention, the jig is up, burn the midnight oil, chip off the old block, diamond in the rough, break new ground,* and so forth.

3. Help students to understand more easily the Shakespearean plays that they read by reviewing with them words used by Shakespeare whose meanings have changed radically.
   EXAMPLES *fond* (foolish, silly), *conceit* (thought, idea), *portly* (grand), *sad* (serious), *abuse* (deceive), *appeal* (accuse), *vantage* (opportunity), *questionable* (able to talk), *rivals* (partners), *competitors* (partners), *extravagant* (wandering outside), *unlucky* (fatal), *perplexed* (mentally tortured), and so forth.

   Another way to facilitate students' understanding of Shakespeare is to have them translate one scene of a play into modern English.

4. Help students to become aware of the dialectal differences of British English through such works as the poems of Robert Burns; the novels of Charles Dickens, Thomas Hardy, and Henry James; Emily Bronte's *Wuhering Heights;* and George Bernard Shaw's *Candida* and *Pygmalion.*
   Discuss with students the differences between regional and social dialects. Ask the students questions like the following.
   EXAMPLE What differences can you detect in the education, social status, regional background, and culture of the characters by their speech?

Preparing for College-Entrance Examinations

While experts agree that studying does not influence college-entrance examination scores, there is some indication that preparation in test-taking strategies does have a positive effect. Use the following suggestions to help students become cognizant of helpful approaches to completing the four different types of test items on the verbal portions of those tests.

The Test as a Whole Because each section of most college-entrance exams generally moves from the less difficult items to the more difficult items, suggest to student that they complete the first third of the items in the sentence-completion and analogy sections before continuing with the items that involve more complex reasoning.

Sentence Completions

1. Suggest to students that an effective way of approaching these items is to read every sentence carefully, looking for context clues within the sentence. They should look for punctuation and signal words, such as coordinating or correlative conjunctions, that provide signposts showing how the ideas are developed. Before considering the five answer choices, students should attempt to insert words of their own that make sense in the blanks.
   EXAMPLE Whereas William Thackeray was a(n) - - - - writer who dissected the foibles of society, Charles Dickens was a(n) - - - - novelist who wept for the frailties of people.
   (A) emotional . . eccentric
   (B) cynical . . sympathetic
   (C) romantic . . triumphant
   (D) skeptical . . pious
   (E) banal . . commonplace

   A student should see that the two writers are being contrasted on the basis of their attitude and approach to society. Since Thackeray *dissected foibles,* students may insert *critical* in the blank to describe him. On the other hand, Dickens *wept for the frailties,* and students might choose *compassionate* to describe him. Looking at the answer choices, the student would then eliminate (A), (C), and (E) since none of these establishes the necessary contrast. While (D) may be a possible answer choice, there is nothing in the sentence to support the idea that Dickens is reverent or devout. These (B), which contains the needed contrast, is the correct choice, and most closely approximates the student's own sentence insertions.

2. Help students to become aware of patterns that appear in sentence-completion items. For example, in a cause-and-effect sentence, the words selected for the blanks must make both parts of the sentence consistent in the sense of cause and effect. Tell students that words like *if, since, for, because, therefore, why, when,* and *then* signal this type of pattern.

   EXAMPLE If we proceed - - - - and decisively, we can maintain science and technology in the - - - - state required by our national welfare and security.
   (A) assiduously . . minimal
   (B) diligently . . flourishing
   (C) capriciously . . sovereign
   (D) overtly . . judicious
   (E) radically . . congenial
   The correct answer is (B).

3. Tell students that contrast is another typical pattern used in sentence-completion items. A sentence that indicates contrast explains what something is not and helps readers to infer what it really is. Tell students to look for words and phrases like *although, even though, even if, never . . . but always, rather than,* and so forth. Remind them that a sentence of contrast is often broken into two sections by a comma or a semicolon.

   EXAMPLE These sporadic raids seem to indicate that the enemy is waging war of - - - - rather than attacking us directly.
   (A) insurgency (B) attrition
   (C) intensity (D) barbarism
   (E) hypocrisy
   The correct answer is (B).

Analogies

1. Remind students that parts of speech are always consistent within individual analogies. If the capitalized words are NOUN : ADJECTIVE, then all the choices will be noun : adjective.

2. Because analogy items test logic as well as vocabulary, have students practice the reasoning process aloud.

   EXAMPLE
   TRANSIENT : ETERNAL : :
   (A) pensive : contemplative
   (B) acute : chronic
   (C) clement : lenient
   (D) replete : hollow
   (E) former : latter

   A student might analyze the analogy in the following way. The two capitalized words are antonyms expressing the relationship of duration. Choices (A) and (C) can be eliminated since *pensive* and *contemplative* and *clement* and *lenient* are synonyms. Choice (D) can be eliminated because the words, while antonyms, refer to capacity. Choice (E), referring to time, establishes a relationship of sequence. Choice (B), *acute* and *chronic,* establish a relationship of duration equivalent to the given pair and therefore is the correct answer.

Reading Comprehension

1. Suggest to students that one way of approaching the reading-comprehension section is to skim quickly the questions following the passage in order to determine generally what to be reading for. Next, the students can read the passage slowly and carefully to determine the main ideas. Finally, when answering the questions, they can return to the passage in order to locate specific details. In this way, students can make the best use of their time.

2. Explain to students that the questions on reading-comprehension passages fall into three major categories. Questions about central ideas may focus on the title that best expresses the author's point, the main idea or theme of the selection, and the author's purpose in writing the passage. Words that signal main ideas and conclusions are *therefore, consequently,* and *hence.*

   Questions about specific details may include identifying correct statements or selecting the one incorrect statement. Remind the students that details are signaled by such phrases as *for example, for instance,* and *in particular.*

   Finally, questions about logical relationships entail drawing conclusions and making assumptions about what is read. These questions will ask what the author implies or what the reader can infer.

VOCABULARY FOR ACHIEVEMENT READING COMPREHENSION PASSAGES

A Reading Comprehension passage appears in each of the 30 vocabulary lessons in each level. The passage is an article, essay, or story that contains all ten vocabulary words of the lesson, thereby giving students an opportunity to understand the new words in a larger context. These passages also lend an entertaining variety to the abundant practice and provide students with enriching information drawn from a wide variety of subject matter. *Vocabulary for Achievement* truly offers students a chance to read across the curriculum while they incorporate newly learned words into their vocabularies. For your convenience, the following is a level-specific list of topics and passages.

Grade 12: Sixth Course

Lesson	Topic	Title of Passage
1	Language	The History of the English Language
2	Myths and Legends	Perseus and Medusa
3	Science and Nature	The Gift of the Nile
4	History	Marco Polo: World Explorer
5	Science and Nature	The Greenhouse Effect: The Warming of the World
6	Science and Nature	Deep-Sea Salvage: The Treasures of History
7	The Arts	María Martínez: Matriarch of Potters
8	Science and Nature	Dr. Charles Drew: Physician and Scientist
9	Science and Nature	The Galápagos Islands: Biological Oddities
10	Literature and Communication	Mary Shelley: Creator of Frankenstein
11	Literature and Communication	Sherlock Holmes: Master Crime Solver
12	History	Bubonic Plague: The Black Death
13	Technology	The Brooklyn Bridge: An Engineering Marvel
14	Literature and Communication	Styles of Public Speaking
15	History	Joan of Arc (1412–1431)
16	Language	The Naming of the New World
17	Sports and Recreation	Pancho Gonzales: Temperamental Tennis Champion
18	The Arts	Jenny Lind: The Swedish Nightingale
19	Literature and Communication	Lincoln's Gettysburg Address
20	History	The Great Wall of China
21	Sports and Recreation	The New Automobile Junkyard
22	Literature and Communication	Anne Sullivan Macy: "Miracle Worker"
23	History	The Mystery of the Nacza Plain
24	Science and Nature	The Atom: Nature's Building Block
25	Technology	The "Unsinkable *Titanic*"
26	Science and Nature	The La Brea Tar Pits: Deathtrap of the Ages
27	Literature and Communication	The Brontë Sisters
28	History	Benjamin Franklin: Statesman and Diplomat
29	The Arts	The Beginnings of Modern Art
30	Social History	Jesters and Fools

COMPLETE WORD LIST FOR SIXTH COURSE

Words from this grade level used on the Verbal Aptitude Tests are marked with a colored asterisk.

SCOPE AND SEQUENCE OF SKILLS

	Introductory	First	Second	Third	Fourth	Fifth	Sixth
Dictionary Skills	**Parts of a Dictionary Entry** (pp. 19–20) **Finding the Right Definition** (pp. 39–40)	**Finding the Appropriate Definition** (pp. 19–20) **Part-of-Speech Labels** (pp. 39–40) **Understanding Etymologies** (pp. 59–60)	**Finding the Appropriate Definition** (pp. 19–20) **Inflected Forms of Words** (pp. 39–40) **Biographical and Geographical Entries** (pp. 59–60)	**Finding the Appropriate Definition** (pp. 19–20) **Usage Notes** (pp. 39–40)	**Synonym Paragraphs** (pp. 19–20)	**Using a Thesaurus** (pp. 19–20)	**Using a Dictionary and a Thesaurus to Find Synonyms** (pp. 19–20)
Test-Taking Skills	**Synonym Tests** (pp. 59–60) **Antonym Tests** (pp. 79–80)	**Sentence-Completion Tests** (pp. 79–80)	**Sentence-Completion Tests** (pp. 79–80) **Synonym Tests** (pp. 99–100) **Analogy Tests** (pp. 119–120)	**Antonym Tests** (pp. 59–60) **Analogy Tests** (pp. 79–80) **Reading-Comprehension Tests** (pp. 99–100)	**Antonym Test Items** (pp. 39–40) **Sentence-Completion Test Items** (pp. 59–60) **Analogy Test Items** (pp. 79–80) **Reading-Comprehension Test Items** (pp. 99–100)	**Antonym Test Items** (pp. 39–40) **SAT Sentence-Completion Test Items** (pp. 59–60) **SAT Analogy Test Items** (pp. 79–80) **SAT Reading-Comprehension Test Items** (pp. 99–100)	**ACT Reading-Comprehension Tests** (pp. 39–40) **Tests of Standard Written English** (pp. 59–60)
Reading Skills	**Context Clues** (pp. 99–100) **Dividing Words into Parts** (pp. 119–120) **The Prefixes *non-, un-*** (pp. 139–140) **The Prefix *trans-*** (pp. 159–160) **The Prefix *de-*** (pp. 179–180) **The Suffixes *-ity, -hood*** (pp. 199–200)	**Context Clues: Definition in the Sentence** (pp. 99–100) **The Prefix *dis-*** (pp. 119–120) **The Prefix *re-*** (pp. 139–140) **The Prefix *sub-*** (pp. 159–160) **The Suffixes *-ance, -ence, -ancy*** (pp. 179–180) **The Suffix *-able*** (pp. 199–200)	**Context Clues: Synonyms** (pp. 139–140) **The Prefix *pre-*** (pp. 159–160) **The Prefix *in-*** (pp. 179–180) **The Suffixes *-ion, -ness*** (pp. 199–200)	**Context Clues: Substitution** (pp. 119–120) **The Prefixes *ex-, e-*** (pp. 139–140) **The Prefixes *ab-, a-, abs-*** (pp. 159–160) **The Suffixes *-ful, -ous*** (pp. 179–180) **Four Verb Suffixes** (pp. 199–200)	**Context Clues: Examples and Appositives** (pp. 119–120) **Context Clues: Contrast** (pp. 139–140) **The Prefix *ad-*** (pp. 159–160) ***Com-* and Related Prefixes** (pp. 179–180) **Five Adjective Suffixes** (pp. 199–200)	**Context Clues and the Reading of American History** (pp. 119–120) **Context Clues and the Reading of American Literature** (pp. 139–140) **The Prefixes *bene-, mal-*** (pp. 159–160) **The Prefixes *inter-, intra-, intro-*** (pp. 179–180) **The Prefixes *ante-, post-*** (pp. 199–200)	**Context Clues and the Reading of Primary Sources** (pp. 79–80) **Context Clues and the Reading of British Literature** (pp. 99–100) **The Prefixes *bi-, semi-*** (pp. 119–120) **Prefixes Indicating Number** (pp. 139–140) **The Prefixes *conter-, contra-, anti-*** (pp. 159–160) **The Prefixes *circum-, peri-*** (pp. 179–180) **The Prefixes *extra-, super-, ultra-*** (pp. 199–200)

Vocabulary for Achievement

SIXTH COURSE

Margaret Ann Richek

Arlin T. McRae

Susan K. Weiler

GREAT SOURCE
WILMINGTON, MA

AUTHORS

Margaret Ann Richek
Professor of Education, Northeastern Illinois University; consultant in reading and vocabulary study; author of The World of Words *(Houghton Mifflin)*

Arlin T. McRae
Supervisor of English, Evansville-Vanderburgh School Corporation, Evansville, Indiana; Adjunct Instructor in English, University of Evansville

Susan K. Weiler
Instructor of Art History at John Carroll University in Cleveland, Ohio; former teacher of Latin, Beaumont School for Girls, Cleveland Heights, Ohio

CONSULTANT

Larry S. Krieger
Social Studies Supervisor, Montgomery Township Public Schools, New Jersey; author of World History *and* U.S. History *(D.C. Heath), co-author of* Mastering the Verbal SAT 1/PSAT *(Great Source)*

CLASSROOM CONSULTANTS

Jack Pelletier
Teacher of English, Mira Loma High School, Sacramento, California

Valerie M. Webster
Teacher of English, Walnut Hill School, Natick, Massachusetts

ACKNOWLEDGMENTS

Definitions for the three hundred words taught in this textbook are based on Houghton Mifflin dictionaries—in particular, the *Houghton Mifflin College Dictionary,* copyright © 1986, and *The American Heritage Dictionary of the English Language, Third Edition,* copyright © 1992. The dictionary passages in the skill lesson on pages 19–20 are adapted from the latter, as is the pronunciation key on the inside front cover. Also on pages 19–20 are passages from *Roget's International Thesaurus,* 4th edition revised by Robert L. Chapman (Thomas Y. Crowell), as follows: entries 630.9 (p. 485), 691.9 (p. 544), and 893.21 (p. 698), as well as index entry for *improve* (p. 1018). Copyright © 1977 by Harper & Row, Publishers, Inc. Reprinted by permission of Harper & Row, Publishers, Inc. The reading passage on pages 39–40 is from Robert F. Biehler and Lynne Hudson, *Developmental Psychology,* Third Edition, copyright © 1986 by Houghton Mifflin Company. Reprinted by permission of Houghton Mifflin Company. The reading passage on pages 79–80 is from *The Journals of Lewis and Clark* by Bernard de Voto. Copyright 1953 by Bernard de Voto. Copyright © renewed 1981 by Avis de Voto. Reprinted by permission of Houghton Mifflin Company. SAT and Scholastic Assessment Test are registered trademarks of the College Entrance Examination Board.

CREDITS

Production: PC&F, Inc.

Illustrations: Nanette Biers: pages 37, 65, 97, 111, 145; Sylvia Giblin: pages 85, 131, 137, 165; Norman Nicholson: pages 25, 45, 51, 71, 77; Phyllis Rockne: pages 17, 57, 171

Printed in the United States of America

ISBN: 0-669-46483-X

1 2 3 4 5 6 7 8 9 10 HS 00 03 02 01 00 99 98

CONTENTS

COMPLETE WORD LIST

LESSON 1 THE SCIENCE OF LANGUAGE

Linguistics, the science of language, sheds light on many fascinating questions. Through studying the similarities of different languages, linguists can determine that peoples who now live far apart share a common history. Although geographically distant, many languages of India, including ancient Sanskrit, show a common ancestry with such European languages as German and French. Surprisingly, Finnish, although spoken in a country relatively close to Germany and France, is a very distant language, pointing to a separate heritage for the Finns. The words in this lesson will help you understand and talk about the development and structure of languages.

WORD LIST

cognate
derivative
diminutive
inflection
orthography
paradigm
philology
phonology
rhetoric
syntax

DEFINITIONS

After you have studied the definitions and example for each vocabulary word, write the word on the line to the right.

1. **cognate** (kôg′nāt′) *adjective* Related by being derived, descended, or borrowed from the same word or root. *noun* A word, word part, or language that is related to another by common descent or derivation. (From the Latin *com-*, meaning "together," and *gnatus,* meaning "born") 1. ______________

Example The English word *father* and the Latin word *pater* are cognate words.

2. **derivative** (dĭ-rĭv′ə-tĭv) *noun* **a.** A word formed from another word or root, such as by adding a prefix or a suffix. **b.** Something taken or received from a specified source. *adjective* Made up of elements that have been borrowed from another source: *a derivative artistic style.* (From the Latin *de-*, meaning "away from," and *rivus,* meaning "stream") 2. ______________

Related Words **derivation** *noun;* **derive** *verb*
Example The words *apparel* and *rampart* are both *derivatives* of a Latin word that means "to equip."

3. **diminutive** (dĭ-mĭn′yə-tĭv) *noun* A word formed by shortening or by adding certain suffixes indicating primarily small size but also youth, affection, or contempt. *adjective* **a.** Relating or referring to a word, suffix, or name that is a diminutive or forms one: *a diminutive suffix.* **b.** Very small in size. (From the Latin *de-*, meaning "away from," and *minuere,* meaning "to lessen") 3. ______________

Related Words **diminution** *noun;* **diminutively** *adverb*
Example The names of many young animals, such as *duckling* and *owlet,* are *diminutives.*

4. **inflection** (ĭn-flĕk'shən) *noun.* **a.** The change in the form of words that indicates a grammatical distinction, such as number, gender, case, person, tense, mood, or voice. **b.** A word form of this kind. **c.** A change in the pitch or tone of the voice. (From the Latin *in-*, an intensive prefix, and *flectere,* meaning "to bend") 4. ____________

Related Words **inflect** *verb;* **inflectional** *adjective*
Example The plural form *books* is formed by the *inflection* of the noun *book,* but the adjective *bookish* and the noun *booklet* are not.

5. **orthography** (ôr-thŏg'rə-fē) *noun* The art or study of correct spelling according to established usage. (From the Greek words *orthos,* meaning "correct" or "straight," and *graphein,* meaning "to write") 5. ____________

Related Words **orthographic** *adjective;* **orthographically** *adverb*
Example English *orthography* was standardized in the eighteenth century.

6. **paradigm** (păr'ə-dīm', (păr'ə-dĭm')*noun* **a.** A list of all the inflectional forms of a particular word. **b.** An example or model, especially one that is typical or particularly clear. (From the Greek words *para,* meaning "alongside," and *deikunai,* meaning "to show") 6. ____________

Example The *paradigm* of the noun *sheep* includes only two different forms, *sheep* and *sheep's.*

7. **philology** (fĭ-lôl'ə-jē) *noun* **a.** The chronological study of language development. **b.** The study of literature and language as used in literature. (From the Greek words *philos,* meaning "loving," and *logos,* meaning "word") 7. ____________

Related Words **philological** *adjective;* **philologist** *noun*
Example *Philology* is regarded as the science of language.

8. **phonology** (fə-nŏl'ə-jē, fō-nol'ə-jē) *noun* The science of speech sounds in a language. (From the Greek words *phōnē,* meaning "sound," and *logos,* meaning "word" or "reason") 8. ____________

Related Words **phonological** *adjective;* **phonologist** *noun*
Example The use of the articles *a* and *an,* depending on the sound that follows, is governed by a rule of English *phonology.*

9. **rhetoric** (rĕt'ər-ĭk) *noun* **a.** The art of using language effectively. **b.** The study of the elements used in composition or discourse. **c.** Insincere and pretentious language. (From the Greek word *rhētōr,* meaning "orator") 9. ____________

Related Words **rhetorical** *adjective;* **rhetorically** *adverb*
Example Students learn the grammar and vocabulary of a language quickly, but mastering its *rhetoric* takes a lifetime.

10. **syntax** (sĭn'tăks') *noun* The way in which words are arranged or combined to form phrases, clauses, and sentences. (From the Greek *sun-,* meaning "together," and *tassein,* meaning "to arrange") 10. ____________

Related Word **syntactic** *adjective*
Example The placement of an adjective between the article and the noun is a rule of English *syntax.*

NAME ______________________________ DATE ______________

EXERCISE 1 WRITING CORRECT WORDS

On the answer line, write the word from the vocabulary list that fits each definition.

1. The art or study of correct spelling according to standard usage — 1. orthography
2. The art of using language effectively — 2. rhetoric
3. The chronological study of language development — 3. philology
4. Related by origin from the same word or root — 4. cognate
5. A change in the form of a word that indicates a grammatical distinction — 5. inflection
6. A list of all the inflected forms of a word; a typical example or model — 6. paradigm
7. The way in which words are arranged in phrases, clauses, and sentences — 7. syntax
8. A word formed from another word or root — 8. derivative
9. The science of speech sounds in a language — 9. phonology
10. A word formed with a suffix that indicates small size, youth, or affection — 10. diminutive

EXERCISE 2 USING WORDS CORRECTLY

Each of the following statements contains an italicized vocabulary word. Decide whether the sentence is true or false, and write *True* or *False* on the answer line.

1. Carelessness about *orthography* is a mark of a good speller. — 1. False
2. *Phonology* is the science of long-distance communication. — 2. False
3. The placement of modifiers is a question of *syntax*. — 3. True
4. A *paradigm* is a grammatical mistake. — 4. False
5. A person skilled in *rhetoric* can use language effectively. — 5. True
6. The word "completely" is a *derivative* of "complete." — 6. True
7. A person interested in *philology* need not be concerned with language. — 7. False
8. French and Spanish are *cognate* languages; both developed from Latin. — 8. True
9. The word "learned" comes from "learn" by *inflection*. — 9. True
10. A *diminutive* is a word that has only one syllable. — 10. False

EXERCISE 3 CHOOSING THE BEST WORD

Decide which vocabulary word or related form best completes the sentence, and write the letter of your choice on the answer line.

1. The suffix *-ie* forms many ______, such as *dearie* and *doggie*. — 1. b
   a. cognates **b.** diminutives **c.** paradigms **d.** inflections
2. Many people are not aware that the poet A. E. Housman was also a ______, who edited the works of the Latin writer Juvenal. — 2. a
   a. philologist **b.** phonologist **c.** derivative **d.** paradigm

3. Shakespeare's _____ causes many common words in his plays to look unfamiliar to the modern reader. 3. c

a. paradigm b. inflection c. orthography d. philology

4. The candidate's speech was nothing but a lot of empty _____. 4. c

a. syntax b. phonology c. rhetoric d. philology

5. Although her pronunciation is perfect, you can tell from certain _____ errors that French is not her native language. 5. d

a. cognate b. diminutive c. orthographic d. syntactic

6. The words *chef* and *chief* are _____; they both come from the Latin word *caput*, meaning "head." 6. b

a. diminutives b. cognates c. paradigms d. inflections

7. That composer's works are not performed today because his style is _____ and his musical ideas lack originality. 7. a

a. derivative b. diminutive c. rhetorical d. inflectional

8. Ellen's mother, a professor of _____, is an expert on the way English was pronounced in the sixteenth century. 8. c

a. orthography b. syntax c. phonology d. rhetoric

9. The _____ of the verb *go* contains the past tense form *went*, which is not related in origin. 9. d

a. derivation b. cognate c. syntax d. paradigm

10. In addition to singular and plural forms, nouns in some languages have _____ for a dual form that is used for two persons or things. 10. c

a. cognates b. derivatives c. inflections d. paradigms

EXERCISE 4 USING DIFFERENT FORMS OF WORDS

Decide which form of the vocabulary word in parentheses best completes the sentence. The form given may be correct. Write your answer on the answer line.

1. The candidate garnished his speech with many _____ flourishes. *(rhetoric)* 1. rhetorical

2. Although it may seem unlikely, it is possible to demonstrate that the English word *night* and the Spanish word *noche* are _____ words. *(cognate)* 2. cognate

3. The *-ing* in *singing* is an _____ suffix. *(inflection)* 3. inflectional

4. Noah Webster introduced _____ changes that distinguish American from British spelling. *(orthography)* 4. orthographic

5. The word *finger* is _____ from the same root as the word *five*. *(derivative)* 5. derived

6. The Grimm brothers' interest in folktales grew out of their _____ studies. *(philology)* 6. philological

7. Natty Bumppo, the central character in Cooper's "Leather-Stocking" novels, is a _____ of the American frontiersman. *(paradigm)* 7. paradigm

8. The pronunciation of the plural suffix *-s* with a *z* sound when it follows a vowel is a _____ rule of English. *(phonology)* 8. phonological

9. Although it denotes a relatively large object, *violoncello* is actually a _____ in its original language, Italian. *(diminutive)* 9. diminutive

10. The _____ form of interrogative sentences has changed since Chaucer's time. *(syntax)* 10. syntactic

NAME ______________________ DATE ____________

(syntax)

READING COMPREHENSION

Each numbered sentence in the following passage contains an italicized vocabulary word or related form. After you read the passage, you will complete an exercise.

THE HISTORY OF THE ENGLISH LANGUAGE

Like everything else that is subject to the effects of time, languages change. (1) Although almost nothing is known about the beginnings of human speech, during the last two centuries ***philologists*** have made important discoveries about how languages change. Their studies have shed much light on the history of English.

The history of English proper began around A.D. 500, when several Germanic tribes migrated to Britain. This first stage in the history of English lasted until about 1100 and is called Old English. (2) In many features Old English resembled German, a ***cognate*** language. (3) The system of verb ***inflections,*** for example, is strikingly similar in the two languages.

During the Old English period, the main foreign influence on the language came from the Danes and Norwegians, who first invaded and later settled in England. (4) Many common words in modern English are ***derived*** from Scandinavian words, including the pronouns *they, their,* and *them,* which replaced the Old English forms.

The Middle English period, which lasted from about 1100 to 1500, was a time of far-reaching and rapid change in language. (5) The ***paradigms*** of nouns and adjectives became simpler, as many inflectional endings either were dropped or were no longer distinguished in pronunciation. By the end of the Middle English period, the inflectional system became very close to what it is today.

Other important changes occurred during Middle English times that gave English its distinctive modern appearance so different from the Germanic shape of Old English. (6) The first was the overhaul of the ***phonological*** system, which occurred in several stages. In time, all the long vowels became diphthongs. Phonetically speaking, modern English, unlike Old English, has no long vowels.

The second great change was the influence of French on English vocabulary. The Norman French conquered England in 1066, and for the next four centuries French language, literature, and culture permeated English life. (7) Many people also became bilingual, and their mixing of the two languages resulted in the ***diminution*** of the Old English word-stock in favor of borrowing from French.

(8) The last change was the beginning of the stabilization of English ***orthography*** in the fifteenth century with the production of printed books. Speakers of modern English complain about the peculiarities of English spelling—that, for example, *eight* and *ate* should be pronounced alike. Yet those spellings represent significant differences in pronunciation that were lost relatively recently.

In the modern period, from about 1500 to the present, English has changed less radically than in earlier times. (9) During the Renaissance there was much experimentation with ***rhetoric*** and style, as well as the importation of many Latin and Greek words. (10) Some changes in ***syntax*** also occurred. One example is the development of the progressive form of the verb, such as *is going.* In the eighteenth and nineteenth centuries, a standard from of the language was established, which, because of Great Britain's political might, became one of the most widespread and important languages of the world.

READING COMPREHENSION EXERCISE

Each of the following statements corresponds to a numbered sentence in the passage. Each statement contains a blank and is followed by four answer choices. Decide which choice fits best in the blank. The word or phrase that you choose must express roughly the same meaning as the italicized word in the passage. Write the letter of your choice on the answer line.

1. _____ have made discoveries about how languages change.
   a. People who use language effectively **c.** Good spellers
   b. People who study language **d.** Careful readers

1. ___b___

2. English and German are _____ languages. 2. a

a. related b. European c. ancient d. difficult

3. German and Old English have similar systems of verb _____. 3. d

a. combinations c. sounds that convey meaning
b. conjugations d. changes that indicate grammatical distinctions

4. Many English words are _____ from Scandinavian words. 4. b

a. different b. descended c. changed d. abbreviated

5. In Middle English times, the _____ of nouns and adjectives became simpler. 5. c

a. meanings b. overall use c. patterns d. spelling

6. One great change in Middle English was the overhaul of the _____ system. 6. a

a. speech-sound b. spelling c. literary d. educational

7. The mixing of French and English led to the _____ of the Old English word-stock. 7. c

a. increase b. preservation c. reduction d. borrowing

8. English _____ began to be stabilized in the fifteenth century. 8. d

a. pronunciation b. word order c. grammar d. spelling

9. During the Renaissance there was much experimentation with _____ and style. 9. b

a. sentence structure c. literary form
b. effective use of language d. word formation

10. Some changes also occurred in _____. 10. c

a. vocabulary c. how words are arranged in sentences
b. literary form d. how borrowed words were incorporated

WRITING ASSIGNMENT

Choose a category of information that interests you and do some library research about the differences between British and American words. For example, if you choose the category of vehicles, you might investigate British terminology for different parts of the automobile, such as *windshield, hood, trunk,* and *fender.* Write a brief report in which you summarize the results of your investigation.

VOCABULARY ENRICHMENT

Rhetoric comes from the Greek word *rhētōr,* meaning "orator." The ancient Greeks, and later the Romans, used this word to describe a teacher of oratory or public speaking. The orator prepared young men for careers in law or politics by teaching them how to argue for and against certain issues and how to use techniques for persuading an audience effectively. Our modern word *rhetoric,* meaning "the art of effective speaking and writing," denotes the specialty of the *rhētōr:* skillful communication through the spoken or written word.

Activity Look up the following words in a dictionary and write their meanings and the words or names they are derived from. Then write an explanation of the connection between the derivation and the meaning.

1. demagogue 2. homily 3. jeremiad 4. mob 5. philippic

LESSON 2 HONESTY AND DECEPTION

2

How many of the following words and phrases do you use to express the concepts of honesty and deception?

Seeing is believing.
the unvarnished truth
true blue
as honest as the day is long
hoodwink
pull the wool over one's eyes
sleight of hand
sell one a bill of goods

The number and variety of expressions for the concepts of truthfulness and trickery illustrate their importance in our lives. The words in this lesson will help you to add more specific terms for honesty and deception to your vocabulary. While you will probably never go to the extremes of Diogenes, the cynical Greek philosopher who wandered through Athens carrying a lantern in broad daylight in order to search for an honest person, these words will help you to distinguish between fact and falsehood.

WORD LIST

belie
clandestine
collusion
dissemble
nefarious
perfidious
probity
scrupulous
spurious
stratagem

DEFINITIONS

After you have studied the definitions and example for each vocabulary word, write the word on the line to the right.

1. **belie** (bĭ-lī′) *trans. verb* **a.** To picture falsely; misrepresent; disguise. **b.** To show to be false; contradict. **c.** To disappoint or leave unfulfilled. 1. ____________

Example The new teacher's strictness *belied* her usual easygoing nature.

2. **clandestine** (klăn-dĕs′tĭn) *adjective* Concealed or kept secret, often for unlawful purposes. (From the Latin word *clandestinus,* meaning "secret") 2. ____________

Related Word **clandestinely** *adverb*
Example Before the practice of the "smoke-filled room" was abolished, presidential candidates were often chosen in *clandestine* meetings held by influential politicians.

3. **collusion** (kə-lo͞o′zhən) *noun* A secret agreement between two or more persons for a deceitful or fraudulent purpose; conspiracy. (From the Latin *com-,* meaning "together," and *ludere,* meaning "to play") 3. ____________

Related Word **collude** *verb*
Example Winters was found guilty of espionage and *collusion* with the enemy.

4. **dissemble** (dĭ-sĕm′bəl) *trans. verb* **a.** To disguise or conceal behind a false appearance: *dissemble one's fears with laughter.* **b.** To make a false show of; feign. *intrans. verb* To conceal one's real motives, nature, or feelings under a pretense. (From the Old French *des-*, indicating reversal, and *sembler*, meaning "to appear" or "to seem")

4. ______________

USAGE NOTE: Do not confuse *dissemble* with *disassemble*, which means "to take apart."

Related Word **dissemblance** *noun*
Example Unable to *dissemble* her annoyance, Beth's dislike of her roommate was apparent to all.

5. **nefarious** (nə-fâr′ē-əs) *adjective* Extremely wicked or infamous; evil; villainous. (From the Latin *ne-*, meaning "not," and *fas*, meaning "something permitted or ordained by law")

5. ______________

Related Words **nefariously** *adverb;* **nefariousness** *noun*
Example During the sixteenth and seventeenth centuries, *nefarious* pirates kidnapped travelers and sold them as slaves.

6. **perfidious** (pûr-fĭd′ē-əs) *adjective* Disloyal; treacherous. (From the Latin *per-*, meaning "through," and *fides*, meaning "faith")

6. ______________

Related Words **perfidiously** *adverb;* **perfidy** *noun*
Example In putting his ambitions before his devotion to Duncan, Macbeth proves to be a *perfidious* servant of his king.

7. **probity** (prō′bĭ-tē) *noun* Complete and confirmed integrity; uprightness. (From the Latin word *probus*, meaning "honest")

7. ______________

Example To assure that his *probity* would never be questioned, the president hired someone to handle his personal finances during his term of office.

8. **scrupulous** (skro͞o′pyə-ləs) *adjective* **a.** Acting in strict regard for what is considered right or proper; having principles. **b.** Very conscientious and exacting: *scrupulous attention to detail.*

8. ______________

Related Words **scruple** *noun;* **scrupulously** *adverb;* **scrupulousness** *noun*
Example When she learned that her brother had entered the photography contest, Mrs. Crowell's *scrupulous* sense of fairness prompted her to resign from the panel of judges.

9. **spurious** (spyo͝or′ē-əs) *adjective* **a.** Lacking authenticity or validity; false. **b.** Constituting a forgery. (From the Latin word *spurius*, meaning "false")

9. ______________

Related Words **spuriously** *adverb;* **spuriousness** *noun*
Example Fred did not realize that he had been swindled until he attempted to cash the *spurious* check.

10. **stratagem** (străt′ə-jəm) *noun* **a.** A clever scheme or trick designed to attain a goal. **b.** A maneuver designed to deceive or surprise an enemy. (From the Greek words *stratos*, meaning "army," and *agein*, meaning "to lead")

10. ______________

Example Harley devised a *stratagem* to ensure Ahmed's attendance at the surprise party.

NAME ____________________ DATE __________

EXERCISE 1 WRITING CORRECT WORDS

On the answer line, write the word from the vocabulary list that fits each definition.

1. Lacking authenticity or validity; false; constituting a forgery — 1. spurious
2. To disguise or conceal behind a false appearance; make a false show of — 2. dissemble
3. Acting in strict regard for what is considered right or proper; conscientious — 3. scrupulous
4. To picture falsely; show to be false; disappoint — 4. belie
5. Disloyal; treacherous — 5. perfidious
6. A clever scheme or trick designed to attain a goal; a maneuver designed to deceive or surprise an enemy — 6. stratagem
7. A secret agreement between two or more persons for a deceitful purpose — 7. collusion
8. Extremely wicked or infamous; evil — 8. nefarious
9. Complete and confirmed integrity; uprightness — 9. probity
10. Concealed or kept secret, often for unlawful purposes — 10. clandestine

EXERCISE 2 USING WORDS CORRECTLY

Each of the following statements contains an italicized vocabulary word. Decide whether the sentence is true or false, and write *True* or *False* on the answer line.

1. Bank officials may be indicted for their *collusion* in suppressing information about major loan defaults. — 1. True
2. A *nefarious* plan would be supported by charitable, compassionate individuals. — 2. False
3. A company's *spurious* transactions would probably be discovered during a yearly audit. — 3. True
4. If the failure of a new restaurant *belies* its owner's expectations, it fulfills them. — 4. False
5. Lying about one's guilt is an excellent way to establish *probity.* — 5. False
6. A *clandestine* rendezvous with an important celebrity would be well publicized prior to the event. — 6. False
7. A candidate who wins an election by a *stratagem* has used a deceptive technique. — 7. True
8. A bored member of an audience who *dissembles* interest shows genuine alertness and involvement. — 8. False
9. Someone who pays *scrupulous* attention to directions follows them carefully. — 9. True
10. If you reveal a friend's secret, he or she may well consider you *perfidious.* — 10. True

EXERCISE 3 IDENTIFYING SYNONYMS AND ANTONYMS

Decide which word has the meaning that is the same as (a synonym) or opposite to (an antonym) that of the capitalized vocabulary word. Write the letter of your choice on the answer line.

1. COLLUSION (synonym): — 1. b
   a. assurance **b.** conspiracy **c.** disorder **d.** approximation

2. NEFARIOUS (antonym):
a. stern b. minute c. infuriated d. virtuous
2. d

3. BELIE (synonym):
a. misrepresent b. vitalize c. preface d. assent
3. a

4. PROBITY (antonym):
a. dishonor b. obedience c. eventuality d. contingency
4. a

5. STRATAGEM (synonym):
a. conviction b. convention c. trick d. anguish
5. c

6. DISSEMBLE (antonym):
a. condone b. disclose c. expend d. victimize
6. b

7. PERFIDIOUS (synonym):
a. passive b. contemplative c. arbitrary d. treacherous
7. d

8. SPURIOUS (antonym):
a. perpetual b. noxious c. genuine d. ruthless
8. c

9. CLANDESTINE (synonym):
a. surreptitious b. ferocious c. judicious d. watchful
9. a

10. SCRUPULOUS (antonym):
a. meticulous b. antagonistic c. turbulent d. remiss
10. d

EXERCISE 4 USING DIFFERENT FORMS OF WORDS

Decide which form of the vocabulary word in parentheses best completes the sentence. The form given may be correct. Write your answer on the answer line.

1. Using a _____, Hector persuaded his friends to meet him at the bowling alley. *(stratagem)* 1. **stratagem**
2. Diamonds were brought into the country _____. *(clandestine)* 2. **clandestinely**
3. Benedict Arnold's _____ in betraying the colonies to the British is remembered even today. *(perfidious)* 3. **perfidy**
4. The border guards immediately detected the _____ passport. *(spurious)* 4. **spurious**
5. During the climb Anna Maria could manage only a _____ of courage. *(dissemble)* 5. **dissemblance**
6. Members of the grand jury _____ consider every detail of evidence before deciding on an indictment. *(scrupulous)* 6. **scrupulously**
7. Despite their attempts to _____ on the test, neither student did very well. *(collusion)* 7. **collude**
8. Lionel is a young man of indisputable _____ whose bluntness sometimes alienates his friends. *(probity)* 8. **probity**
9. The charm and elegance of the restored neighborhood _____ its origin as the site of a rope factory. *(belie)* 9. **belies**
10. The _____ of their stock-market schemes earned them little beyond a poor reputation. *(nefarious)* 10. **nefariousness**

NAME ______________________ DATE __________

READING COMPREHENSION

Each numbered sentence in the following passage contains an italicized vocabulary word or related form. After you read the passage, you will complete an exercise.

PERSEUS AND MEDUSA

Perseus, like all heroes of Greek legend, was a courageous and dedicated young man. (1) Best known for his adventure with the Gorgon Medusa, Perseus fended off evil foes at tremendous risk, struggled against ***nefarious*** kings, outwitted fearsome monsters, and rescued beautiful women.

The son of Danaë and Zeus, Perseus was cast into the sea with his mother when he was only an infant. His grandfather Acrisius, King of Argos, was attempting to protect himself from the prophecy of an oracle, which stated that the king would be killed by his grandson. Under the protection of Zeus, however, Danaë and Perseus were rescued by the citizens of Seripuys. Here, Danaë became a servant and Perseus was raised as a fisherman.

King Polydectes, the ruler of Seripuys, was attracted by Danaë's great beauty and wanted to marry her. Danaë resisted him for years, claiming that raising her son required all of her attention. As Perseus grew to manhood, Polydectes realized that the only way to claim Danaë as his bride was to get rid of Perseus. (2) To lull the young man's suspicions, Polydectes ***dissembled*** interest in marrying a certain noblewoman. As was the tradition, all of the young men of the kingdom assembled to present the king with bridal gifts for his intended. With embarrassment Perseus, the son of a servant, admitted to having nothing to give. (3) A young man of ***probity,*** he pledged, instead, that he would perform any task the king asked of him. (4) This was exactly what the king expected; with hesitation ***belying*** his joy, he claimed that his bride wanted a far-fetched curiosity—something like the head of the Gorgon Medusa.

The Gorgons were three horrible sisters with hands of brass and wings of gold. Two of the sisters had scaly heads and the tusks of a wild boar, while the third, Medusa, had the face of a beautiful woman with hair of writhing serpents. So terrible was the sight of the three sisters that those who saw them were immediately turned to stone.

Perseus had no idea how to find or kill Medusa and did the only thing that he could: he prayed to the wise goddess Athena for guidance. (5) Athena was delighted to ***collude*** with him. (6) First, she instructed him to shine his shield ***scrupulously*** so that he would look only at the Gorgons' reflections on its glossy surface. Next, she gave him her brother Hermes' sword of the hardest rock, the only weapon capable of slicing off Medusa's head. Finally, she instructed him to visit the Graiae, or Gray Sisters. (7) These women were the only ones to know the ***clandestine*** location of the nymphs who guarded the other articles Perseus needed to accomplish his task.

The Graiae were three sisters who shared one eye. (8) They granted no favors except under compulsion, and had Perseus not devised a ***stratagem,*** he would have failed in his mission. Waiting until the sisters were in the process of switching the eye, Perseus grabbed it and refused to return it until they told him where to find the nymphs.

The nymphs, who hated monsters, willingly provided Perseus with some important accessories. On his head they placed the hat of darkness, which would make him invisible. They fitted him with winged sandals to speed his journey and donated a special knapsack to hold the Gorgon's head.

Perseus easily killed Medusa. Coming upon the three sisters as they slept, he followed directions and sliced off Medusa's head. As he made his way home with his prize, Perseus managed to perform several more good deeds. Using the special aids provided by Athena and the nymphs, he killed a sea monster about to devour a beautiful maiden and changed a giant into a mountain of stone.

Having been convinced that Perseus would be killed in his attempt to obtain the Gorgon's head, Polydectes was enraged at the hero's successful return. (9) The ***perfidious*** king had failed to win the hand of Danaë; having asked her to marry him and being refused, he then threatened her, forcing her to escape and hide. (10) Polydectes laughed at Perseus' tale of killing the Gorgon, accusing him of making ***spurious*** claims to honors he did not deserve. Perseus, in turn, was infuriated by the insult and by reports of his mother's persecution. Without hesitation, Perseus withdrew the horrible head from the knapsack and instantly turned King Polydectes to stone. Perseus went on to pursue other adventures, and Medusa's head found a permanent home on Athena's protective shield.

READING COMPREHENSION EXERCISE

Each of the following statements corresponds to a numbered sentence in the passage. Each statement contains a blank and is followed by four answer choices. Decide which choice fits best in the blank. The word or phrase that you choose must express roughly the same meaning as the italicized word in the passage. Write the letter of your choice on the answer line.

1. Perseus struggled against _____ kings and outwitted fearsome monsters. — 1. ___a___
   a. wicked b. weak c. mighty d. wise

2. Polydectes _____ interest in marrying a certain noblewoman. — 2. ___c___
   a. suspected b. plotted c. feigned d. pleaded

3. Perseus was a young man of _____. — 3. ___d___
   a. shame b. wisdom c. tranquillity d. uprightness

4. With hesitation _____ his joy, the king claimed that his bride wanted a far-fetched curiosity. — 4. ___a___
   a. disguising b. disrupting c. banishing d. increasing

5. Athena was delighted to _____ with Perseus. — 5. ___c___
   a. escape b. govern c. conspire d. do battle

6. She instructed him to shine his shield _____. — 6. ___b___
   a. superbly b. conscientiously c. greedily d. gradually

7. The Gray Sisters were the only ones who knew the _____ location of the nymphs. — 7. ___c___
   a. occasional b. improvised c. secret d. official

8. Perseus would have failed in his mission if he had not devised a(n) _____. — 8. ___b___
   a. facsimile b. scheme c. accident d. ordeal

9. The _____ king had failed to win the hand of Danaë. — 9. ___a___
   a. treacherous b. shrewd c. ineffectual d. unhappy

10. Polydectes accused Perseus of making _____ claims to honors he did not deserve. — 10. ___d___
    a. feeble b. dramatic c. absolute d. false

WRITING ASSIGNMENT

You are probably familiar with many stories about heroes fighting against evil. From Hercules and Atalanta to Superman and Princess Leia, there are many examples of the forces of good combating the forces of dishonesty and deception. Create your own legend of a modern superhero, narrating an event in which he or she triumphs over an adversary. Use at least five of the vocabulary words from this lesson and underline each one.

Word History: scrupulous

Latin: *scrupulus* = little stone

The word *scrupulous* comes from the Latin noun *scrupulus,* meaning "a little stone." In ancient Roman times, a *scrupulus* that found its way into a person's sandal would cause discomfort to a sensitive foot. The trouble and pain associated with *scrupulus* gradually overpowered its meaning as "a little stone," and soon people forgot about the "little stone" and simply connected *scrupulus* with the idea of sensitivity to trouble. In modern usage *scrupulous* individuals, because of their heightened sensitivity to what is right and proper, weigh their actions most carefully, live by high principles, and try to stay out of trouble.

LESSON 3 MOVEMENT

3

When you think about the movement of something, you probably envision the activity of a living thing. The cheetah, for example, is the fastest animal, capable of running seventy miles per hour. A hummingbird's wings are only a blur when they move, vibrating at a rate of sixty to seventy-five times a second. The change of position of a garden snail, on the other hand, can barely be detected; it moves at only 0.03 miles per hour.

Although people usually connect movement with living things, all matter is made up of tiny particles that are constantly in motion. The particles of a solid are packed closely together and are not free to move about as much as the particles of liquids and gases. Yet even skyscrapers have a certain amount of sway, and concrete bridges often expand in hot weather. In addition, Earth both turns on its axis and revolves around the sun. Therefore, it may be appropriate to ask if anything actually stands still. The words in this lesson describe a variety of movements.

WORD LIST

emanate
inhibit
meander
retrogress
serpentine
supersede
torpid
transitory
undulate
unremitting

DEFINITIONS

After you have studied the definitions and example for each vocabulary word, write the word on the line to the right.

1. **emanate** (ĕm′ə-nāt′) *intrans. verb* To come forth, as from a source; originate. *trans. verb* To send forth; emit: *Radioactive substances emanate gamma rays.* (From the Latin *ex-*, meaning "out," and *manere*, meaning "to flow") 1. ____________

Related Word **emanation** *noun*
Example A heavy fragrance *emanates* from such flowers as gardenias and narcissuses.

2. **inhibit** (ĭn-hĭb′ĭt) *trans. verb* To restrain or hold back; prevent. (From the Latin *in-*, meaning "in," and *habere*, meaning "to have") 2. ____________

Related Word **inhibition** *noun*
Example Thoughts of our friend's problems *inhibited* our enjoyment of the party.

3. **meander** (mē-ăn′dər) *intrans. verb* **a.** To follow a winding and turning course. **b.** To wander aimlessly and idly without fixed direction. *noun* **a. meanders.** Circuitous windings, as of a stream or path. **b.** Often **meanders.** A circuitous journey or excursion; ramble. (From the Greek word *maiandros*, after *Maeander*, a river in Turkey noted for its winding course) 3. ____________

Example The Jordan River *meanders* approximately seventy-five miles from the Sea of Galilee to the Dead Sea.

4. **retrogress** (rĕt′rə-grĕs′, rĕt′ rə-grĕs′) *intrans. verb* **a.** To return to an earlier, inferior, or less complex condition; revert. **b.** To move or go backward. (From the Latin words *retro*, meaning "back," and *gradi*, meaning "to go") 4. ____________

Related Words **retrogression** *noun*; **retrogressive** *adjective*; **retrogressively** *adverb*
Example After several months of recovery, the economy *retrogressed*, and inflation again became a problem.

5. **serpentine** (sûr′pən-tēn′, sûr′pən-tīn′) *adjective* **a.** Of or resembling a serpent, as in form or movement; sinuous. **b.** Subtly sly and tempting: *a serpentine plot.* (From the Latin word *serpens,* meaning "serpent") 5. ______________

Example The *serpentine* path of the roller coaster criss-crossed itself many times before the ride finished.

6. **supersede** (so͞o′pər-sēd′) *trans verb* **a.** To take the place of; replace. **b.** To cause to be set aside or displaced; supplant. (From the Latin *super-,* meaning "above," and *sedere,* meaning "to sit") 6. ______________

Example Oil, gas and electricity have *superseded* coal as cleaner and more efficient sources of heat.

7. **torpid** (tôr′pĭd) *adjective* **a.** Lacking energy or vigor; lethargic; sluggish. **b.** Deprived of the power of motion or feeling; benumbed. **c.** Dormant; hibernating. (From the Latin word *torpere,* meaning "to be sluggish") 7. ______________

Related Words **torpidly** *adverb;* **torpor** *noun*
Example Members of the audience were in such a *torpid* state following the dull lecture that they could barely summon the energy to applaud.

8. **transitory** (trăn′sĭ-tôr′ē, trăn′zĭ-tôr′ē) *adjective* Existing only briefly; short-lived. (From the Latin word *transire,* meaning "to go across") 8. ______________

Related Word **transitoriness** *noun*
Example In spite of its *transitory* beauty, the day lily is a popular flower found in many gardens.

9. **undulate** (ŭn′jə-lāt′, ŭn′dyə-lāt′) *trans. verb* **a.** To move in waves or with a wavelike motion; ripple. **b.** To have a wavelike appearance or form. *trans. verb* **a.** To cause to move in a smooth wavelike motion. **b.** To give a wavelike appearance or form to. *adjective* (ŭn′jə-lĭt, ŭn′jə-lāt′, ŭn′dyə-lāt′) Having a wavy outline or appearance: *leaves with undulate markings.* (From the Latin word *unda,* meaning "wave") 9. ______________

Related Word **undulation** *noun*
Example The ripened grain *undulated* in the summer breeze.

10. **unremitting** (ŭn′rĭ-mĭt′ĭng) *adjective* Never slackening; persistent. 10. ______________

Related Word **unremittingly** *adverb*
Example Through the *unremitting* efforts of underwater archaeologists, the *Mary Rose,* flagship of King Henry VIII of England, was recovered and reconstructed.

NAME ______________________________ DATE ______________

EXERCISE 1 WRITING CORRECT WORDS

On the answer line, write the word from the vocabulary list that fits each definition.

1. To follow a winding and turning course; wander aimlessly and idly without a fixed course. 1. meander
2. To take the place of; cause to be set aside or displaced 2. supersede
3. Existing only briefly; short-lived 3. transitory
4. To come forth, as from a source; send forth 4. emanate
5. Of or resembling a serpent, as in form or movement; sinuous 5. serpentine
6. Never slackening; persistent 6. unremitting
7. To restrain or hold back 7. inhibit
8. Lacking energy or vigor; deprived of the power of motion or feeling 8. torpid
9. To move in waves or with a wavelike motion; ripple 9. undulate
10. To return to an earlier, inferior, or less complex condition; move or go backward 10. retrogress

EXERCISE 2 USING WORDS CORRECTLY

Decide whether the italicized vocabulary word has been used correctly in the sentence. On the answer line, write *Correct* for correct use and *Incorrect* for incorrect use:

1. Ardis tries to *emanate* everything her older sister does. 1. Incorrect
2. A young child may *retrogress* to babyish behavior when a new sibling arrives. 2. Correct
3. The original rules were *superseded* by the addition of several new directives. 3. Correct
4. Bill, who can labor for hours over a model ship or car, has a *transitory* attention span. 4. Incorrect
5. Leslie enjoyed the challenge of navigating the *serpentine* curves of the mountain road. 5. Correct
6. Still unsteady on their feet, the *torpid* puppies climbed all over each other in their attempts to explore their box. 6. Incorrect
7. Colin and Dirk followed a definite itinerary as they *meandered* through several national parks. 7. Incorrect
8. The lead runner could not maintain the *unremitting* pace and soon dropped back into the middle of the pack. 8. Correct
9. Virtually nothing can *inhibit* Lucy's enthusiasm. 9. Correct
10. Arranged in precise rows, the pencils and pens *undulated* across the top of Peter's desk. 10. Incorrect

EXERCISE 3 IDENTIFYING SYNONYMS AND ANTONYMS

Decide which word has the meaning that is the same as (a synonym) or opposite to (an antonym) that of the capitalized vocabulary word. Write the letter of your choice on the answer line.

1. TRANSITORY (antonym): — 1. b
   a. comprehensive b. permanent c. privileged d. suspicious
2. RETROGRESS (synonym): — 2. d
   a. uncover b. exclude c. propose d. revert
3. INHIBIT (antonym): — 3. a
   a. encourage b. dare c. suppose d. restrain
4. SUPERSEDE (synonym): — 4. d
   a. qualify b. endure c. survey d. supplant
5. TORPID (antonym): — 5. c
   a. sorrowful b. uncommon c. lively d. universal
6. MEANDER (synonym): — 6. a
   a. wander b. dedicate c. augment d. impel
7. UNREMITTING (antonym): — 7. b
   a. forgiving b. fluctuating c. corresponding d. deficient
8. SERPENTINE (synonym): — 8. d
   a. obedient b. obstinate c. evil d. snakelike
9. EMANATE (antonym): — 9. a
   a. withhold b. relinquish c. fascinate d. gratify
10. UNDULATE (synonym): — 10. c
    a. display b. hoard c. ripple d. repair

EXERCISE 4 USING DIFFERENT FORMS OF WORDS

Decide which form of the vocabulary word in parentheses best completes the sentence. The form given may be correct. Write your answer on the answer line.

1. Calvin has lost his shyness and many of his _____. *(inhibit)* — 1. inhibitions
2. Nicole _____ from one job to another. *(meander)* — 2. meanders
3. The _____ of the Arctic summer means that scientists who study animals there must complete their observations within several weeks. *(transitory)* — 3. transitoriness
4. Released from its thick braid, her hair _____ down her back. *(undulate)* — 4. undulated
5. Even though the patient had received the best possible treatment for her disease, her _____ was obvious. *(retrogress)* — 5. retrogression
6. Gail sanded the tabletop _____ until it was smooth. *(remitting)* — 6. unremittingly
7. Aspens and birches grew along the _____ banks of the creek. *(serpentine)* — 7. serpentine
8. During the power loss, Lisa tried to read by the meager _____ of light from a candle. *(emanate)* — 8. emanation
9. The crisp days of autumn relieve the _____ of summer. *(torpid)* — 9. torpor
10. Two years ago more efficient production methods _____ slow, costly procedures. *(supersede)* — 10. superseded

NAME ____________________ DATE __________

READING COMPREHENSION

Each numbered sentence in the following passage contains an italicized vocabulary word or related form. After you read the passage, you will complete an exercise.

THE GIFT OF THE NILE

The Nile is the world's longest, mightiest, and most mysterious river. (1) Twice as long as the Mississippi, it ***meanders*** 4145 miles from the equator through the desert of North Africa to the Mediterranean Sea. (2) Although it flows almost ***unremittingly*** through nine nations and embraces many different climates and topographies, the heart of the Nile lies in Egypt. Here the life-giving river provided both the means and the motivation for the development of a rich civilization.

To the ancient Egyptians, the Nile was Yer-o, the Great River. They worshipped the river whose water and silt nourished their crops and made Egypt the granary of the ancient world. Living along the banks of the river, people had to cooperate and organize in order to survive and control the regular flooding. (3) At first the Egyptians' battle for survival ***inhibited*** cultural growth. As they began to win the battle, however, the river stimulated various kinds of discoveries. They invented the 365-day calendar so that they could keep better track of the patterns of flooding. They developed geometry so that they could lay out ditches and canals to contain the waters. As centuries passed, the Nile served as an indispensable waterway, connecting the Egyptian provinces and stimulating trade and commerce. No other country is so dependent upon a single natural feature as Egypt is upon the Nile.

"Of the source of the Nile no one can give any account," wrote Herodotus, the Greek historian, in 460 B.C. when his exploring party

was halted at a waterfall. For more than two thousand years after that, the source of the river remained a mystery, as well as an enduring geographic preoccupation.

(4) Not until the nineteenth century was it finally established that the Nile actually has two points of ***emanation.***

The longer branch, the White Nile, begins in the mountains of central Africa as the melting of glacial ice. (5) The river ***undulates*** through Lake Victoria, then flows over falls and rapids in Uganda and enters the swamp in southern Sudan known as the Sudd. (6) Here, among a maze of channels and islands of tropical vegetation, the White Nile becomes ***torpid,*** almost losing its forward motion.

The Blue Nile begins in the highlands of Ethiopia. This branch of the river is much wilder, dropping over falls and gorges. It grows wider and calmer as it flows through the desert until it joins the White Nile in Khartoum, the capital of Sudan. (7) Together, the branches of the Nile move in ***serpentine*** course through the Sahara Desert and over the Aswan Dam. (8) The narrow band of water nourishes a lush area that appears to be vulnerable and ***transitory*** in the midst of uncompromising desert. Nevertheless, this region supports 97 percent of Egypt's population and produces year-round crops of fruits, grains, cotton, and vegetables. The Nile valley and delta rank among the world's most fertile farming areas.

(9) Contemporary life along the banks of the Nile seems much like a ***retrogression*** to life in 3100 B.C., when Egypt was the "cradle of civilization." (10) Modern equipment and electrical power have not ***superseded*** simple, ancient practices. Farmers still hack fifteen-foot sugar canes with machetes and turn the soil with wooden plows and hoes. Uncomplicated machines called shadoofs still draw water from the river and splash it into irrigation ditches, and blindfolded water buffalo still turn waterwheels. The eternal Nile has nurtured civilization for over five thousand years. It is the thread that connects the present with the past.

READING COMPREHENSION EXERCISE

Each of the following statements corresponds to a numbered sentence in the passage. Each statement contains a blank and is followed by four answer choices. Decide which choice fits best in the blank. The word or phrase that you choose must express roughly the same meaning as the italicized word in the passage. Write the letter of your choice on the answer line.

1. The Nile ____ from the equator to the Mediterranean Sea. 1. c
   a. includes the sea c. follows a winding course
   b. saturates the land d. flows directly
2. The river flows almost ____ through nine nations. 2. b
   a. slowly b. without slackening c. ultimately d. quickly
3. The Egyptians' battle for survival ____ cultural growth. 3. d
   a. renewed b. supplied c. consolidated d. restrained
4. It was finally established in the nineteenth century that the Nile has two points of ____. 4. c
   a. symmetry b. picturesqueness c. origin d. affluence
5. The river ____ through Lake Victoria, flows over rapids in Uganda, and enters a swamp in southern Sudan. 5. a
   a. ripples c. has a level course
   b. follows a narrow path d. glides quickly
6. The Nile becomes ____, almost losing its forward motion. 6. d
   a. destructive b. relentless c. renewed d. sluggish
7. The branches of the Nile move in a ____ course through the Sahara Desert and over the Aswan Dam. 7. b
   a. direct b. snakelike c. complex d. standard
8. The water nourishes an area that appears to be ____. 8. a
   a. short-lived b. barren c. protected d. uninhabited
9. Contemporary life along the Nile seems like a(n) ____ life in 3100 B.C. 9. c
   a. example of b. criterion for c. reversion to d. key to
10. Modern equipment has not ____ simple, ancient practices. 10. a
    a. replaced b. improved c. interfered with d. compensated for

WRITING ASSIGNMENT

Suppose that you are in charge of your car club's yearly rally. Your first task is to write detailed instructions for the competitors, explaining the general layout of the course (the public roads in your area) and summarizing the normal traffic regulations that will be in effect. Explain that the rally consists of different routes with stops for clues that will provide further directions for drivers. Remind people that speed does not determine the winner; instead, prizes will be awarded to those who collect the largest number of clues and pass the greatest number of checkpoints. In your instructions use at least five of the words from this lesson and underline each one.

The **Test** for Lessons 1, 2, and 3 is on page T1.

NAME ______________________ DATE ____________

A B C

DICTIONARY SKILLS

USING A DICTIONARY AND A THESAURUS TO FIND SYNONYMS

When you need a synonym for a word, you usually consult a dictionary, paying particular attention to **synonym paragraphs,** which differentiate among the related synonyms in a cluster. You can also consult a **thesaurus,** a book of synonyms, which is usually divided into two parts: the *text,* containing numbered idea categories and words associated with them, and an *index* to the idea categories.

Each reference tool, the dictionary and the thesaurus, has a particular advantage. The synonym paragraphs in a dictionary enable you to choose a word with just the right shade of meaning. The thesaurus does not distinguish among the meanings of synonyms; however, its synonym lists in the text are extensive, giving you a wide choice. Sometimes it is wise to use both a thesaurus and a dictionary.

Thesaurus Index Entry

improve
be changed 139.5
change 139.6
excel 36.6
get better 691.7
make better 691.9
make perfect 677.5
recuperate 694.19
take advantage of 665.15
rain 562.14

Portion of Thesaurus Text

.9 (make better) **improve, better,** change for the better, make an improvement; transform, transfigure 139.7; improve upon, refine upon, **mend, amend,** emend [archaic]; meliorate, **ameliorate; advance, promote,** foster, favor, nurture, forward, bring forward; **lift,** elevate, **uplift,** raise, **boost** [informal]; upgrade; **enhance, enrich,** fatten, lard [archaic]; make one's way, better oneself; be the making of; **reform;** reform oneself, turn over a new leaf, mend one's ways, straighten out, straighten oneself out, go straight [informal]; **civilize,** acculturate, socialize; enlighten, edify; **educate** 562.11.

Suppose, for example, that you want a synonym for *improve.* You begin with a thesaurus, finding *improve* in the index. Scanning the list of numbered words and phrases under *improve,* you decide that "make better" best expresses the type of improving that you mean. Using its number, 691.9, you locate the "make better" paragraph in the text.

Within the paragraph you notice that each group of related words appears in a separate cluster set off by semicolons. (You also notice that the most common words appear in boldface type and that such usage labels as "informal" are supplied with some words. Finally, you notice that references to other numbered paragraphs are given after other words.) Reading the synonyms for *improve,* you think that either *better* or *enhance* may be the synonym that you need, but you want to know more about their connotations.

You therefore consult a dictionary and, at the end of the *improve* entry, find a synonym paragraph. Reading through the definitions, you decide on *enhance,* It is the synonym that will best express your meaning in a book review as you explain the way in which illustrations *add to* the text.

Synonym Paragraph in a Dictionary

***Synonyms:** improve, better, help, ameliorate, enhance.* These verbs mean to make more attractive or desirable in some respect. *Improve,* the most general term, refers to an act of raising in quality or value or of relieving an undesirable situation. *Better* is often interchangeable with *improve* in the preceding senses; used reflexively, *better* implies worldly gain: *better himself by changing jobs. Help* usually implies limited relief or change for the better: *medicine that helped her. Ameliorate* refers to improving or bettering conditions that cry out for change. *Enhance,* in contrast, suggests adding to something already attractive or worthy and thus increasing its value.

EXERCISE FINDING APPROPRIATE SYNONYMS

Decide which of the three italicized synonyms in parentheses fits most appropriately in each sentence. To choose the correct answer, study the two thesaurus paragraphs and the synonym paragraph at the foot of the page. You will need to take information from both types of paragraphs. Write your answer on the answer line.

1. Having traveled in twenty-five countries on four continents before she reached the age of thirty, Randy was truly _____. *(reckless, adventurous, hasty)* 1. **adventurous**
2. Driving at seventy-five miles an hour is not only illegal but _____. *(impetuous, foolhardy, enterprising)* 2. **foolhardy**
3. _____ Sarah liked to invest in penny stocks, but she was always aware of the risks. *(Venturesome, Impulsive, Foolhardy)* 3. **Venturesome**
4. In a(n) _____ mood, James invited ten classmates to his home for dinner the next evening. *(impulsive, daring, venturous)* 4. **impulsive**
5. Neither a judge nor a jury should ever make _____ decisions. *(enterprising, confident, precipitate)* 5. **precipitate**
6. The _____ hikers climbed the mountain during a snowstorm. *(daring, reckless, venturesome)* 6. **reckless**
7. She always counsels students not to be _____ when they make a decision about a career. *(daring, venturous, rash)* 7. **rash**
8. In a(n) _____ move, the rebel troops took control of the weakened government. *(audacious, foolhardy, overhasty)* 8. **audacious**
9. With complete assurance the professional skater performed a _____ jump that no one had ever before attempted. *(foolhardy, daring, hasty)* 9. **daring**
10. During his long and distinguished career, the research scientist displayed a _____ spirit. *(venturous, rash, foolhardy)* 10. **venturous**

.9 ADJS **impulsive, impetuous, hasty,** overhasty, quick, sudden, **precipitate,** headlong; **reckless, rash** 894.7–9; impatient 862.6.

.21 daring, audacious, overbold; **adventurous, venturous, venturesome,** adventuresome, enterprising, foolhardy 894.9.

***Synonyms:** reckless, adventurous, rash, precipitate, foolhardy, audacious, daring, venturous, venturesome. Reckless* suggests heedlessness or thoughtlessness in action or decision. *Adventurous* implies willingness to incur risk and danger, but usually not mindlessly. *Rash* and *precipitate* connote haste and lack of deliberation in deed or decision. *Foolhardy* implies absence of sound judgment. *Audacious* and *daring* suggest fearlessness and confidence. *Venturous* and *venturesome* imply inclination to take risk that is recognized as such.

LESSON 4 WORDS FROM OTHER LANGUAGES

4

Throughout its long history, the English language has always been characterized by its flexibility in incorporating new words. Exploration, colonization, and immigration have provided exposure to new people, places, products, and ideas. In encountering the unfamiliar, people have needed words to describe these new experiences; borrowing from other languages has been a natural way to achieve precise expression. Although borrowed words may sometimes be altered or adapted in pronunciation, spelling, or meaning, foreign language borrowings continue to enrich the language. The words in this lesson will acquaint you with ten of the words that have added color and variety to English.

WORD LIST

berserk
jubilee
juggernaut
kowtow
maelstrom
mecca
nabob
saga
shibboleth
trek

DEFINITIONS

After you have studied the definitions and example for each vocabulary word, write the word on the line to the right.

1. **berserk** (bər-sûrk′, bər-zûrk′) *adjective* **a.** Destructively violent. **b.** Deranged; insane. (From the Old Norse word *berserker,* an ancient Scandinavian warrior who fought with insane fury) 1. ____________

   Example Suddenly the prisoner broke away from his captors and attacked them in a *berserk* fashion.

2. **jubilee** (jo͞o′bə-lē′) *noun* **a.** A season or occasion of joyful celebration. **b.** Jubilation; rejoicing. **c.** A special anniversary, especially a fiftieth anniversary. (From the Hebrew word *yobhel,* a year of restoration of property and freeing of slaves observed every fifty years by the ancient Hebrews) 2. ____________

   Example The museum is planning a month-long *jubilee* to celebrate the completion of the new wing.

3. **juggernaut** (jŭg′ər-nôt′) *noun* **a.** An overwhelming and irresistible force or movement. **b.** Something, such as a belief or institution, that elicits blind and destructive devotion. (From the Hindi word *jagannath,* meaning "lord of the world." The word was used as the title of the god Krishna, who aroused such devotion that people were said to have thrown themselves under the wheels of the chariot that carried his idol.) 3. ____________

   Example The *juggernaut* of the barbarian invasion destroyed every civilization in its path.

4. **kowtow** (kou-tou′, kou′tou′) *intrans. verb* To show respect or submission; fawn. *noun* An act or gesture of exaggerated respect or obedience. (From the Chinese words *ke,* meaning "to knock," and *tou,* meaning "head." The ancient Chinese would kneel and touch their foreheads to the ground as an expression of respect or submission.) 4. ____________

Example Employees of Edison National Bank must *kowtow* to the bank president if they expect to be promoted.

5. **maelstrom** (māl′strəm) *noun* **a.** A whirlpool of extraordinary size or violence. **b.** A situation that resembles a whirlpool in the violence or turbulence of feelings, ideas, or conditions: *the maelstrom of war.* (From the Dutch words *malen,* meaning "to whirl," and *stroom,* meaning "stream") 5. ____________

Example Caught in the *maelstrom,* the sailboat was inundated by eight-foot waves.

6. **mecca** (mĕk′ə) *noun* **a.** A place regarded as the center of an activity or interest. **b.** A place visited by many people: *a mecca for tourists.* **c.** A goal to which the followers of a religious faith or practice aspire. (From the Arabian City *Mecca,* the birthplace of the prophet Mohammed and a place of pilgrimage for Muslims) 6. ____________

Example The vital, creative atmosphere of New York City has made it a *mecca* for actors, artists, and musicians.

7. **nabob** (nā′bŏb′) *noun* A person of great wealth and prominence. (From the Arabic word *nawwab,* meaning "a deputy governor under the Mogul empire") 7. ____________

Example The imperious *nabob* always demanded special treatment.

8. **saga** (sä′gə) *noun* **a.** A prose narrative; story. **b.** A long, detailed report: *the saga of four generations of a family.* **c.** A prose narrative of the twelfth and thirteenth centuries recounting historical and legendary events and exploits in Iceland or Norway. (From the Old Norse word *saga,* meaning "a medieval Scandinavian prose narrative") 8. ____________

Example The *saga* of the Alamo is both tragic and heroic.

9. **shibboleth** (shĭb′ə-lĭth, shĭb′ə-lĕth′) *noun* **a.** A slogan or often repeated word or phrase. **b.** A common saying or idea. **c.** A language usage that distinguishes the members of one group or class from another. (From the Hebrew word *shibboleth,* a word which, in the Old Testament, was used to distinguish Ephraimites, who could not pronounce *sh,* from Gileadites) 9. ____________

Example "Any child can grow up to be president" is an example of a *shibboleth.*

10. **trek** (trĕk) *intrans. verb* To make a slow or difficult journey. *noun* **a.** A journey or leg of a journey, especially when it is slow and difficult. **b.** A migration. (From the Dutch word *trekken,* meaning "to travel") 10. ____________

Example Pioneers of the 1800s often endured hunger, cold, and danger as they *trekked* across the frontier.

NAME ______________________ DATE ____________

EXERCISE 1 WRITING CORRECT WORDS

On the answer line, write the word from the vocabulary list that fits each definition.

1. An overwhelming and irresistible force or movement — 1. juggernaut
2. To make a slow or difficult journey — 2. trek
3. A season or occasion of joyful celebration — 3. jubilee
4. A prose narrative; a long, detailed report — 4. saga
5. Destructively violent; deranged — 5. berserk
6. A slogan or often-repeated word or phrase; a language usage that distinguishes the members of one group from another — 6. shibboleth
7. To show respect or submission; an act or gesture of exaggerated respect or obedience — 7. kowtow
8. A person of great wealth and prominence — 8. nabob
9. A place regarded as the center of an activity or interest — 9. mecca
10. A whirlpool of extraordinary size or violence; a situation resembling a whirlpool in the turbulence of feelings, ideas, or conditions — 10. maelstrom

EXERCISE 2 USING WORDS CORRECTLY

Decide whether the italicized vocabulary word has been used correctly in the sentence. On the answer line, write *Correct* for correct use and *Incorrect* for incorrect use.

1. The politician used the same *shibboleths* for all of his campaigns. — 1. Correct
2. The candidate's headquarters were a *maelstrom* of activity. — 2. Correct
3. The sailor took a long *juggernaut* in a small boat. — 3. Incorrect
4. The strain of working long hours drove the prisoners of war *berserk.* — 4. Correct
5. The players showed their *jubilee* at winning the football championship. — 5. Incorrect
6. Marcia is so domineering that she wants to *kowtow* to everyone. — 6. Incorrect
7. The Ginsburgs *trekked* for several hundred miles along the banks of the Nile River. — 7. Correct
8. The boating club is dominated by the local *nabobs,* who try to exclude the less well-to-do. — 8. Correct
9. Orion, once a popular resort, has gone downhill and become a *mecca.* — 9. Incorrect
10. Tom's brother enjoyed "The *Saga* of Robin Hood" on television. — 10. Correct

EXERCISE 3 CHOOSING THE BEST DEFINITION

For each italicized vocabulary word in the following sentences, write the letter of the best definition on the answer line.

1. The *saga* of Hercules deals with his twelve labors for the king of Mycenae. — 1. b
   a. life **b.** prose narrative **c.** lengthy ordeal **d.** ancient play
2. "A Descent into the *Maelstrom*" is Lee's favorite story by Poe. — 2. d
   a. tidal wave **b.** dungeon **c.** cave **d.** whirlpool
3. The soccer fans went *berserk* over their team's unexpected victory. — 3. b
   a. silly **b.** insane **c.** comatose **d.** jubilant

4. A *trek* in the Himalayas takes years to plan and months to carry out.
a. visit b. invasion c. slow, difficult journey d. survival course
4. c

5. When the British ruled India, they expected residents to *kowtow* to them.
a. be submissive b. be amusing c. be helpful d. show kindness
5. a

6. The Paris salon of Gertrude Stein was a *mecca* for artists and writers.
a. tourist trap b. place of conspiracy c. center of activity d. home and studio
6. c

7. Our town will hold a *jubilee* this summer to mark its sesquicentennial, or 150-year anniversary.
a. meeting b. celebration c. election d. contest
7. b

8. Hiram Ellsworth, considered by many to be a *nabob*, is running for mayor.
a. person of great intelligence c. person of doubtful reputation
b. person of great education d. person of wealth and position
8. d

9. The poster featured the old *shibboleth* "Crime does not pay."
a. grammatical error b. foreign term c. common saying d. joke
9. c

10. The beginning of the end for Hitler's *juggernaut* was the invasion of Normandy on D-Day, June 6, 1944.
a. destructive force b. ambition c. battleship d. vice chancellor
10. a

EXERCISE 4 CHOOSING THE BEST WORD

Decide which vocabulary word best completes the sentence, and write the letter of your choice on the answer line.

1. According to an old Norse legend, a _____ swallowed all ships within a wide radius.
a. maelstrom b. mecca c. jubilee d. shibboleth
1. a

2. During World War II, interrogating officers insisted that suspected spies pronounce such _____ as *mellifluous* and *unintelligible.*
a. sagas b. kowtows c. nabobs d. shibboleths
2. d

3. In the eighteenth century, the typical costume of a _____ in India included a brocaded jacket and a jeweled turban.
a. mecca b. berserk c. trek d. nabob
3. d

4. Richard Wagner based the operas of his "Ring" cycle on the Scandinavian Volsungsa _____.
a. Juggernaut b. Saga c. Mecca d. Kowtow
4. b

5. At the teahouse the waitress delivered our tea, performed a _____, and backed quietly out of the room.
a. trek b. mecca c. kowtow d. juggernaut
5. c

6. After ruling for sixty years, Queen Victoria celebrated her diamond _____.
a. jubilee b. maelstrom c. nabob d. saga
6. a

7. Carlo referred to our short walk on the beach as a _____.
a. shibboleth b. trek c. nabob d. maelstrom
7. b

8. Bonaire, a small island in the Netherlands Antilles chain, has become a _____ for scuba divers.
a. juggernaut b. maelstrom c. trek d. mecca
8. d

9. Caught in the _____ of war, the small country was crushed.
a. kowtow b. trek c. juggernaut d. saga
9. c

10. Gillian attacks her work with something resembling _____ intensity.
a. shibboleth b. berserk c. jubilee d. mecca
10. b

NAME ______________________ DATE __________

READING COMPREHENSION

Each numbered sentence in the following passage contains an italicized vocabulary word or related form. After you read the passage, you will complete an exercise.

MARCO POLO: WORLD EXPLORER

At a time when most people stayed fairly close to home, Marco Polo (1254–1324) traveled throughout North Africa and Asia, bringing back tales of strange and distant lands. His account of his adventures was for several decades the primary source of information for European mapmakers and explorers and the stimulus for European interest in Asian trade and science.

(1) Marco Polo was born in Venice, Italy, a ***mecca*** of commerce during the thirteenth century. When his mother died and his father left on a lengthy trading mission, Marco's care fell to an aunt and uncle. He was educated to be a merchant, learning about foreign currency, judging products, and handling cargo ships.

In 1269 Marco Polo's father returned to Venice from Cathay, or present-day China. His accounts of the Mongol empire of Kublai Khan fascinated Marco, who decided to accompany his father on his next trip.

Father and son left Venice in 1271. (2) For the next three years, they ***trekked*** by camel across the deserts and mountains of Asia. (3) Along the way they had the opportunity to learn new languages and customs and talk with the ***nabobs*** of different cultures. (4) The Polos were among the first Europeans to visit such places as Persia; their arrival prompted lavish ***jubilees*** that often lasted for days.

(5) When they finally arrived in China, Marco Polo was deeply impressed with the splendor of the imperial court, where people ***kowtowed*** to him regularly. Kublai Khan was equally impressed with him. Valuing the linguistic ability and resourcefulness of his young guest, the Khan employed Polo for a variety of missions. Over the next seventeen years, Marco Polo exercised his powers of observation in order to make the full reports expected of a traveling official.

With Kublai Khan approaching his eightieth birthday, the Polos decided in 1292 that it was time to return home. (6) A political ***maelstrom*** had characterized the last several years of the Khan's reign, and China was no longer safe for them. (7) The Polos feared that Kublai Khan's death would unleash a ***juggernaut*** that would destroy his supporters.

The Polos returned to Venice to find the city at war with Genoa, its longtime rival in trade. Although little is known about the circumstances, Marco Polo was captured and imprisoned during a skirmish. (8) He made good use of the time in prison; between 1296 and 1298 Polo dictated the ***saga*** of his travels to a fellow prisoner.

The book, whose title has been variously translated as *Description of the World* or *The Travels of Marco Polo*, describes Kublai Khan's prosperous, advanced empire and includes Polo's observations about manufacturing, inventions, customs, government, and religion.

Although filled with specific detail, Marco Polo's book was received with astonishment and disbelief. (9) "Marco's Millions" was the ***shibboleth*** that people used to describe what they felt to be the exaggerated wonders of the book. (10) Many tried to dismiss it as a collection of fabrications and the author as a ***berserk*** liar. Polo lived out the rest of his days as a figure of amusement. It was not until some years later, after other travelers had verified his tales, that the book and Marco Polo were given the respect that they deserved.

READING COMPREHENSION EXERCISE

Each of the following statements corresponds to a numbered sentence in the passage. Each statement contains a blank and is followed by four answer choices. Decide which choice fits best in the blank. The word or phrase that you choose must express roughly the same meaning as the italicized word in the passage. Write the letter of your choice on the answer line.

1. Marco Polo was born in Venice, Italy, which was _____ commerce. 1. b
   a. the capital city of c. the geographical location for
   b. a center of activity in d. a dependable area for

2. Marco and his father _____ across the deserts and mountains of Asia. 2. a
   a. traveled slowly b. rode quickly c. drove d. ambled

3. They had many opportunities to learn new languages and to talk with _____. 3. d
   a. artists c. farmers
   b. the poor d. the wealthy and prominent

4. The Polos' arrival was the occasion for lavish _____. 4. d
   a. works of art b. costumes c. preparations d. celebrations

5. At the imperial court, people _____ Marco Polo. 5. b
   a. charmed b. showed respect to c. spoke to d. ignored

6. Political _____ made China unsafe for the Polos. 6. c
   a. parties b. attacks c. turbulence d. prisoners

7. The Polos feared that Kublai Khan's death would unleash a _____. 7. a
   a. ruthless force b. catastrophe c. pretense d. political change

8. While in prison Polo dictated the _____ of his travels. 8. d
   a. epic poem b. gist c. outline d. long, detailed report

9. People used the _____ "Marco's Millions" to describe his book. 9. c
   a. poetic phrase b. quotation c. slogan d. nickname

10. Many people called Polo a(n) _____ liar. 10. b
    a. perplexing b. insane c. legendary d. skillful

WRITING ASSIGNMENT

For a class presentation on the topic "Our Debt to Other Languages," choose a language and investigate some of its contributions to English. For example, you might use the dictionary and library resources to learn about such German words as *gestalt* and *waltz* or such Arabic words as *elixir* and *gazelle.* Summarize your findings in a brief report.

VOCABULARY ENRICHMENT

Mecca, a city in what is now Saudi Arabia, was the birthplace of the prophet Mohammed, who founded the Islam religion. Although people who practice Islam today live throughout the world, Mecca remains their holy city, to which they are urged to make a pilgrimage at least once in their lifetime. Because of the significance of the city, the word *mecca* was first used to mean "a place or goal to which the followers of a religious faith aspire." However, the word has come to denote any place that is the center of an activity or interest.

Activity Many other English words come from the names of places. Look up the etymologies and definitions of the following words and explain the connections.

1. mall 2. Rubicon 3. shanghai 4. tuxedo 5. worsted

The **Bonus activity** for Lessons 1–4 is on page T3.

LESSON 5 RELATIONSHIPS

5

To a mouse, a cat is a lion. (Albanian proverb)
The smaller the woods, the larger seems the hare. (Dutch proverb)
When the moon is not full, the stars shine more brightly. (Buganda proverb)
Bad is never good until worse happens. (Danish proverb)

All of the proverbs above share a single idea—that people tend to view things in relationship to other things. The unknown is easier to envision when it is compared to something familiar. You have probably experienced this yourself, describing the impact of an event by associating or connecting it with an approximate or equivalent situation. The words in this lesson will help you to explain the parallel and complementary relationships that you encounter.

WORD LIST

adjunct
amalgamate
contiguous
diffuse
diverge
parity
periphery
synergy
transcend
unison

DEFINITIONS

After you have studied the definitions and example for each vocabulary word, write the word on the line to the right.

1. **adjunct** (ăj′ŭngkt′) *noun* **a.** Something attached to another thing but in a dependent or auxiliary capacity. **b.** A person associated with another in a subordinate or auxiliary capacity. *adjective* Attached to a faculty or staff in a temporary or auxiliary capacity: *an adjunct professor.* (From the Latin *ad-*, meaning "to," and *jungere,* meaning "to join") 1. ________

   Example In vocabulary study a thesaurus is a useful *adjunct* to the dictionary.

2. **amalgamate** (ə-măl′gə-māt′) *intrans. verb* **a.** To combine, unite, or consolidate. **b.** To blend with another metal: *Silver amalgamates with mercury to make a dental filling.* *trans. verb* To mix so as to make a unified whole; blend. (From the Greek word *malagma,* meaning "soft mass") 2. ________

   Related Words **amalgam** *noun;* **amalgamation** *noun*
   Example Three local businesses *amalgamated* to form a national corporation.

3. **contiguous** (kən-tĭg′yo͞o-əs) *adjective* **a.** Sharing a boundary or edge; touching. **b.** Adjacent; nearby. **c.** Adjacent in time; immediately preceding or following; serial. **d.** Continuous. (From the Latin *con-*, an intensive prefix, and *tangere,* meaning "to touch") 3. ________

   USAGE NOTE: *Contiguous* means "touching" or "in actual contact," whereas *continuous* suggests a constant recurrence in time.

   Related Words **contiguity** *noun;* **contiguously** *adverb*
   Example The two lakefront properties are *contiguous.*

4. **diffuse** (dĭ-fyo͞os′) *adjective* **a.** Widely spread or scattered. **b.** Characterized by wordiness. *trans. verb* (dĭ-fyo͞oz′) **a.** To pour out and cause to spread freely. **b.** To spread about or scatter; disseminate. *intrans. verb* To spread out or soften. (From the Latin *dis-*, meaning "apart," and *fundere,* meaning "to spread") 4. ________

   Related Word **diffusion** *noun*
   Example The stage was characterized by soft, *diffuse* lighting that created an atmosphere of cozy warmth.

5. **diverge** (dĭ-vûrj′, dī-vûrj′) *intrans. verb* **a.** To go or extend in different directions from a common point; branch out. **b.** To differ, as in opinion or manner. **c.** To depart from a set course or norm; deviate. (From the Latin *dis-*, meaning "apart," and *vergere*, meaning "to bend") 5. ____________

Related Words **divergence** *noun;* **divergent** *adjective*
Example Robert Frost wrote about roads that "*diverged* in a yellow wood."

6. **parity** (păr′ĭ-tē) *noun* Equality, as in amount, status, or value. (From the Latin word *par,* meaning "equal") 6. ____________

Related Word **par** *noun*
Example The naval forces of the two countries had *parity.*

7. **periphery** (pə-rĭf′ə-rē) *noun* **a.** The outermost part or region within a precise boundary. **b.** The region or area immediately beyond a precise boundary. **c.** A zone constituting an inexact boundary. (From the Greek words *peri,* meaning "around," and *pherein,* meaning "to carry") 7. ____________

Related Word **peripheral** *adjective*
Example Soldiers patrolled the *periphery* of the air base.

8. **synergy** (sĭn′ər-jē) *noun* The combined action of two or more agents, substances, organs, or organisms to achieve an effect greater than the total effect that would be produced by each one acting individually; interdependence. (From the Greek word *sunergos,* meaning "working together") 8. ____________

USAGE NOTE: *Synergy* and *synergism* are interchangeable terms.

Related Words **synergistic** *adjective;* **synergistically** *adverb*
Example The *synergy* of the flexor muscles allows us to bend our joints.

9. **transcend** (trăn-sĕnd′) *trans. verb* **a.** To pass beyond or rise above. **b.** To surpass or exceed. **c.** To exist above and independent of (the physical realm). From the Latin *trans-*, meaning "over," and *scandere,* meaning "to climb") 9. ____________

Related Words **transcendence** *noun;* **transcendent** *adjective*
Example Do one's family loyalties *transcend* one's loyalties to a friend?

10. **unison** (yo͞o′nĭ-sən, yo͞o′nĭ-zən) *noun* **a.** The act of speaking or singing the same words simultaneously by two or more people. **b.** An instance of agreement; concord. **c.** Identity of musical pitch. (From the Latin words *unus,* meaning "one," and *sonus,* meaning "sound") 10. ____________

Example "Yes!" the children shouted in *unison* when Mrs. Díaz asked if they wanted to go to the planetarium.

NAME _______________ DATE _______________

EXERCISE 1 WRITING CORRECT WORDS

On the answer line, write the word from the vocabulary list that fits each definition.

1. The act of speaking or singing the same words simultaneously by two or more people; agreement — 1. unison
2. To combine, unite, or consolidate — 2. amalgamate
3. To go or extend in different directions from a common point; differ in opinion or manner — 3. diverge
4. The combined action of two or more agents or organisms to achieve an effect greater than that produced by each acting individually. — 4. synergy
5. Something attached to another thing in a dependent or auxiliary capacity — 5. adjunct
6. The outermost region within a precise boundary; the region immediately beyond a precise boundary — 6. periphery
7. Equality, as in amount, status, or value — 7. parity
8. To pass beyond or rise above; surpass or exceed — 8. transcend
9. Sharing a boundary or edge; adjacent — 9. contiguous
10. Widely spread or scattered; wordy; to pour out and cause to spread freely — 10. diffuse

EXERCISE 2 USING WORDS CORRECTLY

Each of the following questions contains an italicized vocabulary word. Choose the correct answer to the question, and write *Yes* or *No* on the answer line.

1. Could an apprentice be considered an *adjunct* to an experienced plumber? — 1. Yes
2. If Kevin has collected more newspapers for recycling than Jill has, is there *parity* in the amounts that they have collected? — 2. No
3. In a three-part round, in which each voice enters at a different time with the same melody, do people sing in *unison?* — 3. No
4. If the Canadian provinces of Saskatchewan and Manitoba share a border, are they *contiguous?* — 4. Yes
5. If you *transcend* an obstacle that you encounter, do you rise above it? — 5. Yes
6. Would a *synergy* of medical remedies work in opposition to each other? — 6. No
7. In a business might the work of two departments be *amalgamated?* — 7. Yes
8. Would a single drop of food coloring *diffuse* in a cup of water? — 8. Yes
9. If you stand on the *periphery* of a crowd, are you in the center of it? — 9. No
10. If a bicycle path *diverges* from the main highway, does the path run parallel to it? — 10. No

EXERCISE 3 CHOOSING THE BEST WORD

Decide which vocabulary word or related form best completes the sentence, and write the letter of your choice on the answer line.

1. The old adage "Two heads are better than one" is an example of _____. — 1. b
   a. diffusion **b.** synergy **c.** parity **d.** periphery

2. The international trade agreement calls for _____ between imports and exports in five years' time. 2. d
   a. transcendence b. adjunct c. periphery d. parity

3. In 1916 the Daytona Normal School, founded by Mary McLeod Bethune, _____ with Cookman Institute to become the four-year coeducational Bethune-Cookman College. 3. a
   a. amalgamated b. diverged c. transcended d. diffused

4. The restaurant is a(n) _____ of the bookstore. 4. b
   a. divergence b. adjunct c. contiguity d. unison

5. The flutes, violins, and harp play the first melody in _____. 5. c
   a. synergy b. parity c. unison d. diffusion

6. Liam's _____ speech was tiresome; it took him much too long to get to his central point. 6. a
   a. diffuse b. synergistic c. contiguous d. peripheral

7. Sara's instinct for doing the right thing _____ mere etiquette. 7. d
   a. amalgamates b. diffuses c. diverges d. transcends

8. Dwight continually raises _____ issues that have little relevance to the present discussion. 8. c
   a. synergistic b. transcendent c. peripheral d. contiguous

9. _____ red-brick houses are sometimes called Philadelphia row houses. 9. b
   a. Diffused b. Contiguous c. Amalgamated d. Peripheral

10. Maureen's speech was more effective than Liam's because she never _____ from her main topic. 10. a
   a. diverged b. transcended c. diffused d. amalgamated

EXERCISE 4 USING DIFFERENT FORMS OF WORDS

Decide which form of the vocabulary word in parentheses best completes the sentence. The form given may be correct. Write your answer on the answer line.

1. We decided to sell our stock at _____, or monetary face value. *(parity)* 1. par
2. The choral reading required the speakers to present a poem in _____. *(unison)* 2. unison
3. The Painted Desert is a landscape of _____ beauty. *(transcend)* 3. transcendent
4. Dr. Madarese will serve as an _____ professor at the university this semester. *(adjunct)* 4. adjunct
5. There has been an increasing _____ between the Democratic and Republican platforms on many key issues. *(diverge)* 5. divergence
6. The _____ effect of a responsive audience and a talented performer can produce outstanding and satisfying entertainment. *(synergy)* 6. synergistic
7. Platinum is generally _____ with another metal, such as iridium or nickel, to produce electrical components and jewelry. *(amalgamate)* 7. amalgamated
8. The _____ of the two events suggests that cause and effect were operating. *(contiguous)* 8. contiguity
9. Connie's _____ vision is quite acute. *(periphery)* 9. peripheral
10. Mr. Uribe trimmed the _____ branches of the rosebush in order to attach the bush to a trellis. *(diffuse)* 10. diffuse

NAME ______________________ DATE ____________

READING COMPREHENSION

Each numbered sentence in the following passage contains an italicized vocabulary word or related form. After you read the passage, you will complete an exercise.

THE GREENHOUSE EFFECT: THE WARMING OF THE WORLD

Geophysicists at a conference in Calgary, Alberta, applauded enthusiastically when they learned that temperatures throughout the world may increase slightly over the next decade. These scientists were reacting to the possibility of an escape from the frigid winters of the Canadian plains. If the predictions are accurate, however, the warming of the world will mean much more than milder winters in certain areas.

(1) According to climatologists and meteorologists, the key to the regulation of the world's climate lies in the ***synergy*** of gases in the atmosphere that absorb the sun's heat. (2) The ***amalgamation*** of carbon dioxide, ozone, and other gases allows the sun's ultraviolet rays to penetrate and warm the earth. The blanket of gases absorbs the energy that would otherwise radiate back to space. (3) The air that is ***contiguous*** to the earth is warmed by the trapped gases. (4) This complex cycle is called the "greenhouse effect" because the gases in the atmosphere function much like the glass walls of a gardener's greenhouse, trapping warmth inside that would otherwise be ***diffused.***

The importance of the greenhouse effect can be illustrated by examining its influence on the two planets closest to the earth, Venus and Mars. Venus, closer to the sun, intercepts twice as much of the sun's light as does Earth. Its thick blanket of carbon dioxide traps so much heat that the surface temperature of the planet is 800°F, hot enough to melt lead. Mars, on the other hand, is farther away from the sun. With its thin atmosphere, the planet is icy and lifeless.

(5) Today scientists are concerned over maintaining ***parity*** with the current amounts of atmospheric gases. As our use of wood and fossil fuels, such as coal, oil, and natural gas, exceeds that of other generations, we add increasing amounts of carbon dioxide to the atmosphere. The conversion of dense forests into sparsely vegetated farms or communities means that there are fewer plants to absorb the carbon dioxide. Other gases, too, are shifting the balance in the atmosphere.

(6) Although the experts have ***divergent*** views on the overall effects of these atmospheric changes, they seem to agree that if the current rate of releasing carbon dioxide and other gases into the air continues, the earth's temperature will probably rise by 3 to 9°F by the year 2050. (7) While some scientists emphasize positive outcomes, such as lower heating costs and enhanced crop yields, others warn of possible negative ***adjuncts*** of the overall warming trend.

Thus far, the greenhouse effect remains a theory, but evidence is accumulating. Meteorologists have determined that the world has got about a degree warmer during the twentieth century. (8) Some climatologists believe that we may be on the ***periphery*** of a dangerous trend. (9) Weather researchers are in ***unison*** when they speak of the significance of the greenhouse effect on our future. (10) They indicate that further research is of ***transcendent*** importance and that controls should be placed on processes that result in carbon dioxide by-products. Because the atmosphere has no national boundaries, scientists urge a worldwide solution before the greenhouse effect gets out of control.

READING COMPREHENSION EXERCISE

Each of the following statements corresponds to a numbered sentence in the passage. Each statement contains a blank and is followed by four answer choices. Decide which choice fits best in the blank. The word or phrase that you choose must express roughly the same meaning as the italicized word in the passage. Write the letter of your choice on the answer line.

1. The key to the regulation of the world's climate lies in the _____ of gases in the atmosphere. 1. ____d____
   a. presence **b.** absence **c.** partial combination **d.** combined action

2. The _____ of carbon dioxide, ozone, and other gases allows the sun's rays to warm the earth. 2. a
a. union b. magnification c. deterioration d. reduction

3. The air that is _____ the earth is warmed by the trapped gases. 3. a
a. next to b. essential to c. combined with d. far from

4. The glass walls of a gardener's greenhouse capture warmth that would otherwise be _____. 4. d
a preserved b. obscured c. constantly reheated d. widely scattered

5. Scientists are concerned over maintaining _____ with the current amounts of atmospheric gases. 5. a
a. equality b. flexibility c. transparency d. inversion

6. Experts have _____ views on the overall effects of these atmospheric changes. 6. b
a. similar b. differing c. contradictory d. falsely based

7. Scientists are not certain what the _____ of the overall warming trend will be. 7. c
a. secrets b. difficulties c. related effects d. future significance

8. Climatologists believe that we may be approaching the _____ of a dangerous trend. 8. a
a. edge b. inevitability c. continuation d. conclusion

9. Weather researchers are in _____ when they speak of the significance of the greenhouse effect on our future. 9. d
a. controversy b. doubt c. trouble d. agreement

10. Scientists who study weather and climate indicate that further research is of _____ importance. 10. d
a. minor b. no c. moderate d. exceptional

PRACTICE WITH ANALOGIES

See pages 66 and 86 for some other strategies to use with analogies.

A verbal analogy is a similarity between sets of otherwise dissimilar word pairs. An analogy can be written as a sentence or with colons.

Diminutive is to small as colossal is to large.
diminutive : small :: colossal : large

Strategy To complete an analogy, find the relationship between the words in the first pair. The second pair must have the same relationship. In the example above, *diminutive* is very small in the same way as *colossal* is very large. The relationship is one of *degree.*

Directions On the answer line, write the letter of the phrase that best completes each analogy.

1. TRAITOR : PERFIDIOUS :: (A) veteran : enthusiasm (B) neighbor : supportive (C) hypocrite : insincere (D) teammate : competitiveness (E) knight : skillful 1. C

2. SPURIOUS : AUTHENTICITY :: (A) precious : value (B) anonymous : identity (C) imagination : reality (D) ambition : success (E) insecure : doubt 2. B

3. MEANDER : PATH :: (A) block : door (B) veer : course (C) avoid : obstacle (D) overcome : barrier (E) pursue : goal 3. B

4. TORPID : ENERGY :: (A) polished : refinement (B) inefficient : time (C) emotion : anger (D) gravity : force (E) diffuse : concentration 4. E

5. SAGA : STORY :: (A) skit : play (B) draft : essay (C) sketch : drawing (D) epic : poem (E) anecdote : story 5. D

LESSON 6 CLARITY AND VAGUENESS

The English language is filled with idioms that are traditionally used—and overused—to communicate the concepts of clarity and vagueness. For example, you may have used "crystal clear," "as clear as a bell," or "see the light" to describe situations or ideas that are easily perceptible or distinct. Such expressions as "shrouded in mystery," "it's too deep for me," and "clear as mud" are used to describe uncertainties. The words in this lesson will help you to express clarity and vagueness more vividly.

WORD LIST

adumbrate
arcane
covert
educe
fathom
impervious
limpid
manifest
nebulous
translucent

DEFINITIONS

After you have studied the definitions and example for each vocabulary word, write the word on the line to the right.

1. **adumbrate** (ăd'əm-brāt', ə-dŭm'-brāt') *trans. verb* **a.** To give a sketchy outline of. **b.** To disclose partially or guardedly. **c.** To prefigure indistinctly; foreshadow. (From the Latin *ad-*, meaning "to," and *umbra*, meaning "shadow") 1. ____________

Related Word **adumbration** *noun*
Example The details of the marketing plan were kept secret, but the company president briefly *adumbrated* the basic strategy at the staff meeting.

2. **arcane** (är-kān') *adjective* Known or understood only by a few; esoteric. (From the Latin word *arcanus*, meaning "secret") 2. ____________

Example The system of addressing English nobility by different titles seemed *arcane* to the American.

3. **covert** (kûv'ərt, kō'vərt) *adjective* **a.** Concealed; hidden; secret. **b.** Covered or covered over; sheltered *noun* **a.** Covering or cover. **b.** A covered place or shelter; hiding place. **c.** Thick underbrush or woodland affording cover for game. (From the Old French word *covrir*, meaning "to cover") 3. ____________

Related Words **covertly** *adverb;* **covertness** *noun*
Example The man was arrested for making *covert* sales of arms to rebel forces.

4. **educe** (ĭ-do͞os', ĭ-dyo͞os') *trans. verb* **a.** To draw or bring out; elicit. **b.** To assume or work out from given facts; deduce. (From the Latin *ex-*, meaning "out," and *ducere*, meaning "to lead") 4. ____________

Related Words **educible** *adjective;* **eduction** *noun*
Example The director *educed* an emotional performance from the seemingly unresponsive actor.

5. **fathom** (făth′əm) *trans. verb* **a.** To get to the bottom of and understand. **b.** To determine the depth of; sound. *noun* A unit of length equal to six feet used in the measurement of marine depths. (From the Middle English word *fathme,* meaning "outstretched arms.") 5. ________________

Related Words **fathomable** *adjective;* **fathomless** *adjective*
Example With painstaking effort Marion ultimately *fathomed* the confusing passage of Descarte's mathematical philosophy.

6. **impervious** (ĭm-pûr′vē-əs) *adjective* **a.** Incapable of being penetrated. **b.** Incapable of being affected. **c.** Not open to argument or suggestion. (From the Latin *in-,* meaning "not," *per,* meaning "through," and *via,* meaning "way") 6. ________________

Related Words **imperviously** *adjective;* **imperviousness** *noun*
Example Jolene's raincoat is made of a new fabric that is *impervious* to water and wind.

7. **limpid** (lĭm′pĭd) *adjective* **a.** Characterized by transparent clearness. **b.** Easily intelligible: *a limpid explanation.* **c.** Calm and untroubled; serene. (From the Latin word *limpidus,* meaning "clear") 7. ________________

Related Words **limpidly** *adverb;* **limpidness** *noun*
Example Snorkeling in *limpid* water helps one appreciate the variety of fish in the ocean.

8. **manifest** (măn′ə-fĕst′) *adjective* Clearly apparent to the sight or understanding; obvious. *trans. verb* **a.** To show or demonstrate plainly; reveal. **b.** To be evidence of; prove. *noun* A list of cargo or passengers for a ship or airplane. (From the Latin word *manifestus,* meaning "obvious") 8. ________________

Related Words **manifestation** *noun;* **manifestly** *adverb*
Example The gratefulness of the people rescued from the storm was *manifest* in every smiling face.

9. **nebulous** (nĕb′yə-ləs) *adjective* **a.** Lacking definite form or limits; vague. **b.** Cloudy, misty, or hazy. (From the Latin word *nebula,* meaning "cloud") 9. ________________

Related Words **nebulously** *adverb;* **nebulousness** *noun*
Example Until Monica could confirm her theory, she kept the *nebulous* idea to herself.

10. **translucent** (trăns-lo͞o′sənt, trănz-lo͞o′sənt) *adjective* Transmitting light but causing sufficient diffusion to make impossible the perception of distinct images. (From the Latin *trans-,* meaning "through," and *lucere,* meaning "to shine") 10. ________________

Related Words **translucence** *noun;* **translucently** *adverb*
Example Behind the *translucent* window shade, shadowed figures moved back and forth.

NAME ______________________________ DATE ______________

EXERCISE 1 WRITING CORRECT WORDS

On the answer line, write the word from the vocabulary list that fits each definition.

1. Concealed; hidden; sheltered — 1. covert
2. Characterized by transparent clearness; easily intelligible — 2. limpid
3. To get to the bottom of and understand; determine the depth of — 3. fathom
4. Transmitting light but causing sufficient diffusion to make impossible the perception of distinct images — 4. translucent
5. To give a sketchy outline of; disclose partially; foreshadow — 5. adumbrate
6. Incapable of being penetrated; incapable of being affected — 6. impervious
7. Clearly apparent to the sight or understanding of; to show or demonstrate plainly — 7. manifest
8. Known or understood only by a few; esoteric — 8. arcane
9. Lacking definite form or limits; cloudy or hazy — 9. nebulous
10. To draw or bring out; assume or work out from given facts — 10. educe

EXERCISE 2 USING WORDS CORRECTLY

Decide whether the italicized vocabulary word has been used correctly in the sentence. On the answer line, write *Correct* for correct use and *Incorrect* for incorrect use.

1. Monica couldn't *fathom* her friends' delight in snow until she, too, learned cross-country skiing. — 1. Correct
2. *Arcane* laws are those that are no longer current or applicable. — 2. Incorrect
3. Ever since his accident, Luis has had a terrible *limpid* and a sore elbow. — 3. Incorrect
4. The science teacher's questions *educed* many facts about the atom. — 4. Correct
5. The architect used large panes of *translucent* glass in the dining room windows so that we could admire the view as we ate. — 5. Incorrect
6. Charles's interest in becoming a veterinarian is *manifest.* — 6. Correct
7. Federal agents successfully carried out *covert* operations against the spy ring. — 7. Correct
8. Babe Ruth could easily *adumbrate* a baseball into the outfield stands. — 8. Incorrect
9. The heavy backing on some curtains makes them *impervious* to light. — 9. Correct
10. After setting twelve national records, Robbie was voted one of the most *nebulous* passers in football history. — 10. Incorrect

EXERCISE 3 IDENTIFYING SYNONYMS AND ANTONYMS

Decide which word or phrase has the meaning that is the same as (a synonym) or opposite to (an antonym) that of the capitalized vocabulary word. Write the letter of your choice on the answer line.

1. LIMPID (antonym): — 1. a
   a. murky **b.** petite **c.** flaccid **d.** firm

2. ARCANE (synonym):
   a. illogical **b.** indispensable **c.** noisy **d.** esoteric
   2. d

3. ADUMBRATE (antonym):
   a. elaborate **b.** generalize **c.** desiccate **d.** soar
   3. a

4. EDUCE (synonym):
   a. exert **b.** accept **c.** elicit **d.** beautify
   4. c

5. MANIFEST (antonym):
   a. depreciated **b.** resolute **c.** concealed **d.** plentiful
   5. c

6. COVERT (synonym):
   a. believable **b.** hidden **c.** virtuous **d.** disdainful
   6. b

7. IMPERVIOUS (antonym):
   a. pitiless **b.** zealous **c.** formidable **d.** penetrable
   7. d

8. FATHOM (synonym):
   a. waste **b.** persist **c.** humiliate **d.** discern
   8. d

9. TRANSLUCENT (antonym):
   a. elevated **b.** submerged **c.** opaque **d.** dreary
   9. c

10. NEBULOUS (synonym):
    a. sentimental **b.** vague **c.** oppressive **d.** powerful
    10. b

EXERCISE 4 USING DIFFERENT FORMS OF WORDS

Decide which form of the vocabulary word in parentheses best completes the sentence. The form given may be correct. Write your answer on the answer line.

1. Nance chose an _____ novel by a South American writer for her report. *(arcane)* 1. **arcane**
2. The solution to the puzzle was not _____ from the clues that were given. *(educe)* 2. **educible**
3. The _____ of the explanation satisfied the audience. *(limpid)* 3. **limpidness**
4. The author's constant _____ of doom were more annoying than suspenseful. *(adumbrate)* 4. **adumbrations**
5. The _____ of Matt's alibi aroused the suspicions of the authorities. *(nebulous)* 5. **nebulousness**
6. Throughout the meal Martine gazed _____ at the stack of gifts on the floor. *(covert)* 6. **covertly**
7. Worried frowns and soothing words were the _____ of the pet owners' concerns for their animals. *(manifest)* 7. **manifestations**
8. Arthur believed that the situation was _____ only if he could regain his objectivity. *(fathom)* 8. **fathomable**
9. The _____ of the stained-glass window provides both light and privacy. *(translucent)* 9. **translucence**
10. Vera's _____ to gossip has won her the trust and respect of many people. *(impervious)* 10. **imperviousness**

NAME ______________________ DATE __________

READING COMPREHENSION

Each numbered sentence in the following passage contains an italicized vocabulary word. After you read the passage, you will complete an exercise.

DEEP-SEA SALVAGE: THE TREASURES OF HISTORY

Archaeologists regard shipwrecks as microcosms of maritime culture, commerce and social structure, while salvage professionals view sunken vessels as opportunities for dazzling profit. Although the two groups historically have operated at cross-purposes, advanced underwater techniques now enable both to attain their goals.

The story of the Spanish galleon *Nuestra Señora de Atocha* and its sister ship, the *Santa Margarita,* illustrates the cooperative efforts of archaeologists and salvage teams. These two ships, en route to Spain with cargoes of wealth from the New World, sank in a hurricane in 1622. Efforts to recover the treasure began almost immediately. (1) Using a bronze diving bell that trapped air like an inverted bucket, Spanish treasure hunters were lowered to the ocean floor, where they peered through tiny windows, trying to discern the ***nebulous*** shape of the wrecks in the sand. (2) In an area of open ocean with no visible landmarks, however, a wreck site can easily be missed by a few hundred yards, even in ***limpid*** water. It took two years for the Spanish divers to locate the remains of the *Santa Margarita.* Although they brought up some gold and silver ingots and coins, they never located the *Atocha* or the bulk of the treasure.

(3) Several ***covert*** operations allegedly were mounted by divers of other nationalities. (4) However, the wrecks and the great wealth of the *Atocha* and the *Santa Margarita* remained ***impervious*** to all salvage operations until 1971. (5) At that time a historian who was examining ***arcane*** documents in Spain found a handwritten account of a survivor of the shipwreck. (6) The survivor had ***adumbrated*** some of the events of the disaster. (7) The historian ***educed*** the theory that the galleons had sunk off the western tip of the Florida Keys.

Even with a more exact location and the help of advanced technology, it took a team of American salvage experts and archaeologists nine years to locate the wrecks and begin to unearth the treasure. (8) Using sidescan sonar, which scatters sound pulses along the ocean floor, the team was able to ***fathom*** the site. Protruding objects returned echoes, which were transformed into a visual outline that clarified the contours of the bottom and pinpointed the hulls of the galleons. (9) Electromagnetic detectors, which emit one type of signal in the presence of iron and another type of signal for other metals, such as silver, gold and bronze, were used to make large buried objects ***manifest*** on a screen.

Once the shipwreck sites were identified and the salvage team was assured of the presence of treasure, they were prepared to blast holes in the sand by using large tubes attached to the propellers of boats. These devices can cut through five feet of sand in thirty minutes.

(10) The archaeologists, however, favored a much slower approach, insisting that the tubes would scatter artifacts and leave the remains of the vessels jumbled in the ***translucent*** water. Instead, they placed a metal grid over the wreck site, dividing it into coded quadrants. Within the separate sections, divers then fanned away sand slowly. When they uncovered objects, each was placed in a numbered plastic bag. Back in the laboratory, archaeologists could study the collected objects in relation to one another and to their location in the hulls of the galleons.

To date the salvage experts and archaeologists have located more than twenty million dollars of treasure, including gold and silver coins and ingots, jewelry, precious stones, and cutlery. While the archaeologists scientifically reconstruct life aboard the galleons, divers continue to search under twenty feet of sand for the scattered treasures of history.

READING COMPREHENSION EXERCISE

Each of the following statements corresponds to a numbered sentence in the passage. Each statement contains a blank and is followed by four answer choices. Decide which choice fits best in the blank. The word or phrase that you choose must express roughly the same meaning as the italicized word in the passage. Write the letter of your choice on the answer line.

1. Spanish treasure hunters tried to discern the _____ shape of the wrecks through a diving bell. 1. a
   a. indistinct b. concrete c. unusual d. conspicuous

2. A wreck site can easily be missed, even in _____ water. 2. d
   a. deep b. murky c. rough d. clear

3. Several _____ operations were mounted by divers of other nationalities. 3. a
   a. secret b. efficient c. economical d. serious

4. The great wealth of the galleons remained _____ to all salvage operations. 4. c
   a. nonexistent b. a symbol c. impenetrable d. unparalleled

5. A historian who was examining _____ documents in Spain found a survivor's account of the shipwreck. 5. b
   a. ancient b. specialized c. mysterious d. genuine

6. The survivor had _____ some of the events of the disaster. 6. a
   a. outlined b. recalled c. forgotten d. condoned

7. The historian _____ that the galleons had sunk off the Florida Keys. 7. d
   a. acknowledged b. announced c. implied d. reasoned

8. The team was able to _____ the site by using sidescan sonar. 8. a
   a. determine the depth of c. locate
   b. examine in detail d. excavate

9. Electromagnetic detectors were used to make buried objects _____ on a screen. 9. c
   a. larger b. attractive c. apparent d. predominant

10. The archeologists insisted that the tubes would leave the remains of the structure of the vessels jumbled in the _____ water. 10. b
    a. polluted b. cloudy c. encompassing d. tranquil

WRITING ASSIGNMENT

Stendahl, the nineteenth-century French novelist and biographer, once said, "I see but one rule: to be clear. If I am not clear, all my world crumbles to nothing." Using the quotation as a starting point, write a brief story or an essay based on personal experience to illustrate how a lack of clarity had unfortunate results. Use at least five of the words from this lesson in your story or essay and underline each one.

Word History: adumbrate

Latin: *ad* = to + *umbra* = shade or shadow

Numerous derivatives of *umbra* have found their way into the English language, and each derivative contains the notion of "shade" or "shadow." For example, an *umbrageous* tree gives plentiful "shade," while *umbrageous* people take offense easily because they don't like to be "overshadowed" or excelled by others. The *penumbra* is the "half-shadow" that outlines the dark shadow produced during an eclipse, while an *umbrella* gives "shade" from the sun as well as protection from the rain.

The **Test** for Lessons 4, 5, and 6 is on page T4.

TEST-TAKING SKILLS

SAT AND ACT READING COMPREHENSION TESTS

A test of reading comprehension is part of both the Scholastic Assessment Test (SAT) and the American College Testing (ACT) Assessment Program. In a reading comprehension test, you are asked to read one or more paragraphs and then answer questions about them. Both the SAT and the ACT test contain reading passages from the humanities, the social sciences, and the natural sciences. The test items below are closer in format to the SAT than to the ACT test, but the strategies that follow apply to both.

STRATEGIES

1. *Determine the main idea of the passage as you read.* It may not be stated directly in the passage. Understanding the main idea will give you a better understanding of the information that you are reading and of the test items that follow.
2. *Note sentences that support the main idea.* Such sentences contain reasons and examples. You will return to some supporting sentences in order to answer test items; be sure to do so instead of relying on your memory alone.
3. *Distinguish conclusions from support sentences.* Conclusions are general statements that sum up the ideas presented in prior sentences. Such words and phrases as *thus, therefore,* and *in summary* may signal conclusions.
4. *Be prepared to make inferences about what you have read.* An inference is an *unstated* conclusion that can reasonably be drawn from what is stated.
5. *Read as fast as you can and still retain the meaning.* Read the passage before looking at the questions. As you do each item, read all of the answer choices before selecting one of them. Verify each answer by quickly checking the relevant part of the passage. Guess if you think you may know the answer; there is no penalty for wrong answers, as there is in the comparable SAT test section.

EXERCISE ANSWERING READING COMPREHENSION TEST ITEMS

Read the following passage and then answer the questions about it. For each question write the letter of your choice on the answer line.

In keeping with the laws of developmental direction, the brain develops, for the most part, from the bottom to the top and from the inside to the outside. That is, the brain stem develops before the cortex, and the inside of the cortex develops before the outside. The cerebellum, however, which is responsible for regulation and coordination of complex voluntary muscular movements, is an exception to the general trends of neurological development. The cerebellum is the last of the brain to develop, even though it is just in back of the spinal cord and below the cortex. The development of the brain is thought to occur as neurons multiply, migrate (to use a term favored by developmental neurologists), and interact. Individual neurons that make up the human nervous system communicate with each other through dendrites and axons. Dendrites are branched projections of the nucleus of nerve cells that function to *receive* signals from other cells. The axon is a long fibrous projection that *transmits* information to other cells. The area of communication between neurons is called a *synapse.*

As neurons develop and pathways between them are established, the brain becomes capable of controlling a greater variety of physical and cognitive activities. It appears that the brain is genetically programmed to develop according to a timetable that prepares the maturing organism to process appropriate stimulation at particular stages of development (Parmalee and Sigman, 1983). If stimulation occurs before the nervous system is ready for it, neurons seem to protect themselves by rejecting the sensory input. Premature infants, for example, are exposed to many more stimuli than infants who develop in utero for the full nine-month gestation period. Despite receiving an abnormal amount of stimulation compared to full-term infants, preterm babies do not exhibit accelerated neurological or physiological growth. Once the nervous system is ready to respond, however, it appears that "appropriate" stimulation facilitates normal development.

1. The main idea of the passage is that — 1. **C**

(A) the parts of the brain develop independently of one another.
(B) the development of the brain is a result of the multiplication, migration, and interaction of neurons.
(C) the brain has a fixed pattern of development.
(D) the communication of information takes place through the action of dendrites and axons.

2. The cerebellum is located — 2. **B**

(A) at the top of the brain.
(B) at the bottom of the brain.
(C) in front of the spinal cord.
(D) above the cortex.

3. Neurons are — 3. **C**

(A) axons.
(B) dendrites.
(C) nerve cells.
(D) synapses.

4. The brain develops — 4. **D**

(A) from the bottom to the top and from the outside to the inside.
(B) from the top to the bottom and from the outside to the inside.
(C) from the top to the bottom and from the inside to the outside.
(D) from the bottom to the top and from the inside to the outside.

5. Brain development takes place according to — 5. **A**

(A) an inherited timetable.
(B) body size.
(C) outside stimulation.
(D) muscular movement.

6. That the neurological growth of premature babies is not more rapid than that of full-term babies is — 6. **C**

(A) a trend of neurological development.
(B) a result of a flexible timetable for development.
(C) a type of inborn protection.
(D) a result of abnormal stimulation.

LESSON 7 THE ROOT -*CAP*-

7

The Latin root -*cap*- and its alternate forms -*cip*-, -*capt*-, -*cept*-, and -*ceiv*- are all derived from the Latin word *capere,* meaning "to take." This word has served as the basis of many English words. For example, if the trunk of a car has a large *capacity,* it takes or holds many objects. When you *anticipate* an event, you take it in mentally or realize it beforehand. The *receiver* of a telephone is the mechanism that takes in electromagnetic signals. In this lesson you will learn other words that relate in some way to the action of taking.

WORD LIST

capacious
captious
captivate
cater
concept
inception
perceptible
precept
receptacle
recipient

DEFINITIONS

After you have studied the definitions and example for each vocabulary word, write the word on the line to the right.

1. **capacious** (kə-pā′shəs) *adjective* Capable of holding a large quantity; spacious; roomy. (From the Latin word *capere,* meaning "to take")

   Related Word **capaciousness** *noun*
   Example The living room was *capacious* enough to accommodate a concert grand piano as well as the other furniture.

1. ______________

MEMORY CUE: Something that is *capacious* has a large *capacity.*

2. **captious** (kăp′shəs) *adjective* **a.** Inclined to find fault and make petty criticisms. **b.** Intending to entrap or confuse; deceptive: *a captious question.* (From the Latin word *capere*)

   Related Words **captiously** *adverb;* **captiousness** *noun*
   Example Nothing could please Mrs. Weitzen when she was in a *captious* mood.

2. ______________

3. **captivate** (kăp′tĭ-vāt′) *trans. verb* To fascinate by special charm, wit, intelligence, or beauty; enrapture. (From the Latin word *capere*)

   Related Word **captivation** *noun*
   Example The cast *captivated* the audience with their unusual interpretation of the classical play.

3. ______________

4. **cater** (kā′tər) *intrans. verb* **a.** To provide food, services, or entertainment. **b.** To provide anything wished for or needed. *trans. verb* To provide food service for. (From the Latin word *capere*)

   Related Word **caterer** *noun*
   Example The Nelsons hired a company called The Glorious Gourmet to *cater* the large banquet.

4. ______________

5. **concept** (kŏn′sĕpt′) *noun* **a.** A general idea or understanding, especially one derived from specific instances or occurrences; abstraction. **b.** A thought or notion. (From the Latin word *concipere,* meaning "to conceive") 5. ____________

Related Words **conceptual** *adjective;* **conceptualize** *verb;* **conceptually** *adverb*
Example Paul could not grasp the *concept* of how a computer stores information.

6. **inception** (ĭn-sĕp′shən) *noun* The beginning of something; commencement. (From the Latin *in-,* meaning "in," and *capere)* 6. ____________

Example Hot-air ballooning had its *inception* in eighteenth-century France.

7. **perceptible** (pər-sĕp′tə-bəl) *adjective* Capable of being grasped by the senses or mind; noticeable; discernible. (From the Latin *per-,* an intensive prefix, and *capere)* 7. ____________

Related Words **perceptibly** *adverb;* **perception** *noun*
Example The flaw in the skater's performance was *perceptible* only to the judges.

8. **precept** (prē′sĕpt′) *noun* A rule that imposes a particular standard of action or conduct; guiding principle. (From the Latin *prae-,* meaning "before," and *capere)* 8. ____________

Example *Poor Richard's Almanack,* by Benjamin Franklin, contains many *precepts* for success in life.

9. **receptacle** (rĭ-sĕp′tə-kəl) *noun* Something that holds or contains; a container. (From the Latin *re-,* meaning "again," and *capere)* 9. ____________

Example None of the trash *receptacles* was large enough to hold all of the litter that accumulated during the parade.

10. **recipient** (rĭ-sĭp′ē-ənt) *noun* One that receives or is capable of receiving. *adjective* Functioning as a receiver; receptive. (From the Latin *re-,* meaning "again," and *capere)* 10. ____________

Example In a blood transfusion, the donor and the *recipient* must have compatible blood types.

NAME ______________________ DATE ____________

EXERCISE 1 MATCHING WORDS AND DEFINITIONS

Match the definition in Column B with the word in Column A. Write the letter of the correct definition on the answer line.

Column A

1. perceptible
2. captious
3. concept
4. capacious
5. precept
6. inception
7. receptacle
8. recipient
9. captivate
10. cater

Column B

a. capable of holding a large quantity; spacious
b. something that holds or contains
c. to fascinate by charm, wit, intelligence, or beauty; enrapture
d. a general idea or understanding derived from specific instances; a thought or notion
e. to provide food, services, or entertainment; provide anything wished for or needed
f. inclined to find fault and make petty criticisms
g. one that receives or is capable of receiving
h. the beginning of something; commencement
i. capable of being grasped by the senses or mind; noticeable
j. a rule that imposes a particular standard of action or conduct; guiding principle

1. i
2. f
3. d
4. a
5. j
6. h
7. b
8. g
9. c
10. e

EXERCISE 2 USING WORDS CORRECTLY

Decide whether the italicized vocabulary word has been used correctly in the sentence. On the answer line, write *Correct* for correct use and *Incorrect* for incorrect use.

1. At the zoo the children were *captivated* by the pygmy hippopotamus. — 1. Correct
2. Leon's *captious* remarks were overheard by his colleagues, who were surprised at his ill humor. — 2. Correct
3. From beginning to *inception,* it took six months to build our house. — 3. Incorrect
4. Etiquette books are full of social *precepts.* — 4. Correct
5. "Mary Hamilton is the *recipient* of a full scholarship to the state university," announced the principal at graduation. — 5. Correct
6. The *capacious* elevator could hold only three people. — 6. Incorrect
7. The sound of the train whistle frightened the horses, and they *catered* off in all directions. — 7. Incorrect
8. We had no *concept* of how a commodity exchange operates until we visited the grain exchange in Sioux City. — 8. Correct
9. The sky was so cloudy last night that only a few stars were *perceptible.* — 9. Correct
10. Only cans and bottles should be returned to the store; all *receptacles* should be thrown away. — 10. Incorrect

EXERCISE 3 CHOOSING THE BEST DEFINITION

For each italicized vocabulary word in the following sentences, write the letter of the best definition on the answer line.

1. In late winter metal *receptacles* attached to maple trees collect the sap. — 1. b
   a. spouts **b.** containers **c.** tubes **d.** recesses

2. "Do unto others as you would have them do unto you" is a familiar *precept* that has always influenced Meredith's courteous behavior. 2. d
   a. virtue b. chant c. favorite quotation d. guiding principle

3. Zeke decided against the small carry-on bag and chose, instead, a more *capacious* suitcase. 3. a
   a. roomy b. elegant c. suitable d. distinctive

4. The new magazine *caters to* to city gardeners with small plots of land. 4. b
   a. was established for b. provides what is needed for c. guides d. influences

5. In the recesses of the cave, daylight was barely *perceptible.* 5. d
   a. important b. necessary c. beautiful d. noticeable

6. Johanna can *captivate* an audience with her dynamic personality. 6. c
   a. mislead b. manipulate c. fascinate d. overpower

7. In management training courses, the *concepts* of cooperation and interaction are often taught through role-playing activities. 7. a
   a. general ideas b. specific skills c. excesses d. foundations

8. The neighbors enjoy being the *recipients* of Mr. Gomez's homemade pickles. 8. a
   a. receivers b. testers c. judges d. witnesses

9. The new architectural critic is knowledgeable but *captious.* 9. d
   a. inferior b. conventional c. naive d. fault-finding

10. The year 1972 saw the *inception* of the company's employee evaluation program. 10. b
    a. culmination b. beginning c. restriction d. burden

EXERCISE 4 USING DIFFERENT FORMS OF WORDS

Decide which form of the vocabulary word in parentheses best completes the sentence. The form given may be correct. Write your answer on the answer line.

1. In dry, powdery snow, each snowflake is _____ different from other snowflakes. *(perceptible)* 1. **perceptibly**
2. At its _____ a snowflake consists of a few thousand molecules grouped around a tiny core of ice or a speck of dust. *(inception)* 2. **inception**
3. On a microscopic level, a snowflake has a certain _____, comprising finally about a million trillion molecules. *(capacious)* 3. **capaciousness**
4. It is difficult for us to _____ the number one million trillion. *(concept)* 4. **conceptualize**
5. The snowflake is _____ for child and scientist alike. *(captivate)* 5. **captivating**
6. The value of hard work was the most important _____ in his life. *(precept)* 6. **precept**
7. "I apologize for my _____," said Rona, "but I'm eager for this song to be performed properly." *(captious)* 7. **captiousness**
8. All of the _____ of the high school art award will be honored at a reception next week. *(recipient)* 8. **recipients**
9. Mr. Stoneman keeps the computer diskettes in a protective _____ in the closet. *(receptacle)* 9. **receptacle**
10. Mrs. Wheeler will be the _____ for the father-daughter banquet. *(cater)* 10. **caterer**

NAME ______________________ DATE ____________

READING COMPREHENSION

Each numbered sentence in the following passage contains an italicized vocabulary word. After you read the passage, you will complete an exercise.

MARÍA MARTÍNEZ: MATRIARCH OF POTTERS

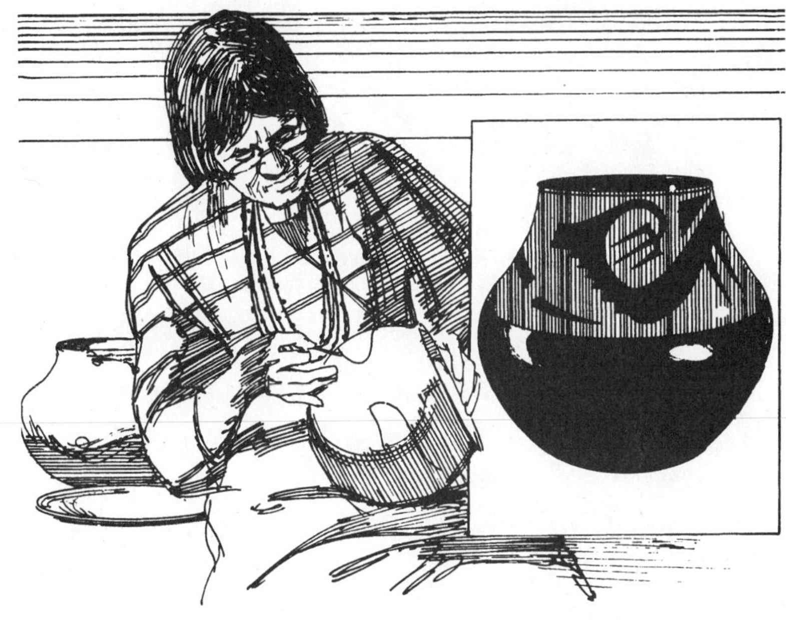

In 1908 Dr. Edgar Lee Hewett, professor of archaeology and director of the Museum of New Mexico, was commissioned to excavate several ancient pueblos of the Tewa Indians. In Frijoles Canyon, northwest of Santa Fe, he and other members of his research team turned up a kind of pottery fragment not found before in the Southwest. Unlike the characteristic black-on-red, black-on-cream, or undecorated pottery of the area, these shards were highly polished jet- or charcoal-black. (1) Excited by his unusual find, Dr. Hewett needed someone to help him recreate the ***receptacles*** from which the fragments had come. María Martínez, a local potter, was recommended to him.

María Montoya Martínez (1887?–1980), a Tewa Indian herself, lived close to the excavation site in the San Ildefonso pueblo. (2) Having learned to make pottery at the age of ten by following the ***precepts*** of her aunt, she was a master at making perfectly symmetrical vessels without using a potter's wheel. (3) Using design ***concepts*** inherited from her ancestors, Martínez made a variety of functional vessels out of red clay. (4) Although most of the pottery was made for daily use, she would often sell ***capacious*** pieces to augment the family's income.

When Dr. Hewett asked for María Martínez's help, she viewed her task with some misgivings. The pots themselves were easy to reproduce because the configuration of the pieces provided clues to the original shapes. (5) Achieving the unique black sheen was considerably more difficult; the pottery shards provided no ***perceptible*** information about the source of the color or shine. However, through experimentation, María Martínez contrived a solution. (6) This was the ***inception*** of the famous black pottery of San Ildefonso.

Martínez produced the first black ware in 1910. (7) She refused to show the experimental pots to visitors who came to the pueblo shop that ***catered*** to tourists, because she believed that the black pots were not representative of San Ildefonso pottery. (8) However, Dr. Hewett and his associates from the Museum of New Mexico were ***captivated*** by the glowing surfaces. They encouraged her to continue experimenting with different clays, firing techniques, and decorative touches.

(9) Although never ***captious,*** María Martínez was a perfectionist. After ten years of practice, she finally achieved the distinctive process that has had such a strong influence on the course of ceramic artistry in the Southwest. After each pot was shaped and dried, she spent hours polishing each piece with a smooth stone. The pots were then placed in a pile, shielded with sheet metal, and layered over with dried cow and horse manure. The entire pile was then set on fire. Once the fire was at its peak, the pile was smothered in ash and additional manure so that the heat and smoke from the rich fuel could carbonize the surface of the pots. The finished products glowed with a silver-black intensity.

Within her lifetime, María Martínez was greatly honored for her artistic achievements. (10) In addition to being entertained by four Presidents at the White House, she was the ***recipient*** of many prizes and honorary degrees. Her pottery is displayed throughout the world in museums and private collections. Today her descendants carry on the techniques that have formed a new tradition in American art.

READING COMPREHENSION EXERCISE

Each of the following statements corresponds to a numbered sentence in the passage. Each statement contains a blank and is followed by four answer choices. Decide which choice fits best in the blank. The word or phrase that you choose must express roughly the same meaning as the italicized word in the passage. Write the letter of your choice on the answer line.

1. Dr. Hewett wanted to know what the ____ might have looked like. 1. ____c____
   a. geographical regions c. containers
   b. shelters d. normal conditions

2. Martínez learned to make pottery by imitating the ____ of her aunt. 2. ____a____
   a. guiding principles c. disciples
   b. meager examples d. representations

3. Martínez used ____ inherited from her ancestors. 3. ____d____
   a. tools c. materials
   b. specific instructions d. general ideas

4. She would often sell ____ pieces to augment the family's income. 4. ____a____
   a. large b. balanced c. miniature d. life-size

5. The pottery shards provided no ____ information about the source of the color or shine. 5. ____a____
   a. discernible b. satisfactory c. encouraging d. useful

6. This was the ____ of the famous black pottery of San Ildefonso. 6. ____c____
   a. termination b. importance c. beginning d. distortion

7. She would not show the black pots to those who visited the shop that ____ tourists. 7. ____b____
   a. excited b. served c. enlightened d. admitted

8. Dr. Hewett and his associates were ____ the pottery. 8. ____d____
   a. not happy with c. made prosperous by
   b. outraged by d. fascinated by

9. María Martínez was never ____, but she was a perfectionist. 9. ____c____
   a. complimentary c. pettily critical
   b. satisfied d. falsely encouraging

10. María Martínez was the ____ of many prizes and honorary degrees. 10. ____b____
    a. donor b. receiver c. bearer d. inheritor

WRITING ASSIGNMENT

An amphitheater is a round or oval structure with an open space or arena surrounded by rising rows of seats. Through the ages people have used amphitheaters for such diverse events as chariot races, circuses, football games, dramatic productions, and concerts. Imagine that you live during some previous time in history. For your neighbors write an announcement of the latest event at your local amphitheater. Use at least five of the words from this lesson to describe the featured performance and its setting. Underline each vocabulary word that you use.

LESSON 8 PERSUASION AND ARGUMENT

The art of persuasion has many practical applications. Whether you are defending your point of view, demonstrating the truth or falsehood of something, or trying to influence another person's thinking, you use logic and fact in order to be convincing. While some people may be swayed by emotional appeals or by personal forcefulness, the reasonable presentation of proof or evidence is likely to be much more effective. The words in this lesson will help you to express the ways in which persuasive powers are exercised.

WORD LIST

axiomatic
definitive
empirical
hypothetical
presuppose
rationalize
rebuttal
repudiate
synthesis
verifiable

DEFINITIONS

After you have studied the definitions and example for each vocabulary word, write the word on the line to the right.

1. **axiomatic** (ăk′ sē-ə-măt′ĭk) *adjective* Self-evident; pertaining to an accepted principle or established rule. (From the Greek word *axiōma,* meaning "a self-evident proposition") 1. ______________

Related Word **axiom** *noun*
Example The fact that a room will become dark at night unless the light is turned on is *axiomatic.*

2. **definitive** (dĭ-fĭn′ĭ-tĭv) *adjective* **a.** Determining finally; decisive. **b.** Authoritative and complete. **c.** Precisely outlining; explicit. (From the Latin word *definire,* meaning "to define") 2. ______________

Related Words **define** *verb;* **definition** *noun;* **definitively** *adverb*
Example Sara claims that she has the *definitive* answer to the question of the meaning of life.

3. **empirical** (ĕm-pĭr′ĭ-kəl) *adjective* **a.** Relying solely on practical experience without regard for theory. **b.** Relying upon or derived from observation or experiment: *empirical data.* (From the Greek work *empeirikos,* meaning "experienced") 3. ______________

Related Words **empirically** *adverb;* **empiricism** *noun*
Example Not believing in any one theory of finance, Mr. Mitchell makes *empirical* decisions about his investments.

4. **hypothetical** (hī′ pə-thĕt′ĭ-kəl) *adjective* **a.** Based on a belief or theory that accounts for a set of facts and that can be tested; theoretical. **b.** Based on something that is merely supposed or guessed at: *a hypothetical case.* (From the Greek word *hupotithenai,* meaning "to suppose") 4. ______________

Related Words **hypothesis** *noun;* **hypothesize** *verb*
Example She set up her experiment so that each part would satisfy the *hypothetical* conditions.

5. **presuppose** (prē′sə-pōz′) *trans. verb* **a.** To assume in advance; take for granted. **b.** To require as a necessary condition. 5. ________________

Related Word **presupposition** *noun*
Example Ted wrote his report *presupposing* that the data in the experiment would show the desired effect.

6. **rationalize** (răsh′ə-nə-līz′) *noun* **a.** To devise self-satisfying but incorrect reasons for (one's behavior). **b.** To interpret from a reasonable standpoint. *intrans. verb* To devise self-satisfying but incorrect reasons for one's behavior. 6. ________________

Related Words **rational** *adjective;* **rationalization** *noun*
Example When she got a speeding ticket, Naomi *rationalized* that everyone had to get one sometime.

7. **rebuttal** (rĭ-bŭt′l) *noun* **a.** A statement or statements that present opposing evidence or arguments. **b.** The act of presenting such evidence. 7. ________________

Related Word **rebut** *verb*
Example In his *rebuttal* Mr. Meyers refuted his opponent's argument with such conviction that he won over his audience.

8. **repudiate** (rĭ-pyo͞o′dē-āt′) *trans. verb* **a.** To reject the validity of. **b.** To refuse to recognize or pay. **c.** To reject as untrue: *to repudiate an accusation.* **d.** To disown. (From the Latin word *repudiare,* meaning "to divorce") 8. ________________

Related Word **repudiation** *noun*
Example Brad *repudiated* his brother's objections to classical music by reminding him that he did not like any music.

9. **synthesis** (sĭn′thĭ-sĭs) *noun* **a.** The combining of separate elements or substances to form a coherent whole. **b.** Reasoning from the general to the particular; logical deduction. (From the Greek word *suntithenai,* meaning "to put together") 9. ________________

Related Word **synthesize** *verb*
Example Amy's persuasive essay was a *synthesis* of facts that she had compiled from separate sources.

10. **verifiable** (vĕr′ə-fī′ə-bəl) *adjective* **a.** Able to be proved true by the presentation of evidence or testimony. **b.** Able to be tested for accuracy as by comparison or investigation. (From the Latin words *verus,* meaning "true," and *facere,* meaning "to make") 10. ________________

Related Words **verification** *noun;* **verify** *verb*
Example Due to the thorough records that Dr. Ling kept of all his experiments, his results were *verifiable* by other scientists.

NAME ______________________ DATE __________

EXERCISE 1 WRITING CORRECT WORDS

On the answer line, write the word from the vocabulary list that fits each definition.

1. Determining finally; authoritative and complete — 1. **definitive**
2. Based on a theory that accounts for a set of facts and that can be tested — 2. **hypothetical**
3. To assume in advance; require as a necessary condition — 3. **presuppose**
4. To reject the validity of; refuse to recognize or pay — 4. **repudiate**
5. Relying on practical experience without regard for theory — 5. **empirical**
6. Self-evident; pertaining to an accepted principle or established rule — 6. **axiomatic**
7. A statement that presents opposing evidence or arguments — 7. **rebuttal**
8. The combining of separate elements or substances to form a coherent whole — 8. **synthesis**
9. Able to be proved true by the presentation of evidence or testimony — 9. **verifiable**
10. To devise self-satisfying but incorrect reasons for (one's behavior) — 10. **rationalize**

EXERCISE 2 USING WORDS CORRECTLY

Decide whether the italicized vocabulary word has been used correctly in the sentence. On the answer line, write *Correct* for correct use and *Incorrect* for incorrect use.

1. Maurice has obtained most of his work experience through such *empirical* methods as reading about others' jobs. — 1. **Incorrect**
2. Because prehistoric peoples kept few records, their patterns of trade are easily *verifiable.* — 2. **Incorrect**
3. Many authors have created *hypothetical* societies, called utopias, in which there are no social ills. — 3. **Correct**
4. The defense attorney brought in three witnesses to *repudiate* the charges against the defendant. — 4. **Correct**
5. Mrs. Santiago *rationalized* her failure to attend the party by saying that no one would miss her. — 5. **Correct**
6. The mean was a *synthesis* of representative dishes from many cultures. — 6. **Correct**
7. Thomas Jefferson included in the Declaration of Independence several truths that the new republic considered *axiomatic.* — 7. **Correct**
8. Mrs. Greenstein, our history teacher, hopes that her new book about "Seward's folly" will be the *definitive* work on the subject. — 8. **Correct**
9. Yasuko's excellence as a pianist *presupposes* great musical talent. — 9. **Correct**
10. Jon's agreement with Denise's argument was presented in a witty *rebuttal.* — 10. **Incorrect**

EXERCISE 3 CHOOSING THE BEST WORD

Decide which vocabulary word or related form best expresses the meaning of the italicized word or phrase in the sentence. On the answer line, write the letter of the correct choice.

1. According to my grandmother, "Nothing ventured, nothing gained" is *self-evident.* — 1. **c**
   a. hypothetical b. presupposed c. axiomatic d. definitive

2. For his *statement of opposing evidence,* Nicholas offered statistics that contradicted his opponent's generalizations. 2. a
a. rebuttal b. rationalization c. synthesis d. presupposition

3. In her opening address to the jury, the district attorney suggested a *supposed* motive for the defendant. 3. d
a. repudiated b. definitive c. verifiable d. hypothetical

4. The prize-winning weaving was a *coherent whole* of such fabrics as silk, jute, and canvas. 4. b
a. axiom b. synthesis c. repudiation d. verification

5. The invention of glass in 3000 B.C. probably occurred by methods that were *derived from observation or experiment.* 5. c
a. rationalized b. repudiated c. empirical d. axiomatic

6. Connie *devised self-satisfying but incorrect reasons for* her purchase by saying that she really needed a new jacket. 6. d
a. synthesized b. repudiated c. presupposed d. rationalized

7. Ladislaw's *decisive* victory in the chess championship earned him front-page coverage in the local newspaper. 7. a
a. definitive b. rational c. axiomatic d. hypothetical

8. Because no footnotes accompanied the quotations in the book, these alleged conversations were not *able to be tested for accuracy.* 8. c
a. repudiated b. empirical c. verifiable d. definitive

9. *Assuming in advance* that he could get Friday off from work, Mr. Herrera made plans to leave on vacation early in the morning. 9. a
a. presupposing b. hypothesizing c. synthesizing d. verifying

10. The senator will appear at a press conference to *reject as untrue* the charges made against him. 10. b
a. define b. repudiate c. rationalize d. presuppose

EXERCISE 4 USING DIFFERENT FORMS OF WORDS

Each sentence contains an italicized vocabulary word in a form that does not fit the sentence. On the answer line, write the form of the word that does fit the sentence.

1. Carol's *presuppose* about how the story would end led to her failure to finish the novel. 1. **presupposition**

2. The *hypothetical* of Copernicus held that the planets spin on their axes and revolve around the sun. 2. **hypothesis**

3. Our knowledge of science and technology had its roots in Greek *empirical.* 3. **empiricism**

4. In geometry class we had to memorize an *axiomatic* and use it to solve problems. 4. **axiom**

5. Mr. and Mrs. Ravich hope that an expert on antiques will be able to *verifiable* the authenticity of the old pine cabinet. 5. **verify**

6. Once the individual surveys are complete, Julie will tally the results and *synthesis* her data. 6. **synthesize**

7. Instead of having a *rationalize* reaction, Carl flew into a rage when he learned the game had been canceled. 7. **rational**

8. The Declaration of Independence, proclaimed on July 4, 1776, was a *repudiate* of Britain's control over the American colonies. 8. **repudiation**

9. The Continental Congress voted *definitive* to declare independence on July 2. 9. **definitively**

10. In a debate, after each team has presented its case, team members *rebuttal* the arguments of their opponents. 10. **rebut**

NAME ______________________ DATE __________

READING COMPREHENSION

Each numbered sentence in the following passage contains an italicized vocabulary word or related form. After you read the passage, you will complete an exercise.

DR. CHARLES DREW: PHYSICIAN AND SCIENTIST

Dr. Charles Richard Drew (1904–1950), an American physician and scientist, was internationally recognized as the leading authority on the preservation of human blood for transfusion. Without his work on blood plasma, numerous lives would have been lost needlessly during World War II. His pioneering efforts in blood research were also responsible for the foundation of blood banks.

Charles Drew began his medical career at McGill University in Montreal, Quebec. He became interested in blood research as an intern. In 1938 a Rockefeller fellowship for advanced training allowed him to pursue this interest at Columbia University's Presbyterian Hospital, where two years later he would be awarded the Doctor of Medical Science degree, actually a Ph.D. in medicine. Charles Drew was the first African American to earn this degree.

(1) Working on techniques for ***synthesizing*** and preserving blood, Dr. Drew paid close attention to the special properties of plasma, the fluid portion of blood. (2) ***Presupposing*** that plasma could be preserved for future emergency transfusions, he spent as much as eighteen hours a day gathering data to support this idea. (3) In 1939 he tested his theory ***empirically*** by setting up an experimental blood bank. (4) His ***hypothesis*** was valid; unlike whole blood, plasma could be stored more than one week and could be administered to a person of any blood type. Drew's doctoral thesis, *Banked Blood: A Study in Blood Preservation,* dealt with the development of the blood bank and with the preservation and transportation of plasma. (5) The treatise remains a ***definitive*** study of the subject.

(6) As World War II began in Europe, Dr. Drew had further opportunity to ***verify*** his findings. He was appointed medical supervisor of the "Blood for Britain" project, which supplied Britain with badly needed blood plasma. (7) Although some physicians at first ***rationalized*** that whole blood was preferable, Drew showed them that plasma was more efficient, especially in emergencies. After Britain no longer needed American aid, Drew was appointed director of the American Red Cross program for collecting and banking blood for the American armed services.

(8) Dr. Drew's work for both programs constituted a ***rebuttal*** to the conventional assumption that wartime casualties could be treated only in hospitals. (9) Formerly it had been ***axiomatic*** that battlefield transfusions were impossible. (10) Now emergency use of plasma ***repudiated*** this idea. Trained technicians could administer the life-saving plasma.

In peacetime Drew's work remained important as blood banks continued to save lives. Drew spent the rest of his career in various teaching and administrative posts at Howard University, where he became head of the department of surgery.

Dr. Charles Drew died of injuries resulting from a car accident. His death was ironic: in desperate need of a blood transfusion, he did not reach a hospital in time.

READING COMPREHENSION EXERCISE

Each of the following statements corresponds to a numbered sentence in the passage. Each statement contains a blank and is followed by four answer choices. Decide which choice fits best in the blank. The word or phrase that you choose must express roughly the same meaning as the italicized word in the passage. Write the letter of your choice on the answer line.

1. Dr. Drew was working on techniques for ____ and preserving blood. 1. b
   a. detecting certain proportions in **c.** observing
   b. combining individual elements of **d.** liquefying

2. Drew ____ that plasma could be preserved for future emergency transfusions. 2. d
   a. did not know **c.** informed others
   b. denied **d.** assumed in advance

3. He tested his theory ____ by setting up an experimental blood bank. 3. a
   a. in practice **b.** step by step **c.** partially **d.** irregularly

4. His ____ was valid. 4. b
   a. modification **b.** theory **c.** motive **d.** arrangement

5. Drew's doctoral thesis remains a(n) ____ study of blood banks. 5. a
   a. authoritative **b.** most famous **c.** pioneering **d.** least-known

6. Dr. Drew had further opportunity to ____ his findings at the start of World War II. 6. c
   a. reassess **c.** prove the truth of
   b. conceal **d.** promote financially

7. Some physicians ____ that whole blood was preferable to plasma. 7. b
   a. argued **b.** reasoned **c.** were certain **d.** were pleased

8. Dr. Drew's work constituted a(n) ____ the assumption that wartime casualties could be treated only in hospitals. 8. d
   a. exception to **c.** separation from
   b. warning about **d.** opposing argument to

9. Formerly it had been ____ that battlefield transfusions were impossible. 9. a
   a. self-evident **b.** a consideration **c.** a disgrace **d.** controversial

10. The emergency use of plasma ____ this idea. 10. c
    a. supported **b.** questioned **c.** rejected **d.** tolerated

PRACTICE WITH ANALOGIES

See pages 32, 66, and 86 for some strategies to use with analogies.

Directions On the answer line, write the vocabulary word or a form of it that completes each analogy.

1. APPRAISE : VALUE :: ____ : depth *(Lesson 6)* 1. fathom
2. INDESTRUCTIBLE : BROKEN :: ____ : penetrated *(Lesson 6)* 2. impervious
3. PRECIOUS : VALUABLE :: ____ : clear *(Lesson 6)* 3. limpid
4. CRAMPED : CONFINED :: ____ : roomy *(Lesson 7)* 4. capacious
5. INTUITIVE : INSTINCT :: ____ : evidence *(Lesson 8)* 5. empirical
6. SPY : COVERT :: nitpicker : ____ *(Lesson 7)* 6. captious

The **Bonus activity** for Lessons 5–8 is on page T6.

LESSON 9 NORMALITY AND ABNORMALITY

Whether someone or something conforms to customary patterns or deviates from them depends on one's point of view. Behind the concepts of normality and abnormality is the assumption that there is a single standard by which to judge everything. What may be normal to one group, however, may be unacceptable to another. For example, Americans generally cut their food with the knife in the right hand and the fork in the left. For them, transferring the fork to the right hand to carry food to the mouth is comfortable. In contrast, Europeans, who commonly leave the fork in the left hand, find the American method odd and inefficient. For the many Asians who hold a bowl of food in the left hand and manipulate a set of chopsticks with the right, both of these methods may be out of the ordinary. The words in this lesson will help you to express the relative nature of the normal and abnormal circumstances that you encounter.

WORD LIST

aberrant
anomaly
eccentricity
endemic
incongruous
mundane
outlandish
paragon
ubiquitous
unwonted

DEFINITIONS

After you have studied the definitions and example for each vocabulary word, write the word on the line to the right.

1. **aberrant** (ă-bĕr'ənt) *adjective* **a.** Deviating from what is normal; atypical **b.** Deviating from the proper or expected course. (From the Latin *ab-*, meaning "from," and *errare*, meaning "to wander") 1. ______________

Related Word **aberration** *noun*
Example The dog's sudden *aberrant* eating patterns alerted its owner to a possible health problem.

2. **anomaly** (ə-nŏm'ə-lē) *noun* **a.** A deviation or departure from the normal or common order, form, or rule. **b.** Something that is irregular, abnormal, or unusual. (From the Greek *an-*, meaning "not," and *homos*, meaning "same") 2. ______________

Related Word **anomalous** *adjective*
Example It was an *anomaly* that all registered voters in Gladstone, though typically apathetic, cast their ballots on election day.

3. **eccentricity** (ĕk'sĕn-trĭs'ĭ-tē) *noun* **a.** Odd, peculiar, or whimsical behavior. **b.** An example or instance of diverging from customary or conventional practices. (From the Greek *ex-*, meaning "out," and *kentron*, meaning "center") 3. ______________

Related Word **eccentric** *adjective*
Example Geraldine's particular *eccentricity* was her extensive collection of frogs; the amphibians dominated every room of her house.

4. **endemic** (ĕn-dĕm'ĭk) *adjective* **a.** Prevalent in or peculiar to a particular locality or people. **b.** Native. (From the Greek *en-*, meaning "in," and dēmos, meaning "people") 4. ______________

Related Word **endemically** *adverb*
Example Measles, at first *endemic* to the eastern hemisphere, spread to the Americas after European voyages there in the late 1400s.

5. **incongruous** (ĭn-kŏng'gro͞o-əs) *adjective* **a.** Not consistent with what is logical, customary, or expected; inappropriate. **b.** Not corresponding; disagreeing: *a plan incongruous with good sense.* **c.** Made up of distinct, inconsistent, or discordant parts or qualities. (From the Latin *in-*, meaning "not," and *congruere,* meaning "to agree")

5. ____________

Related Words **incongruity** *noun;* **incongruously** *adverb*
Example The modern furniture looked *incongruous* in the ancient castle.

6. **mundane** (mŭn′ dān′, mŭn'dān′) *adjective* **a.** Typical of or concerned with the ordinary, practical, or usual. **b.** Of, relating to, or typical of this world; worldly. (From the Latin word *mundus,* meaning "world")

6. ____________

Related Word **mundanely** *adverb*
Example Although cooking can be a creative task, laundry and cleaning tend to be *mundane* chores.

7. **outlandish** (out-lăn'dĭsh) *adjective* **a.** Conspicuously unconventional; bizarre; absurd. **b.** Strikingly foreign, unfamiliar. **c.** Geographically remote from the familiar world.

7. ____________

Related Words **outlandishly** *adverb;* **outlandishness** *noun*
Example At the party a prize was awarded to the wearer of the most *outlandish* costume.

8. **paragon** (păr'ə-gŏn′, păr'ə-gən) *noun* A model of perfection or excellence; peerless example. (From the Italian word *paragone,* meaning "a touchstone")

8. ____________

USAGE NOTE: Compare with a *paradigm* (page 2), which may simply be "a typical or a particularly clear model."

Example To Homer, author of the *Iliad,* Helen of Troy was a *paragon* of beauty.

9. **ubiquitous** (yo͞o-bĭk'wĭ-təs) *adjective* Being or seeming to be everywhere at the same time; omnipresent. (From the Latin word *ubique,* meaning "everywhere")

9. ____________

Related Words **ubiquitously** *adverb;* **ubiquity** *noun*
Example Bomb shelters were *ubiquitous* in London during World War II.

10. **unwonted** (ŭn-wôn'tĭd, ŭn-wōn'tĭd, ŭn-wŭn'tĭd) *adjective* Not habitual, customary, or common; unusual. (From the Old English word *wurian,* meaning "to be used to")

10. ____________

Related Words **unwontedly** *adverb;* **unwontedness** *noun*
Example Isaac responded with *unwonted* rudeness, surprising everyone in the room.

NAME ______________________ DATE ____________

EXERCISE 1 MATCHING WORDS AND DEFINITIONS

Match the definition in Column B with the word in Column A. Write the letter of the correct definition on the answer line.

Column A

1. incongruous
2. ubiquitous
3. aberrant
4. eccentricity
5. mundane
6. paragon
7. anomaly
8. unwonted
9. endemic
10. outlandish

Column B

a. a departure from the normal or common order, form, or rule
b. deviating from what is normal; atypical
c. conspicuously unconventional; strikingly foreign
d. not consistent with what is logical, customary, or expected; not corresponding
e. being or seeming to be everywhere at the same time
f. odd, peculiar, or whimsical behavior
g. concerned with the ordinary, practical, or usual
h. prevalent in or peculiar to a particular locality or people; native
i. not habitual, customary, or common
j. a model of perfection or excellence

1. d
2. e
3. b
4. f
5. g
6. j
7. a
8. i
9. h
10. c

EXERCISE 2 USING WORDS CORRECTLY

Decide whether the italicized vocabulary word has been used correctly in the sentence. On the answer line, write *Correct* for correct use and *Incorrect* for incorrect use.

1. When the questionnaires were analyzed, the researchers discovered that 80 percent of the *aberrant* responses came from one geographical area. — 1. Correct
2. "This snowstorm is an *anomaly*," said the farmer. "We get one like it every year." — 2. Incorrect
3. Unexpected or *incongruous* things—a child carrying a briefcase, for example—often make us laugh. — 3. Correct
4. Because many people travel widely today, doctors must be knowledgeable about diseases *endemic* in many different locales. — 4. Correct
5. To the ancient Athenians, Theseus was a *paragon* of the wise ruler. — 5. Correct
6. Carolee loves to cook exotic, *mundane* dishes using unusual ingredients. — 6. Incorrect
7. In an *unwonted* move, the president signed the bill that he had earlier opposed. — 7. Correct
8. Saul's one *eccentricity* was conforming to the expectations of his friends. — 8. Incorrect
9. Eleanor's *outlandish* behavior surprised those who knew her as a sedate young woman. — 9. Correct
10. Gas street lamps had become *ubiquitous;* they were located only in the restored historical section of the city. — 10. Incorrect

EXERCISE 3 IDENTIFYING SYNONYMS AND ANTONYMS

Decide which word has the meaning that is the same as (a synonym) or opposite to (an antonym) that of the capitalized vocabulary word. Write the letter of your choice on the answer line.

1. ABERRANT (antonym):
   a. deviant **b.** abhorrent **c.** exclusive **d.** normal — 1. d

2. INCONGRUOUS (synonym): 2. a
a. inconsistent b. appropriate c. insincere d. pessimistic

3. ENDEMIC (antonym): 3. d
a. stately b. diseased c. peculiar d. widespread

4. PARAGON (synonym): 4. c
a. subordinate b. reprieve c. ideal d. tranquility

5. UNWONTED (antonym): 5. b
a. unimportant b. customary c. rare d. overused

6. MUNDANE (synonym): 6. a
a. ordinary b. infinite c. heavy d. refined

7. OUTLANDISH (antonym): 7. c
a. clear b. exact c. commonplace d. obvious

8. ANOMALY (synonym): 8. b
a. example b. irregularity c. rule d. naturalness

9. ECCENTRICITY (antonym): 9. d
a. peculiarity b. competence c. verity d. conventionality

10. UBIQUITOUS (synonym): 10. a
a. omnipresent b. absent c. imaginary d. questionable

EXERCISE 4 USING DIFFERENT FORMS OF WORDS

Decide which form of the vocabulary word in parentheses best completes the sentence. The form given may be correct. Write your answer on the answer line.

1. A snowfall in southern Florida is an ____. *(aberrant)* 1. **aberration**

2. The new employee was placed in an ____ position of leadership when her boss suddenly resigned. *(anomaly)* 2. **anomalous**

3. The ____ of wearing a fur coat with a bathing suit had obviously escaped the movie star. *(incongruous)* 3. **incongruity**

4. The malaria outbreak spread only ____ and was quickly contained. *(endemic)* 4. **endemically**

5. Leonardo da Vinci was a ____ of the artist, the scientist, and the engineer. *(paragon)* 5. **paragon**

6. William Randolph Hearst was considered by many to be ____ when he began collecting wild animals on his California estate. *(eccentricity)* 6. **eccentric**

7. The room was ____ decorated in purple and green. *(outlandish)* 7. **outlandishly**

8. The ____ of the reporters made it impossible to conceal the discovery of the treasure for long. *(ubiquitous)* 8. **ubiquity**

9. Kevin and Erica were delighted when their ____ conversation was interrupted by the arrival of the guests. *(mundane)* 9. **mundane**

10. We usually sleep late on weekends, but we arose ____ early last Saturday to take a sunrise hike. *(unwonted)* 10. **unwontedly**

NAME ______________________ DATE __________

READING COMPREHENSION

Each numbered sentence in the following passage contains an italicized vocabulary work or related form. After you read the passage, you will complete an exercise.

THE GALÁPAGOS ISLANDS: BIOLOGICAL ODDITIES

Six hundred miles off the coast of Ecuador lie the islands of the Galápagos, home of some of the most unusual plants and animals in the world. Nowhere but in the sixteen islands of this volcanic archipelago can one find sunflowers that have evolved into trees, penguins and fur seals living at the equator, and the only four-eyed fish, marine lizards, and nocturnal sea gulls that exist.

(1) What partially accounts for such biological ***incongruities*** are the two Pacific Ocean currents that cut through the islands. The cold Humboldt Current, which originates in the Antarctic, and the warm El Niño Current, which begins off the coast of South America, combine off the Galápagos. (2) Their meeting produces such climatic ***anomalies*** as low rainfall along the coast, cool air and surface-water temperatures, and heavy mists that periodically blanket the Galápagos.

(3) While the unusual combination of the two currents explain some of the biological ***aberrations,*** the extent of the diversity is attributed to the isolation of the Galápagos. The islands, never connected to the mainland, are believed to have arisen from the ocean floor ten million years ago as the tops of volcanoes. Plants, insects, and small animals probably made the long journey from South America to the Galápagos on rafts of vegetation or driftwood or were carried there by early pirates, whalers, or Spanish explorers. (4) While some of the creatures, such as herons, crabs, and turtles, are familiar and ***mundane,*** others, though descended from mainland species, developed for countless millennia in virtual isolation from evolutionary processes on the continent. (5) Scientists regard the Galápagos as the world's best laboratory for studying how ***endemic*** species came to be differentiated.

Charles Darwin was the first scientist to discover the distinctive nature of species adaptation. Visiting the islands in 1835, the naturalist speculated about the relationship of the Galápagos species to those he had seen on the continent of South America. He found an astounding number of species that not only differed from those on the mainland but also differed from island to island. Each island, in fact, had its own distinctive wildlife and plants.

(6) Darwin was regarded as ***eccentric*** when he first advanced his theory of natural selection based on his observations of the Galápagos. In Darwin's time it was accepted scientific fact that an animal species was something fixed and unalterable. Darwin, however, pointed out that specific conditions, such as climate and food, affect isolated populations in different ways and promote change. Over long periods of time, a species will adapt to the special conditions and evolve into a new species.

(7) One of the most striking examples that Charles Darwin cited as support for his theory of evolution was the ***ubiquitous*** tortoise, for which the Galápagos were named. Darwin observed that one type of tortoise had the deep, rounded shell of its mainland ancestors, whereas a second type, having a saddle-shaped shell and a longer neck, bore little resemblance to other land tortoises. From observing the habitats of both varieties, he concluded that the second type of tortoise, living on the more arid islands, was forced during droughts to stretch upwards to feed on cactus pads and fruit. Those tortoises that could stretch survived, while those with shorter necks did not.

(8) The same adaptation gave finches an ***outlandish*** appearance. Although all thirteen of the species he observed seemed to have had a common ancestor, the birds differed from island to island in size and beak shape. On one island the finches have slender beaks for probing the pulpy centers of cacti; on another the birds have developed sturdy feet, legs, and heads to push against large rocks to get at insects underneath. (9) Adapting to local conditions, these birds have developed seemingly ***unwonted*** physical differences. The genetic traits that have survival value have been preserved.

Anyone who visits these enchanted isles, as the Galápagos were once called, automatically becomes a naturalist of sorts. (10) This group of islands is the ***paragon*** of a natural laboratory, where species adaptation is the key to the development of so many unique biological wonders.

READING COMPREHENSION EXERCISE

Each of the following statements corresponds to a numbered sentence in the passage. Each statement contains a blank and is followed by four answer choices. Decide which choice fits best in the blank. The word or phrase that you choose must express roughly the same meaning as the italicized word in the passage. Write the letter of your choice on the answer line.

1. Two Pacific currents partially account for the biological ____. — 1. b
   a. controls b. inconsistencies c. enhancements d. considerations

2. The two currents combine to produce climatic ____. — 2. d
   a. comparisons b. consistency c. turbulence d. irregularities

3. The two currents explain only some of the biological ____. — 3. a
   a. deviations b. restrictions c. applications d. spectacles

4. Some of the creatures are familiar and ____. — 4. b
   a. domestic b. ordinary c. independent d. essential

5. Scientists regard the islands as the best place for studying ____ species. — 5. c
   a. authoritative b. comprehensive c. native d. systematized

6. Darwin was considered ____ when he first advanced his theory. — 6. d
   a. deranged b. optimistic c. accurate d. unconventional

7. Darwin cited the ____ tortoise as support for his theory of evolution. — 7. b
   a. little-known b. omnipresent c. land d. extinct

8. Darwin noted the same ____ adaptation among finches. — 8. a
   a. conspicuously unusual c. perceptible
   b. poorly understood d. unexplained

9. The finches have developed seemingly ____ physical differences. — 9. d
   a. typical b. majestic c. critical d. unusual

10. This group of islands is the ____ of natural laboratories. — 10. c
    a. restoration c. peerless example
    b. beginning d. original proof

WRITING ASSIGNMENT

Whether something is normal or abnormal depends to a great extent on one's point of view. Write a brief newspaper article that presents a situation from the perspective of a reporter who sees the event as natural or typical. Then, using the same situation, rewrite the article from the point of view of someone who interprets the event as odd. In each article use (and underline) at least four vocabulary words from this lesson.

VOCABULARY ENRICHMENT

The word *paragon* comes from the Italian word *paragone,* meaning "a touchstone." A touchstone was a standard for testing the purity of gold. By rubbing the gold against a dark stone, people could determine the amount of gold present by the type of mark that was made. In time the use of the touchstone disappeared, but people continued to associate the word *paragon* with a model for determining the true worth of something.

Activity Other English words are associated with metals. Look up the following words in a dictionary, and write their roots and definitions. Then write an explanation of the connection between the root and the meaning.

1. Argentina 2. aureole 3. chrysanthemum 4. nickel 5. plummet

The **Test** for Lessons 7, 8, and 9 is on page T7.

NAME ______________________ DATE __________

TEST-TAKING SKILLS

TESTS OF STANDARD WRITTEN ENGLISH

In addition to the verbal and mathematical parts, some standardized tests contain a section that tests a student's knowledge of standard written English. The SAT II Writing Test has some of these questions as part of its Revision-in-Context section, as does the English Test in the American College Testing (ACT) Assessment Program.

Tests of standard written English usually contain usage questions and sentence-correction questions. These items test your knowledge of the following areas of English.

1. Agreement, of subject and verb and of pronoun and antecedent
2. Correct form, tense, and mood of verbs
3. Correct case of pronouns
4. Correct use of modifiers, including degree of comparison
5. Correct use of words sometimes confused (example: *accept/except*) or used unacceptably (example: a double negative)
6. Complete sentences, as opposed to run-ons and fragments
7. Correct placement of modifiers and participial phrases
8. Use of parallel structure when called for
9. Clear, logical, and correct style

A *usage question* requires you to look at four underlined parts of a sentence and determine whether one of them is faulty.

I rung the bell three times before anyone answered. No error
A (rung) B (before) C (anyone) D (answered.) E (No error)

Read the entire sentence. Then reread it, making a judgment about each underlined part. (No more than one part can be incorrect.) If you find no errors, choose E as the answer. Choice A is the answer in the sample test item; *rang* would be the correct form of the verb.

A *sentence-correction question* presents you with a sentence and alternative versions of the underlined part of it. Your task is to select the correct version. Choice A is always the same as the original and means "make no change." In the sample test item that follows, Choice C is correct. Choice A has a dangling participial phrase, and choice B is not a complete sentence. *On account of* in choice D is used unacceptably, and choice E does not have a logical time sequence.

Detonating a nuclear bomb, people on Bikini Atoll had to be evacuated.
(A) Detonating a nuclear bomb,
(B) Detonating a nuclear bomb, and
(C) Before a nuclear bomb was detonated,
(D) On account of a nuclear bomb was detonated,
(E) A nuclear bomb was detonated, and so

EXERCISE TAKING USAGE AND SENTENCE-CORRECTION TESTS

On the answer line, write the letter of the correct answer for each of the following test items.

1. I knew that Jesse was a better writer than me. No error
   A B C D E

   1. D

2. "Whom shall I say is calling?" Carol asked. No error
   A B C D E

   2. A

3. Either carrot cake or strawberries was chosen for dessert. No error
   A B C D E

   3. C

4. Jeannie's twin sister, Melinda, is tallest, but Jeannie is more conspicuous
   A B C

   because of her brilliant red hair. No error
   D E

   4. B

5. I left the phone ring for two minutes before someone answered irritably,
   A B C

   "There's no one here!" No error
   D E

   5. A

6. Coming down the hill, my house is the first one on the right.
   (A) Coming down the hill, my house
   (B) Coming down the hill, you will find that my house
   (C) My house, coming down the hill,
   (D) Coming down the hill, and my house
   (E) You will find my house, coming down the hill,

   6. B

7. The uniforms that they wore were bright green.
   (A) uniforms that they wore
   (B) uniforms, that they wore,
   (C) uniforms they are wearing
   (D) uniforms that they wearing
   (E) uniforms, which they wore,

   7. A

8. I am reading a book, it is interesting and humorous.
   (A) a book, it is interesting and humorous.
   (B) a book, which is interesting and humorous.
   (C) a book it is interesting and humorous.
   (D) a book, for it is interesting and humorous.
   (E) an interesting and humorous book.

   8. E

9. The Roman Empire fell in the late fifth century, and it left an enduring legacy of culture and law.
   (A) The Roman Empire fell in the late fifth century, and
   (B) Although the Roman Empire fell in the late fifth century,
   (C) Since the Roman Empire fell in the late fifth century,
   (D) The Roman Empire fell in the late fifth century
   (E) The fall of the Roman Empire occurred in the late fifth century, and

   9. B

10. Accustomed to the noise of trucks, and sirens, and the sound of radios, she could not get used to the music of chirping crickets and calling birds.
    (A) Accustomed to the noise of trucks, sirens, and the sound of radios,
    (B) Accustomed to the noise of trucks, sirens, and radios,
    (C) Being as she was accustomed to the noise of trucks, sirens, and radios,
    (D) She was accustomed to the noise of trucks, sirens, and radios, so
    (E) Because she was accustomed to the noise of trucks, sirens, and the sound of radios,

    10. B

LESSON 10 THE ROOTS *-CORP-* AND *-ANIM-*

10

The root *-corp-* comes from the Latin word *corpus,* meaning "body." The root *-anim-* comes from the Latin word *anima,* meaning "soul." It is closely related to the Latin word *animus,* meaning "spirit," "mind," or "alive." Both of these Latin roots serve as the basis for many English words. A *corps,* for example, is a body of persons acting together or associated under common direction, while a *corpse* is a dead body. An *animated* person is filled with life, activity, vigor, or spirit, while a *unanimous* vote indicates that the voters are in agreement. In this lesson you will learn other words derived from these two Latin roots. These words describe complementary aspects of existence—the body and the mind.

WORD LIST

animus
corpulent
corpus
corpuscle
equanimity
inanimate
incorporate
incorporeal
magnanimous
pusillanimous

DEFINITIONS

After you have studied the definitions and example for each vocabulary word, write the word on the line to the right.

1. **animus** (ăn′ə-məs) *noun* **a.** A feeling of animosity; bitter hostility or hatred. **b.** An intention or purpose; moving spirit behind an action. (From the Latin word *animus,* meaning "soul" or "mind") 1. ____________

Example His *animus* toward his enemy made him refuse any attempts at reconciliation.

2. **corpulent** (kôr′pyə-lənt) *adjective* Having a large, overweight body; obese. (From the Latin word *corpus,* meaning "body") 2. ____________

Related Word **corpulence** *noun*
Example Appearing in both *The Merry Wives of Windsor* and *Henry IV,* the *corpulent* Sir John Falstaff is one of Shakespeare's most famous comic characters.

3. **corpus** (kôr′pəs) *noun* **a.** A large collection of writings of a specific kind or on a specific subject. **b.** A human or animal body, especially when dead. **c.** A structure constituting the main part of an organ: *the corpus of the jaw.* (From the Latin word *corpus*) 3. ____________

Example The scholar made a thorough study of the *corpus* of sixteenth-century Italian literature.

4. **corpuscle** (kôr′pə-səl, kôr′pŭs′əl) *noun* **a.** A cell, such as a blood or lymph cell, in a liquid, as distinguished from a cell fixed in tissue. **b.** A minute globular particle. (From the Latin word *corpusculum,* meaning "little particle") 4. ____________

Related Word **corpuscular** *adjective*
Example *Corpuscles* provide oxygen for cartilage and bone tissue.

5. **equanimity** (ē′kwə-nĭm′ĭ-tē, ĕk′wə-nĭm′ĭ-tē) *noun* The quality of being calm and even-tempered; composure. (From the Latin words *aequus,* meaning "even," and *animus,* meaning "soul" or "mind") 5. ____________

Example Nothing disturbs Adela's *equanimity,* not even the trying antics of her five-year-old brother.

6. **inanimate** (ĭn-ăn′ə-mĭt) *adjective* **a.** Not having the qualities associated with active, living organisms. **b.** Not exhibiting life; appearing lifeless or dead. **c.** Not animated or energetic; dull; listless. (From the Latin *in-,* meaning "not," and *anima,* meaning "soul") 6. ____________

Related Words **inanimately** *adverb;* **inanimateness** *noun*
Example Lester has the habit of talking to *inanimate* objects, such as his typewriter and his car.

7. **incorporate** (ĭn-kôr′pə-rāt′) *trans verb* **a.** To unite with or blend indistinguishably into something already in existence. **b.** To cause to merge or combine together into a united whole. **c.** To give substance or material form to; embody. *intrans. verb* **a.** To become united or combined into an organized body. **b.** To form a legal corporation. (From the Latin *in-,* meaning "in," and *corpus*) 7. ____________

Related Words **incorporated** *adjective;* **incorporation** *noun*
Example The members of the club *incorporated* three new laws into their constitution.

8. **incorporeal** (ĭn′kôr-pôr′ē-əl) *adjective* **a.** Lacking material form or substance. **b.** Intangible, as a legal right or patent. (From the Latin *in-,* meaning "not," and *corpus*) 8. ____________

Example In *Macbeth* an *incorporeal* being, Banquo's ghost, appears at a great banquet and is seen by no one but Macbeth.

9. **magnanimous** (măg-năn′ə-məs) *adjective* Noble of mind and heart, especially generous in forgiving; unselfish; gracious. (From the Latin words *magnus,* meaning "great," and *animus*) 9. ____________

Related Words **magnanimity** *noun;* **magnanimously** *adverb*
Example After the tennis match, the *magnanimous* victor ran to the net to congratulate her opponent on a well-played game.

10. **pusillanimous** (pyo͞o′sə-lăn′ə-məs) *adjective* Cowardly; lacking courage. (From the Latin word *pusillus,* meaning "weak," and *animus*) 10. ____________

Related Word **pusillanimity** *noun*
Example The *pusillanimous* athlete made a habit of criticizing his teammates when he talked to reporters.

NAME ______________________________ DATE ______________

EXERCISE 1 WRITING CORRECT WORDS

On the answer line, write the word from the vocabulary list that fits each definition.

1. Having a large, overweight body; obese — 1. corpulent
2. A cell capable of free movement in a liquid; minute globular particle — 2. corpuscle
3. Not having qualities associated with active, living organisms — 3. inanimate
4. An intention or purpose; feeling of animosity — 4. animus
5. Cowardly; lacking courage — 5. pusillanimous
6. Lacking material form or substance; intangible — 6. incorporeal
7. Noble of mind and heart; generous; unselfish — 7. magnanimous
8. A large collection of writings of a specific kind — 8. corpus
9. The quality of being calm and even-tempered; composure — 9. equanimity
10. To unite with something already in existence; cause to combine into a united whole — 10. incorporate

EXERCISE 2 USING WORDS CORRECTLY

Each of the following statements contains an italicized vocabulary word. Decide whether the sentence is true or false, and write *True* or *False* on the answer line.

1. A *corpuscle* is an organ, such as the appendix, that is no longer necessary to the functioning of the body. — 1. False
2. Being excessively *corpulent* can endanger one's health. — 2. True
3. The *animus* is the end result or effect of an action. — 3. False
4. Rocks, books, and bicycles are all *inanimate* objects. — 4. True
5. In folklore phantoms are always *incorporeal.* — 5. True
6. The sonnets of John Keats added significantly to the *corpus* of English poetry of the Romantic period. — 6. True
7. In a *magnanimous* gesture, the winner of an election usually criticizes his or her opponent. — 7. False
8. A race-car driver must be *pusillanimous* if he or she is ever going to win a race. — 8. False
9. Most people's personalities *incorporate* both positive and negative characteristics. — 9. True
10. An anxious person can face all problems with *equanimity.* — 10. False

EXERCISE 3 IDENTIFYING SYNONYMS AND ANTONYMS

Decide which word or phrase has the meaning that is the same as (a synonym) or opposite to (an antonym) that of the capitalized vocabulary word. Write the letter of your choice on the answer line.

1. INCORPOREAL (antonym): — 1. c
   a. disreputable **b.** obscure **c.** tangible **d.** spontaneous

2. ANIMUS (synonym): 2. a
a. intention b. perplexity c. weakness d. intonation

3. PUSILLANIMOUS (antonym): 3. d
a. untainted b. meager c. imperial d. courageous

4. CORPUS (synonym): 4. c
a. group of dancers
b. group of soldiers
c. body of writings
d. thicket of trees

5. EQUANIMITY (antonym): 5. a
a. frenzy b. enmity c. passivity d. hostility

6. CORPUSCLE (synonym): 6. c
a. fixed cell b. dominant organ c. moving cell d. medical condition

7. INANIMATE (antonym): 7. d
a. deficient b. reckless c. vehement d. alive

8. MAGNANIMOUS (synonym): 8. d
a. spiteful b. exalted c. victorious d. generous

9. CORPULENT (antonym): 9. a
a. lean b. petulant c. incessant d. modest

10. INCORPORATE (synonym): 10. c
a. expel b. separate c. unite d. conspire

EXERCISE 4 USING DIFFERENT FORMS OF WORDS

Decide which form of the vocabulary word in parentheses best completes the sentence. The form given may be correct. Write your answer on the answer line.

1. Mother's _____ has helped the family through many crises. *(equanimity)* 1. **equanimity**

2. Calmly and without _____, Martin explained the seriousness of the errors. *(animus)* 2. **animus**

3. The _____ of King George IV made it necessary for him to be lowered onto his horse by a mechanical device. *(corpulent)* 3. **corpulence**

4. In *The Wizard of Oz,* the lion hopes to receive courage in place of his _____. *(pusillanimous)* 4. **pusillanimity**

5. The _____ of Rebecca's ideas into the rebuttal strengthened the debate team's position. *(incorporate)* 5. **incorporation**

6. The _____ of Bach's work has been increased by the recent discovery of some thirty chorales. *(corpus)* 6. **corpus**

7. Mr. Quezada welcomed us _____ to the neighborhood. *(magnanimous)* 7. **magnanimously**

8. The blood test revealed that Kayla lacked enough white _____ to fight infection. *(corpuscle)* 8. **corpuscles**

9. The story was about gremlins, _____ creatures that supposedly live in mechanical devices and are responsible for their breakdown. *(incorporeal)* 9. **incorporeal**

10. After her first aerobics workout, Lisa was so tired that she sat slumped _____ against the wall. *(inanimate)* 10. **inanimately**

NAME ____________________ DATE ____________

READING COMPREHENSION

Each numbered sentence in the following passage contains an italicized vocabulary word. After you read the passage, you will complete an exercise.

MARY SHELLEY: CREATOR OF FRANKENSTEIN

Mary Wollstonecraft Godwin Shelley (1797–1851) was the daughter of two of the most liberal thinkers of the eighteenth century, the wife of an English poet, and the friend of some of the most creative writers and artists of her time. Besides being important in the lives of many famous people, she earned her own place in literary history. At the age of eighteen, she wrote *Frankenstein,* the first and most enduring work of science fiction. More than 150 years after its original publication, *Frankenstein* continues to fascinate and frighten its readers

Mary Godwin had an unusual childhood. After her mother, a pioneering feminist author, died in childbirth, her father remarried. The family was constantly in debt, and Mary received little attention. (1) Her ***equanimity,*** positive nature, and high standards of duty were tested by the demands of her step- and half-brothers and sisters. Although she had no formal schooling, she did live in an atmosphere of scholarship and ideas, absorbing the social and political theories championed by her father.

Mary was sixteen when the poet Percy Bysshe Shelley, attracted by the philosophy of her father, visited the family in London. They fell instantly in love and eloped. The Shelleys became colleagues as well as companions, offering each other mutual encouragement in their writing. Because Shelley was hounded by financial and legal difficulties, the couple had no permanent home; instead, they wandered throughout Europe.

It was while they were visiting Lord Byron, another famous English poet, in Switzerland that Mary conceived the idea for *Frankenstein,* (2) One evening, as they read aloud German tales of ***incorporeal*** beings, Byron suggested that his company try writing their own ghost stories. Only Mary's story was ever completed.

Frankenstein is the tale of a Swiss chemist, Dr. Victor Frankenstein, who discovers the secret of life and decides to create a man. (3) Collecting ***inanimate*** matter from laboratories, he constructs a body that is grotesque but mechanically sound. (4) The creature's yellow skin scarcely covers the muscles and arteries of its large, though not ***corpulent,*** body. (5) As electricity is shot through every ***corpuscle,*** the nameless creature is activated. Dr. Frankenstein is horrified with his results. (6) Although he once saw himself as a ***magnanimous*** benefactor of the world, he now realizes his mistake. His idea of producing a new and happy species has resulted in the creation of a monster. (7) The ***pusillanimous*** doctor flees from this knowledge and from his creation.

The monster is actually a gentle creature, but everyone fears and mistreats him because of his hideous appearance. (8) Desperately lonely, he feels an ***animus*** against human beings and seeks revenge by murdering those closest to Dr. Frankenstein. Frankenstein dies while trying to track down and kill his creation, who disappears into the Arctic. Mary Shelley concludes the novel ambiguously, leaving the reader to decide whether the monster destroys itself or continues to pursue vengeance.

Published anonymously in 1818, the novel was considered a minor classic by the time it was republished in 1831 under Mary Shelley's name. If *Frankenstein* had been only entertainment, it would long since have been forgotten as a period piece. (9) Mary Shelly, however, ***incorporates*** several timeless themes into her novel. The monster illustrates the suffering caused by judging only appearances. By fashioning what is beyond his control, Dr. Frankenstein shows that science and knowledge are in themselves neither creative nor destructive forces. The theme that it is our responsibility to use them wisely for the promise of a better life is as valid today as it was in the early nineteenth century.

Widowed at the age of twenty-five, when Percy Bysshe Shelley drowned in a boating accident, Mary Shelley supported their one surviving child by writing. Partially through her efforts at collecting and annotating her husband's poetry, he received the recognition he deserved. (10) Although she produced other novels, plays, and travel books, *Frankenstein* is the only work in her entire ***corpus*** that remains timelessly popular.

READING COMPREHENSION EXERCISE

Each of the following statements corresponds to a numbered sentence in the passage. Each statement contains a blank and is followed by four answer choices. Decide which choice fits best in the blank. The word or phrase that you choose must express roughly the same meaning as the italicized word in the passage. Write the letter of your choice on the answer line.

1. Mary's _____ was tested by the demands of her new family. — 1. c
   a. courage b. good sense c. even temper d. endurance
2. After reading German tales about beings _____, Lord Byron suggested that they try writing their own stories. — 2. a
   a. lacking material form
   b. lacking realism
   c. that made mischief
   d. that were mysterious
3. Dr. Frankenstein collects _____ matter from laboratories. — 3. d
   a. unstable b. contaminated c. counterfeit d. lifeless
4. The creature's body is large, though not _____. — 4. b
   a. strong b. obese c. splendid d. flawless
5. The creature is activated when electricity is shot through every _____. — 5. c
   a. organ b. limb c. moving cell d. nerve ending
6. Dr. Frankenstein had seen himself as a(n) _____ benefactor of the world. — 6. a
   a. generous b. eminent c. imaginary d. principal
7. The _____ doctor flees from the monster. — 7. d
   a. corrupt b. greedy c. foolhardy d. cowardly
8. The monster has _____ human beings. — 8. b
   a. responsibility for
   b. bitterly hostile attitude toward
   c. delight in
   d. deep understanding of
9. Mary Shelley _____ several timeless themes in her novel. — 9. a
   a. combines b. experiments with c. advances d. treats
10. *Frankenstein* is the only work in her entire _____ that remains popular. — 10. c
    a. volume b. library c. body of writings d. range of experience

PRACTICE WITH ANALOGIES

See pages 32 and 86 for some other strategies to use with analogies.

Verbal Aptitude Test I is on page T9.

Strategy Check grammatical relationships. If the given words are a noun-verb pair, the answer must be a noun-verb pair.

Incorrect quarterback : pass :: batter : strong
Correct quarterback : pass :: batter : swing

Directions On the answer line, write the letter of the phrase that best completes the analogy. Some of the items use the strategy explained above.

1. ABERRATION : NORM :: (A) apology : regret (B) anomaly : rule (C) pledge : donation (D) trophy : victory (E) bonus : gift — 1. B
2. ECCENTRIC : BEHAVIOR :: (A) unwonted : attitude (B) revolutionary : justice (C) righteous : indignation (D) resilient : character (E) outlandish : costume — 2. E
3. INANIMATE : MOTION :: (A) arid : moisture (B) jubilant : joy (C) compassion : sympathy (D) precious : wealth (E) vital : energy — 3. A
4. INCORPOREAL : SUBSTANCE :: (A) inefficient : time (B) vital : energy (C) sluggish : fatigue (D) shallow : depth (E) ardent : passion — 4. D
5. MAGNANIMOUS : GRACIOUS :: (A) aimless : consistent (B) cautious : impatient (C) pusillanimous : cowardly (D) contiguous : distant (E) intricate : simple — 5. C

LESSON 11 WRONGDOING AND JUSTICE

11

Although our modern system of justice is not perfect, we have only to consider what justice was like in the Middle Ages to determine how far society has come. In those times, people accused of crimes would often have to exonerate themselves by getting eleven people to swear to their innocence or even by waging an actual battle. In the 1100s, Henry II of England ensured the great reform of trial by a jury through evidence. His son, King John, later extended legal reforms through the Magna Carta (1215) which, among other things, assured that those accused could not be kept in jail indefinitely without being charged. These ancient reforms are part of the basis of our legal system today.

WORD LIST

abscond
bilk
clemency
contrite
impute
iniquity
redress
reprehensible
restitution
vindicate

DEFINITIONS

After you have studied the definitions and example for each vocabulary word, write the word on the line to the right.

1. **abscond** (ăb-skŏnd') *intrans. verb* To leave quickly and secretly and hide oneself, especially to avoid arrest or prosecution. (From the Latin *ab-*, meaning "away," and *condere,* meaning "to put") 1. ________

Example The criminal *absconded* with the stolen goods.

2. **bilk** (bĭlk) *trans. verb* **a.** To cheat or swindle. **b.** To evade payment of. 2. ________

Example The Smiths were *bilked* by a smooth-talking salesperson who sold them aluminum siding for their brick house.

3. **clemency** (klĕm'ən-sē) *noun* **a.** Mercy, especially toward an offender or enemy; leniency. **b.** Mildness: *the clemency of the weather.* 3. ________

Related Word **clement** *adjective*
Example The judge showed *clemency* by imposing a fine on the defendant instead of sending him to jail.

4. **contrite** (kən-trīt', kŏn'trīt') *adjective* Sincerely sorry for one's sins or inadequacies. (From the Latin *com-*, an intensive prefix, and *terere,* meaning "to grind" or "to wear out") 4. ________

Related Words **contritely** *adverb;* **contrition** *noun*
Example After her brother tripped over her toys, the small child was *contrite* about leaving them in the hallway.

5. **impute** (ĭm-pyo͞ot') *trans verb* **a.** To attribute (a crime or fault) to another; blame without proof. **b.** To attribute to a cause or source. (From the Latin *in-*, meaning "in," and *putare,* meaning "to reckon") 5. ________

Related Word **imputation** *noun*
Example The prisoner *imputed* his life of crime to his inability to earn a steady income.

6. **iniquity** (ĭ-nĭk′wĭ-tē) *noun* **a.** Wickedness; sinfulness. **b.** A grossly immoral act. (From the Latin *in-*, meaning "not," and *aequus*, meaning "equal") 6. ________________

Related Word **iniquitous** *adjective*
Example Ramón finds it hard to accept *iniquity* in the world.

7. **redress** (rĭ-drĕs′) *trans. verb* To set right; rectify. *noun* (rē′drĕs) Satisfaction or amends for wrong done. (From the Old French *re-*, meaning "back," and *dresser*, meaning "to arrange") 7. ________________

Example Elizabeth sought to *redress* the wrong she had done by personally apologizing to everyone concerned.

8. **reprehensible** (rĕp′rĭ-hĕn′sə-bəl) *adjective* Deserving of blame. (From the Latin word *reprehendere*, meaning "to blame") 8. ________________

Related Word **reprehend** *verb*
Example Norman's *reprehensible* habit of talking about people behind their backs got him into trouble.

9. **restitution** (rĕs′tĭ-to͞o′shən, rĕs′tĭ-tyo͞o′shən) *noun* **a.** The act of restoring or returning to the rightful owner something that has been taken away, lost, or surrendered. **b.** The act of compensating for loss, damage, or injury. (From the Latin *re-*, meaning "back," and *statuere*, meaning "to set up") 9. ________________

Example The embezzler was ordered to make full *restitution* to the company.

10. **vindicate** (vĭn′dĭ-kāt′) *trans. verb* **a.** To clear of accusation, blame, or suspicion by means of evidence or proof. **b.** To justify or support: *to vindicate one's claim.* **c.** To prove the worth of, especially in the light of later developments. (From the Latin word *vindicare*, meaning "to lay claim to" or "to avenge") 10. ________________

Related Word **vindication** *noun*
Example Elaine was *vindicated* when it was revealed that she was on a plane heading for Sacramento when the jewel robbery occurred.

NAME ______________________ DATE ____________

EXERCISE 1 MATCHING WORDS AND DEFINITIONS

Match the definition in Column B with the word in Column A. Write the letter of the correct definition on the answer line.

Column A	Column B	
1. iniquity	a. deserving of blame	1. b
2. restitution	b. wickedness; sinfulness	2. f
3. clemency	c. to cheat or swindle; evade payment of	3. j
4. redress	d. to clear of accusation, blame, or suspicion by means of evidence or proof	4. i
5. abscond	e. sincerely sorry for one's sins or inadequacies	5. h
6. contrite	f. the act of restoring to the rightful owner something that has been taken away, lost, or surrendered	6. e
7. reprehensible	g. to attribute (a crime or fault) to another; attribute to a cause or source	7. a
8. bilk	h. to leave quickly and secretly to avoid arrest or prosecution	8. c
9. vindicate	i. to set right; rectify	9. d
10. impute	j. mercy, especially toward an offender or enemy; leniency	10. g

EXERCISE 2 USING WORDS CORRECTLY

Decide whether the italicized vocabulary word has been used correctly in the sentence. On the answer line, write *Correct* for correct use and *Incorrect* for incorrect use.

1. A *contrite* person refuses to acknowledge his or her mistakes. — 1. Incorrect
2. The treasurer *bilked* the stockholders by gambling with the company's investments. — 2. Correct
3. Acting on the evidence of check forgery, the grand jury *vindicated* Erroll and recommended that he be brought to trial. — 3. Incorrect
4. The Bazermans made several *iniquities* about the neighborhood and the school system. — 4. Incorrect
5. According to Monica, carelessness is a *reprehensible* habit. — 5. Correct
6. Chase *imputed* that his weekend guests had arrived uninvited. — 6. Incorrect
7. The two children were forced to make *restitution* for the damage they had done to the garden. — 7. Correct
8. The airline *redressed* the error by providing free tickets for several travelers. — 8. Correct
9. Emphasizing the previously clean record of the defendant, the attorney pleaded for *clemency.* — 9. Correct
10. During snow emergencies, all parking policies are *absconded.* — 10. Incorrect

EXERCISE 3 CHOOSING THE BEST DEFINITION

For each italicized vocabulary word in the following sentences, write the letter of the best definition on the answer line.

1. During the night several animals invaded the campsite, found the backpackers' food, and *absconded* with it. — 1. d
   a. made caches b. played c. feasted d. fled

2. Sally wrote a *contrite* letter of apology. 2. b
a. deceitful b. remorseful c. sarcastic d. responsible

3. I don't know which was more *reprehensible*—borrowing my bracelet without asking or lying about it. 3. a
a. blameworthy b. cautious c. desperate d. appropriate

4. The testimony of a witness *vindicated* the driver, who had been charged with criminal negligence. 4. a
a. cleared b. accused c. cheated d. discriminated against

5. Claiming that the painting had been stolen, the owner of the art gallery *bilked* the insurance company of ten thousand dollars. 5. c
a. opposed b. implored c. swindled d. reimbursed

6. Grandfather humorously refers to his basement workshop as his "den of *iniquity*." 6. b
a. power b. wickedness c. wisdom d. torment

7. To Sam, Joellen *imputed* the damage to one of her favorite records. 7. c
a. misrepresented c. attributed
b. complained about d. denied

8. Judge Singh is an advocate of *clemency* to first offenders. 8. d
a. harshness b. hostility c. preaching d. mercy

9. The angry owner demanded the *restitution* of her car, which had been mistakenly towed by the police. 9. a
a. return b. repair c. evaluation d. retention

10. Bankrupt farm owners plan to petition the government for the *redress* of their grievances. 10. b
a. distress b. rectification c. vigilance d. disgrace

EXERCISE 4 USING DIFFERENT FORMS OF WORDS

Decide which form of the vocabulary word in parentheses best completes the sentence. The form given may be correct. Write you answer on the answer line.

1. After weeks of gray skies and dismal cold, we looked forward to more _____ weather. *(clemency)* 1. clement
2. Niccolò Machiavelli advanced political theories that were considered _____ by many people. *(iniquity)* 2. iniquitous
3. The politician was severely _____ for her role in the bribery scandal. *(reprehensible)* 3. reprehended
4. Private detectives searched for the employee who had _____ with the secret documents. *(abscond)* 4. absconded
5. Marcy denied the _____ that her poor grades were related to her poor study habits. *(impute)* 5. imputation
6. Sir Isaac Newton's experiments with physics were the _____ of Galileo's early theories of motion. *(vindicate)* 6. vindication
7. The First Amendment to the Constitution guarantees the right of individuals to seek _____. *(redress)* 7. redress
8. Full of _____ for her negative attitude, Barbara tried to make amends by being especially enthusiastic. *(contrite)* 8. contrition
9. _____ of the stolen property was made possible by an anonymous note. *(restitution)* 9. Restitution
10. The merchant _____ his clients by overcharging them on credit-card purchases. *(bilk)* 10. bilked

NAME ______________________________ DATE ____________

(bilk)

READING COMPREHENSION

Each numbered sentence in the following passage contains an italicized vocabulary word or related form. After you read the passage, you will complete an exercise.

SHERLOCK HOLMES: MASTER CRIME SOLVER

One hundred years ago, the adventures of Sherlock Holmes initiated an enthusiasm for detective fiction that has never waned. Holmes and his remarkable powers of deduction were the creation of a Scottish physician, Sir Arthur Conan Doyle. Struggling to establish a private medical practice, Doyle began writing about baffling crimes and the man who could solve them. Since the first story, "A Study in Scarlet," appeared in 1887, millions of readers have followed Sherlock Holmes's career in seventy other stories, delighting in his brilliant imagination, sharp reasoning, and keen powers of observation.

(1) Even though he is an amateur, Sherlock Holmes is hired to investigate crimes, to find missing valuables, and to ***redress*** wrongdoings. (2) With brilliant analytical faculties and an indefatigable curiosity, he is invariably able to bring ***reprehensible*** criminals to justice, leaving the police and Scotland Yard detectives to pursue misleading clues.

(3) In "The Adventure of the Speckled Band," for example, a sinister stepfather tries to ***bilk*** his stepdaughters of their inheritance. When one stepdaughter dies mysteriously after announcing her engagement, the other fears for her life. (4) In desperation she seeks the help of Holmes, who quickly draws conclusions from minute details. Within a short time, he solves the mystery and helps to correct the ***iniquitous*** family situation. (5) In "The Musgrave Ritual," a butler tries to ***abscond*** with a hidden treasure, the valuable crown of King Charles II. (6) Sherlock Holmes fits together an odd assortment of clues, enabling him to catch the butler and ensure the ***restitution*** of the crown to the family that had been entrusted with it.

(7) Sherlock Holmes is also called upon to ***vindicate*** those who are wrongfully accused of terrible deeds. (8) In "The Naval Treaty," a man seeks Holmes's assistance because the theft of government plans has been ***imputed*** to him. Drawing on his knowledge of geology, botany, chemistry, anatomy, and British law, Holmes proves the man's innocence.

(9) Despite his clever pursuit of justice, there is an element of ***clemency*** in Holmes's treatment of criminals. (10) Sometimes, as in "The Adventure of the Three Students," he allows a ***contrite*** wrongdoer to leave the country, particularly if the culprit is motivated to change.

The character of Sherlock Holmes was so realistically drawn that many people have thought he actually existed. At one point, when the author decided to put an end to the detective by having him killed in a plunge from a cliff, his admirers raised such an outcry that Sir Arthur Conan Doyle was forced to write another story in which it turned out that Holmes had not perished but had merely eluded the criminal chasing him. This classic sleuth of detective fiction, whose ingenious methods for solving crimes actually helped to advance criminology, continues to fascinate contemporary readers.

READING COMPREHENSION EXERCISE

Each of the following statements corresponds to a numbered sentence in the passage. Each statement contains a blank and is followed by four answer choices. Decide which choice fits best in the blank. The word or phrase that you choose must express roughly the same meaning as the italicized word in the passage. Write the letter of your choice on the answer line.

1. Sherlock Holmes is hired to _____ wrongdoings and investigate crimes. — 1. d
a. delineate **b.** exclude **c.** confer about **d.** rectify

2. He is able to bring _____ criminals to justice. — 2. b
a. unknown **b.** blameworthy **c.** ordinary **d.** dangerous

3. In "The Adventure of the Speckled Band," a sinister stepfather tries to _____ his stepdaughters out of their inheritance. — 3. b
a. claim **b.** swindle **c.** disown **d.** invest

4. Holmes solves the mystery and helps to correct the _____ family situation. — 4. a
a. wicked **b.** uncivilized **c.** rigid **d.** awkward

5. In "The Musgrave Ritual," a butler tries to _____ the crown of King Charles II. — 5. d
a. govern with **b.** quietly surrender **c.** please others with **d.** flee secretly with

6. Sherlock Holmes ensures the _____ of the crown. — 6. c
a. registration **b.** immunity **c.** return **d.** safety

7. Holmes is also called upon to _____ those who are wrongfully accused. — 7. a
a. clear of blame **b.** pass judgment on **c.** punish **d.** petition

8. In "The Naval Treaty," a man seeks Holmes's help when the theft of government plans has been _____ him. — 8. c
a. contemplated by **b.** arranged by **c.** attributed to **d.** carried out by

9. There is an element of _____ in Holmes's treatment of criminals. — 9. b
a. humor **b.** mercy **c.** hostility **d.** reverence

10. Sometimes he allows a _____ wrongdoer to leave the country. — 10. a
a. sincerely sorry **b.** basically honest **c.** subdued **d.** bewildered

WRITING ASSIGNMENT

Mystery and detective stories are among the most popular choices of fiction and nonfiction. For your school or community newspaper, write a review of a book, movie, or television program about a puzzling crime. In addition to summarizing the plot briefly, give your opinion of the quality of this example of the genre. Use at least five of the words from this lesson in your review and underline each one.

LESSON 12 HEALTH

12

People of today are healthier than ever before. We live longer, eat better, have fewer cavities, and even grow taller than people did fifty years ago. Whereas the emphasis during earlier periods of history was on the treatment of disease, today preventive medicine is also practiced. Scientists have gained a greater understanding of the human body, and doctors now specialize in distinct branches of medical science. The conquest of many infectious diseases, the development of complex surgical techniques, and the emphasis on public health all contribute to our well-being. The words in this lesson will enable you to express information and ideas about health and illness.

WORD LIST

atrophy
debilitate
livid
moribund
noxious
pestilent
prostrate
salubrious
scourge
unscathed

DEFINITIONS

After you have studied the definitions and example for each vocabulary word, write the word on the line to the right.

1. **atrophy** (ăt′rə-fē) *intrans. verb* To waste away; wither. *trans. verb* To cause to wither. *noun* **a.** The emaciation or wasting away of tissues, organs, or the entire body. **b.** Any wasting away or diminution: *atrophy of one's unused talents.* (From the Greek *a-*, meaning "without," and *trophē*, meaning "food") 1. ______________

Example Yolanda underwent extensive physical therapy to exercise the leg that had *atrophied* while in a cast.

2. **debilitate** (dĭ-bĭl′ĭ-tāt′) *trans. verb* To make feeble; weaken. (From the Latin word *debilis,* meaning "weak") 2. ______________

Related Word **debilitation** *noun*
Example Heavy blood loss during surgery had *debilitated* Mr. Suarez and impeded his recovery.

3. **livid** (lĭv′ĭd) *adjective* **a.** Discolored, as from a bruise; black-and-blue. **b.** Ashen or very pale, as from anger. **c.** Extremely angry. (From the Latin word *livere,* meaning "to be bluish") 3. ______________

Related Words **lividly** *adverb;* **lividness** *noun*
Example After falling off her bike, Nell's shins were *livid* for a week.

4. **moribund** (môr′ə-bŭnd′) *adjective* In a condition approaching death or an end. (From the Latin word *mori,* meaning "to die") 4. ______________

Example The *moribund* pelican was revived by the veterinarian.

5. **noxious** (nŏk'shəs) *adjective* **a.** Injurious or harmful to health. **b.** Injurious or harmful to the mind or morals; corrupting: *noxious ideas.* (From the Latin word *noxa,* meaning "damage") 5. ____________

Related Words **noxiously** *adverb;* **noxiousness** *noun*
Example The chemical solvent should be used outside so that you are not overcome by the *noxious* fumes.

6. **pestilent** (pĕs'tə-lənt) *adjective* **a.** Tending to cause death; fatal **b.** Likely to cause an epidemic disease. **c.** Infected or contaminated with a contagious disease. (From the Latin word *pestis,* meaning "plague") 6. ____________

Related Word **pestilence** *noun*
Example Vaccination has eradicated *pestilent* diseases in most parts of the world.

7. **prostrate** (prŏs'trāt') *trans. verb* **a.** To weaken or render helpless; overcome. **b.** To make (oneself) bow or kneel down in humility or adoration. *adjective* **a.** Physically or emotionally exhausted; helpless. **b.** Lying face-down, as in submission or adoration. **c.** Lying down full-length. (From the Latin *pro-,* meaning "forward," and *sternere,* meaning "to cast down") 7. ____________

Related Word **prostration** *noun*
Example A tropical fever *prostrated* three members of the scientific expedition.

8. **salubrious** (sə-lo͞o'brē-əs) *adjective* Favorable to health or well-being. (From the Latin word *salus,* meaning "health") 8. ____________

Related Words **salubriously** *adverb;* **salubriousness** *noun*
Example Moderate exercise has a *salubrious* effect.

9. **scourge** (skûrj) *noun* **a.** A cause of great suffering or harm. **b.** Any instrument, such as a whip, used for inflicting punishment, suffering, or vengeance. *trans. verb* **a.** To afflict severely; devastate. **b.** To punish severely. **c.** To beat, whip, or flog. (From the Latin word *corrigia,* meaning "thong") 9. ____________

Example Cyclical attacks of plant-eating locusts were the *scourge* of farmers.

10. **unscathed** (ŭn-skāthd') *adjective* Unharmed; uninjured. 10. ____________

Example The race-car driver emerged from the burning vehicle miraculously *unscathed.*

Word History: salubrious

Latin: *salus*=health

Eating five or more servings of fruit and vegetables each day has a *salubrious* effect on your body. In other words, such foods make you "healthy." The word *salubrious* comes from the Latin *salus,* meaning "favorable to health or well-being." In the English language, a *salute* is "a greeting with an expression of welcome and good will" and implies a wish of "good health," as does a letter's *salutation.* In some languages, the idea of one person wishing "good health" to another occurs in a word of greeting. The Romans used to say, "Salve!" and the French still say, "Salut!" Both words literally mean, "Hello, good health to you!"

NAME ______________________ DATE ____________

EXERCISE 1 COMPLETING DEFINITIONS

On the answer line, write the word from the vocabulary list that best completes each definition.

1. Something that is harmful to health, morals, or the mind is _____. 1. noxious
2. To make feeble or to weaken is to _____. 2. debilitate
3. If you are uninjured or unharmed, you are _____. 3. unscathed
4. When something wastes away or withers, it can be said to _____. 4. atrophy
5. To weaken, render helpless, or overcome is to _____. 5. prostrate
6. Something approaching death or an end is _____. 6. moribund
7. A cause of great suffering or harm is called a _____. 7. scourge
8. If something causes death or is likely to cause an epidemic disease, it is considered _____. 8. pestilent
9. Something that is favorable to health or well-being is _____. 9. salubrious
10. Something that is discolored or ashen may be described as _____. 10. livid

EXERCISE 2 USING WORDS CORRECTLY

Decide whether the italicized vocabulary word has been used correctly in the sentence. On the answer line, write *Correct* for correct use and *Incorrect* for incorrect use

1. Bloodletting was once a surgical procedure for treating those who were *prostrated* by fever and other maladies. 1. Correct
2. Muscle tissue will *atrophy* if it is not nourished and exercised. 2. Correct
3. The first antibiotic, a moldy curd of soy beans, was used by the Chinese to treat boils and other *salubrious* infections. 3. Incorrect
4. Ancient peoples often believed that *pestilent* forces were punishments from the gods. 4. Correct
5. The School of Salerno, which flourished in Italy from the tenth through the thirteenth centuries, was the first *unscathed* medical school in Europe. 5. Incorrect
6. Rest and a balanced diet can easily *debilitate* even the strongest person. 6. Incorrect
7. *Moribund* tales of surgery without anesthesia horrify modern readers. 7. Incorrect
8. The work of Robert Koch introduced a new era of public health by showing how *noxious* bacteria could be controlled by water filtration. 8. Correct
9. The *scourge* of yellow fever was all but eradicated by a vaccine. 9. Correct
10. Pam turned *livid* before she fainted. 10. Correct

EXERCISE 3 CHOOSING THE BEST WORD

Decide which vocabulary word or related form best expresses the meaning of the italicized word or phrase in the sentence. On the answer line, write the letter of the correct choice.

1. Arteriosclerosis, a *weakening* disease that causes the hardening of the walls of the arteries, is directly related to the amount of saturated fats in the diet. 1. b

   a. noxious **b.** debilitating **c.** livid **d.** pestilent

2. As a result of the accident, the construction worker was *approaching death.* 2. d
a. unscathed b. noxious c. salubrious d. moribund

3. Heat *exhaustion* can be dangerous if not treated. 3. a
a. prostration b. atrophy c. debilitation d. lividness

4. Bedridden patients often require physical therapy so that their muscles will not *waste away.* 4. b
a. debilitate b. atrophy c. prostrate d. scourge

5. Clean air and fresh food are considered *favorable to health and well-being.* 5. c
a. livid b. unscathed c. salubrious d. noxious

6. *Unhealthful* chemical wastes have polluted many wells in the area. 6. b
a. Salubrious b. Noxious c. Moribund d. Unscathed

7. Mom calls our cat Feisty the *cause of harm or suffering* of the neighborhood. 7. a
a. scourge b. pestilence c. prostration d. debilitation

8. We found it hard to believe that people could actually walk barefoot over hot coals and emerge *unharmed.* 8. d
a. livid b. moribund c. salubrious d. unscathed

9. As the car came to an abrupt stop at the edge of the cliff, the motorist's face turned *ashen* from fear or shock. 9. c
a. noxious b. moribund c. livid d. pestilent

10. *Tending to cause death* smallpox killed over sixty million people in the eighteenth century alone. 10. b
a. Debilitating b. Pestilent c. Prostrating d. Salubrious

EXERCISE 4 USING DIFFERENT FORMS OF WORDS

Decide which form of the vocabulary word in parentheses best completes the sentence. The form given may be correct. Write your answer on the answer line.

1. Many people retire to California or Florida because of the _____ of the climate. *(salubrious)* 1. salubriousness

2. Monica is convinced that her low-level job will lead to the _____ of her intellect. *(atrophy)* 2. atrophy

3. The Halseys hoped to protect their children from what they considered to be the _____ influence of television. *(noxious)* 3. noxious

4. After four days without sleep the patient suffered from _____. *(prostrate)* 4. prostration

5. Despite his fear Gregory emerged _____ from his ride on the roller coaster. *(unscathed)* 5. unscathed

6. Returning from the battle, the conquering tribe found its own territory in a state of _____ due to famine. *(debilitate)* 6. debilitation

7. The _____ of his injuries did not disappear entirely for a long time. *(livid)* 7. lividness

8. The new vice-president was the _____ of incompetent managers. *(scourge)* 8. scourge

9. Derek kept watch over his _____ gerbils. *(moribund)* 9. moribund

10. The _____ ship was quarantined outside the harbor. *(pestilent)* 10. pestilent

NAME ______________________ DATE __________

READING COMPREHENSION

Each numbered sentence in the following passage contains an italicized vocabulary word. After you read the passage, you will complete an exercise.

BUBONIC PLAGUE: THE BLACK DEATH

Although many epidemics are known to have decimated large groups of people throughout history, no other disease can compare with the plague both in its devastating effects and in the profound impression left on history. (1) Striking Europe in the fourteenth century, bubonic plague was a ***pestilent*** disease that brought terror to millions.

(2) Transmitted by fleas from infected rats, the ***scourge*** was carried to Europe from Asia and the Middle East by rodents on merchant vessels. (3) Arriving in southern Italy in the summer of 1347, the ***noxious*** malady soon spread by trade routes to Spain and France. (4) By the end of 1350, few people remained ***unscathed.*** Although the exact mortality figures are unknown, it has been estimated that roughly two thirds of the population of Europe contracted bubonic plague and that twenty-five million people died. No one was immune; the plague killed kings, queens, archbishops, farmers, and serfs. Recurrent epidemics prevented Europe's population from reaching preplague levels until at least the mid-fifteenth century.

There were actually two forms of plague. (5) Within two to ten days after a fleabite, bubonic plague left its victims ***prostrate*** with chills, fever, headache, and painful swelling of the buboes, or lymph nodes, in the neck, armpits, and groin. Although delirium and coma were common, bubonic plague was usually of short duration; death or recovery occurred within a few days of the onset of the symptoms.

(6) Pneumonic, or pulmonary, plague was far more ***debilitating,*** contagious, and dangerous. (7) It was characterized by a high fever, lung congestion, heavy cough, ***livid*** complexion, and black spots caused by under-the-skin hemorrhages. (8) Within a day or two, patients were ***moribund.*** The name Black Death may have referred to the dusky blue color of the dying victim, to the black plague spots, or to the sinister, hopeless quality of the disease. Although every sort of treatment was tried, there was no medical cure for either form of the plague.

When the plague struck, Europe was helpless to combat it. Standards of public health and personal hygiene were nonexistent. Houses were abandoned by surviving members of families. (9) Some families fled to country homes, in search of more ***salubrious*** living places.

Bubonic plague had far-reaching effects on the economic and political stability of Europe. Because the disease hit seaports first, trade underwent a serious slump. As the plague traveled into cities, many regions experienced an acute shortage of labor, and the prices of commodities rose alarmingly. (10) With little farming going on, rural areas ***atrophied,*** and the landowning classes were ruined. Public hysteria and a constant fear of death led to unhealthy morbidness, excesses of religious severity, and hysterical dancing manias. The Black Death left generations of Europeans distressed and insecure.

Epidemics of the magnitude of the fourteenth-century spread of bubonic plague have not occurred in modern times. Antiplague vaccine can now prevent outbreaks, and such antibiotics as streptomycin can lessen the severity of the illness if it is diagnosed early enough. Measures to exterminate rats and fumigate cargoes as well as the control of infectious diseases by sanitation and strict quarantine techniques have eliminated the plague in most parts of the world.

READING COMPREHENSION EXERCISE

Each of the following statements corresponds to a numbered sentence in the passage. Each statement contains a blank and is followed by four answer choices. Decide which choice fits best in the blank. The word or phrase that you choose must express roughly the same meaning as the italicized word in the passage. Write the letter of your choice on the answer line.

1. Bringing terror to millions, bubonic plague was ____. 1. c
   a. exaggerated b. rare c. likely to be fatal d. likely to be mild

2. The ____ was carried by rodents on merchant vessels. 2. a
   a. cause of suffering c. germ
   b. form of pollution d. virus

3. The ____ malady soon spread to Spain and France. 3. d
   a. unpleasant b. atrocious c. unfamiliar d. harmful

4. Few people remained ____ by the end of 1350. 4. c
   a. helpless b. alive c. unharmed d. productive

5. Bubonic plague left its victims ____ chills, fever, and swelling of the lymph nodes. 5. b
   a. prone to b. overcome by c. uncomfortable with d. corrupted by

6. Pulmonary plague was far more ____. 6. d
   a. complicated b. unusual c. common d. weakening

7. It was characterized by a high fever, lung congestion, and a ____ complexion. 7. a
   a. discolored b. clear c. blotchy d. grim

8. Within a day or two, patients were ____. 8. c
   a. increasingly ill c. approaching death
   b. unchanged d. approaching recovery

9. Some families fled to country homes, in search of more ____ living places. 9. b
   a. discrete b. healthful c. advanced d. zestful

10. Rural areas ____ as farming decreased. 10. a
    a. diminished b. multiplied c. were crowded d. changed greatly

WRITING ASSIGNMENT

Medical science has made much progress in controlling, preventing, and curing many diseases. Your health class has decided to write and publish a pamphlet entitled "One Hundred Years of Progress" in which the class members will record some of the gains made in medicine. Do some research in the library about a disease that interests you, such as cholera, yellow fever, smallpox, tuberculosis, or polio. Then write a report describing the symptoms of the disease and the way in which it can be treated, prevented, or controlled. Use at least five of the vocabulary words from this lesson in your report and underline each one.

The **Bonus activity** for Lessons 9–12 is on page T14.
The **Test** for Lessons 10, 11, and 12 is on page T15.

NAME ______________________ DATE __________

READING SKILLS

CONTEXT CLUES AND THE READING OF PRIMARY SOURCES

As you study history in greater depth, you will probably begin to read **primary sources,** actual writings from the period that you are studying. Such works may be anything from books to diaries, letters, and census records of the period. The following strategies will help you to use the context to determine the meaning of unfamiliar words.

STRATEGIES

1. *Consider the date of the work.* Remember that a word may have had a special meaning in the period during which the work was written. Today the meaning may be different, or the word may not be in use at all. For example, the meaning of the word *nice* has gone from "foolish" to "fastidious" to "pleasant."
2. *Consider the country in which the work was written.* Meanings of an English word sometimes vary enormously according to country. In Britain, for example, *governor* can mean "warden of a penitentiary," whereas *warden* usually refers to an officer of a university or hospital.
3. *Make allowances for unusual spellings and punctuation.* Spelling was not standardized in the United States until the last century; also, in previous times fewer people had access to a good education.
4. *If you are unsure of the meaning of a word, look it up in a dictionary.* If necessary, use an unabridged dictionary.

EXERCISE USING CONTEXT CLUES IN READING PRIMARY SOURCES

The following passage is from the journal kept by Meriwether Lewis and George Rogers Clark during their famous exploration of the American West. Written by Lewis, this passage is dated April 7, 1805. Begin by reading the entire passage. *Step 1:* Write your own definition of each italicized word in the passage. *Step 2:* Write the appropriate dictionary definition of the word.

> Our vessels consisted of six small canoes, and two large (1) *perogues*. This little fleet altho' not quite so rispectable as those of Columbus or Capt. Cook, were still viewed by us with as much pleasure as those deservedly famed adventurers ever (2) *beheld* theirs; and I (3) *dare say* with quite as much anxiety for their safety and preservation. we were now about to penetrate a country at least two thousand miles in width, on which the foot of civilized man had never (4) *trodden;* the good or evil it had in store for us was for experiment yet to determine, and these little vessells contained every article by which we were to expect to (5) *subsist* or defend ourselves. however, as the state of mind in which we are, generally gives the (6) *colouring* to events, when the imagination is (7) *suffered* to wander into futurity, the picture which now presented itself to me was a most pleasing one. enterta[in]ing as I do, the most confident hope of succeeding in a voyage which had formed a (8) *da[r]ling* project of mine for the last ten years, I could but esteem this moment of my departure as among the most happy of my life. The party are in excellent health and sperits, (9) *zealously* attached to the

enterprise, and anxious to proceed; not a whisper of murmur or discontent to be heard among them, but all act in unison, and with the most perfict harmony. Capt. Clark myself the two Interpretters and the woman [Sacajawea] and child sleep in a tent of dressed skins. this tent is in the Indian stile, formed of a number of dressed Buffaloe skins sewed together with **(10)** *sinues.*

1. *perogues (pirogues)*

   Your Definition boats of some kind

   Dictionary Definition canoes made from hollowed tree trunks

2. *beheld*

   Your Definition looked at

   Dictionary Definition gazed at; looked upon

3. *dare say*

   Your Definition suppose

   Dictionary Definition consider very likely or almost certain

4. *trodden*

   Your Definition walked

   Dictionary Definition walked

5. *subsist*

   Your Definition live

   Dictionary Definition live

6. *colouring*

   Your Definition impression

   Dictionary Definition appearance, aspect, or tone

7. *suffered*

   Your Definition allowed

   Dictionary Definition permitted; allowed

8. *darling*

   Your Definition favorite

   Dictionary Definition regarded with special favor; favorite

9. *zealously*

   Your Definition enthusiastically

   Dictionary Definition enthusiastically; fervently

10. *sinues (sinews)*

    Your Definition tendons

    Dictionary Definition tendons

LESSON 13 THE ROOTS *-PEND-*, *-PENS-*, AND *-POND-* 13

The root *-pend-* comes from the Latin word *pendere,* meaning "to weigh," "to hang," or "to pay." The roots *-pens-* and *-pond-* come from the Latin words *pensare* and *ponderare,* which both mean "to weigh." These roots have given us many English words. For example, if you *compensate* for a mistake, you weigh against it or counterbalance it. If something is *ponderous,* it has great weight. When you incur *expenses,* you are forced to pay out sums of money. In this lesson you will learn other words from these roots that share the meaning of hanging, weighing, or paying.

WORD LIST

append
dispense
expendable
expenditure
impend
pending
perpendicular
preponderance
recompense
suspension

DEFINITIONS

After you have studied the definitions and example for each vocabulary word, write the word on the line to the right.

1. **append** (ə-pĕnd′) *trans verb* **a.** To add as a supplement. **b.** To fix to; attach. (From the Latin *ad-,* meaning "to," and *pendere,* meaning "to hang") 1. ________

Related Word **appendage** *noun*
Example Rachel *appended* a bibliography to her research paper.

2. **dispense** (dĭ-spĕns′) *trans. verb* **a.** To prepare and distribute in parts or portions. **b.** To administer: *dispense justice.* **c.** To exempt or release, as from a duty or obligation. (From the Latin *dis-,* meaning "apart," and *pensare,* meaning "to weigh out") 2. ________

USAGE NOTE: The idiom *dispense with* means "to do without" or "to do away with."

Related Word **dispensation** *noun*
Example The machine *dispensed* fruit juices.

3. **expendable** (ĭk-spĕn′də-bəl) *adjective* **a.** Viewed as not worth keeping or maintaining. **b.** Subject to use or consumption. (From the Latin *ex-,* meaning "out," and *pendere,* meaning "to pay") 3. ________

Related Word **expend** *verb*
Example Paper plates are *expendable* dishes.

4. **expenditure** (ĭk-spĕn′də-chər) *noun* **a.** The act or process of consuming or using (something) up; outlay. **b.** An expense. (From the Latin *ex-,* meaning "out," and *pendere,* meaning "to pay") 4. ________

Related Word **expend** *verb*
Example The manager had not anticipated that completion of the project would require such a large *expenditure* of staff time.

5. **impend** (ĭm-pĕnd′) *intrans. verb* **a.** To hang or hover menacingly. **b.** To be about to take place. (From the Latin *in-*, meaning "against," and *pendere*, meaning "to hang") 5. ______________

Example In the winter a heavy, overcast sky is a sign that snow *impends*.

6. **pending** (pĕn′dĭng) *adjective* Not yet decided; awaiting conclusion. *preposition* While awaiting; until. (From the Latin word *pendere*, meaning "to hang") 6. ______________

Example Until Shana improved her grades in chemistry, her place on the varsity soccer team would be *pending*.

7. **perpendicular** (pûr′pən-dĭk′yə-lər) *adjective* **a.** Intersecting at or forming right angles. **b.** At right angles to a horizontal line or plane; vertical; exactly upright. *noun* **a.** A line or plane perpendicular to a given line or plane. **b.** A perpendicular position. (From the Latin *per-*, an intensive prefix, and *pendere*, meaning "to hang") 7. ______________

Related Word **perpendicularly** *adverb*
Example Victorio held the crosspiece *perpendicular* while his brother nailed it in place.

8. **preponderance** (prĭ-pŏn′dər-əns) *noun* Superiority in weight, quantity, power, or importance. (From the Latin *prae-*, meaning "in front of," and *ponderare*, meaning "to weigh") 8. ______________

Related Word **preponderant** *adjective*
Example Trevor was relieved to see the *preponderance* of A's on his report card.

9. **recompense** (rĕk′əm-pĕns′) *trans. verb* **a.** To award compensation to, as for services rendered. **b.** To make a return for (an action). *noun* **a.** Payment to compensate for another's loss. **b.** Payment in return for something given or done. (Form the Latin *re-*, meaning "back," *com* , meaning "together," and *pensare*, meaning "to weigh") 9. ______________

Example We *recompensed* our elderly neighbor for his many kindnesses by shoveling his sidewalk during the winter.

10. **suspension** (sə-spĕn′shən) *noun* **a.** The temporary deferment of an action. **b.** The period during which one is excluded from privilege, office, or position, usually as punishment. **c.** A device from which a mechanical part is hung. (From the Latin *sub-*, meaning "under" or "from below," and *pendere*, meaning "to hang") 10. ______________

Related Word **suspend** *verb*
Example The Traffic Division put into effect a *suspension* of the usual parking regulations on Sundays.

NAME ______________________________ DATE ____________

EXERCISE 1 WRITING CORRECT WORDS

On the answer line, write the word from the vocabulary list that fits each definition.

1. To award compensation to; payment for loss or in return for something done — 1. recompense
2. Not yet decided; awaiting conclusion; until — 2. pending
3. Viewed as not worth keeping or maintaining; subject to use — 3. expendable
4. Superiority in weight, quantity, power, or importance — 4. preponderance
5. To add as a supplement; fix to; attach — 5. append
6. To hang or hover menacingly; be about to take place — 6. impend
7. The temporary deferment of an action; a period of exclusion — 7. suspension
8. To prepare and distribute in parts or portions; administer — 8. dispense
9. Intersecting at or forming right angles; at right angles to a horizontal line or plane; vertical; exactly upright — 9. perpendicular
10. The act or process of consuming or using (something) up; outlay; expense — 10. expenditure

EXERCISE 2 USING WORDS CORRECTLY

Decide whether the italicized vocabulary word has been used correctly in the sentence. On the answer line, write *Correct* for correct use and *Incorrect* for incorrect use.

1. "This mystery I'm reading is very complicated and drawn out, and the *suspension* is killing me!" exclaimed Matt. — 1. Incorrect
2. The city-wide referendum sought to block the *expenditure* of city funds to repave private roads. — 2. Correct
3. The police hoped that they would not have to use tear gas to *dispense* the angry mob. — 3. Incorrect
4. Mr. Scott believes that his employees are *expendable.* — 4. Correct
5. The organization follows legislation about women and children that is *pending* before Congress. — 5. Correct
6. The *preponderance* of the evidence pointed to his innocence. — 6. Correct
7. By reading carefully, Maura is able to *append* the complex philosophy of Friedrich Nietzsche. — 7. Incorrect
8. Leroy heard a *perpendicular* noise in the attic and went to investigate. — 8. Incorrect
9. As *recompense* for our dog's having ruined the Axelrods' garden, we are helping our neighbors replant their flower beds. — 9. Correct
10. From the very beginning, trouble over the project *impended.* — 10. Correct

EXERCISE 3 CHOOSING THE BEST WORD

Decide which vocabulary word or related form best expresses the meaning of the italicized word or phrase in the sentence. On the answer line, write the letter of the correct choice.

1. "Be sure to *attach* your photograph to your application," Ann reminded her friend. — 1. a

   a. append **b.** impend **c.** suspend **d.** expend

2. Coal and gas were once regarded as *not worth maintaining* natural resources. 2. c
a. pending b. perpendicular c. expendable d. impending

3. Mrs. Turner owns a *superior number* of conservative business suits. 3. d
a. expenditure b. recompense c. suspension d. preponderance

4. Jason tutored a neighbor child in math for a month and received four dollars as *payment for services rendered.* 4. c
a. preponderance b. suspension c. recompense d. expenditure

5. While the contract was *awaiting conclusion,* the owners of the two businesses refused to discuss the details of the merger. 5. b
a. impending b. pending c. suspended d. dispensed

6. During the Great Depression, soup kitchens *gave out* hot meals to the hungry. 6. d
a. expended b. appended c. impended d. dispensed

7. The city treasurer's *exclusion for a time from his position* while the books were audited shocked everyone. 7. b
a. expenditure b. suspension c. recompense d. preponderance

8. Consumer *outlays* for recreation jumped from $41 billion in 1970 to over $106 billion in 1980. 8. a
a. expenditures b. recompenses c. appendages d. dispensations

9. Jan's street is *at right angles* to ours and only one block away. 9. b
a. preponderant b. perpendicular c. suspended d. impending

10. As the hour of the exam approached, Felicia felt an increasing sense of *hovering* doom. 10. d
a. expendable b. recompensed c. suspended d. impending

EXERCISE 4 USING DIFFERENT FORMS OF WORDS

Decide which form of the vocabulary word in parentheses best completes the sentence. The form given may be correct. Write your answer on the answer line.

1. The athletic-shoe company _____ millions of dollars on the promotion of its new line. *(expendable)* 1. expended

2. Because of a lack of time, we decided to _____ with the reading of the minutes of the last meeting. *(dispense)* 2. dispense

3. Red oaks, once the _____ trees in this area, have been subject to a blight. *(preponderance)* 3. preponderant

4. The Treaty of Versailles (1919) declared Germany's guilt in World War I and ordered the country to _____ the Allies. *(recompense)* 4. recompense

5. We had to _____ our names and grade to our art project before entering it in the competition. *(append)* 5. append

6. To have a balanced budget, a worker must not _____ more than he or she earns. *(expenditure)* 6. expend

7. The gymnast hung _____ from the bar until she could swing her legs up over it. *(perpendicular)* 7. perpendicularly

8. The rural newspaper was forced to _____ publication briefly when it ran out of newsprint. *(suspension)* 8. suspend

9. The airline will hold your luggage _____ your arrival on a later flight. *(pending)* 9. pending

10. Charelle is very excited about her _____ trip to Florida. *(impend)* 10. impending

NAME ______________________ DATE __________

READING COMPREHENSION

Each numbered sentence in the following passage contains an italicized vocabulary word or related form. After you read the passage, you will complete an exercise.

THE BROOKLYN BRIDGE: AN ENGINEERING MARVEL

(1) In prehistoric times, when the need arose to cross a river or gorge, people contrived various methods of weaving vines and ***suspending*** them from trees or rocks on either side. In principle, today's suspension bridges are based on this practical solution. (2) A suspension bridge is basically a long roadway hung from wire cables that are attached to two ***perpendicular*** towers. The idea is to create constant tension, which keeps the bridge steady yet flexible. (3) Except for the heavy deck that is ***appended*** to the cables in order to carry traffic, a suspension bridge resembles an elaborate clothesline.

While the suspension bridge evolved from those made of woven bamboo, rope, or chains of iron to the massive steel structures of the twentieth century, the pioneering engineers faced setbacks and disasters. (4) In fact, the ***preponderance*** of public opinion held that suspension bridges were unsuitable for long spans, would not withstand high winds, and would not bear the weight of traffic. Because arch bridges were thought to be sounder, John Roebling's proposal in 1857 to build a suspension bridge across New York's East River seemed mad.

(5) Ten years passed ***pending*** approval of Roebling's proposal. The engineering problems were dramatic. The bridge, spanning the 1600 feet from Manhattan to Brooklyn, would need to be far longer than any bridge yet constructed. In addition, the center of the bridge would have to rise 135 feet above the water to allow tall ships to sail beneath it. Roebling had to defy not only gravity but considerable public skepticism as well. (6) Approval of the plan, however, was some ***recompense*** for Roebling's efforts of more than a decade. Tragically, he died soon after approval was finally given to build the Brooklyn Bridge.

(7) Further trouble ***impended*** when Washington Roebling took over his father's project. For fourteen years he battled forces of nature, dishonest contractors and politicians, prejudiced newspaper editors, and critical engineers. Yet somehow the huge bases for the towers were sunk, the towers built, and the steel wire cables strung. Known as the eighth wonder of the world, the Brooklyn Bridge was opened on May 24, 1883.

(8) Completed after the ***expenditure*** of eighteen million dollars, the Brooklyn Bridge was a triumph of engineering. (9) Washington Roebling, who had dared to ***dispense*** with iron and use steel cable instead, paved the way for lighter and longer suspension bridges. (10) With few exceptions, John Roebling's design has been retained, except for certain ***expendable*** elements that have been altered or eliminated from modern suspension bridges. Designed for the horse-drawn and rail traffic of the nineteenth century, the Brooklyn Bridge today supports hundreds of thousands of cars, bicyclists, and pedestrians each day.

In an effort to honor the Roeblings for building such a famous, graceful, and efficient link between Manhattan and Brooklyn, New Yorkers held a gala centennial celebration in 1983. An artist was commissioned to create a commemorative sculpture that will be installed near the bridge. The monument that best honors the Roeblings, however, is the Brooklyn Bridge itself.

READING COMPREHENSION EXERCISE

Each of the following statements corresponds to a number sentence in the passage. Each statement contains a blank and is followed by four answer choices. Decide which choice fits best in the blank. The word or phrase that you choose must express roughly the same meaning as the italicized word in the passage. Write the letter of your choice on the answer line.

1. People contrived various methods for weaving vines and _____ them from trees in order to cross a river or gorge. 1. ___a___
   a. hanging b. cutting c. lowering d. ejecting
2. A suspension bridge is a long roadway hung from wire cables that are attached to _____ towers. 2. ___c___
   a. concrete b. massive c. vertical d. concentric
3. A suspension bridge resembles a clothesline except for a heavy deck that is _____ the cables. 3. ___b___
   a. outlined by b. attached to c. behind d. transformed by
4. In fact, the _____ of public opinion held that suspension bridges were unsuitable for long spans. 4. ___a___
   a. great amount b. minimum c. pandemonium d. assault
5. Ten years passed _____ approval of Roebling's proposal. 5. ___d___
   a. after b. since c. during d. while awaiting
6. Approval of the plan was some _____ for Roebling's efforts. 6. ___b___
   a. hope b. repayment c. excuse d. support
7. Further trouble _____ when Washington Roebling took over his father's project. 7. ___c___
   a. was anticipated b. ended c. threatened d. was avoided
8. The bridge was completed after the _____ of eighteen million dollars. 8. ___b___
   a. initial fee b. outlay c. commission d. gamble
9. Washington Roebling _____ iron and used steel instead. 9. ___d___
   a. considered b. refurbished c. experimented with d. did away with
10. John Roebling's design has been retained, except for certain _____ elements. 10. ___a___
    a. unnecessary b. ridiculous c. expensive d. obsolete

PRACTICE WITH ANALOGIES

See pages 32 and 66 for some other strategies to use with analogies.

Strategy Watch out for reversed elements in analogies.

Incorrect ship : hull :: wing : airplane
Correct ship : hull :: airplane : wing

Directions On the answer line, write the letter of the phrase that best completes the analogy. Some of the items use the strategy explained above.

1. REPREHENSIBLE : BLAME :: (A) historical : approval (B) virtuous : censure (C) concise : praise (D) questionable : ignorance (E) notable : attention 1. ___E___
2. PENITENT : CONTRITE :: (A) visionary : practical (B) conformist : original (C) hypocrite : sincerity (D) bigot : biased (E) miser : generosity 2. ___D___
3. ATROPHY : MUSCLE :: (A) narrow : mind (B) amplify : sound (C) nibble : food (D) stretch : fiber (E) wither : leaf 3. ___E___
4. DEBILITATE : STRENGTH :: (A) deplore : misbehavior (B) depreciate : value (C) restore : confidence (D) organize : victory (E) depict : event 4. ___B___
5. LIVID : ANGER :: (A) juvenile : maturity (B) astonish : surprise (C) delicate : texture (D) agile : stiffness (E) despondent : hope 5. ___B___

LESSON 14 SPEAKING

14

According to psychologists the greatest human fear is not of heights or snakes, as you might assume, but of speaking in front of a group. Many people feel uncomfortable and apprehensive about how an audience will respond to what they have to say. Whether delivering a formal presentation or an informal report, however, people can overcome their nervousness and insecurity by planning, organizing, and practicing the speech.

In this lesson you will learn about different types of speeches and different methods of delivery. The vocabulary words will help you to realize that, as Ralph Waldo Emerson said, "Speech is power: speech is to persuade, to convert, to compel."

WORD LIST

eulogy
exalt
exhort
expatiate
garrulous
gist
histrionic
laconic
peremptory
polemic

DEFINITIONS

After you have studied the definitions and example for each vocabulary word, write the word on the line to the right.

1. **eulogy** (yo͞o′lə-jē) *noun* **a.** A speech praising another; tribute. **b.** Great praise. (From the Greek *eu-*, meaning "well," and *-logia*, meaning "discourse")

   Related Word **eulogize** *verb*
   Example A close friend of Mrs. Acala delivered a moving *eulogy* at the memorial service.

   1. ________________

2. **exalt** (ĭg-zôlt′) *trans. verb* **a.** To glorify; praise; honor. **b.** To raise in rank, character, or status; elevate. (From the Latin *ex-*, meaning "up," and *altus*, meaning "high")

   Related Words **exaltation** *noun;* **exalted** *adjective*
   Example Many readers *exalt* Shakespeare to the extent that they would never allow a present-day dramatist to tamper with his plays.

   2. ________________

3. **exhort** (ĭg-zôrt′) *trans. verb* To urge or incite by strong argument, advice, or appeal. (From the Latin *ex-* an intensive prefix, and *hortari,* meaning "to encourage")

   Related Word **exhortation** *noun*
   Example At the PTA meeting, the director of athletics *exhorted* parents to raise funds for sports programs.

   3. ________________

4. **expatiate** (ĭk-spā′shē-āt′) *intrans. verb* To speak or write at length; elaborate. (From the Latin *ex-*, meaning "out," and *spatiari,* meaning "to spread")

   Example She thought that she was providing vital supplementary information when she was actually *expatiating* on an unrelated topic.

   4. ________________

   USAGE NOTE: *Expatiate* is usually followed by the preposition *on* or *upon.*

5. **garrulous** (găr'ə-ləs, găr'yə-ləs) *adjective* Habitually talkative, especially excessively so. (From the Latin word *garrire,* meaning "to chatter") 5. ______________

Related Words **garrulously** *adverb;* **garrulousness** *noun*
Example Since all the passengers on the bus were in a hurry that day, they avoided Greg, who had a reputation for being quite *garrulous* in his morning greetings.

6. **gist** (jĭst) *noun* The central idea of a matter; essence. 6. ______________

Example The *gist* of the conversation was that Eddie had just gotten a part-time job.

7. **histrionic** (hĭs′trē-ŏn'ĭk) *adjective* **a.** Excessively dramatic or emotional; affected. **b.** Of or pertaining to actors or acting. (From the Latin word *histrio,* meaning "actor") 7. ______________

USAGE NOTE: The noun *histrionics* usually means "exaggerated, theatrical behavior."

Related Word **histrionics** *noun*
Example Gina did not expect Larry's *histrionic* reaction to the news that she had lost his chemistry notes.

8. **laconic** (lə-kŏn'ĭk) *adjective* Using or marked by the use of few words; terse. (From the Greek word *Lakōnikos,* meaning "Spartan"; Spartans had a reputation for brevity of speech.) 8. ______________

Related Word **laconically** *adverb*
Example When May asked him about his job interview, Mark gave a *laconic* reply: "Nothing."

9. **peremptory** (pə-rĕmp'tə-rē) *adjective* **a.** Not allowing contradiction or refusal; imperative. **b.** Having the nature of expressing a command; urgent. **c.** Putting an end to all debate or action. (From the Latin word *perimere,* meaning "to take away") 9. ______________

USAGE NOTE: Do not confuse *peremptory* with *preemptory,* which means "taking or acting before others."

Related Word **peremptorily** *adverb*
Example Dana made the *peremptory* statement that no matter what was decided, she would do as she thought best.

10. **polemic** (pə-lĕm'ĭk) *noun* A controversy or argument, especially one that is a refutation of or an attack upon the opinions or doctrines of another. *adjective* Of or pertaining to a controversy, argument, or refutation. (From the Greek word *polemos,* meaning "war") 10. ______________

Related Word **polemics** *noun*
Example The Roman orator Cicero was famous for his *polemic* against the politician Cataline.

NAME ______________________ DATE ____________

EXERCISE 1 MATCHING WORDS AND DEFINITIONS

Match the definition in Column B with the word in Column A. Write the letter of the correct definition on the answer line.

Column A	Column B	
1. garrulous	a. using or marked by the use of few words; terse	1. h
2. peremptory	b. a speech praising another; tribute; great praise	2. g
3. eulogy	c. to speak or write at length; elaborate	3. b
4. histrionic	d. to glorify; raise in rank, character, or status	4. f
5. exhort	e. a controversy or argument, especially one that is an attack on the opinions of another	5. i
6. polemic	f. excessively dramatic or emotional; pertaining to actors or acting	6. e
7. laconic	g. not allowing contradiction or refusal; having the nature of expressing a command	7. a
8. expatiate	h. habitually and excessively talkative	8. c
9. gist	i. to urge or incite by strong argument, advice, or appeal	9. j
10. exalt	j. the central idea of a matter; essence	10. d

EXERCISE 2 USING WORDS CORRECTLY

Each of the following statements contains an italicized vocabulary word. Decide whether the sentence is true or false, and write *True* or *False* on the answer line.

1. A shy student is usually the most *garrulous* one in the class. 1. False
2. If someone *exhorts* you to do something, he or she is offering you a casual suggestion. 2. False
3. A *eulogy* is the opening address at a large gathering, such as a political convention. 3. False
4. An aggressive rebuttal to the argument of another is a *polemic.* 4. True
5. Employees would not be likely to offer their bosses *peremptory* suggestions on how to improve the office environment. 5. True
6. If you *expatiate* on a particular subject, you deliberately fail to bring it up. 6. False
7. When you grasp the *gist* of a topic, you understand the central idea. 7. True
8. A *histrionic* individual is overly dramatic. 8. True
9. A *laconic* speaker tends to be verbose and repetitive. 9. False
10. A newspaper article that *exalts* a person's achievements praises that individual. 10. True

EXERCISE 3 CHOOSING THE BEST DEFINITION

For each italicized vocabulary word in the following sentences, write the letter of the best definition on the answer line.

1. Maxwell often quotes *laconic* proverbs to emphasize his point. 1. b
   a. subtle b. terse c. colorful d. striking

2. Joan's *histrionic* fits of temper have alienated nearly every member of the team. 2. d
   a. tearful b. overly critical c. competitive d. excessively dramatic

3. At Mr. Yong's funeral, several of his colleagues delivered stirring *eulogies*. 3. a
   a. tributes c. poems
   b. good-by messages d. suggestions

4. Mrs. Lockwood asked Alex to repeat the *gist* of her comments so that she could be certain that he understood them. 4. d
   a. range b. contradiction c. exact wording d. central idea

5. Nance *expatiated* on the delights of scuba diving. 5. c
   a. wavered b. wrote c. elaborated d. depended

6. Luz dared not argue with the *peremptory* edicts of her grandmother. 6. c
   a. sensible b. popular c. imperative d. discerning

7. Little progress was made in the negotiations while both sides insisted on trading hostile *polemics*. 7. b
   a. inquiries b. arguments c. glances d. grievances

8. Before presenting the award to Dr. Grodin, the university president *exalted* her triumphs in medical research. 8. a
   a. praised b. recalled c. promoted d. predicted

9. Tiresias *exhorted* Oedipus not to seek to know who murdered Laius, but Oedipus ignored the seer's pleas. 9. a
   a. urged b. told c. advised d. commanded

10. A *garrulous* radio announcer never seems to run out of things to say. 10. c
    a. quiet b. nervous c. talkative d. happy

EXERCISE 4 USING DIFFERENT FORMS OF WORDS

Decide which form of the vocabulary word in parentheses best completes the sentence. The form given may be correct. Write your answer on the answer line.

1. The coach's _____ to make a supreme effort did not go unheeded. *(exhort)* 1. exhortation
2. Representative Barnes is a master at writing _____. *(polemic)* 2. polemics
3. Beth's _____ often makes people avoid talking to her if they are in a hurry. *(garrulous)* 3. garrulousness
4. Zeke is the epitome of conceit: he never ceases to _____ on his own virtues. *(expatiate)* 4. expatiate
5. Meredith thought that Nick was bored with their conversation when he responded so _____. *(laconic)* 5. laconically
6. Congress _____ declared a moratorium on testing alternative energy sources. *(peremptory)* 6. peremptorily
7. The suspect's _____ did not deter the arresting officer. *(histrionic)* 7. histrionics
8. The president _____ the firefighter's alertness and bravery. *(eulogy)* 8. eulogized
9. We needed a translator so that we could understand the _____ of the visitor's impassioned speech. *(gist)* 9. gist
10. Lou found the _____ atmosphere of the conservatory challenging and invigorating. *(exalt)* 10. exalted

NAME ______________________________ DATE ____________

READING COMPREHENSION

Each numbered sentence in the following passage contains an italicized vocabulary word or related form. After you read the passage, you will complete an exercise.

STYLES OF PUBLIC SPEAKING

The difference between a good speech and a great one is how well a speaker accomplishes the purpose. Whether delivered to inform, inspire, entertain, or persuade, a speech must be instantly intelligible to the audience, appropriate for the occasion, and expressive. Although stylistic conventions in public speaking have differed throughout history, the most memorable speeches share the characteristic of having influenced people's thoughts and feelings.

Whatever public speakers wish to express or in what manner, they must have a definite purpose in mind. In ancient Greece citizens learned to devise and arrange plausible arguments that would persuade judges to grant them rights to confiscated property. (1) In making a serious ***polemic*** for or against declaring war, such famous speakers as Patrick Henry, Winston Churchill, and Franklin Delano Roosevelt emphasized their points through the logical organization of ideas and forceful language. (2) These men were successful in ***exhorting*** their listeners to think about, to believe in, and to act for a specific cause. (3) Audiences expect to hear somber speeches for serious occasions; lighter, informal presentations for social events; or ***peremptory*** remarks in a debate or political speech. (4) An audience prepared for a ***eulogy,*** for example, would undoubtedly be confused and disturbed by negative, sarcastic comments.

Another key ingredient in effective public speaking is the speaker's choice of words and his or her style. (5) When Franklin D. Roosevelt substituted the sentence "We are going to make a country in which no one is left out" for the more ***exalted*** language of "We are trying to construct a more inclusive society," he chose a more direct, conversational style to influence his listeners. (6) If John F. Kennedy had ***expatiated*** on the virtues of patriotism rather than stating "Ask not what your country can do for you—ask what you can do for your country," his eloquent message might have been forgotten. The best speakers balance the grace and elegance of language with its precision and clarity. As the Arabian proverb suggests, good speakers "make [others] see with their ears."

Successful public speakers develop a style that best suits them and the purpose of their speeches. (7) Early Roman orators believed in the power of the address and were masters of physical gesture and ***histrionic*** displays. (8) Other speakers, such as the American statesman Daniel Webster, adopted a ***garrulous*** approach. Convinced that words speak louder than silence, Webster chose a lengthy, ornate mode of presentation. (9) Still others were subdued and ***laconic,*** such as President Lincoln, who delivered his Gettysburg Address in three minutes. A speaking style may be elaborately formal, such as that of William Jennings Bryan, or simple but dignified, as was that of Chief Joseph of the Nez Percé tribe. Regardless of the style, a speaker's ease, confidence, and authority of delivery continue to be factors in how listeners respond and how the purpose is achieved.

(10) Although all speakers intend to communicate the ***gist*** of their topic, the greatest speechmakers are able to accomplish more. Providing lasting inspiration, they change opinions, excite emotions, draw out deep feelings, and stir listeners to action. Using mere words, Patrick Henry stirred the colonists to revolt, Winston Churchill bolstered the spirits of the British during World War II, and Martin Luther King, Jr., demanded equality for all.

READING COMPREHENSION EXERCISE

Each of the following statements corresponds to a numbered sentence in the passage. Each statement contains a blank and is followed by four answer choices. Decide which choice fits best in the blank. The word or phrase that you choose must express roughly the same meaning as the italicized word in the passage. Write the letter of your choice on the answer line.

1. Famous speakers used forceful language when they made a(n) _____ for or against declaring war. 1. c
   a. supplication b. effort c. argument d. excuse

2. These speakers succeeded in _____ their listeners to think and to act. 2. a
   a. urging b. begging c. forcing d. permitting

3. Audiences expect to hear _____ remarks in a debate. 3. b
   a. trite b. commanding c. hesitant d. exaggerated

4. An audience prepared for a _____ would be confused by negative comments. 4. c
   a. resolution b. sacrifice c. tribute d. justification

5. Franklin D. Roosevelt substituted a direct statement for more _____ language. 5. d
   a. vague b. commonplace c. repetitive d. elevated

6. If John F. Kennedy had _____ patriotism, his eloquent message might have been forgotten. 6. b
   a. lectured about b. elaborated on c. ignored d. restored

7. Early Roman orators were masters of _____ displays. 7. a
   a. dramatic b. opinionated c. tactful d. timid

8. Other speakers adopted a(n) _____ approach. 8. a
   a. excessively talkative b. plainly superior c. sarcastic d. antagonistic

9. Still others were subdued and _____. 9. d
   a. weak b. honest c. obscure d. terse

10. All speakers intend to communicate the _____ of their topic. 10. b
    a. emotion b. central idea c. tone d. nature

WRITING ASSIGNMENT

"Speech is the mirror of the soul; as a man speaks, so he is." (Publilius Syrus, Latin writer of the first century B.C.)

Using at least five of the words from this lesson, explain in a composition why and how this quotation is or is not true to human experience. Underline each vocabulary word that you use.

VOCABULARY ENRICHMENT

The word *polemic* comes from the Greek word *polemos*, meaning "war." During the seventeenth century, the meaning of the word gradually shifted from the aggressiveness of physical combat to the controversial nature of discussion or argument between opposing sides.

Activity Many other English words have etymologies that are closely connected with the idea of war. Look up the following words in a dictionary and write their origins and definitions. Then write a sentence in which you use each word.

1. Armageddon 2. bellicose 3. blitz 4. martial 5. pugnacious

LESSON 15 REVERENCE AND IRREVERENCE 15

Reverence, a feeling of profound awe or respect, is expected or mandated in certain situations. People are expected to show proper solemnity during a marriage ceremony, for example, or at a state funeral. British subjects are required to show esteem for a member of the royal family by bowing or curtseying. Often, however, reverence is individually motivated. One person visiting a national monument for the first time may be moved by the grandeur of the marble structure, whereas another may regard the experience as simply viewing another statue. Graffiti on a fence may be seen by some as witty decoration, while others interpret them as showing a lack of respect for property. The words in this lesson will help you to describe instances of reverence and irreverence.

WORD LIST

consecrate
credo
desecrate
laudable
pious
sacrilegious
sanctimony
sanctity
supplicate
venerate

DEFINITIONS

After you have studied the definitions and example for each vocabulary word, write the word on the line to the right.

1. **consecrate** (kŏn′sĭ-krāt′) *trans. verb* **a.** To declare or set apart as holy or sacred: *consecrate a burial ground.* **b.** To dedicate to a worthy goal or service: *consecrated his life to helping the poor.* **c.** To confirm officially by religious or civil ceremonies. (From the Latin *com-*, an intensive prefix, and *sacer,* meaning "sacred") 1. ______________

Related Word **consecrated** *noun*
Example The ancient Romans *consecrated* the Pantheon as a place of worship of all the gods.

2. **credo** (krē′dō, krā′dō) *noun* **a.** A system of fundamental beliefs or guiding principles; creed. **b.** A formal statement of religious belief. (From the Latin word *credere,* meaning "to believe") 2. ______________

Example Honesty with herself and others is a vital part of Monica's *credo.*

3. **desecrate** (dĕs′ĭ-krāt′) *trans. verb* **a.** To violate or abuse the sacredness of; profane. **b.** To treat irreverently or contemptuously, thereby arousing outrage in others: *land development that desecrates the wilderness.* 3. ______________

Related Word **desecration** *noun*
Example Vandals had *desecrated* the cemetery.

4. **laudable** (lô′də-bəl) *adjective* Deserving praise; commendable. (From the Latin word *laus,* meaning "praise") 4. ______________

USAGE NOTE: The adjective form *laudatory* means "expressing praise."

Related Words **laud** *verb;* **laudably** *adverb;* **laudatory** *adjective*
Example Musicians' efforts on behalf of the poor, the hungry, and the homeless have been *laudable.*

5. **pious** (pī′əs) *adjective* **a.** Having or exhibiting reverence and earnest compliance in the observance of religion; devout. **b.** Professing or exhibiting a strict, traditional sense of virtue and morality; high-minded. **c.** Marked by false devoutness; solemnly hypocritical: *pious fraud.* (From the Latin word *pius,* meaning "dutiful") 5. ________

Related Words **piety** *noun;* **piously** *adverb*
Example The Greek worship of the Olympian gods was characterized by such *pious* practices as making sacrifices and seeking the advice of oracles.

6. **sacrilegious** (săk′rə-lē′jəs, săk′rə-lĭj′əs) *adjective* Disrespectful or irreverent toward something sacred. (From the Latin words *sacer,* meaning "sacred," and *legere,* meaning "to gather") 6. ________

USAGE NOTE: Do not confuse the spelling of *sacrilegious* with that of *religious.*

Related Words **sacrilege** *noun;* **sacrilegiously** *adverb*
Example In Homer's *Iliad* two Greeks are guilty of *sacrilegious* behavior when they steal an image of Athena from the Trojans.

7. **sanctimony** (săngk′tə-mō′nē) *noun* Pretended devoutness or righteousness; a hypocritical show of holiness. (From the Latin word *sanctus,* meaning "holy") 7. ________

Related Words **sanctimonious** *adjective;* **sanctimoniously** *adverb*
Example Harry was surprised to learn that the lives of his noble ancestors had been free of *sanctimony* and ostentatious display.

8. **sanctity** (săngk′tĭ-tē) *noun* **a.** The quality or condition of being considered sacred; inviolability. **b.** Holiness of life; saintliness. (From the Latin word *sanctus,* meaning "holy") 8. ________

Example During the wedding ceremony, the bride and groom were reminded of the *sanctity* of their marriage vows.

9. **supplicate** (sŭp′lĭ-kāt′) *trans. verb* **a.** To make a humble entreaty to; beseech. **b.** To ask for humbly or earnestly, as by praying. *intrans. verb* To make a humble and earnest petition; beg. (From the Latin *sub-,* meaning "down," and *plicare,* meaning "to fold up") 9. ________

Related Words **supplicant** *noun;* **supplication** *noun;* **supplicatory** *adjective*
Example Caught stealing food, the serfs *supplicated* the lord of the manor for mercy.

10. **venerate** (vĕn′ə-rāt′) *trans. verb* To regard with respect, reverence, or deference. 10. ________

Related Words **venerable** *adjective;* **veneration** *noun*
Example Throughout the world, people *venerated* Mother Teresa for her work among the needy.

NAME ______________________ DATE __________

EXERCISE 1 WRITING CORRECT WORDS

On the answer line, write the word from the vocabulary list that fits each definition.

1. To violate or abuse the sacredness of; treat irreverently or contemptuously — 1. desecrate
2. The quality or condition of being considered sacred; saintliness — 2. sanctity
3. Deserving praise; commendable — 3. laudable
4. To regard with respect, reverence, or deference — 4. venerate
5. To declare holy or sacred; dedicate to a worthy goal or service — 5. consecrate
6. Disrespectful or irreverent toward something sacred — 6. sacrilegious
7. A system of fundamental beliefs or guiding principles; creed; formal statement of religious belief — 7. credo
8. To make a humble entreaty to; ask for humbly, as by praying — 8. supplicate
9. Exhibiting reverence and earnest compliance in the observation of religion — 9. pious
10. Pretended devoutness or righteousness; hypocritical show of holiness — 10. sanctimony

EXERCISE 2 USING WORDS CORRECTLY

Decide whether the italicized vocabulary word has been used correctly in the sentence. On the answer line, write *Correct* for correct use and *Incorrect* for incorrect use.

1. Mr. Whitman is very kind and wise; he seems to have a certain *sanctity* about him. — 1. Correct
2. Sandy is a *pious* practitioner of yoga, believing that the daily exercises will help her to attain tranquillity. — 2. Correct
3. The detective caught the people who broke in and *consecrated* the historic house of worship. — 3. Incorrect
4. Members of the Indian nation believed that the new dam would *desecrate* their land. — 4. Correct
5. Ed asked his father for a five-dollar loan to *supplicate* his allowance. — 5. Incorrect
6. She wore an expression of such *sanctimony* that we instantly admired her. — 6. Incorrect
7. The coach decided that the team needed a pep rally to *venerate* enthusiasm for the last games of the season. — 7. Incorrect
8. During the Middle Ages, a person whose life was in danger could find shelter in a church and claim the right of sanctuary; it would have been considered *sacrilegious* to harm such a person. — 8. Correct
9. We didn't believe that Jamie was *laudable* of making a twenty-five-mile hike. — 9. Incorrect
10. According to the Inuit *credo,* no stranger can be denied food or shelter. — 10. Correct

EXERCISE 3 IDENTIFYING SYNONYMS AND ANTONYMS

Decide which word has the meaning that is the same as (a synonym) or opposite to (an antonym) that of the capitalized vocabulary word. Write the letter of your choice on the answer line.

1. SANCTITY (synonym): — 1. c
   a. uniqueness **b.** perseverance **c.** sacredness **d.** abundance

2. DESECRATE (antonym):
a. purify b. scheme c. affirm d. divulge
2. a

3. CREDO (synonym):
a. restraint b. belief c. objective d. resolve
3. b

4. LAUDABLE (antonym):
a. blameworthy b. soothing c. arbitrary d. exempt
4. a

5. SANCTIMONY (synonym):
a. subordination b. suspicion c. prediction d. hypocrisy
5. d

6. PIOUS (antonym):
a. vehement b. irreverent c. noble d. tedious
6. b

7. CONSECRATE (synonym):
a. undermine b. dedicate c. crave d. disclose
7. b

8. VENERATE (antonym):
a. disconcert b. instill c. malign d. augment
8. c

9. SACRILEGIOUS (synonym):
a. irreverent b. inconsistent c. unstable d. tortuous
9. a

10. SUPPLICATE (antonym):
a. incriminate b. fascinate c. foster d. disdain
10. d

EXERCISE 4 USING DIFFERENT FORMS OF WORDS

Decide which form of the vocabulary word in parentheses best completes the sentence. The form given may be correct. Write your answer on the answer line.

1. The book describes the ____ of the oak groves where ancient druids conducted mysterious ceremonies. *(consecrate)* 1. **consecration**

2. Creating beauty from junkyard debris was part of the artist's ____. *(credo)* 2. **credo**

3. "Allowing countless species of animals to become extinct is almost a ____," exclaimed the naturalist. *(sacrilegious)* 3. **sacrilege**

4. In A.D. 135 Roman legions carried out the Emperor Hadrian's orders for the destruction of Jerusalem and the ____ of the houses of worship. *(desecrate)* 4. **desecration**

5. The king ignored the ____ of his serfs. *(supplicate)* 5. **supplications**

6. We learned about the ____ and dedication of Cotton Mather, an eighteenth-century American theologian and writer. *(pious)* 6. **piety**

7. Everyone was impressed by the unselfish ____ of her life. *(sanctity)* 7. **sanctity**

8. Professor Cummins had nearly turned the ____ of Shakespeare into idolatry. *(venerate)* 8. **veneration**

9. Luanne sometimes resents her older sister's ____ self-assurance. *(sanctimony)* 9. **sanctimonious**

10. Because the Sullivans expect their children to help out, they do not ____ the children for cleaning their rooms. *(laudable)* 10. **laud**

NAME ______________________ DATE ____________

READING COMPREHENSION

Each numbered sentence in the following passage contains an italicized vocabulary word or related form. After you read the passage, you will complete an exercise.

JOAN OF ARC (1412–1431)

(1) The brief, dramatic life of Joan of Arc, a French peasant girl who won strategic victories against the English during the Hundred Years' War, has long aroused popular imagination and ***veneration.*** Her tenacity, her sense of divine mission, and the apparently miraculous success she achieved made her a symbol of French national unity and a popular heroine.

Although Joan received no formal schooling, she evidently was an immensely capable and sensible young girl. (2) Known for her gentleness, charity, and ***piety,*** she was hardworking and self-disciplined. Until she was sixteen years old, she took pleasure in domestic accomplishments, such as sewing and spinning, which she learned from her mother.

As a child Joan was accustomed to conflict, as English troops repeatedly devastated the countryside around her village. The throne of France was under dispute between the English king, Henry VI, whose troops occupied the northern part of the French kingdom, and its king, Charles. Charles, inactive and apathetic, did little to assert the powers of his kingship. In fact, he could not even strengthen his claim to the throne by actually being crowned; Reims, the traditional location for the coronation, was in enemy-held territory.

(3) When the English laid siege to the French city of Orléans in 1428, Joan of Arc believed that the ***desecration*** of her country had gone far enough. Believing herself to be inspired by divine command, she wanted to go to Orléans, raise the siege, and lead the king to Reims to be crowned. (4) Charles was skeptical at first about her claims to divine intervention; however, after the ***sanctity*** of her religious beliefs had been tested by his theologians and clergy, he gave Joan the command of a force of troops.

Although she knew nothing of military tactics or strategy, Joan of Arc inspired her troops to fight fiercely. Utterly fearless in battle, Joan had a presence that seemed to assure success. The English gave way within a short time. The siege of Orléans was raised on May 8, 1429, and the French advanced, encountering little opposition. Charles entered Reims on July 16, 1429, escorted by Joan and her army. (5) She stood at his side the following day when he was ***consecrated*** as Charles VII, King of France.

The news of the liberation of Orléans and the coronation of Charles VII spread quickly and injected a spirit of hope and resolution into the oppressed French population. (6) Although Joan and her military leaders ***supplicated*** Charles to press their advantage and to take Paris, the king believed that diplomatic negotiations would be more effective than fighting. (7) He did little to help Joan in her continuing ***laudable*** effort to drive the English from France.

In 1430 Joan of Arc was captured by French troops loyal to the enemy. When Charles VII made no offers of ransom, she was sold to the English, who viewed her as a serious impediment to their conquest of France. Although her crimes were political in nature, she was brought to trial in a church court. (8) Her interrogators intended to destroy her claim to divine guidance, making her seem to be only a foolish, ***sanctimonious*** girl. (9) The seventy charges, which included witchcraft, were based mainly on the contention that her whole attitude and behavior showed ***sacrilegious*** presumption. By submitting to the authority of the church, she would have had to admit that her divine mission was false. (10) For refusing to denounce her ***credo*** and renounce her belief in her divinely inspired mission, Joan of Arc was burned at the stake in the public square of the city of Rouen on May 30, 1431.

READING COMPREHENSION EXERCISE

Each of the following statements corresponds to a numbered sentence in the passage. Each statement contains a blank and is followed by four answer choices. Decide which choice fits best in the blank. The word or phrase that you choose must express roughly the same meaning as the italicized word in the passage. Write the letter of your choice on the answer line.

1. The brief dramatic life of Joan of Arc has aroused popular _____. 1. ___b___
   a. confusion b. respect c. rebellion d. satisfaction

2. She was known for her gentleness and _____. 2. ___d___
   a. vigor b. obedience c. brilliance d. devoutness

3. When the English seized Orléans, Joan believed that the _____ of her country had gone far enough. 3. ___a___
   a. abuse b. exclusion c. restraint d. reorganization

4. Charles had his theologians and clergy test the _____ of her religious beliefs. 4. ___b___
   a. structure b. inviolability c. origin d. validity

5. When Charles was _____ as King of France, Joan of Arc stood at his side. 5. ___c___
   a. denounced c. officially confirmed
   b. decorated d. magnificently displayed

6. Joan and her military leaders _____ Charles to take Paris. 6. ___a___
   a. beseeched b. forced c. ordered d. coaxed

7. He did little to help Joan in her continuing _____ efforts. 7. ___d___
   a. useless b. ruthless c. patient d. commendable

8. Her interrogators wanted to make her seem to be only a foolish, _____ girl. 8. ___b___
   a. totally inept c. uncompromising
   b. hypocritically holy d. pessimistic

9. The charges were based on the contention that her attitude and behavior showed _____ presumption. 9. ___c___
   a. unmistakable b. eternal c. irreverent d. overwhelming

10. Joan of Arc refused to denounce her _____. 10. ___a___
    a. fundamental beliefs c. friends
    b. conclusive opinions d. persecutors

WRITING ASSIGNMENT

The pharaohs of ancient Egypt had a special status. Respected as rulers of the state, the pharaohs were also believed to be the embodiment of divinity and so were treated like gods. Imagine that you could go back in time to observe a pharaoh and his court. Incorporating facts that you have obtained from library research, write the script for a radio program in which you question an ancient Egyptian ruler about the behavior and attitude of his subjects toward him. Use at least five of the words from this lesson in your script and underline each one.

The **Test** for Lessons 13, 14, and 15 is on page T17.

NAME ______________________ DATE __________

READING SKILLS

CONTEXT CLUES AND THE READING OF BRITISH LITERATURE

As you continue your study of literature, you will read more literary works from Britain and other countries. Many works will be from earlier periods. The following strategies suggest ways of using context clues to determine the meanings of unfamiliar words.

STRATEGIES

1. *Consider the period in which the work was written.* Some words in an older work may not be in use today or may have different meanings. For example, when you read Jane Austen's novels, you will encounter a *barouche landau,* recognizable in context as a type of carriage, and a *ha-ha,* harder to identify as a walled ditch that serves as a fence.
2. *Consider the author and his or her style.* Be on the alert for an author's use of metaphors. Also be sure that you understand the literary allusions in a work; the poet Milton, for example, used many.
3. *Consider the genre (type of literature) and the subject of the work.* If the work is fiction, for example, when and where is the story set? The setting and the subject of a work help to determine its vocabulary.
4. *Use a desk dictionary or an unabridged dictionary.* Use it to check meanings that you have tentatively assigned to words, working from context clues. Also check meanings of words without helpful context.

EXERCISE USING CONTEXT CLUES IN READING LITERATURE

The following passage is from *A Tale of Two Cities,* by Charles Dickens (1812–1870), a novel set during the French Revolution of the late eighteenth century. In the countryside "four fierce figures" have set fire to the chateau of an oppressive marquis, or noble. Begin by reading the entire passage. *Step 1:* Write your own definition of each italicized word. *Step 2:* Write the appropriate dictionary definition of the word.

> The (1) *chateau* was left to itself to flame and burn. In the roaring and raging of the (2) *conflagration,* a red-hot wind, driving straight from the infernal regions, seemed to be blowing the (3) *edifice* away. With the rising and falling of the blaze, the stone faces showed as if they were in torment. When great masses of stone and timber fell, the face of the two (4) *dints* in the nose became obscured: (5) *anon* struggled out of the smoke again, as if it were the face of the cruel Marquis, burning at the stake and (6) *contending* with the fire.
>
> The chateau burned; the nearest trees, laid hold of by the fire, scorched and shrivelled; trees at a distance, fired by the four fierce figures, (7) *begirt* the blazing edifice with a new forest of smoke. Molten lead and iron boiled in the marble basin of the fountain; the water ran dry; the extinguisher tops of the towers vanished like ice before the heat, and trickled down into four rugged wells of flame. Great (8) *rents* and splits branched out in the solid walls, like crystallisation; stupefied birds wheeled about, and dropped into the furnace;

four fierce figures trudged away, East, West, North, and South, along the night-(9) *enshrouded* roads; guided by the beacon they had lighted, towards their next destination. The illuminated village had seized hold of the (10) *tocsin*, and, abolishing the lawful ringer, rang for joy.

1. *chateau*

   Your Definition large country home; castle

   Dictionary Definition French castle or manor house

2. *conflagration*

   Your Definition fire

   Dictionary Definition large and destructive fire

3. *edifice*

   Your Definition building

   Dictionary Definition building, especially one of imposing appearance or size

4. *dints*

   Your Definition dents

   Dictionary Definition dents

5. *anon*

   Your Definition then

   Dictionary Definition in a short time; soon

6. *contending*

   Your Definition struggling; suffering

   Dictionary Definition fighting; disputing

7. *begirt*

   Your Definition covered

   Dictionary Definition encircled; surrounded

8. *rents*

   Your Definition tears

   Dictionary Definition openings; rips

9. *enshrouded*

   Your Definition covered

   Dictionary Definition covered with, or as with, a burial cloth

10. *tocsin*

    Your Definition bell

    Dictionary Definition alarm bell

LESSON 16 THE ROOTS *-ONYM-* AND *-NOMIN-* 16

Although the roots *-onym-* and *-nomin-* share the same meaning, they are derived from different languages. The root *-onym-* comes from the Greek word *onyma,* meaning "name," whereas *-nomin-* is derived from the Latin word *nomen,* which also means "name." Such words as *synonym, antonym,* and *pseudonym* reflect their Greek heritage, while *nominate, noun,* and *pronoun* show their Latin derivation. In this lesson you will learn other words that come from both of these roots.

WORD LIST

anonymous
cognomen
denomination
homonym
ignominy
metonymy
misnomer
nomenclature
nominal
renown

DEFINITIONS

After you have studied the definitions and example for each vocabulary word, write the word on the line to the right.

1. **anonymous** (ə-nŏn'ə-məs) *adjective* **a.** Having unknown or withheld authorship or agency. **b.** Having an unknown or unacknowledged name. **c.** Lacking individuality, distinction, or recognizability. (From the Greek *an-,* meaning "without," and *onyma,* meaning "name") 1. ______________

Related Words **anonymity** *noun;* **anonymously** *adverb*
Example Folk ballads such as "The Wife of Usher's Well" are *anonymous.*

2. **cognomen** (kŏg-nō'mən) *noun* **a.** A name, especially a descriptive nickname acquired through usage. **b.** A family name; a surname. (From the Latin *com-,* meaning "together," and *nomen,* meaning "name") 2. ______________

Example Because David's favorite sport has been baseball ever since he saw his first game, his friends have given him the *cognomen* "Slugger."

3. **denomination** (dĭ-nŏm'ə-nā'shən) *noun* **a.** The name of a class or group. **b.** A name; designation. **c.** The act of naming. **d.** An organized group of religious congregations. **e.** A class of units having specified values: *coins of small denominations.* (From the Latin *de-,* an intensive prefix, and *nomen)* 3. ______________

USAGE NOTE: *Denominate* means "to give a name to"; *denominator* means "a common characteristic," but in math a denominator is the bottom in a fraction.

Related Words **denominate** *verb;* **denominational** *adjective;* **denominator** *noun*
Example The *denomination* of the species of turtle came from the name of the zoologist who first studied them.

4. **homonym** (hŏm'ə-nĭm') *noun* One of two or more words that have the same sound and often the same spelling but differ in meaning. (From the Greek words *homos,* meaning "same," and *onyma)* 4. ______________

Example *Bear,* meaning "to support" and *bear,* meaning "a large omnivorous mammal," are *homonyms,* but in context they are seldom confused.

5. **ignominy** (ĭg′nə-mĭn′ē) *noun* **a.** Great personal dishonor or humiliation. **b.** Shameful or disgraceful action, conduct, or character. (From the Latin *in-*, meaning "not," and *nomen*) 5. ____________

Related Word ignominious *adjective*
Example In colonial times wrongdoers were often subjected to the *ignominy* of being put into the stocks.

6. **metonymy** (mə-tŏn′ə-mē) *noun* A figure of speech in which an attribute or commonly associated feature is used to name or designate something. (From the Greek *meta-*, meaning "changing," and *onyma*) 6. ____________

Example In the days of sailing vessels, people used *metonymy* when they referred to ships as "sails."

7. **misnomer** (mĭs-nō′mər) *noun* **a.** A name wrongly or unsuitably applied to a person, place, or thing. **b.** An error in naming a person or place. (From the Old French *mes-*, meaning "wrongly," and *nommer*, meaning "to name"; the Old French *nommer* comes from the Latin word *nomen*) 7. ____________

Example The Thrifty Traveler is certainly a *misnomer* for an expensive motel.

8. **nomenclature** (nō′mən-klā′chər) *noun* A system of names used in the arts and sciences. (From the Latin words *nomen* and *calare*, meaning "to call") 8. ____________

Example The diagram gave the *nomenclature* for the parts of a cell.

9. **nominal** (nŏm′ə-nəl) *adjective* **a.** Existing in name only and not in actuality. **b.** Insignificantly small: *a nominal fee.* **c.** Of, like, or pertaining to a name or names; bearing a person's name. (From the Latin word *nomen*) 9. ____________

Example The manager's title of "consultant" was a *nominal* one, since his colleagues rarely asked for his opinions.

10. **renown** (rĭ-noun′) *noun* The quality of being widely honored and acclaimed; fame. (From the Latin *re-*, meaning "again," and *nomen*) 10. ____________

Related Word renowned *adjective*
Example Because Dr. Miller was a physicist of great *renown*, her advice was widely sought by others in the field.

NAME ______________________ DATE __________

EXERCISE 1 MATCHING WORDS AND DEFINITIONS

Match the definition in Column B with the word in Column A. Write the letter of the correct definition on the answer line.

Column A	Column B	Answer
1. denomination	a. having an unknown or withheld name, authorship, or agency; lacking individuality, distinction, or recognizability	1. i
2. metonymy	b. a name wrongly or unsuitably applied to a person, place, or thing; an error in naming	2. h
3. homonym	c. one of two or more words that have the same sound and often the same spelling but differ in meaning	3. c
4. anonymous	d. the quality of being widely honored and acclaimed; fame	4. a
5. nominal	e. personal dishonor or humiliation; shameful or disgraceful action, conduct, or character	5. g
6. cognomen	f. a system of names used in the arts and sciences	6. j
7. nomenclature	g. existing in name only and not in actuality; insignificantly small	7. f
8. renown	h. a figure of speech in which an attribute or feature is used to name or designate something	8. d
9. misnomer	i. the name of a class or group; an organized group of religious congregations	9. b
10. ignominy	j. a name, especially a descriptive nickname acquired through usage	10. e

EXERCISE 2 USING WORDS CORRECTLY

Decide whether the italicized vocabulary word has been used correctly in the sentence. On the answer line, write *Correct* for correct use and *Incorrect* for incorrect use.

1. When using *metonymy,* remember that the part represents the whole. — 1. Correct
2. The word *celebrity* is a *homonym* for *fame.* — 2. Incorrect
3. In an old popular song, Hardhearted Hannah was the *cognomen* of an unfeeling young woman. — 3. Correct
4. The bald brother of the Three Stooges was given the *misnomer* Curly. — 4. Correct
5. The *anonymous* letter was signed by Jorge Orlando. — 5. Incorrect
6. It took several weeks for Ian to become familiar with the *nomenclature* of graphic arts. — 6. Correct
7. Juanita's family cheered her *ignominy* when she was named class valedictorian. — 7. Incorrect
8. The evil deeds of the bandit king won him *renown* that lasted for decades. — 8. Incorrect
9. The *nominal* leader of a group is often called a figurehead. — 9. Correct
10. "Coordinator" was the *denomination* used for Michele's new job category. — 10. Correct

EXERCISE 3 CHOOSING THE BEST WORD

Decide which vocabulary word or related form best expresses the meaning of the italicized word or phrase in the sentence. On the answer line, write the letter of the correct choice.

1. An *unidentified* caller tipped off the police about the robbery. 1. b
   a. renowned b. anonymous c. denominational d. nominal

2. The *system of names* of biology classifies plants and animals in increasingly specific categories: kingdom, phylum, class, order, family, genus, and species. 2. d
   a. ignominy b. denomination c. misnomer d. nomenclature

3. The *naming* of a new product is a vital consideration in marketing. 3. b
   a. nomenclature b. denomination c. homonym d. cognomen

4. The telephone book lists over five pages of people who share the *family name* of Smith. 4. a
   a. cognomen b. homonym c. misnomer d. ignominy

5. People are allowed to enter the town museum for the *insignificant* fee of twenty-five cents. 5. d
   a. denominational b. renowned c. ignominious d. nominal

6. The heavyweight boxer's fans used a humorous *error in naming* when they dubbed the fighter "Slim." 6. c
   a. nomenclature b. homonym c. misnomer d. renown

7. Although Christopher Columbus enjoyed great *acclaim* soon after his first voyage to the Americas, he died forgotten and neglected by his contemporaries. 7. d
   a. cognomen b. anonymity c. ignominy d. renown

8. The words "rain" and "reign" are English *words that sound the same but differ in meaning*. 8. b
   a. metonymy b. homonyms c. misnomers d. denominations

9. The most *humiliating* experience I can recall is locking myself out of the house while still in my pajamas. 9. a
   a. ignominious b. anonymous c. nominal d. renowned

10. Newspaper reporters tend to overuse *associated features that name something,* as, for example, when they write about citizen groups that demand action from City Hall or the White House. 10. b
    a. anonymity b. metonymy c. denomination d. misnomer

EXERCISE 4 USING DIFFERENT FORMS OF WORDS

Decide which form of the vocabulary word in parentheses best completes the sentence. The form given may be correct. Write your answer on the answer line.

1. Erica's favorite use of _____ is the quotation "The pen is mightier than the sword." *(metonymy)* 1. metonymy

2. *Pause* and *paws* are _____. *(homonym)* 2. homonyms

3. To suggest a more hopeful future, the Sahims bestowed the _____ "Lucky" on the kitten they had pulled from a well. *(cognomen)* 3. cognomen

4. In Hawthorne's *The Scarlet Letter,* Hester Prynne has an _____ position in seventeenth-century Boston. *(ignominy)* 4. ignominious

5. Clergy from many _____ attended the series of meetings on world problems. *(denomination)* 5. denominations

NAME ______________________ DATE ____________

6. Aristotle, who tried to classify animals in the fourth century B.C., was the first to establish a system of _____. *(nomenclature)* 6. **nomenclature**

7. The money to build the new hospital wing was donated _____. *(anonymous)* 7. **anonymously**

8. The Watsons paid the city the _____ sum of one dollar for the historic house. *(nominal)* 8. **nominal**

9. Although he was a _____ prime minister and statesman, Winston Churchill was nevertheless voted out of office after World War II. *(renown)* 9. **renowned**

10. Columbus and others thought that the Americas were the outer reaches of the East Indies: therefore, they gave native Americans the _____ "Indian." *(misnomer)* 10. **misnomer**

READING COMPREHENSION

Each numbered sentence in the following passage contains an italicized vocabulary word or related form. After you read the passage, you will complete an exercise.

THE NAMING OF THE AMERICAS

(1) *Toponymy,* a word that is part of geographical ***nomenclature,*** means the process and study of naming places. Toponymy is a fascinating topic that yields information about geography, history, archaeology, linguistics, and folklore in different regions of the world. The naming of places arises from a single motivation—the desire to identify a particular place and distinguish it from others. To fulfill this practical purpose, place names come from a variety of sources. They may be based on sensory descriptions, such as size, color, or configuration, or on location. For example, Ecuador was named for its proximity to the equator, and the Black Hills of South Dakota for the dark appearance of the pines that cover the mountains. (2) Other place names commemorate the ***cognomens*** of the people who discovered them or a major incident that occurred there. Still others may evolve from metaphors—*cape, point, run.* (3) A few place names have more than one pronunciation; for example, some speakers pronounce the word *creek* like its ***homonym*** *creak,* and others pronounce it to rhyme with *brick.*

(4) The naming of the Americas apparently occurred as the result of a ***misnomer.*** Christopher Columbus, who sailed to the Americas, lost the opportunity to name them when he was unwilling to accept the concept of the area as two separate continents. Beginning with the idea of reaching China and Japan by sailing westward from Spain, he believed that he had reached the fringes of Asia rather than the Americas.

(5) Five years after Columbus's ***renowned*** journey, Amerigo Vespucci, an Italian merchant and navigator, claimed to have reached "a new world." During the course of his expeditions, Vespucci wrote letters to the Italian art patron and statesman Lorenzo de Medici in which he vividly described a continent and revealed previously unknown information about the extent of its coastline. (6) Using ***metonymy,*** he informed de Medici that he had "claimed the land for the crown." Published as *Mundus Novus* (New World) and translated into French, German, Flemish, and Latin, Vespucci's letter established his credibility and fame.

In 1507 the German mapmaker and geographer Martin Waldseemüller, who was familiar with Vespucci's letter and travels, included a map of the new region in an appendix to an atlas. (7) Because he did not want to present an ***anonymous*** land mass, Waldseemüller labeled it "America," noting in the margin that since Amerigo Vespucci had reached the fourth part of the world, the continent was aptly named for him.

(8) Later information proved that Vespucci was only the ***nominal*** "discoverer" of America. Although he may have sailed on voyages led by other explorers that touched on the shores of the Americas, it appears that Vespucci gathered facts and details from Columbus, whose ships he had helped outfit. (9) By the time the public learned the truth of Columbus's voyage, the ***ignominious*** error of Martin Waldseemüller had been repeated by other mapmakers. (10) The ***denomination*** *America* credits and commemorates the wrong person.

READING COMPREHENSION EXERCISE

Each of the following statements corresponds to a number sentence in the passage. Each statement contains a blank and is followed by four answer choices. Decide which choice fits best in the blank. The word or phrase that you choose must express roughly the same meaning as the italicized word in the passage. Write the letter of your choice on the answer line.

1. *Toponymy* is a word that is part of a geographical _____. 1. a
   a. system of names c. atlas
   b. system of notation symbols d. index
2. Other place names commemorate the _____ of the people who discovered them. 2. d
   a. titles b. professions c. explorations d. family names
3. Some speakers pronounce *creek* like its _____, *creak.* 3. b
   a. working having a similar etymology
   b. word having the same sound but a different meaning
   c. word having the opposite meaning
   d. word having the same vowel pattern
4. The designation of the Americas was the result of _____. 4. a
   a. an error in naming c. confusion
   b. a controversy about location d. outdated information
5. Amerigo Vespucci claimed to have reached "a new world" five years after Columbus's _____ journey. 5. c
   a. likely b. dubious c. famous d. prior
6. He informed de Medici of his claim to the continent by using _____. 6. a
   a. a figure of speech in which an associated feature names something
   b. a figure of speech in which words imitate what they denote
   c. elaborate language
   d. outrageous exaggerations
7. Waldseemüller did not want to present a(n) _____ land mass. 7. d
   a. shapeless b. separate c. conclusive d. unidentified
8. Vespucci was merely the _____ discoverer of America. 8. c
   a. primary b. chance c. in name only d. legendary
9. Other mapmakers repeated the _____ error made by Waldseemüller. 9. a
   a. shameful b. careless c. minor d. little-known
10. The _____ *America* commemorates the wrong person. 10. c
    a. nickname c. name
    b. picturesque term d. location

PRACTICE WITH ANALOGIES

See pages 32, 66, and 86 for some strategies to use with analogies.

Directions On the answer line, write the vocabulary word or a form of it that completes each analogy.

1. ELEGY : LAMENT :: _____ : praise *(Lesson 14)* 1. eulogy
2. LACONIC : BRIEF :: _____ : talkative *(Lesson 14)* 2. garrulous
3. REPREHENSIBLE : BLAME :: _____ : praise *(Lesson 15)* 3. laudable
4. COWARD : FEAR :: saint : _____ *(Lesson 15)* 4. piety
5. EMPTY : CONTENT :: _____ : name *(Lesson 16)* 5. anonymous
6. MISCONCEPTION : IDEA :: _____ : name *(Lesson 16)* 6. misnomer

The **Bonus activity** for Lessons 13–16 is on page T19.

LESSON 17 THE AGREEABLE AND THE DISAGREEABLE

17

How many of the following expressions do you use to describe reactions or situations that are agreeable or disagreeable?

meeting of the minds
hit it off with
fit like a glove
against the grain
turn thumbs down
at cross-purposes
pointblank refusal

These idioms are among the many phrases used to express the kinds of harmonious or antagonistic circumstances that we all encounter. Although compatibility and consensus are preferable to discord, circumstances cannot always be to one's liking. The words in this lesson will enable you to express the agreeable and disagreeable accurately and specifically.

WORD LIST

convivial
ebullience
felicitous
irascible
placid
querulous
sardonic
surly
truculent
unctuous

DEFINITIONS

After you have studied the definitions and example for each vocabulary word, write the word on the line to the right.

1. **convivial** (kən-vĭv'ē-əl) *adjective* **a.** Sociable; fond of feasting and good company. **b.** Festive. (From the Latin *com-*, meaning "together," and *vivere*, meaning "to live") — 1. ______

Related Word **conviviality** *noun*
Example Everyone liked Eddie because he had a *convivial* manner.

2. **ebullience** (ĭ-bo͝ol'yəns, ĭ-bŭl'yəns) *noun* The quality of expressing feelings or ideas in an enthusiastic and lively manner; exuberance. (From the Latin *ex-*, meaning "up," and *bullire*, meaning "to boil") — 2. ______

Related Words **ebullient** *adjective;* **ebulliently** *adverb*
Example After a time the *ebullience* of the child made even the most energetic of baby sitters weary.

3. **felicitous** (fĭ-lĭs'ĭ-təs) *adjective* **a.** Well-chosen; apt. **b.** Yielding great pleasure or delight. (From the Latin word *felix*, meaning "happy") — 3. ______

Related Words **felicitously** *adverb;* **felicity** *noun*
Example Rosalinda handled the delicate situation in a *felicitous* manner that was respected by everyone.

4. **irascible** (ĭ-răs'ə-bəl) *adjective* **a.** Prone to outbursts of temper; easily angered. **b.** Characterized by or resulting from anger. (From the Latin word *irasci*, meaning "to be angry") — 4. ______

Related Words **irascibility** *noun;* **irascibly** *adverb*
Example The *irascible* Yosemite Sam has always been one of Sarah's favorite cartoon characters.

5. **placid** (plăs′ĭd) *adjective* **a.** Having an undisturbed surface or aspect; outwardly calm or composed. **b.** Self-satisfied. (From the Latin word *placere,* meaning "to please") 5. ________________

Related Words **placidly** *adverb;* **placidness** *noun*
Example Nothing ever seemed to disturb Kathy's *placid* nature.

6. **querulous** (kwĕr′ə-ləs, kwĕr′yə-ləs) *adjective* **a.** Given to complaining; peevish. **b.** Expressing or showing a complaint: a *querulous voice.* (From the Latin word *queri,* meaning "to complain") 6. ________________

MEMORY CUE: A *querulous* person has a *quarrel* with everything.

Related Words **querulously** *adverb;* **querulousness** *noun*
Example The shopkeeper grew tired of the customer's *querulous* remarks about the quality of the merchandise.

7. **sardonic** (sär-dŏn′ĭk) *adjective* Scornfully mocking and derisive. (From the Greek word *sardonios,* meaning "bitter" or "scornful") 7. ________________

Related Word **sardonically** *adverb*
Example Jennifer's *sardonic* remarks about the standards of judging at the competition caused others to criticize her attitude.

8. **surly** (sûr′lē) *adjective* Sullenly ill-humored; gruff. 8. ________________

Related Word **surliness** *noun*
Example Because of his *surly* behavior, Gerald was not promoted as quickly as he had hoped to be.

9. **truculent** (trŭk′yə-lənt) *adjective* **a.** Savage and cruel; fierce. **b.** Disposed to fight; pugnacious. (From the Latin word *trux,* meaning "fierce") 9. ________________

Related Word **truculence** *noun;* **truculently** *adverb*
Example At the meeting we were shocked when one of the delegates made a *truculent* attack on the competence of the steering committee.

10. **unctuous** (ŭngk′cho͞o-əs) *adjective* **a.** Characterized by affected, exaggerated, or insincere earnestness. **b.** Having the quality or characteristics of oil or ointment; greasy. 10. ________________

Related Words **unctuously** *adverb;* **unctuousness** *noun*
Example Dicken's character Uriah Heep is notable for his *unctuous* insistence that he is a humble person.

Word History: unctuous

Latin: *unctum* = ointment < *ungere* = to annoint

The idea of "grease" contained within *unctuous* comes from the Latin noun *unctum,* "ointment," which in turn comes from the Latin verb *ungere,* to "anoint." When the ancient Romans attended the popular public baths, somewhat like our modern health clubs, they would have their slaves anoint their bodies with grease after soaking in a huge marble tub filled with very hot water. Since they had no soap, grease made from olive oil was used instead. The slaves, known as "unctores" or "anointers," rubbed the olive oil into their masters' skin and then scraped it off with a blunt metal tool. This process removed the skin's impurities and left it soft and clean.

NAME ______________________ DATE ____________

EXERCISE 1 WRITING CORRECT WORDS

On the answer line, write the word from the vocabulary list that fits each definition.

1. Given to complaining; expressing or showing a complaint — 1. querulous
2. Well-chosen; apt; yielding great pleasure or delight — 2. felicitous
3. Savage and cruel; fierce; disposed to fight — 3. truculent
4. Sociable; fond of feasting and good company; festive — 4. convivial
5. Prone to outbursts of temper; easily angered — 5. irascible
6. Characterized by affected, exaggerated, or insincere earnestness; having the quality of oil or ointment; greasy — 6. unctuous
7. Having an undisturbed surface or aspect; outwardly calm or composed — 7. placid
8. Sullenly ill-humored; gruff — 8. surly
9. The quality of expressing feelings or ideas in an enthusiastic and lively manner; exuberance — 9. ebullience
10. Scornfully mocking and derisive — 10. sardonic

EXERCISE 2 USING WORDS CORRECTLY

Each of the following questions contains an italicized vocabulary word. Choose the correct answer to the question, and write *Yes* or *No* on the answer line.

1. Would a *sardonic* review of a book please the book's author? — 1. No
2. Is a *convivial* occasion likely to be marked by a quiet, somber mood? — 2. No
3. Would you expect a *surly* salesperson to make many sales? — 3. No
4. Should a person question the validity of an *unctuous* compliment? — 4. Yes
5. Is a *truculent* temperament an important asset for a diplomat? — 5. No
6. Does a *querulous* person have a tendency to find fault with everything? — 6. Yes
7. Might the *ebullience* of a crowd be contagious? — 7. Yes
8. Would a *placid* horse appear to be a gentle mount for an inexperienced rider? — 8. Yes
9. Would you expect an *irascible* person to control his or her temper at all times? — 9. No
10. Is a *felicitous* letter one that arrives on time entirely by chance? — 10. No

EXERCISE 3 IDENTIFYING SYNONYMS AND ANTONYMS

Decide which word has the meaning that is the same as (a synonym) or opposite to (an antonym) that of the capitalized vocabulary word. Write the letter of your choice on the answer line.

1. PLACID (synonym): — 1. b
   a. priceless **b.** unruffled **c.** exacting **d.** wretched
2. TRUCULENT (antonym): — 2. a
   a. mild **b.** unwieldy **c.** compelling **d.** habitual

3. EBULLIENCE (synonym): 3. d

a. disobedience b. triviality c. alliance d. exuberance

4. IRASCIBLE (antonym): 4. a

a. patient b. unprecedented c. contorted d. blemished

5. SARDONIC (synonym): 5. c

a. tactful b. impaired c. scornful d. durable

6. CONVIVIAL (antonym): 6. b

a. tolerant b. reclusive c. greedy d. lenient

7. QUERULOUS (synonym): 7. d

a. nimble b. deceptive c. dignified d. fretful

8. FELICITOUS (antonym): 8. b

a. youthful b. ill-chosen c. industrious d. secretive

9. SURLY (synonym): 9. a

a. snappish b. motionless c. current d. extraordinary

10. UNCTUOUS (antonym): 10. c

a. absolute b. sturdy c. sincere d. costly

EXERCISE 4 USING DIFFERENT FORMS OF WORDS

Decide which form of the vocabulary word in parentheses best completes the sentence. The form given may be correct. Write your answer on the answer line.

1. The waitresses at the famous old waterfront restaurant have a reputation for _____ with customers. *(surly)* 1. surliness

2. The _____ of the graduation party was dampened by the realization that the friends would soon go their separate ways. *(convivial)* 2. conviviality

3. Grinning _____, the Wicked Witch of the West watched as Dorothy and her friends grew sleepy in the field. *(sardonic)* 3. sardonically

4. Maggie greeted her parents _____, waving her letter of acceptance from the university. *(ebullience)* 4. ebulliently

5. The conflict among the committee members had little effect on the _____ disposition of the chairperson. *(placid)* 5. placid

6. Once we complained to the manager about the service, the waiter _____ overwhelmed us with attention. *(unctuous)* 6. unctuously

7. The woman's _____ frustrated the flight attendant and annoyed the other passengers. *(querulous)* 7. querulousness

8. The Richmans looked forward to sharing the _____ of their fiftieth anniversary with their many friends and relatives. *(felicitous)* 8. felicity

9. Referred to as the "Wicked Wasp of Twickenham," Alexander Pope was known for the wit and _____ of his poetry. *(truculent)* 9. truculence

10. When Donald is in an _____ mood, it's best to stay out of his way. *(irascible)* 10. irascible

NAME ______________________________ DATE ____________

READING COMPREHENSION

Each numbered sentence in the following passage contains an italicized vocabulary word or related form. After you read the passage, you will complete an exercise.

PANCHO GONZALES: TEMPERAMENTAL TENNIS CHAMPION

Lawn tennis, which was patented in 1873, began as a genteel game for young ladies and gentlemen. Played with decorum and ritualized courtesy by relatively small numbers of people, it was the sport of the wealthy, who belonged to clubs or owned estates with lawns large enough to accommodate courts. (1) Since its beginnings as a ***convivial*** game that was played in a leisurely manner, tennis has evolved into a sport of power, agility, and speed. (2) It has grown from a ***felicitous*** social event to a pressure-filled business and profession.

In the 1980s, perhaps in response to the competition for the attention of restless audiences, promoters, and equipment sponsors, players became increasingly temperamental. (3) For example, the ***querulous*** John McEnroe enraged fans and judges alike with his frequent outbursts, and the behavior of Ilie Nastase earned him the nickname of Nasty Nastase. (4) in comparison, the actions of a player like Ivan Lendl seemed relatively ***placid.*** Although these moody players were in the minority, they changed the tone of the game.

Richard Alonzo Gonzales (b. 1928), nicknamed Pancho by a fellow player and known by that name ever since, was one of the first players whose personality and unique style attracted the attention of the crowd. From the time that he received his first racket at the age of twelve, Pancho has been dedicated to the sport. (5) ***Truculent*** and volatile, he often played his most breathtaking tennis after losing his temper.

Untrained and uncoached, Gonzales observed good players and imitated their moves, practicing their best shots and inventing some of his own. He developed a "killer instinct," finding and attacking his opponents' weaknesses. By the age of fifteen, he was the top-ranked player in his age group in southern California.

Among Gonzales's talents was his ability to serve a tennis ball at over 112 miles per hour. His stamina and his ability to react quickly to another player's strategies made him an expert retriever. Most importantly, Gonzales had the competitive edge that contributed to his many victories. (6) As he often noted ***sardonically,*** he *had* to win. Banned from tournament play in 1944 because of frequent absences from school, he dropped out soon after. Pancho Gonzales believed that he could do nothing but play tennis.

Gonzales won the men's singles title at Forest Hills in 1948 and 1949 and was a member of the U.S. Davis Cup team that defeated Australia. Turning professional at the age of twenty-one, he went on to win eight championship titles.

Perhaps the only "'flaw" in Gonzales's versatile, solid tennis game was his short temper. (7) However, as some of his competitors have pointed out, the ***irascible*** Pancho could use his temper to advantage. His outbursts gave him a surge of power.

(8) One hundred years ago, it would have been unthinkable for a tennis player to be as ***surly*** or as excitable as Pancho Gonzales was. (9) In fact, Major Wingfield, the British officer who sought to standardize the rules of tennis, envisioned the game as having an almost ***unctuous*** air of politeness and propriety.

As tennis has grown, however, players like Pancho Gonzales, in their bids for money and media coverage, have brought emotion and intensity to the game. Gonzales's mental attitude and disposition, as well as his strength and grace, aided him in developing a nearly unbeatable game. (10) His talent and disposition also earned him a longstanding reputation as one of the sport's most ***ebullient,*** and most respected, players.

READING COMPREHENSION EXERCISE

Each of the following statements corresponds to a numbered sentence in the passage. Each statement contains a blank and is followed by four answer choices. Decide which choice fits best in the blank. The word or phrase that you choose must express roughly the same meaning as the italicized word in the passage. Write the letter of your choice on the answer line.

1. Tennis began as a _____ game that was played in a leisurely manner. 1. d
   a. convenient b. satisfying c. robust d. sociable

2. It has grown from a _____ social event to a pressure-filled profession. 2. a
   a. pleasurable b. snobbish c. tolerant d. commanding

3. The _____ John McEnroe enraged fans and judges alike. 3. c
   a. inept b. proper c. complaining d. inconsistent

4. The actions of a player like Ivan Lendl were considered _____ in comparison with the antics of others. 4. a
   a. composed b. deceptive c. modest d. cautious

5. Pancho Gonzales was a(n) _____, volatile player. 5. b
   a. indifferent b. fierce c. reckless d. zealous

6. Gonzales often noted _____ that he *had* to win. 6. d
   a. shyly b. gleefully c. anxiously d. derisively

7. The _____ Pancho could use his temper to advantage. 7. c
   a. unbeatable b. inspired c. easily angered d. easily pacified

8. One hundred years ago it would have been unthinkable for a player to be as _____ as Gonzales. 8. a
   a. sullenly ill-humored
   b. quickly outraged
   c. competitive
   d. animated

9. According to Major Wingfield, the game should have an almost _____ air of politeness. 9. d
   a. uncomfortable
   b. intolerable
   c. inoffensively determined
   d. insincerely earnest

10. Gonzales has a long-standing reputation as one of the sport's most _____ players. 10. a
    a. exuberant b. expensive c. famous d. intriguing

WRITING ASSIGNMENT

In English class you have been discussing character development and change in literature. Choose a fictional character from a book, movie, or television program who begins as an agreeable or disagreeable person and then, because of a particular situation, undergoes some sort of change. Write a composition in which you show how the character is plausibly motivated, believable, and realistic. Use at least five of the words from this lesson in your composition and underline each one.

LESSON 18 WILLINGNESS AND UNWILLINGNESS 18

There is nothing so easy but that it becomes difficult when you do it reluctantly. Terence (Roman author, 190?–59 B.C.)

Where the willingness is great, the difficulties cannot be great. Niccolò Machiavelli

Although separated by many centuries, both Terence and Machiavelli seem to agree that a task accepted readily is easier to bear than one performed grudgingly. You have probably experienced this yourself—your own positive or negative attitude influences the way in which you do something. The words in this lesson will help you to express the willing and unwilling inclinations that you experience and encounter.

WORD LIST

audacious
contumacy
dour
éclat
indefatigable
irresolute
obdurate
obsequious
pertinacity
stoic

DEFINITIONS

After you have studied the definitions and example for each vocabulary word, write the word on the line to the right.

1. **audacious** (ô-dā'shəs) *adjective* **a.** Fearlessly daring; bold. **b.** Unrestrained by what is considered acceptable or appropriate; insolent. (From the Latin word *audere,* meaning "to dare") 1. ________________

Related Words **audaciously** *adverb;* **audacity** *noun*
Example For his *audacious* expeditions to the Antarctic and his explorations of the polar frontier, Admiral Richard Byrd is considered a national hero.

2. **contumacy** (kŏn'to͞o-mə-sē, kŏn'tyo͞o-mə-sē) *noun* Obstinate or contemptuous resistance to authority; stubborn rebelliousness; insubordination. (From the Latin word *contumax,* meaning "insolent") 2. ________________

Related Words **contumacious** *adjective;* **contumaciously** *adverb*
Example There is nothing that irritates Ms. Garrison more than disrespect and *contumacy.*

3. **dour** (do͝or, dour) *adjective* **a.** Marked by stubborn sternness or harshness; forbidding. **b.** Silently ill-humored; glum. (From the Latin word *durus,* meaning "hard") 3. ________________

Example In spite of countless questions from reporters, the senator maintained a *dour* silence.

4. **éclat** (ā-klä', ā'klä') *noun* **a.** Great brilliance, as of performance or achievement. **b.** Conspicuous success. **c.** Great acclamation or applause. (From the Old French word *esclater,* meaning "to burst") 4. ________________

Example The pianist performed the difficult concerto with rare *éclat.*

5. **indefatigable** (ĭn′dĭ-făt′ĭ-gə-bəl) *adjective* Incapable of being fatigued; tireless. (From the Latin *in-*, meaning "not," *de-*, meaning "thoroughly," and *fatigare*, meaning, "to weary") 5. ________________

Related Words **indefatigability** *noun;* **indefatigably** *adverb*
Example Because of the *indefatigable* and precise efforts of Noah Webster, his dictionary, first published in 1828, has never gone out of print.

6. **irresolute** (ĭ-rĕz′ə-lo͞ot′) *adjective* Undecided or uncertain as to action or procedure; vacillating. 6. ________________

Related Words **irresolutely** *adverb;* **irresolution** *noun*
Example After lengthy debate, the *irresolute* town council postponed further discussion about the shopping center until the next meeting.

7. **obdurate** (ŏb′do͝o-rĭt, ŏb′dyo͞o-rĭt) *adjective* **a.** Not giving in to persuasion; inflexible. **b.** Hardened against feeling; hardhearted. **c.** Hardened in wrongdoing or wickedness. (From the Latin *ob-*, an intensive prefix, and *durare*, meaning "to harden") 7. ________________

Related Words **obduracy** *noun;* **obdurately** *adverb*
Example We were disappointed by Helen's *obdurate* refusal to admit her mistake.

8. **obsequious** (ŏb-sē′kwē-əs, əb-sē′kwē-əs) *adjective* Excessively eager to serve, obey, or ingratiate oneself; fawning. (From the Latin *ob-*, meaning "to," and *sequi*, meaning "to follow") 8. ________________

Related Words **obsequiously** *adverb;* **obsequiousness** *noun*
Example The *obsequious* attention of the salesperson annoyed Mr. Sanchez, who preferred to browse through the merchandise by himself.

9. **pertinacity** (pûr′tn-ăs′ĭ-tē) *noun* **a.** The quality or state of holding firmly to a purpose, belief, or opinion. **b.** Stubborn persistence. (From the Latin *per-*, an intensive prefix, and *tenere*, meaning "to hold") 9. ________________

Related Words **pertinacious** *adjective;* **pertinaciously** *adverb*
Example Conservationists need *pertinacity* in order to re-educate those who see our natural resources as expendable.

10. **stoic** (stō′ĭk) *adjective* Seemingly indifferent to or unaffected by pleasure or pain; impassive. *noun* **a.** A stoic person. **b. Stoic** A member of a Greek school of philosophy, founded by Zeno about 308 B.C., holding that human beings should calmly accept all occurrences as the unavoidable result of fate. (From the Greek word *stoa*, meaning "porch" or "portico") 10. ________________

Related Word **stoicism** *noun*
Example Her *stoic* acceptance of misfortune served as an inspiration to all who knew her.

NAME ______________________ DATE __________

EXERCISE 1 WRITING CORRECT WORDS

On the answer line, write the word from the vocabulary list that fits each definition.

1. Not giving in to persuasion; inflexible; hardened against feeling — 1. **obdurate**
2. Marked by stubborn sternness or harshness; silently ill-humored — 2. **dour**
3. Fearlessly daring; bold; unrestrained by what is considered acceptable or appropriate — 3. **audacious**
4. The quality or state of holding firmly to a purpose, belief, or opinion; stubborn persistence — 4. **pertinacity**
5. Obstinate or contemptuous resistance to authority; stubborn rebelliousness — 5. **contumacy**
6. Seemingly indifferent to or unaffected by pleasure or pain; impassive — 6. **stoic**
7. Incapable of being fatigued; tireless — 7. **indefatigable**
8. Great brilliance, as of performance or achievement; conspicuous success — 8. **éclat**
9. Excessively eager to serve, obey, or ingratiate oneself; fawning — 9. **obsequious**
10. Undecided or uncertain as to action or procedure; vacillating — 10. **irresolute**

EXERCISE 2 USING WORDS CORRECTLY

Decide whether the italicized vocabulary word has been used correctly in the sentence. On the answer line, write *Correct* for correct use and *Incorrect* for incorrect use.

1. Kerry would not be so *indefatigable* if he got a reasonable amount of sleep. — 1. **Incorrect**
2. The crowd applauded the *audacious* feats of the tightrope walker. — 2. **Correct**
3. Grace emerged from the icy lake, attempting to appear *stoic* but unable to control her shivering. — 3. **Correct**
4. Roger found the *contumacy* of his work schedule repetitive but reassuring. — 4. **Incorrect**
5. People who lack self-confidence may welcome *obsequious* flattery. — 5. **Correct**
6. The Felizes welcomed their guests with warm smiles and *dour* comments. — 6. **Incorrect**
7. Terriers, originally bred for hunting animals that live in burrows, are well known for their *pertinacity.* — 7. **Correct**
8. The hikers stood at the fork in the trail, *irresolute* about which branch would take them to the waterfall. — 8. **Correct**
9. The fifteen-year-old chess champion defeated her older opponent with *éclat.* — 9. **Correct**
10. "The answer to your question is *obdurate,*" snapped the detective. — 10. **Incorrect**

EXERCISE 3 IDENTIFYING SYNONYMS AND ANTONYMS

Decide which word has the meaning that is the same as (a synonym) or opposite to (an antonym) that of the capitalized vocabulary word. Write the letter of your choice on the answer line.

1. INDEFATIGABLE (synonym): — 1. **c**
   a. turbulent **b.** apparent **c.** tireless **d.** modest

2. AUDACIOUS (antonym):
a. meek b. memorable c. tedious d. customary

2. a

3. PERTINACITY (synonym):
a. restraint b. reprieve c. composure d. perseverance

3. d

4. STOIC (antonym):
a. offensive b. dubious c. emotional d. primary

4. c

5. DOUR (synonym):
a. severe b. casual c. distinguished d. marginal

5. a

6. ÉCLAT (antonym):
a. nonchalance b. failure c. restoration d. glorification

6. b

7. IRRESOLUTE (synonym):
a. imperative b. congenial c. pretentious d. vacillating

7. d

8. CONTUMACY (antonym):
a. folly b. anxiety c. cooperativeness d. resemblance

8. c

9. OBSEQUIOUS (synonym):
a. ingratiating b. contrary c. noxious d. tyrannical

9. a

10. OBDURATE (antonym):
a. buoyant b. contradictory c. menacing d. agreeable

10. d

EXERCISE 4 USING DIFFERENT FORMS OF WORDS

Decide which form of the vocabulary word in parentheses best completes the sentence. The form given may be correct. Write your answer on the answer line.

1. The _____ of the author's novel earned her well-deserved praise. *(éclat)* 1. éclat
2. The owner of the store tried to avoid his _____ creditors. *(pertinacity)* 2. pertinacious
3. Several members of the election committee _____ questioned the motive behind a major corporation's campaign contribution. *(audacious)* 3. audaciously
4. "Let me take your hat and coat, Madame," said the butler _____. *(obsequious)* 4. obsequiously
5. Tanya's _____ about her vacation plans frustrated her friend, who was waiting impatiently for Tanya to decide. *(irresolute)* 5. irresolution
6. The out-of-state visitors were horrified at the _____ disregard of the speed limit. *(contumacy)* 6. contumacious
7. The _____ of the defendant's testimony influenced the jury negatively. *(obdurate)* 7. obduracy
8. The _____ active toddler was difficult to keep up with. *(indefatigable)* 8. indefatigably
9. In spite of our efforts to be pleasant, our _____ neighbor is often irritable and unfriendly. *(dour)* 9. dour
10. With _____ patience, Melissa listened to her brother rehearse his speech ten times a day. *(stoic)* 10. stoic

NAME ______________________________ DATE ____________

READING COMPREHENSION

Each numbered sentence in the following passage contains an italicized vocabulary word or related form. After you read the passage, you will complete an exercise.

JENNY LIND: THE SWEDISH NIGHTINGALE

Jenny Lind (1820–1887) was probably the most famous and adored personality of the nineteenth century. (1) Known as much for her kindness and charity as for the ***éclat*** of her singing, Jenny Lind inspired a mania throughout Europe and the United States. Never before had an artist so appealed to the public imagination or exerted such an impact on society.

(2) Because her parents could not afford to take care of her, Jenny was raised by her ***dour*** grandmother and a succession of foster parents in Stockholm, Sweden. Her only escape from the loneliness of her childhood was in music. By the age of four, Jenny claimed to have "felt music in my fingers"; she could re-create by ear any melody she heard.

One day, as she was playing the piano and singing, the maid of a dancer at the Royal Opera House heard her. At this time in Sweden, members of the theater were expected to help recruit new talent for the Royal Opera House School, where gifted children were trained. When the maid reported the wonder of the eight-year-old's voice, the dancer met with Jenny's parents and grandmother to persuade them to permit Jenny to enter the school. (3) The family remained ***obdurately*** opposed to the idea for two years, however. (4) They felt that theatrical performers were barely respectable, and were convinced that a career in the theater was much too ***audacious*** for Jenny. Finally, when Jenny was ten years old, her family was persuaded that her voice was a gift that should be shared, and she was admitted to the school.

(5) Jenny proved to be a receptive, ***pertinacious*** pupil. Having never indulged in children's games, she found her lessons in dancing, acting, music, elocution, and French to be delightful play. (6) Her fine intelligence and ***indefatigability*** enabled her to perform almost miraculous feats of learning words and music while studying a role and perfecting a performance. Between 1831 and 1838 Jenny appeared in a variety of musical performances. She was well received by audiences and critics both for her pure, lilting voice and for her mastery of the other dramatic arts.

In 1841, as a result of overwork, Jenny began to notice a roughening of her voice. Advised to go to Paris to see Manuel García, the greatest voice teacher in the world at that time, she was horrified to be told that her voice had been ruined. (7) Jenny, however, was ***contumacious*** and refused to give up; promising total silence for six weeks, she asked García to listen to her again after that period. Her voice was smoother and stronger after the rest, and García agreed to teach her.

After a year's work in Paris, Jenny Lind returned to Stockholm and tumultuous acclaim. The sheer magnetism of her performances attracted huge crowds, and she was welcomed into Sweden's highest social circles. (8) Shy in company and hating ***obsequious*** attention by publicity seekers, she was unspoiled by success. She began contributing most of her income to a variety of charities and would sing outside the theater for anyone to whom singing gave special pleasure.

Before long, opera managers and concert promoters from all over the world sought out Jenny Lind to perform in their countries. (9) She was ***irresolute*** about signing contracts; her insecurity made her feel unworthy of attention, and she feared that aspiring to more renown was an invitation to failure. (10) Nevertheless, she fought stage fright with ***stoic*** fortitude and performed throughout Europe and the British Isles as well as the United States. A Jenny Lind mania soon arose. Souvenirs with her picture were created, and children and animals were named for her. On three different occasions in England, the House of Commons had to suspend its sessions because so many of its members were attending her concerts.

In 1849 Jenny Lind retired from opera. Even though she always refused any role that she considered degrading, she came to see the theater as increasingly frivolous. She devoted the remaining years of her career to concerts and benefit performances for scholarship funds and charities. Although she commanded high ticket prices and attracted massive crowds, she was never too busy or too important to share the gift of her voice with those who were less fortunate.

READING COMPREHENSION EXERCISE

Each of the following statements corresponds to a numbered sentence in the passage. Each statement contains a blank and is followed by four answer choices. Decide which choice fits best in the blank. The word that you choose must express roughly the same meaning as the italicized word in the passage. Write the letter of your choice on the answer line.

1. Jenny Lind was known for the _____ of her singing. 1. d
   a. nature b. range c. mildness d. brilliance

2. Jenny was raised by her _____ grandmother and foster parents. 2. b
   a. hardy b. forbidding c. animated d. impartial

3. Her family was _____ opposed to Jenny's entering the theater school. 3. a
   a. inflexibly b. never c. ultimately d. somewhat

4. They considered a career in the theater much too _____. 4. b
   a. sinful b. bold c. merciless d. unfashionable

5. Jenny was a _____ pupil. 5. c
   a. sensitive b. restless c. persistent d. perfect

6. Her _____ enabled her to perform almost miraculous feats of learning words and music. 6. a
   a. tirelessness b. forcefulness c. incentive d. independence

7. Jenny was _____ and refused to give up. 7. d
   a. indignant b. apathetic c. offended d. obstinate

8. Jenny hated _____ attention by publicity seekers. 8. c
   a. superfluous b. devious c. fawning d. undignified

9. She was _____ about signing contracts. 9. b
   a. unwise b. undecided c. clever d. lax

10. She fought stage fright with _____ fortitude. 10. c
    a. insistent b. infinite c. impassive d. lasting

WRITING ASSIGNMENT

Suppose that you have a managerial job in which one of your responsibilities is to supervise the work performance of a small staff. Write a brief report in which you explain how one person's willing or unwilling attitude affects the quality of his or her work. Use at least five of the words from this lesson in your report; underline each one.

VOCABULARY ENRIGHMENT

The word *stoic* comes from the Greek word *stoa,* meaning "porch" or "portico." The Stoa Poikilē was an open-air structure located in the marketplace of Athens. Here the philosopher Zeno taught the basic principles of his theory. Stoicism was a philosophy that urged calm acceptance of life. Zeno held that the world is governed by fate and cannot be changed. Therefore, the best that human beings can do is to accept this fate without reaction. Today the word *stoic* has come to mean "unaffected by pleasure or pain."

Activity Many other English words derive from Greek philosophy. Look up the following words in a dictionary and write the origin, philosophical definition, and current meaning of each.

1. cynic 2. epicurean 3. peripatetic 4. platonic 5. skeptic

The **Test** for Lessons 16, 17, and 18 is on page T20.

NAME ________________ DATE ________

READING SKILLS

THE PREFIXES *BI-* AND *SEMI-*

A **prefix** is a letter or group of letters that is added to the beginning of a root to change its meaning. (A **root** is the part of a word containing its basic meaning. A root can be a complete word.) The prefixes *bi-* and *semi-* form such words as *biped, bimonthly, semicircle,* and *semiskilled. Bi-* and *semi-* add meanings to English or Latin roots as shown in the table that follows.

Prefix Meaning	Root Word	Word	Word Definition
bi: two, occurring at intervals of two	*pes,* "foot"	biped	an animal with two feet
or twice during	month	bimonthly	every two months
semi: half; partial	circle	semicircle	half circle
	skill	semiskilled	partially skilled

Be aware that *bimonthly* and *biweekly* are special cases. Their preferred meanings are "every two months" and "every two weeks." However, the words are sometimes used to mean "twice a month" and "twice a week"—the same as *semimonthly* and *semiweekly.*

A knowledge of prefixes and roots can help you determine the meaning of unfamiliar words. Use the following procedure to analyze the meaning of words that begin with *bi-* or *semi-* or with some other prefix.

PROCEDURE

1. *Substitute the prefix and root definitions for the prefix and root.* For example, the adjective *bicameral* is formed from the prefix *bi-*, meaning "two," and the Latin root word *camera,* meaning "chamber."

2. *Think of a possible definition of the entire word.* "Having two chambers" is a reasonable definition.

3. *If the word appears in a sentence, use the context to help you develop the possible definition.* Suppose that you came across the word *bicameral* in the sentence "Forty-nine out of the fifty states of the Union have bicameral legislatures." The "two chambers" must refer to the division of a state legislature into a house of representatives and a senate.

4. *Check your definition of the word in a dictionary.* A dictionary definition of *bicameral* is "composed of two legislative chambers or branches."

EXERCISE USING THE PREFIXES *BI-* AND *SEMI-*

Each sentence in this exercise contains an italicized word beginning with *bi-* or *semi-*. When appropriate, the root word and its meaning are given in parentheses after the sentence. *Step 1:* Taking the context into consideration, write your own definition of the word. *Step 2:* Write the dictionary definition of the word. *Step 3:* Write a sentence of your own in which you use the word correctly.

1. The Activities Committee holds its general meeting *semiannually.*

   Your Definition **Every half year**

   Dictionary Definition **Happening or issued twice a year**

   Sentence **The school literary magazine is published semiannually.**

2. The United States celebrated its *bicentennial* in 1976. (Root word: *centum,* "hundred")

   Your Definition **Two-hundredth anniversary**

   Dictionary Definition **A 200th anniversary or its celebration**

   Sentence **Our city will observe its bicentennial in 2005 with a week-long festival.**

3. The jeweler surrounded the diamond with *semiprecious* stones.

   Your Definition **Partially precious**

   Dictionary Definition **Of less value than a precious stone**

   Sentence **On a geology field trip, Kip found eight semiprecious stones.**

4. The *bilingual* students are able to converse in both English and Spanish. (Root word: *lingua,* "language")

   Your Definition **Knowing two languages**

   Dictionary Definition **Able to speak two languages with equal skill**

   Sentence **Many Canadians are bilingual, speaking both French and English.**

5. At eighty-five my great uncle is *semiretired* and has no plans to stop working.

   Your Definition **Partially retired**

   Dictionary Definition **Working on a part-time basis only**

   Sentence **Of the eight people in the camera club, six are semiretired and two are retired.**

6. The *semiaquatic* catfish is fond of climbing trees. (Root word: *aqua,* "water")

   Your Definition **Living partially in water and partially on land**

   Dictionary Definition **Adapted for living or growing in or near water; not entirely aquatic.**

   Sentence **The alligator is well suited to its semiaquatic life in swampy areas.**

7. The snowstorms that came every other year were *biennial* events. (Root word: *annus,* "year")

   Your Definition **Occurring at intervals of every two years**

   Dictionary Definition **Happening every second year**

   Sentence **Because the festival was biennial, we could not attend each year.**

8. People from both sides joined a *bipartisan* group to investigate the disaster.

   Your Definition **From two parties**

   Dictionary Definition **Consisting of or supported by members of two political parties**

   Sentence **The bipartisan committee members forgot their political differences and worked together.**

LESSON 19 THE ROOTS *-DIC-* AND *-LOCU-*

19

The Latin root *-dic-* and its alternate form *-dict-* come from the word *dicere,* meaning "to say." The Latin root *-locu-* and its alternate form *-loq-* come from the word *loqui,* meaning "to speak." Many English words are derived from these two roots. For example, if you *predict* that something will occur, you state or tell about it in advance. If you *contradict* someone, you express the opposite of what that person has said. An *eloquent* speaker is one who is persuasive, fluent, and graceful in expression. *Ventriloquism* is a method of producing vocal sounds so that they seem to originate from a source other than the speaker. In this lesson you will learn other words that include the meaning of speaking or saying.

WORD LIST

benediction
colloquium
edict
elocution
grandiloquence
indict
interdict
interlocutor
loquacious
soliloquy

DEFINITIONS

After you have studied the definitions and example for each vocabulary word, write the word on the line to the right.

1. **benediction** (bĕn′ĭ-dĭk′shən) *noun* **a.** An invocation of divine blessing, usually at the end of a religious service. **b.** A blessing; expression of good wishes. (From the Latin words *bene,* meaning "well," and *dicere,* meaning "to say")

   Example At the end of the banquet, a member of the clergy gave a *benediction.*

1. ________________

2. **colloquium** (kə-lō′kwē-əm) *noun* **a.** An academic seminar on a broad field of study, usually led by a different lecturer at each meeting; conference. **b.** An informal meeting for the exchange of views. (From the Latin *com-,* meaning "together," and *loqui,* meaning "to speak")

   Related Words **colloquial** *adjective;* **colloquy** *noun*
   Example A week-long *colloquium* for senior citizens was held at our branch of the state university.

2. ________________

USAGE NOTE: Either *colloquiums* or *colloquia* is correct as the plural form of this word.

3. **edict** (ē′dĭkt) *noun* **a.** A formal proclamation, command, or decree. **b.** A decree or proclamation issued by an authority and having the force of law. (From the Latin *ex-,* meaning "out," and *dicere*)

   Example The head of the new government issued an *edict* forbidding citizens to hold public meetings.

3. ________________

4. **elocution** (ĕl′ə-kyōō′shən) *noun* **a.** The art of public speaking, emphasizing gesture, vocal production, and delivery. **b.** Style or manner, especially of public speaking. (From the Latin *ex-,* meaning "out," and *loqui*)

   Example When the class studied *elocution,* Rachel presented Keats's "Ode on a Grecian Urn."

4. ________________

5. **grandiloquence** (grăn-dĭl'ə-kwəns) *noun* Pompous or bombastic speech or expression. (From the Latin words *grandis,* meaning "exalted" or "lofty," and *loqui*)

Related Words **grandiloquent** *adjective;* **grandiloquently** *adverb*
Example The *grandiloquence* of the mayor's speech at the groundbreaking ceremony for the new town library embarrassed the townspeople.

5. ________
USAGE NOTE: Do not confuse the spelling and meaning of *grandiloquence* with that of *eloquence.*

6. **indict** (ĭn-dīt') *trans. verb* **a.** To accuse of a crime or other offense; charge. **b.** To make a formal accusation against by the findings of a grand jury. **c.** To attack or condemn. (From the Latin word *indicere,* meaning "to proclaim")

Related Words **indictable** *adjective;* **indictment** *noun*
Example The government prosecutor *indicted* an important official for the misuse of public funds.

6. ________
USAGE NOTE: Notice the unusual pronunciation of this word. The last syllable rhymes with *write.*

7. **interdict** (ĭn'tər-dĭkt') *trans. verb* To prohibit or forbid; place under a legal or ecclesiastical sanction. (From the Latin *inter-,* meaning "between," and *dicere*)

Related Word **interdiction** *noun*
Example Laws have *interdicted* advertising of certain products on television.

7. ________
USAGE NOTE: Unlike *indict,* this word is pronounced the way it is spelled.

8. **interlocutor** (ĭn'tər-lŏk'yə-tər) *noun* Someone who takes part in a conversation. (From the Latin *inter-,* meaning "between" and *loqui*)

Example Holmes chuckled at his *interlocutor's* observation that the detective's deductions were "extraordinary."

8. ________

9. **loquacious** (lō-kwā'shəs) *adjective* Very talkative; garrulous. (From the Latin word *loqui*)

Related Words **loquaciously** *adverb;* **loquaciousness** *noun*
Example Since Linda was so *loquacious,* people always heard her before they saw her.

9. ________

10. **soliloquy** (sə-lĭl'ə-kwē) *noun* **a.** A literary or dramatic form of discourse in which a character reveals his or her thoughts in the form of a monologue without addressing a listener. **b.** The act of speaking to oneself. (From the Latin words *solus,* meaning "alone," and *loqui*)

Example "To be or not to be; that is the question" is the beginning of one of the famous *soliloquies* from Shakespeare's *Hamlet.*

10. ________
MEMORY CUE: A *soliloquy* is a kind of spoken *solo.*

NAME ______________________ DATE __________

EXERCISE 1 WRITING CORRECT WORDS

On the answer line, write the word from the vocabulary list that fits each definition.

1. An academic seminar on a broad field of study: conference; informal meeting for an exchange of views — 1. colloquium
2. An invocation of divine blessing, usually at the end of a religious service; blessing; expression of good wishes — 2. benediction
3. Pompous or bombastic speech or expression — 3. grandiloquence
4. A literary or dramatic form of discourse in which a character reveals thoughts in the form of a monologue without addressing a listener — 4. soliloquy
5. The art of public speaking, emphasizing gesture, vocal production, and delivery; style or manner — 5. elocution
6. One who takes part in a conversation — 6. interlocutor
7. Very talkative; garrulous — 7. loquacious
8. To prohibit or forbid; place under a legal or ecclesiastical sanction — 8. interdict
9. A formal proclamation, command, or decree; a decree or proclamation issued by an authority and having the force of law — 9. edict
10. To accuse of a crime or other offense; make a formal accusation against by the findings of a grand jury — 10. indict

EXERCISE 2 USING WORDS CORRECTLY

Decide whether the italicized vocabulary word has been used correctly in the sentence. On the answer line, write *Correct* for correct use and *Incorrect* for incorrect use.

1. During the heated *soliloquy* among four people, Lucy tried to interject irrelevant observations. — 1. Incorrect
2. Before the baron disappeared, he was seen conversing with a strange woman; Scotland Yard had to find this mysterious *interlocutor.* — 2. Correct
3. Julio and Mimeiko interrupted their private *colloquium* long enough to say good-by to Marianne. — 3. Incorrect
4. "Only three people had the correct *elocution* to this problem," said Mr. Stickler, "and it wasn't very difficult." — 4. Incorrect
5. After Janet's successful operation, her family and friends offered a *benediction.* — 5. Correct
6. So as not to give advance warning, the authorities kept secret the convening of the grand jury until they were ready to *indict* the suspects. — 6. Correct
7. Uncle Ned has always been *loquacious,* speaking only when spoken to and then answering briefly. — 7. Incorrect
8. Many mass transit systems now *interdict* the playing of radios without earphones. — 8. Correct
9. The dictator issued an *edict* making it illegal to whistle in public. — 9. Correct
10. The *grandiloquence* of Harold's everyday speech made people consider him a snob. — 10. Correct

EXERCISE 3 CHOOSING THE BEST WORD

Decide which vocabulary word or related form best completes the sentence, and write the letter of your choice on the answer line.

1. Before the invention of printing, handwritten royal _____ were often posted in central locations. 1. d
   a. interlocutors b. soliloquies c. colloquiums d. edicts

2. The international _____ on maritime law discussed numerous issues about fishing rights and protected waters. 2. b
   a. grandiloquence b. colloquium c. benediction d. loquaciousness

3. Marlene's sophisticated _____ allows her to manipulate an audience effectively. 3. a
   a. elocution b. edict c. colloquium d. indictment

4. _____ moviegoers are inconsiderate of other members of the audience who are trying to watch a film. 4. d
   a. Colloquial b. Grandiloquent c. Indictable d. Loquacious

5. After he graduated from college, Harris departed on a journey around the world with his parents' _____. 5. c
   a. grandiloquence b. soliloquy c. benediction d. interlocutor

6. Paul and Judy were the primary _____; the other members of the committee contributed very little. 6. b
   a. indictments b. interlocutors c. colloquies d. edicts

7. Leslie did not realize that in Shakespeare's *As You Like It* Jacques's famous _____ about the seven ages of man is not heard by the other characters. 7. a
   a. soliloquy b. benediction c. elocution d. interdiction

8. At the awards ceremony, the winner's speech was a(n) _____ and boastful collection of statements about his accomplishments. 8. c
   a. indictable b. colloquial c. grandiloquent d. benediction

9. During the riots the temporary government issued _____ against public gatherings and established a curfew for all citizens. 9. b
   a. colloquiums b. interdictions c. soliloquies d. interlocutors

10. The newspaper editorial was a(n) _____ of mounting malpractice insurance rates. 10. d
    a. grandiloquence b. benediction c. elocution d. indictment

EXERCISE 4 USING DIFFERENT FORMS OF WORDS

Decide which form of the vocabulary word in parentheses best completes the sentence. The form given may be correct. Write your answer on the answer line.

1. Grand juries investigating the Watergate incident in the early 1970s _____ several top administration officials. *(indict)* 1. **indicted**

2. After the banquet the ambassador spoke _____ about the merits of his country. *(grandiloquence)* 2. **grandiloquently**

3. According to most composition textbooks, _____ expressions have no place in formal writing. *(colloquium)* 3. **colloquial**

4. In Jane Austen's *Pride and Prejudice,* Elizabeth Bennet initially perceives Mr. Darcy as an arrogant, disdainful _____. *(interlocutor)* 4. **interlocutor**

5. Alejandro's boss issues _____ just as a czar or dictator would. *(edict)* 5. **edicts**

6. The comedian studied _____ in order to improve his timing and voice control. *(elocution)* 6. **elocution**

NAME ______________________ DATE __________

7. Peggy's _____ earned her the dubious distinction in the school yearbook of being named the "most talkative." *(loquacious)* 7. loquaciousness

8. Following the _____ the bride and bridegroom slowly made their way up the aisle. *(benediction)* 8. benediction

9. Trying to achieve a positive attitude, Cindy delivered a _____ to her mirror. *(soliloquy)* 9. soliloquy

10. In India there is an _____ against killing cattle, which are considered sacred. *(interdict)* 10. interdiction

READING COMPREHENSION

Each numbered sentence in the following passage contains an italicized vocabulary word or related form. After you read the passage, you will complete an exercise.

LINCOLN'S GETTYSBURG ADDRESS

The Battle of Gettysburg was an important but costly turning point in the Civil War. When the three-day battle was over, more than seven thousand Union and Confederate soldiers were buried in temporary graves near where they had fallen. Four months later a national commission was formed to purchase land for a permanent military cemetery and to create an appropriate memorial. On November 19, 1863, the National Soldiers' Cemetery in Gettysburg, Pennsylvania, was dedicated. President Abraham Lincoln, Cabinet members, governors of the northern states, and other civil and military officials joined thousands of private citizens for the commemorative ceremonies.

Edward Everett, a former senator and governor of Massachusetts and one-time president of Harvard, was the principal speaker. (1) Renowned for his skillful ***elocution,*** Everett spoke for two hours. (2) As if lecturing at a scholarly ***colloquium,*** he traced the roots of the war and offered many classical illusions and historical parallels. (3) His ***grandiloquent*** oration was intended both to honor the memory of the dead soldiers and to stir his audience.

(4) President Lincoln's brief speech of dedication contrasted sharply with Everett's ***loquaciousness.*** (5) In less than five minutes, the president summarized the purpose of the war and issued what amounted to an ***edict*** to those who remained alive. He reminded his listeners of the founding principle of the nation—equality for all—and pointed out that it was not enough simply to recognize the nobility of this cause or to honor those who died for it. Rather, by renewing their own dedication to the cause of liberty, Americans must reunite the nation.

The audience received the president's speech without enthusiasm and with little applause. (6) Eleven days earlier, when shown a draft of Everett's speech, Lincoln had told an ***interlocutor,*** a newspaper reporter, that his own remarks would be "short, short, short." The ten graceful sentences of the Gettysburg Address were out of keeping with the full-blown oratory of the time. (7) Unfriendly journalists ***indicted*** the speech as "dishwatery," "ludicrous," "silly," and even in "bad taste." Lincoln himself thought that his speech had been a failure.

Only gradually did the true eloquence and grandeur of the address impress the American public and the world. (8) To some who read the speech, it seemed almost a ***benediction*** following a terrible battle. Even Edward Everett later wrote to Lincoln: "I should be glad if I could flatter myself that I came as near to the central idea of the occasion in two hours as you did in two minutes."

With the passage of time, Lincoln's speech has come to be considered—in the words of the American poet Carl Sandburg—"among the supreme utterances of democratic peoples of the world." (9) Its language is considered to equal that of the ***soliloquies*** of William Shakespeare or the poetry of William Wordsworth. Lincoln's belief that his audience would soon forget his speech proved to be false. (10) Today the world still remembers the closing words that Lincoln uttered almost as an ***interdiction:*** "that we here highly resolve that these dead shall not have died in vain—that this nation, under God, shall have a new birth of freedom—and that government of the people, by the people, for the people, shall not perish from the earth." Abraham Lincoln's simple, noble words continue to stir the deepest feelings.

READING COMPREHENSION EXERCISE

Each of the following statements corresponds to a numbered sentence in the passage. Each statement contains a blank and is followed by four answer choices Decide which choice fits best in the blank. The word or phrase that you choose must express roughly the same meaning as the italicized word in the passage. Write the letter of your choice on the answer line.

1. Edward Everett was renowned for his skillful ____.
   a. historical sense b. public speaking c. politics d. poetry writing
   1. b

2. He spoke as if lecturing at a scholarly ____.
   a. university b. association c. community d. seminar
   2. d

3. His ____ oration was calculated to honor the memory of the dead soldiers.
   a. pompous b. intellectual c. impressive d. valuable
   3. a

4. Lincoln's short speech contrasted with the ____ of Everett.
   a. delivery b. garrulousness c. eloquence d. fervor
   4. b

5. The president gave a(n) ____ to those who were still alive.
   a. familiar quotation c. command
   b. inspirational thought d. rule
   5. c

6. Lincoln had told ____ that his remarks would be brief.
   a. a Cabinet member c. a longtime opponent
   b. an unreceptive audience d. someone taking part in a conversation
   6. d

7. Some journalists ____ the president's speech.
   a. attacked b. praised c. ignored d. commented on
   7. a

8. The speech seemed to some to be a(n) ____.
   a. failure b. essay c. blessing d. poem
   8. c

9. The language of the Gettysburg Address is considered as fine as that of Shakespeare's ____.
   a. monologues b. lively dialogue c. sonnets d. best writing
   9. a

10. The world remembers Lincoln's words almost as a(n) ____.
    a. prophecy of a nation's future c. enigma for the world to ponder
    b. order that forbids something d. statement of a personal credo
    10. b

PRACTICE WITH ANALOGIES

See pages 32, 66 and 86 for some strategies to use with analogies.

Directions On the answer line, write the vocabulary word or a form of it that completes each analogy.

1. GARRULOUS : TALKATIVE :: ____ : enthusiastic *(Lesson 17)* — 1. **ebullient**
2. DECEITFUL : CHEAT :: ____ : complain *(Lesson 17)* — 2. **querulous**
3. EXULTATION : JOY :: ____ : boldness *(Lesson 18)* — 3. **audacity**
4. INDOLENT : WORK :: ____ : tire *(Lesson 18)* — 4. **indefatigable**
5. ELUSIVE : CATCH :: ____ : persuade *(Lesson 18)* — 5. **obdurate**
6. BRAGGART : BOASTFUL :: toady : ____ *(Lesson 18)* — 6. **obsequious**
7. EXTRAVAGANT : SPEND :: ____ : talk *(Lesson 19)* — 7. **loquacious**
8. VAIN : FLATTERY :: ____ : company *(Lesson 17)* — 8. **convivial**

LESSON 20 BUILDING AND DESTROYING

The processes of building and destroying can be observed in the natural world, in human institutions, and in all aspects of life. Since ancient times these forces have been seen as part of the ordinary cycle of existence:

> To every thing there is a season,
> And a time to every purpose under the heaven . . .
> A time to break down, and a time to build up . . .

Natural disasters such as earthquakes, floods, and fires destroy communities that have taken centuries to build, and in time newly constructed environments develop in the devastated areas. The processes of building and destroying are exemplified even by our own bodies, in which old cells are constantly replaced with new cells that ensure our well-being. Throughout the centuries the human institutions of nations and governments rise and fall.

The words in this lesson will help you to describe and to explain the processes of building and destroying that are an inescapable and important part of life.

WORD LIST

deleterious
despoil
effectual
jettison
obviate
pinnacle
raze
stultify
surmount
wrest

DEFINITIONS

After you have studied the definitions and example for each vocabulary word, write the word on the line to the right.

1. **deleterious** (dĕl′ĭ-tîr′ē-əs) *adjective* Having a harmful effect; injurious. 1. ______

Related Words **deleteriously** *adverb;* **deleteriousness** *noun*
Example When the pesticide DDT was found to be *deleterious* to humans, it was removed from the market.

2. **despoil** (dĭ-spoil′) *trans. verb* To deprive of possessions or property by force; plunder; rob. (From the Latin *de-*, meaning "away," and *spoilium,* meaning "booty") 2. ______

Related Word **despoliation** *noun*
Example The army of Alexander the Great *despoiled* the ancient city of Tyre.

3. **effectual** (ĭ-fĕk′cho͞o-əl) *adjective* Producing or sufficient to produce a desired result; fully adequate. 3. ______

Related Word **effectually** *adverb*
Example Ms. Sung knew that her methods of encouraging students to do independent research were *effectual.*

4. **jettison** (jĕt′ĭ-sən, jĕt′ĭ-zən) *trans. verb* **a.** To discard as unwanted or burdensome. **b.** To cast off or overboard. (From the Latin word *jacere,* meaning "to throw") 4. ______

Example After listening to her staff's objections, the manager *jettisoned* the marketing plan.

5. **obviate** (ŏb′vē-āt′) *trans. verb* To prevent by anticipating; make unnecessary. (From the Latin *ob-*, meaning "against," and *via,* meaning "way") 5. ______

Related Word **obviation** *noun*
Example By careful planning, the operators of the new business *obviated* many of the difficulties often encountered by young entrepreneurs.

6. **pinnacle** (pĭn′ə-kəl) *noun* **a.** The highest point; summit; acme. **b.** A tall, pointed formation, such as a mountain peak. **c.** A small turret or spire on a roof or buttress. (From the Latin word *pinna,* meaning "feather")

6. ____________________
MEMORY CUE: The point of a *pin* is in *pinnacle.*

Example The *pinnacle* of achievement for many dramatic actors is to perform the role of Hamlet.

7. **raze** (rāz) *trans. verb* **a.** To tear down or demolish; level to the ground. **b.** To scrape or shave off. (From the Latin word *radere,* meaning "to scrape")

7. ____________________

Example During World War II, bombs *razed* many cities in Europe.

8. **stultify** (stŭl′tə-fī′) *trans. verb* **a.** To render useless or inadequate; cripple. **b.** To cause to appear stupid, inconsistent, or ridiculous. (From the Latin words *stultus,* meaning "foolish," and *facere,* meaning "to make")

8. ____________________

Related Word **stultification** *noun*
Example Forcing a reluctant piano student to practice may *stultify* a natural interest in music.

9. **surmount** (sər-mount′) *trans. verb* **a.** To overcome (an obstacle, for example); conquer. **b.** To ascend to the top of; climb. **c.** To place something above; top. (From the Old French *sur-,* meaning "above," and *monter,* meaning "to mount")

9. ____________________

Related Word **surmountable** *adjective*
Example In his poem "Invictus," William Ernest Henley wrote of his determination to *surmount* all difficulties.

10. **wrest** (rĕst) *trans. verb* **a.** To obtain by or as by pulling with violent twisting movements. **b.** To usurp forcefully: *to wrest power.* **c.** To extract by force, guile, or persistent effort; wring: *to wrest the meaning from an obscure poem.*

10. ____________________
USAGE NOTE: *Wrestle,* a closely related word, means "to struggle"; if you *wrest* something away, however, your struggle to get it has succeeded.

Example In North America, the British eventually *wrested* Canada from French control.

NAME ______________________ DATE ____________

EXERCISE 1 MATCHING WORDS AND DEFINITIONS

Match the definition in Column B with the word in Column A. Write the letter of the correct definition on the answer line.

Column A	Column B	
1. pinnacle	a. producing or sufficient to produce a desired result	1. i
2. raze	b. having a harmful effect; injurious	2. c
3. obviate	c. to tear down or demolish; level to the ground	3. j
4. surmount	d. to obtain by or as by pulling with violent twisting movements; usurp forcefully	4. h
5. deleterious	e. to discard as burdensome; cast off or overboard	5. b
6. stultify	f. to render useless or inadequate; cause to appear stupid, inconsistent, or ridiculous	6. f
7. wrest	g. to deprive of possessions by force; plunder	7. d
8. jettison	h. to overcome; conquer; ascend to the top of	8. e
9. effectual	i. the highest point; summit; a tall, pointed formation, such as a mountain peak	9. a
10. despoil	j. to prevent by anticipating; make unnecessary	10. g

EXERCISE 2 USING WORDS CORRECTLY

Decide whether the italicized vocabulary word has been used correctly in the sentence. On the answer line, write *Correct* for correct use and *Incorrect* for incorrect use.

1. Not being chosen for the opera company represented the *pinnacle* of Robin's career as a singer. — 1. Incorrect
2. Senator Walters was able to *surmount* the lack of campaign funds to win the election. — 2. Correct
3. After extended brainstorming the committee chose a strategy and *jettisoned* the remainder of the ideas. — 3. Correct
4. When Ethan decided to *obviate* the color of his house from pink to brown, his neighbors cheered. — 4. Incorrect
5. Elaine's bluntness *stultified* our discussion. — 5. Correct
6. After presenting her closing argument, the lawyer *wrested* her case. — 6. Incorrect
7. If you don't refrigerate meat, it will *despoil* quickly in hot weather. — 7. Incorrect
8. Did you know that a sunburn is the result of overexposure to the sun's ultraviolet *raze?* — 8. Incorrect
9. Ted discovered that the most *effectual* way of disposing of his trash was to burn it. — 9. Correct
10. When food additives were shown to have *deleterious* effects, the chemicals were approved for human consumption. — 10. Incorrect

EXERCISE 3 CHOOSING THE BEST DEFINITION

For each italicized vocabulary word in the following sentences, write the letter of the best definition on the answer line.

1. For Isaac Bashevis Singer, winning the 1978 Nobel Prize for literature represented the *pinnacle* of success. — 1. a
   a. high point **b.** exciting aspect **c.** apparent moment **d.** profile

2. Before construction crews can begin to dig the foundation for the new civic center, the crumbling remains of the hotel must be *razed*. 2. d

a. elevated b. redesigned c. modified d. demolished

3. Until her cat ate a leaf of the dieffenbachia plant, Amelia was unaware of its *deleterious* effects on animals. 3. c

a. remarkable b. external c. injurious d. improbable

4. Realizing that their boat was about to be inundated by the huge waves, the crew *jettisoned* all nonessential supplies. 4. c

a. disregarded b. collected c. cast overboard d. spontaneously claimed

5. Theodore has devised an alternate but *effectual* method for proving the Pythagorean theorem. 5. c

a. scientific b. expensive c. adequate d. monotonous

6. Glenn Cunningham was able to *surmount* his handicap and set a world record for the mile run. 6. d

a. ignore b. succumb to c. heal d. overcome

7. Corrective surgery will *obviate* the problems associated with Aunt Melinda's condition. 7. b

a. complicate b. prevent c. make noticeable d. make unavoidable

8. Too many hours of rehearsal can *stultify* an actor's spontaneity. 8. d

a. affect b. increase c. restore d. stifle

9. Although he was considered a respectable citizen of New York, Captain William Kidd was a pirate who *despoiled* French ships. 9. a

a. plundered b. outfitted c. capsized d. destroyed

10. The Australian mixed doubles team was able to *wrest* the tennis match from the Americans in the third set. 10. a

a. take by persistent effort b. suspend c. win easily d. conserve

EXERCISE 4 USING DIFFERENT FORMS OF WORDS

Decide which form of the vocabulary word in parentheses best completes the sentence. The form given may be correct. Write your answer on the answer line.

1. A US Secret Service agent's job is the _____ of harm to the president. *(obviate)* 1. obviation

2. Excessively loud music over extended time periods is known to affect one's hearing _____. *(deleterious)* 2. deleteriously

3. The developers are responsible for _____ this beautiful forest. *(raze)* 3. razing

4. The conquering army promised no _____ of land or dwellings. *(despoil)* 4. despoliation

5. After the _____ of his efforts to improve the city planning board, Mr. Summers resigned. *(stultify)* 5. stultification

6. Each spring the Manteos hold a yard sale to _____ the accumulation of articles from their attic and garage. *(jettison)* 6. jettison

7. Having proven to herself that Half Dome was _____, Paloma went on to climb El Capitan and other granite peaks of Yosemite. *(surmount)* 7. surmountable

8. Hoodoos are natural _____ of rock that result from weathering. *(pinnacle)* 8. pinnacles

9. _____ a small harvest from the rocky and infertile soil was a challenging task for the settlers. *(wrest)* 9. Wresting

10. Enid's recommendation has _____ resolved the dilemma about when to present the institute's awards. *(effectual)* 10. effectually

NAME ________________________ DATE __________

READING COMPREHENSION

Each numbered sentence in the following passage contains an italicized vocabulary word. After you read the passage, you will complete an exercise.

THE GREAT WALL OF CHINA

Curving across China like an immense dragon, the Great Wall is one of the most remarkable construction projects ever accomplished. Covering over four thousand miles of varied landscape—from mountain ranges to the edges of the Gobi Desert—the Great Wall served for centuries as a boundary between the stable, agricultural civilization of China and the primitive culture of the nomadic tribes of the north.

The wall's construction began during the Warring States Period (403–221 B.C.), when feudal lords built separate sections of the wall in scattered strategic areas. (1) Following China's unification under the Ch'in Dynasty, Emperor Shih Huang-ti believed that an ***effectual*** military defense system could be created by joining together and extending the separate walls. (2) He foresaw a barrier that would prevent foreign invaders from ***despoiling*** the land. (3) However, the Great Wall's existence did not ***obviate*** the need for defense. (4) After Genghis Khan was able to ***surmount*** the wall in a weakly defended area, Shih Huang-ti ordered improvements. Hundreds of observation and beacon towers, fortresses, and military posts were constructed. (5) From the ***pinnacles*** of the forty-foot-tall watchtowers built every hundred to two hundred yards along the wall, guards kept watch and lit fires to warn the Chinese military of approaching enemies.

Erected entirely by hand, the Great Wall of China took centuries to complete and involved a tremendous expenditure of labor. (6) Peasants, who were ***wrested*** from their villages, and convicts were forced to join soldiers, making up a total work force of more than a million people. (7) Nothing was allowed to ***stultify*** the efforts of these laborers. In Chinese popular thought, each stone of the wall is equated with a human life lost during the massive project.

Although building the Great Wall was an enormous undertaking, the construction techniques were fairly simple. Workers dug furrows approximately twenty-five feet apart and laid a foundation. The outer walls were then fashioned of granite blocks, hard-baked brick, and limestone mortar, while the inner roadway was made of compacted earth, clay, wood, tile, and pebbles. (8) Not a thing that could strengthen the wall was ***jettisoned;*** whatever workers could find locally was employed to reinforce the fifteen- to fifty-foot-high structure. Building materials were transported by handcarts pulled by donkeys or were handled by workers in "assembly lines," who passed the materials along hand by hand.

Almost fifteen feet wide, the wall formed a roadway from the eastern coast to the north-central part of China, allowing for traffic of all kinds. Wide enough to accommodate carts or small groups of soldiers, the Great Wall not only prevented invasion but also improved internal travel in China.

Ch'in Shih Huang-ti predicted that the Great Wall of China would last ten thousand generations. Certainly the wall seems likely to endure for many years. (9) Despite the ***deleterious*** effects of weathering, many sections of the wall are still well-preserved. (10) Today tourists can view how the ancient builders gracefully followed the natural, irregular contours of the land rather than ***razing*** them. The impressive barrier seems to prove the popular myth that a kind dragon walked across China to trace the route of the Great Wall.

READING COMPREHENSION EXERCISE

Each of the following statements corresponds to a numbered sentence in the passage. Each statement contains a blank and is followed by four answer choices. Decide which choice fits best in the blank. The word or phrase that you choose must express roughly the same meaning as the italicized word in the passage. Write the letter of your choice on the answer line.

1. Emperor Shih Huang-ti believed that he could create a(n) _____ defense system by joining the separate walls. 1. c
   a. exceptional b. unmatched c. adequate d. legendary

2. He foresaw a barrier that would prevent foreign invaders from _____ the land. 2. d
   a. farming b. developing c. colonizing d. plundering

3. The Great Wall's existence did not _____ the need for defense. 3. a
   a. make unnecessary c. reveal
   b. adequately fulfill d. overlook

4. Genghis Khan was able to _____ the wall in a weakly defended area. 4. c
   a. tear down b. ignore c. climb d. tunnel through

5. Guards kept watch from the _____ of forty-foot-tall watchtowers. 5. b
   a. lowest openings b. highest points c. stations d. porches

6. Peasants _____ from their villages, convicts, and soldiers made up the work force. 6. a
   a. forcefully pulled b. transported c. specially chosen d. isolated

7. Nothing was allowed to _____ the efforts of these laborers. 7. c
   a. intensify b. prevent c. cripple d. monopolize

8. Not a thing that could strengthen the wall was _____. 8. d
   a. utilized b. forgotten c. fabricated d. discarded

9. Many sections of the wall are well-preserved, despite the _____ effects of weathering. 9. d
   a. beneficial b. unquestionable c. obvious d. injurious

10. Ancient builders followed the contours of the land rather than _____ them. 10. a
   a. leveling b. uncovering c. obscuring d. regulating

WRITING ASSIGNMENT

Each historical period seems to have its list of remarkable structures. Choose a renowned structure of ancient times (such as the Pyramid of Cheops, the Colossus of Rhodes, the Hanging Gardens of Babylon, the Great Wall of China, or Stonehenge) or a structure of medieval times (such as the Hagia Sophia of Constantinople, Mont-Saint-Michel, Chartres, the Alhambra, or London Bridge). Do research on the topic. Then write a composition in which you explain the engineering skill that went into its construction. In your composition use at least five of the words from this lesson and underline each one.

The **Bonus activity** for Lessons 17–20 is on page T22.
Verbal Aptitude Test 2 is on page T23.

LESSON 21 PLENTY AND EXCESS

21

Throughout the centuries philosophers and writers have advised that moderation in all things is the key to happiness. An anonymous Greek writer commanded, "Nothing in excess," while a Chinese philosopher, Lao-tse, recommended, "Manifest plainness and embrace simplicity. . . . To have plenty is to be perplexed." Even the legendary King Midas learns his lesson about greed when he nearly loses his daughter. The words in this lesson will help you to describe situations characterized by excess and to determine whether moderation is really "the happy medium."

WORD LIST

avarice
insatiable
inundate
myriad
parsimony
prodigal
replete
surfeit
tumult
voluminous

DEFINITIONS

After you have studied the definitions and example for each vocabulary word, write the word on the line to the right.

1. **avarice** (ăv'ə-rĭs) *noun* An extreme desire for wealth; greed. (From the Latin word *avarus,* meaning "greedy") 1. ______________

Related Words **avaricious** *adjective;* **avariciously** *adverb*
Example The couple's *avarice* caused them to ignore requests from all charitable organizations.

2. **insatiable** (ĭn-sā'shə-bəl, ĭn-sā'shē-ə-bəl) *adjective* Incapable of being fully satisfied. (From the Latin *in-,* meaning "not," and *satis,* meaning "enough") 2. ______________

Related Word **insatiably** *adverb*
Example The scientist's *insatiable* curiosity compelled her to question many of the theories of her time.

3. **inundate** (ĭn'ŭn-dāt') *trans. verb* **a.** To overwhelm as if with a flood; swamp. **b.** To cover with water, especially flood water; overflow. (From the Latin *in-,* meaning "in," and *unda,* meaning "wave") 3. ______________

Related Word **inundation** *noun*
Example Most presidents are *inundated* with requests from universities seeking a prestigious commencement speaker.

4. **myriad** (mĭr'ē-əd) *adjective* **a.** Constituting a very large, indefinite number; innumerable. **b.** Comprised of numerous diverse elements or facets. *noun* A vast number. (From the Greek word *myrios,* meaning "countless") 4. ______________

Example In Greek mythology the horrifying appearance of Medusa, with *myriad* snakes growing from her head, turned any viewer to stone.

5. **parsimony** (pär′sə-mō′ nē) *noun* Unusual or excessive frugality; stinginess. (From the Latin word *parcere,* meaning "to spare") 5. ____________

Related Words **parsimonious** *adjective;* **parsimoniously** *adverb*
Example In Dickens's *A Christmas Carol,* Scrooge's *parsimony* is transformed into generosity after the visits of the three Christmas spirits.

6. **prodigal** (prŏd′ĭ-gəl) *adjective* **a.** Recklessly wasteful; extravagant; lavish. **b.** Profuse in giving; exceedingly abundant. (From the Latin word *prodigere,* meaning "to squander") 6. ____________

Related Words **prodigality** *noun;* **prodigally** *adverb*
Example It would be unwise for elderly parents to relinquish the management of their finances to a *prodigal* son or daughter.

7. **replete** (rĭ-plēt′) *adjective* **a.** Plentifully supplied; abounding. **b.** Filled to satisfaction; gorged. (From the Latin *re-,* meaning "again," and *plere,* meaning "to fill") 7. ____________

USAGE NOTE: The adjective *complete* implies having all that is necessary; *replete* implies having more than is necessary.

Related Word **repletion** *noun*
Example A sports-car race is *replete* with thrills, chills, and spills.

8. **surfeit** (sûr′fĭt) *noun* **a.** An excessive amount. **b.** Overindulgence in food or drink. *trans. verb* To feed or supply to fullness or excess; satiate. (From the Old French *sur-,* meaning "over," and *faire,* meaning "to do") 8. ____________

Example There were many leftovers from the *surfeit* of food at the banquet.

9. **tumult** (to͞o′mŭlt′, tyo͞o′mŭlt′) *noun* **a.** A disorderly, noisy movement of people. **b.** Noise and commotion, as of a crowd. **c.** Agitation of the mind or emotions. 9. ____________

Related Words **tumultuous** *adjective;* **tumultuously** *adverb*
Example The frustrated fans were in a *tumult* as the box office announced that the last concert ticket had been sold.

10. **voluminous** (və-lo͞o′mə-nəs) *adjective* **a.** Having great volume, fullness, size, or number. **b.** Of unusual length in speech or writing. **c.** Filling or capable of filling volumes. (From the Latin word *volumen,* meaning "roll of writing") 10. ____________

Related Words **voluminously** *adverb;* **voluminousness** *noun*
Example From the *voluminous* folds of his academic gown, the speaker drew the manuscript of his address.

NAME ______________________ DATE ____________

EXERCISE 1 COMPLETING DEFINITIONS

On the answer line, write the word from the vocabulary list that best completes each definition.

1. If a novel contains such incidents as secret messages and a car chase, it is _____ with the traditional ingredients of a suspense story. 1. replete
2. When you have too many things to do, you may feel _____. 2. inundated
3. A disorderly, noisy movement of people is a _____. 3. tumult
4. Unusual or excessive frugality is _____. 4. parsimony
5. A person who has an extreme desire for wealth suffers from _____. 5. avarice
6. Something that has great volume, fullness, size, or number is described as _____. 6. voluminous
7. If you are recklessly wasteful or extravagant, you are _____. 7. prodigal
8. When a desire for knowledge cannot be fully satisfied, it is _____. 8. insatiable
9. An excessive amount is a _____. 9. surfeit
10. If you have a very large, indefinite number of goals, you have _____ objectives. 10. myriad

EXERCISE 2 USING WORDS CORRECTLY

Decide whether the italicized vocabulary word has been used correctly in the sentence. On the answer line, write *Correct* for correct use and *Incorrect* for incorrect use.

1. An *insatiable* thirst is easily quenched by a small amount of liquid. 1. Incorrect
2. Many hungry people returned to the buffet for second and third helpings after consuming a *surfeit* of food. 2. Incorrect
3. The reporter spent weeks reading the *voluminous* transcripts of the trial. 3. Correct
4. Robert is so *parsimonious* that he spends more money than he earns. 4. Incorrect
5. The poet drew an analogy between the *myriad* stars in the galaxy and the grains of sand on a beach. 5. Correct
6. The *tumult* of the storm awakened the children. 6. Correct
7. Before the Aswan Dam was built, the Nile River habitually *inundated* its banks each spring. 7. Correct
8. People display their *avarice* by generously donating money to a variety of worthy causes. 8. Incorrect
9. His paper was *replete* with metaphors and literary allusions. 9. Correct
10. Caroline found nothing suitable to buy during last week's *prodigal* shopping spree. 10. Incorrect

EXERCISE 3 CHOOSING THE BEST WORDS

Decide which vocabulary word or related form best expresses the meaning of the italicized word or phrase in the sentence. On the answer line, write the letter of the correct choice.

1. I understand why *incapable of being satisfied* curiosity is the downfall of the cat. 1. b

   a. prodigal **b.** insatiable **c.** voluminous **d.** replete

2. The museum could not handle the *overflow* of art lovers who visited the gallery during the latest exhibit. 2. d
a. avarice b. tumult c. parsimony d. inundation

3. The *noise and commotion* in City Hall Plaza made concentration difficult, even on the twenty-eighth floor of a nearby building. 3. c
a. parsimony b. repletion c. tumult d. surfeit

4. As Miranda listened to the prelude, *innumerable* images flashed across her mind. 4. a
a. myriad b. inundation c. tumult d. surfeit

5. In Guy de Maupassant's short story "A Piece of String," the *excessive frugality* of Maitre Hauchecorne has ironic consequences. 5. c
a. avarice b. prodigality c. parsimony d. voluminousness

6. Eloise has thus far completed only two of the *unusually lengthy* diaries of Anaïs Nin. 6. b
a. replete b. voluminous c. tumultuous d. insatiable

7. The four-course meal left us *filled to satisfaction* and sleepy. 7. a
a. replete b. inundated c. avaricious d. parsimonious

8. Dwayne's grandparents tend to be *extravagant* with birthday gifts. 8. d
a. insatiable b. tumultuous c. myriad d. prodigal

9. "I believe that there is an *excessive number* of situation comedies this season," remarked the television critic. 9. b
a. avarice b. surfeit c. parsimony d. tumult

10. Mr. Constantine's life-long *greed* resulted in the accumulation of a great fortune but the loss of friends and family. 10. a
a. avarice b. parsimony c. prodigality d. repletion

EXERCISE 4 USING DIFFERENT FORMS OF WORDS

Decide which form of the vocabulary word in parentheses best completes the sentence. The form given may be correct. Write your answer on the answer line.

1. After working for two years at minimum wage, Lila finally realized that her _____ employer would probably never give her a raise. *(parsimony)* 1. parsimonious

2. Ben enjoyed his job as a waiter; each night he took _____ delight in counting his tips. *(avarice)* 2. avaricious

3. Connie was often difficult to work with because she _____ demanded praise and reassurance. *(insatiable)* 3. insatiably

4. Lee's speech was so _____ with jokes and puns that his main point was lost in all the laughter. *(replete)* 4. replete

5. In the days before women wore trousers, the _____ of their skirts forced them to ride horses sidesaddle. *(voluminous)* 5. voluminousness

6. The community experienced an _____ of new residents. *(inundate)* 6. inundation

7. In her marine biology class, Phoebe studies a _____ of underwater life forms. *(myriad)* 7. myriad

8. Political journalists who accompany candidates on the campaign trail soon experience a _____ of travel. *(surfeit)* 8. surfeit

9. Alma seems to thrive in the _____ setting of the stock exchange. *(tumult)* 9. tumultuous

10. The twelve-course dinner, towering ice sculptures, fifty-piece orchestra, and hundred-dollar guest gifts were examples of the _____ of the formal party. *(prodigal)* 10. prodigality

NAME ____________________ DATE ____________

READING COMPREHENSION

Each numbered sentence in the following passage contains an italicized vocabulary word or related form. After you read the passage, you will complete an exercise.

THE NEW AUTOMOBILE JUNKYARD

(1) Whether it is due to ***parsimony*** or nostalgia, Americans have long had a serious infatuation with old cars. Cars built between the 1930s and the 1960s are modern enough to be comfortable, dependable, and serviceable; unlike new cars, they lend themselves to being tinkered with by amateur mechanics. Of course, maintaining an old car often means spending weekends exploring obscure rural junkyards for replacement parts. (2) It takes a particularly dedicated or ***avaricious*** car buff to sort through piles of rusted frames and scrap metal for still-workable parts.

The contemporary junkyard is no longer a dirty, noisy, frustrating place. (3) Though still ***inundated*** with old parts and wrecks, today's salvage yard is an organized, clean big business. Instead of dismantling a suitable wreck by themselves, customers today depend on a staff and professional service. After mechanics take a car apart, the components are cleaned, tested, and rebuilt if necessary. Catalogued and filed for easy access, these guaranteed parts are sold for a fraction of what new parts cost.

(4) The new salvage yards are still crowded with ***insatiable*** car aficionados intent upon locating a special mechanism for an antique auto and with consumers hopeful of rejuvenating their vehicles. Salvagers, however, have become receptive to new ideas in marketing, inventory control, and management. (5) Now customers can go to specialized salvage dealers who carry only hubcaps or doors or certain makes and models of cars instead of hunting for hours through a ***myriad*** of car skeletons. (6) Computers provide instantaneous inventory listings, and telephone circuits called "long lines" automatically connect a junkyard with dozens of other junkyards in order to locate an elusive part or to advertise a ***surfeit*** of supplies. (7) One salvage yard in Washington state has a ***voluminous*** library of parts catalogues that date back to the early 1900s; said to be a one-of-a-kind collection, it is stored in a fire-proof vault.

(8) Aware of the competition in the used auto-part market provided by swap meets, insurance company auctions, and police garage sales, many salvage operators have gone to ***prodigal*** extremes. Chromed auto parts are displayed in velvet-lined glass cases in certain boutique-like showrooms. Wrecks occupy separate concrete pads or are lined up in neat rows, organized by make and model. (9) Other dealers even have buyers who travel the country to locate new parts for old cars; with the skills of a detective, they manage to keep warehouses ***replete*** with still-packaged merchandise unearthed from attics, basements, and out-of-business car dealerships.

(10) Far removed from the ***tumult*** of the traditional neighborhood junk heap, salvage yards are efficiently run businesses that have changed the image of junk. They have managed to widen the used-part clientele to include more than the backyard mechanic. Because of the contributions of new junkyards, countless people with diverse backgrounds now enjoy the ownership, restoration, and maintenance of old automobiles.

READING COMPREHENSION EXERCISE

Each of the following statements corresponds to a numbered sentence in the passage. Each statement contains a blank and is followed by four answer choices. Decide which choice fits best in the blank. The word or phrase that you choose must express roughly the same meaning as the italicized word in the passage. Write the letter of your choice on the answer line.

1. Americans' infatuation with old cars has been attributed to ____ or nostalgia. — 1. c
   a. necessity c. excessive frugality
   b. fads d. mechanical aptitude

2. Sorting through piles of scrap metal takes a particularly dedicated and ____ car buff. — 2. a
   a. greedy b. optimistic c. extroverted d. innocent

3. Today's salvage yards are still ____ with parts and wrecks. — 3. d
   a. on view b. offensive c. inflicted d. overflowing

4. The new salvage yards are still crowded with ____ car aficionados. — 4. c
   a. wholesome b. irritable c. never-satisfied d. shameful

5. Customers can go to specialized dealers instead of hunting through a ____ of car skeletons. — 5. b
   a. limited supply b. vast number c. deposit d. predominance

6. Telephone circuits are used to advertise a(n) ____ of supplies. — 6. a
   a. excessive number c. occasional stock
   b. meager number d. inventory

7. One salvage yard's library of parts catalogues is ____. — 7. d
   a. peculiar c. capable of earning money
   b. outstanding d. capable of filling volumes

8. Many salvage dealers have gone to ____ extremes. — 8. c
   a. ridiculous b. noticeable c. extravagant d. enticing

9. Buyers manage to keep warehouses ____ with still-packaged merchandise. — 9. a
   a. plentifully supplied c. understocked
   b. occasionally overwhelmed d. uniformly crowded

10. Salvage yards are now far from removed from the ____ of the traditional neighborhood junkyard. — 10. b
    a. influence b. commotion c. configuration d. regulation

WRITING ASSIGNMENT

Gold is among the most valuable and desirable of metals. Imagine that you are among the first successful gold prospectors in California or Alaska. Write a letter home to your family in which you describe the reaction to your first find. Use at least five of the words from this lesson in your letter and underline each one.

The **Test** for Lessons 19, 20, and 21 is on page T28.

NAME ______________________ DATE ____________

READING SKILLS

PREFIXES INDICATING NUMBER

The table below shows the prefixes that denote the numbers from one to ten and the number one hundred. If a number has two prefixes, one comes from Latin and the other from Greek. Following each prefix, in the third column, is a word that begins with it. The meaning of each such word appears in the fourth column. Once you have learned these prefixes, you can determine the meaning of unfamiliar words that contain them. To do so, use the procedure that follows the table.

Prefix	Meaning	Word with Prefix	Meaning of Word with Prefix
uni-	one	unique	being the only one of its kind
mono-	one	monotheism	belief that there is only one God
bi-	two	bicuspid	tooth with two cusps, or points
di-	two	diatomic	made up of two atoms
tri-	three	trilogy	group of three literary works
quadr-	four	quadrangle	four buildings enclosing a square
tetr-	four	tetrameter	poetic line with four metrical feet
quin-	five	quintuple	to multiply by five
pent-	five	pentagon	five-sided figure
sex-, ses-	six	sextuplet	one of six in a single birth
hex-	six	hexagonal	having six sides
sept-	seven	septennial	occurring every seven years
hept-	seven	heptarchy	government by seven persons
oct-	eight	octahedron	solid with eight plane faces
nov-	nine	novena	prayer offered for nine days
dec-	ten	decathlon	athletic contest with ten events
cent-	hundred	centenary	hundredth anniversary

PROCEDURE

1. *Substitute the prefix definition for the prefix and—if you know it—the root definition for the root.*
2. *Think of a possible definition of the entire word.*
3. *Use the context to help you develop the possible definition.*
4. *Check your definition of the word in a dictionary.*

EXERCISE IDENTIFYING NUMERICAL PREFIXES

Each sentence contains an italicized word beginning with a numerical prefix. When appropriate, the root word and its meaning are given in parentheses after the sentence. *Step 1:* Taking the context into consideration, write your own definition of the word. *Step 2:* Write the dictionary definition of the word. Choose the definition that fits the way in which the word is used in the sentence.

1. She was able to find only four copies of the *quintuplicate* invoice.

   Your Definition **Having five parts**

   Dictionary Definition **Multiplied by five; fivefold**

2. My uncle, who is a *septuagenarian,* will celebrate his seventy-fifth birthday soon. (Latin root word: *genus,* "kind")

Your Definition **A person between seventy and eighty years of age**

Dictionary Definition **A person who is seventy years old or between the ages of seventy and eighty**

3. He was not content with his stereo but wanted a *quadraphonic* system. (Greek root word: *phone,* "sound")

Your Definition **Pertaining to a four-speaker stereo system**

Dictionary Definition **An extension of stereophonic sound reproduction with two additional channels**

4. In some countries one may have many spouses, but in the United States *monogamy* is the rule. (Greek root word: *gamos,* "marriage")

Your Definition **The custom of having only one spouse**

Dictionary Definition **The custom of being married to only one person at a time**

5. The insect's body was *tripartite,* consisting of head, body, and tail. (Latin root word: *partire,* "to divide")

Your Definition **Having three parts**

Dictionary Definition **Composed or divided into three parts**

6. Ancient laws governing moral conduct are contained in the *Decalogue* (Greek root word: *logos,* "word; speech")

Your Definition **The Ten Commandments**

Dictionary Definition **The Ten Commandments**

7. Having written eight lines of the sonnet, he had only the *sestet* to complete.

Your Definition **The last six lines of a sonnet**

Dictionary Definition **A stanza containing the last six lines of an Italian sonnet**

8. The terms of the peace treaty called for *unilateral* disarmament. (Latin root word: *latus,* "side")

Your Definition **One-sided**

Dictionary Definition **Of, on, pertaining to, involving, or affecting only one side**

9. "To be or not to be" was Hamlet's *dilemma.* (Greek root word: *lemma,* "proposition")

Your Definition **The situation of not being able to choose between two things**

Dictionary Definition **A situation in which one must choose between two equally balanced alternatives**

10. Richard Wagner's "Ring of the Nibelungen" is a *tetralogy* of operas. (Greek root word: *logos,* "word; speech")

Your Definition **Group of four**

Dictionary Definition **A series of four related dramatic, operatic, or literary works**

11. "How many loved your moments of glad grace" is an example of *pentameter.*

Your Definition **A line of poetry with five metrical feet**

Dictionary Definition **A line of verse composed of five metrical feet**

12. The word "antiauthoritarian" is *octosyllabic.*

Your Definition **Having eight syllables**

Dictionary Definition **Containing eight syllables**

LESSON 22 THE ROOT -*TEN*- 22

The root -*ten*- actually comes from two related Latin words: *tendere,* meaning "to stretch," and *tenere,* meaning "to hold onto." Many words in the English language come from this root. For example, an *attentive* person is observant; he or she holds on to what is going on. The *extent* of a book's coverage is the way in which the material is stretched or spread out to its fullest length. *Tension* is the act or process of stretching. In this lesson you will learn other words directly or indirectly derived from the root -*ten*- that share the common meaning of stretching or holding.

WORD LIST

extenuation
portent
pretentious
retentive
retinue
sustenance
tenable
tenacious
tenuous
tenure

DEFINITIONS

After you have studied the definitions and example for each vocabulary word, write the word on the line to the right.

1. **extenuation** (ĭk-stĕn′yo͞o-ā′shən) *noun* **a.** The act of attempting to lessen the seriousness of by providing a partial justification or excuse. **b.** A partial justification or excuse. (From the Latin *ex-,* meaning "out," and *tenuare,* meaning "to make thin") 1. ____________

Related Words **extenuate** *verb;* **extenuating** *adjective*
Example The member of Congress wrote to her constituents in *extenuation* of her recent stand on the foreign trade bill.

2. **portent** (pôr′tĕnt′) *noun* An indication of something momentous or calamitous about to occur; omen. (From the Latin *pro-,* meaning "before," and *tendere,* meaning "to stretch") 2. ____________

MEMORY CUE: Notice that *portentous,* which is very close to *pretentious,* has no *i* after the second *t.*

Related Words **portend** *verb;* **portentous** *adjective*
Example Karen suspected that the broken typewriter ribbon was a *portent* of the difficulty she would have in writing her term paper.

3. **pretentious** (prĭ-tĕn′shəs) *adjective* **a.** Making an extravagant outward show; ostentatious. **b.** Claiming a position of distinction or merit, especially when unjustified. (From the Latin *prae-,* meaning "in front," and *tendere*) 3. ____________

Related Words **pretentiously** *adverb;* **pretentiousness** *noun*
Example The Joneses' ownership of three expensive sports cars seems *pretentious* to their neighbors.

4. **retentive** (rĭ-tĕn′tĭv) *adjective* Having the ability to remember or store. (From the Latin *re-,* meaning "back," and *tenere,* meaning "to hold onto") 4. ____________

Related Words **retain** *verb;* **retention** *noun*
Example Thanks to his *retentive* memory, Luis recalled the doctor's telephone number without having to consult the directory.

5. **retinue** (rĕt'n-o͞o', rĕt'n-yo͞o') *noun* The attendants accompanying a high-ranking person. (From the Latin *per-*, an intensive prefix, and *tenere*, "to hold." A *retinue* was "held" in service for pay.) 5. ____________

Example The president is surrounded by a *retinue* of Secret Service agents whenever he leaves the White House.

6. **sustenance** (sŭs'tə-nəns) *noun* **a.** Something, especially food, that supports life, health, and good spirits. **b.** The supplying of the necessities of life. **c.** The condition of being supplied with these necessities. (From the Latin *sub-*, meaning "under" or "from below," and *tenere*, "to hold." *Sustenance* enables us to "hold onto" life.) 6. ____________

Related Word **sustain** *verb*
Example Survivors of the shipwreck had been without *sustenance* of any kind for five days.

7. **tenable** (tĕn'ə-bəl) *adjective* Capable of being defended or sustained; logical; reasonable. (From the Latin word *tenere*) 7. ____________

Related Word **tenably** *adverb*
Example Maxwell took the *tenable* viewpoint that Shakespeare was easily the most influential playwright in Western literature.

8. **tenacious** (tə-nā'shəs) *adjective* **a.** Holding firmly; persistent. **b.** Cohesive. **c.** Adhesive; clinging to another object or surface. **d.** Tending to retain: *a tenacious memory.* (From the Latin word *tenere*) 8. ____________

Related Words **tenaciously** *adverb;* **tenacity** *noun*
Example Kathy was becoming a nuisance to the store manager by her *tenacious* demands for the refund of her money.

9. **tenuous** (tĕn'yo͞o-əs) *adjective* Having little substance; flimsy. (From the Latin word *tenuis,* meaning "thin" or "stretched") 9. ____________

Related Words **tenuously** *adverb;* **tenuousness** *noun*
Example Mai's love of Mexican food has only a *tenuous* connection with her love of the Spanish language.

10. **tenure** (tĕn'yər, tĕn'yo͝or') *noun* **a.** The period of holding something, such as property or an office; occupation. **b.** Permanence of position: *academic tenure.* (From the Latin word *tenere*) 10. ____________

Example During his *tenure* as senator, Miller was responsible for the passage of many bills that improved the quality of life in our state.

NAME ______________________ DATE ____________

EXERCISE 1 WRITING CORRECT WORDS

On the answer line, write the word from the vocabulary list that fits each definition.

1. Capable of being defended or sustained; logical; reasonable — 1. tenable
2. The act of attempting to lessen the seriousness of by providing a partial justification or excuse — 2. extenuation
3. Having the ability to remember or store — 3. retentive
4. Having little substance; flimsy — 4. tenuous
5. An indication of something momentous or calamitous about to occur; omen — 5. portent
6. Holding firmly; persistent; cohesive — 6. tenacious
7. The attendants accompanying a high-ranking person — 7. retinue
8. The period of holding something, such as property or an office; permanence of position — 8. tenure
9. Something, especially food, that supports life, health, and good spirits; the supplying of the necessities of life — 9. sustenance
10. Making an extravagant outward show; claiming a position of distinction or merit, especially when unjustified — 10. pretentious

EXERCISE 2 USING WORDS CORRECTLY

Decide whether the italicized vocabulary word has been used correctly in the sentence. On the answer line, write *Correct* for correct use and *Incorrect* for incorrect use.

1. Caleb's claim to have been on the winning team seemed *tenuous.* — 1. Correct
2. A larder full of fruits and vegetables from the garden will provide much of the *sustenance* for winter. — 2. Correct
3. A beautiful sunset is generally interpreted as a *portent* of evil. — 3. Incorrect
4. Twenty-five ladies in waiting made up the queen's *retinue.* — 4. Correct
5. Soil lightened with perlite or moss is *retentive* of moisture. — 5. Correct
6. The *tenacious* dog ran from the spitting cat. — 6. Incorrect
7. A *pretentious* speech is concise and well-organized. — 7. Incorrect
8. Ignorance of the law is never an *extenuation* of a crime. — 8. Correct
9. A volunteer's *tenure* in the Peace Corps usually lasts two years. — 9. Correct
10. LaToya chose a *tenable* position for the debate and researched her argument thoroughly. — 10. Correct

EXERCISE 3 IDENTIFYING SYNONYMS AND ANTONYMS

Decide which word has the meaning that is the same as (a synonym) or opposite to (an antonym) that of the capitalized vocabulary word. Write the letter of your choice on the answer line.

1. PORTENT (synonym): 1. b
   a. blindness b. omen c. memento d. discrimination
2. RETENTIVE (antonym): 2. a
   a. forgetful b. pliant c. obstinate d. naive
3. RETINUE (synonym): 3. b
   a. menagerie b. followers c. parade d. crowd
4. PRETENTIOUS (antonym): 4. d
   a. unrestrained b. berserk c. elaborate d. modest
5. SUSTENANCE (synonym): 5. a
   a. nourishment b. remedy c. hope d. activity
6. TENUOUS (antonym): 6. d
   a. flimsy b. applicable c. taut d. substantial
7. TENACIOUS (synonym): 7. c
   a. rebellious b. hesitant c. persistent d. irresolute
8. EXTENUATION (antonym): 8. b
   a. reprieve b. incrimination c. authority d. customary
9. TENURE (synonym): 9. c
   a. demotion b. retirement c. term d. promotion
10. TENABLE (antonym): 10. c
    a. logical b. tangible c. indefensible d. primary

EXERCISE 4 USING DIFFERENT FORMS OF WORDS

Decide which form of the vocabulary word in parentheses best completes the sentence. The form given may be correct. Write your answer on the answer line.

1. Some people claim that a black cat crossing their path ____ disaster. *(portent)* 1. portends
2. Your ____ of facts will improve if you memorize and review over several days. *(retentive)* 2. retention
3. The ____ of Mr. Clyde's office suggested that he played a more important role in the company than he actually did. *(pretentious)* 3. pretentiousness
4. The fortress of Quebec was thought to be ____ situated on a high plateau. *(tenable)* 4. tenably
5. To gourmet cooks food is more than just ____. *(sustenance)* 5. sustenance
6. The silken threads of the spider web clung ____ to the window. *(tenuous)* 6. tenuously
7. Supreme Court judges have lifetime ____. *(tenure)* 7. tenure
8. The movie star traveled with a ____ of maids, hairdressers, tailors, and advisers. *(retinue)* 8. retinue
9. Several large burs were ____ entangled in the puppy's shaggy coat. *(tenacious)* 9. tenaciously
10. "Due to ____ circumstances, tonight's performance has been canceled," announced the manager of the theater. *(extenuation)* 10. extenuating

NAME ______________________ DATE __________

READING COMPREHENSION

Each numbered sentence in the following passage contains an italicized vocabulary word or related form. After you read the passage, you will complete an exercise.

ANNE SULLIVAN MACY: "MIRACLE WORKER"

Throughout most of her life, Anne Mansfield Sullivan Macy (1866–1936) was often overshadowed by the achievements of her famous pupil, Helen Keller. (1) Many of Anne Sullivan Macy's contemporaries viewed her only as a member of Keller's ***retinue,*** some even accusing her of seeking to use Helen for selfish purposes. (2) Others, who exaggerated the miracle of Helen Keller's achievement, dismissed the teacher's role as a ***pretentious*** one. (3) Although these slights wounded Anne Sullivan Macy's ***tenuous*** self-confidence, they did not detract from her remarkable accomplishment. With sensitivity and determination, this patient teacher and companion was initially responsible for Helen Keller's success.

(4) Before Anne ever met the Kellers, she endured a tragic childhood that certainly held no ***portent*** of her impressive career. Partially blind herself from a childhood infection, she was raised in a state institution after her mother died and her father abandoned his children. A spirited, rebellious girl with a passion for knowledge, Anne begged to attend the Perkins Institution for the Blind in Boston, from which she graduated first in her class in 1886. While attending Perkins, Anne had corrective surgery and regained some of her sight, although she was plagued by eye trouble all her life.

In 1887 twenty-year-old Anne Sullivan traveled to Tuscumbia, Alabama, to become the governess for Helen Keller, a child who was blind, deaf, and unable to speak. (5) Although the Keller family and professionals who had examined Helen held the ***tenable*** position that the six-year-old was uneducable, Anne recognized Helen's curiosity. (6) Anne Sullivan felt that the child's handicaps were not an ***extenuation*** of the failure to teach her. She quickly taught Helen table manners, civilized behavior, and self-control.

Anne Sullivan made contact with her student through the sense of touch. (7) ***Tenaciously*** and patiently, she used a sign vocabulary to spell words into Helen's hand. (8) Once Helen grasped that everything has its own special name, she showed a remarkably ***retentive*** mind and made astounding progress. With the same stubborn persistence, Sullivan taught her to read Braille and to speak.

(9) In her forty-nine-year ***tenure*** as Helen's teacher and companion, Anne Sullivan did everything from attending Radcliffe College classes with Helen to accompanying her on speech-making tours and working with her for charitable organizations. (10) ***Sustained*** by her belief that in the event of her own death Helen would have a mentor and friend, she even agreed to marry John Macy in 1905. In time the Macys separated, and Anne Sullivan Macy lived out the rest of her life with her beloved student and friend.

In 1955 Helen Keller wrote *Teacher,* a memoir and a tribute to the extraordinary, selfless woman who had made such a difference in her life. The 1957 hit play *The Miracle Worker,* which was made into a famous film, immortalizes the special relationship of pupil and teacher. Any account of Keller's ability to surmount her handicaps is inspirational, yet those who encounter her story cannot forget the role of Anne Sullivan Macy. With commitment, determination, and perseverance, she was singlehandedly responsible for bringing Helen Keller out of darkness.

READING COMPREHENSION EXERCISE

Each of the following statements corresponds to a numbered sentence in the passage. Each statement contains a blank and is followed by four answer choices. Decide which choice fits best in the blank. The word or phrase that you choose must express roughly the same meaning as the italicized word in the passage. Write the letter of your choice on the answer line.

1. Many people viewed Anne Sullivan Macy only as a member of Helen Keller's _____. 1. a
   a. group of attendants **c.** family
   b. group of friends **d.** organization

2. Others, inspired by Helen Keller's achievements, dismissed the teacher as _____. 2. d
   a. unimportant **b.** inadequate **c.** harmful **d.** self-important

3. These slights wounded Anne Sullivan Macy's _____ self-confidence. 3. b
   a. enormous **b.** flimsy **c.** authoritative **d.** external

4. Her childhood certainly held no _____ of her impressive career. 4. a
   a. indication **b.** definition **c.** hope **d.** advancement

5. Many people held the _____ position that Helen Keller was uneducable. 5. c
   a. opinionated **b.** occasional **c.** reasonable **d.** negative

6. Anne Sullivan felt that Helen's handicaps were not a _____ of the failure to teach her. 6. c
   a. guideline **b.** sign **c.** justification **d.** pretense

7. Sullivan _____ used sign vocabulary to spell out words. 7. a
   a. persistently **b.** knowledgeably **c.** cleverly **d.** originally

8. Helen's mind was remarkably _____. 8. d
   a. patient **c.** quick to understand
   b. complex **d.** good at remembering

9. Anne Sullivan had a forty-nine-year _____ as Helen's teacher and companion. 9. b
   a. learning experience **c.** lifetime
   b. career **d.** challenge

10. Sullivan was _____ by her belief that if she died, John Macy would be Helen's friend and mentor. 10. c
    a. influenced **b.** interrupted **c.** supported **d.** made anxious

PRACTICE WITH ANALOGIES

See pages 32, 66, and 86 for some strategies to use with analogies.

Directions On the answer line, write the vocabulary word or a form of it that completes each analogy.

1. ILLOGICAL : CONFUSION :: _____ : harm *(Lesson 20)* 1. deleterious
2. CREST : WAVE :: _____ : mountain *(Lesson 20)* 2. pinnacle
3. FELL : TREE :: _____ : house *(Lesson 20)* 3. raze
4. IRRESISTIBLE : REFUSED :: _____ : satisfied *(Lesson 21)* 4. insatiable
5. HYPERBOLE : LANGUAGE :: _____ : spending *(Lesson 21)* 5. prodigality
6. VULNERABLE : INJURED :: _____ : defended *(Lesson 22)* 6. tenable
7. TRIVIAL : SIGNIFICANCE :: _____ : modesty *(Lesson 22)* 7. pretentious
8. DISCARD : TRASH :: _____ : cargo *(Lesson 20)* 8. jettison

LESSON 23 PROBLEMS AND SOLUTIONS

23

Each time that you complete a crossword puzzle, unravel the clues of a mystery, or work out a personal decision, you are grappling with a question or situation that presents some degree of uncertainty, perplexity, or difficulty. Regardless of the nature of the problem, however, strategies for resolution are basically the same. After examining the situation carefully and logically, you will most likely decide on several possible alternatives. After evaluating the alternatives and perhaps soliciting the advice and opinions of other people, you will choose the solution that makes the most sense. The words in this lesson will enhance your understanding of the different types of problems that you encounter, as well as tactics for arriving at solutions.

WORD LIST

adduce
confound
construe
conundrum
cryptic
equivocate
paradox
patent
perspicacity
rudimentary

DEFINITIONS

After you have studied the definitions and example for each vocabulary word, write the word on the line to the right.

1. **adduce** (ə-do͞os′, ə-dyo͞os′) *trans. verb* To cite as an example or means of proof in an argument; bring forward for consideration. (From the Latin *ad-*, meaning "to," and *ducere*, meaning "to lead") 1. ____________

Example In her lecture the chemist *adduced* gasoline as one of the best-known carbon compounds.

2. **confound** (kən-found′, kŏn-found′) *trans. verb* **a.** To cause (a person) to become confused; bewilder. **b.** To fail to distinguish; mix up: *confound fact and fiction.* (From the Latin *com-*, meaning "together," and *fundere*, meaning "to pour") 2. ____________

Related Word **confounded** *adjective*
Example The strange results of the experiment *confounded* the scientist.

3. **construe** (kən-stro͞o′) *trans. verb* To place a certain meaning on; interpret. (From the Latin word *construere*, meaning "to build") 3. ____________

Example Allison *construed* her cousin's silence as support of her plan.

4. **conundrum** (kə-nŭn′drəm) *noun* **a.** A problem with no satisfactory solution. **b.** A difficult and complicated problem. **c.** A riddle in which a fanciful question is answered by a pun: *What's the difference between a bird with one wing and a bird with two? It's a matter of a pinion.* 4. ____________

Example The cause of the epidemic was a *conundrum* to state health officials.

5. **cryptic** (krĭp'tĭk) *adjective* **a.** Having an ambiguous or hidden meaning; enigmatic. **b.** Of a secret nature; mystifying. (From the Greek word *kryptein,* meaning "to hide")

Related Word **cryptically** *adverb*
Example Scholars have provided several interpretations of the ancient poet's *cryptic* verses.

5. ______

USAGE NOTE: A *crypt* is an underground (i.e., hidden) vault or chamber, especially one beneath a church and used as a burial place.

6. **equivocate** (ĭ-kwĭv'ə-kāt') *intrans. verb* **a.** To use ambiguous and misleading language intentionally; hedge. **b.** To avoid making an explicit statement. (From the Latin words *aequus,* meaning "equal," and *vocare,* meaning "to call")

Related Words **equivocal** *adjective;* **equivocally** *adverb;* **equivocation** *noun*
Example The witness *equivocated* to such an extent that members of the jury were unable to evaluate the validity of his testimony.

6. ______

ETYMOLOGY NOTE: A literal translation from the Latin might be "to speak with two voices," or, put another way, "to speak out of both sides of one's mouth."

7. **paradox** (păr'ə-dŏks') *noun* **a.** A seemingly contradictory statement that may nonetheless be true. **b.** An assertion that is essentially self contradictory, although based on a valid deduction from acceptable premises. **c.** A person with inexplicable or contradictory qualities. (From the Greek words *para,* meaning "beyond," and *dokein,* meaning "to think")

Related Words **paradoxical** *adjective;* **paradoxically** *adverb*
Example William Wordsworth's assertion that "The child is father of the man" is an example of a *paradox.*

7. ______

8. **patent** (păt'nt) *adjective* Obvious; plain. (From the Latin word *patere,* meaning "to be opened")

Related Word **patently** *adverb*
Example Afraid of their reaction, Morgan made *patent* attempts to avoid his friends.

8. ______

9. **perspicacity** (pûr'spĭ-kăs'ĭ-te) *noun* Acuteness of perception, discernment, or understanding. (From the Latin word *perspicere,* meaning "to look through")

Related Words **perspicacious** *adjective;* **perspicaciously** *adverb*
Example For a twelve-year-old, Rafaela's *perspicacity* about human motivation is quite amazing.

9. ______

10. **rudimentary** (ro͞o'də-mĕn'tə-rē, ro͞o'də-mĕn'trē) *adjective* **a.** Of or relating to basic facts or principles that must be learned first; elementary; fundamental. **b.** In the earliest stages of development; incipient. (From the Latin word *rudis,* meaning "rough" or "unformed")

Related Word **rudiment** *noun*
Example Before going into detail, Mrs. Ling outlined the *rudimentary* aspects of the advertising promotion.

10. ______

Word History: equivocate

Latin: *aequus*=equal + *vocare*=to call

Equivocate literally means "to call equally" or "hedge" by going first in one direction and then in another. This notion of "equal" occurs in numerous other *aequus* derivatives with the spelling *equi-* or *equa-*. For example, *equidistant* describes a point "equally distant" from two other points; the *equator* refers to the line that divides "equally" the Southern and Northern hemispheres; and the *equinox* is the time of the year when the length of the day and the night are "equal."

NAME ______________________ DATE __________

EXERCISE 1 MATCHING WORDS AND DEFINITIONS

Match the definition in Column B with the word in Column A. Write the letter of the correct definition on the answer line.

Column A	Column B	
1. cryptic	a. to use ambiguous and misleading language intentionally; avoid making an explicit statement	1. f
2. construe	b. to cite as an example or proof in an argument	2. h
3. patent	c. a seemingly contradictory statement that nonetheless may be true	3. i
4. perspicacity	d. of or relating to basic facts or principles; in the earliest stages of development	4. g
5. adduce	e. to cause (a person) to become confused; mix up	5. b
6. paradox	f. having an ambiguous or hidden meaning	6. c
7. rudimentary	g. acuteness of perception or understanding	7. d
8. conundrum	h. to place a certain meaning on; interpret	8. j
9. confound	i. obvious; plain	9. e
10. equivocate	j. a problem with no satisfactory solution; a difficult or complicated problem	10. a

EXERCISE 2 USING WORDS CORRECTLY

Decide whether the italicized vocabulary word has been used correctly in the sentence. On the answer line, write *Correct* for correct use and *Incorrect* for incorrect use.

1. The clues for the treasure hunt were so *cryptic* that everyone found the treasure almost immediately. — 1. Incorrect
2. *Rudimentary* experience with a potter's wheel is a prerequisite for the ceramics class. — 2. Correct
3. Part of Eliott's *perspicacity* in playing chess is his ability to capitalize on his opponent's weaknesses. — 3. Correct
4. Olivia's error was so *patent* that no one even noticed. — 4. Incorrect
5. Ms. Petry *adduced* us to consider tutoring elementary school students. — 5. Incorrect
6. "This play has such a convoluted plot that it *confounds* me totally," complained Caroline. — 6. Correct
7. Different people will *construe* the same poem differently. — 7. Correct
8. Jack likes to play with words and especially enjoys concocting *conundrums.* — 8. Correct
9. Sharon *equivocates* so frequently that her friends no longer expect a straightforward response from her. — 9. Correct
10. "You can solve this *paradox* by using simple arithmetic," said Mr. Ashley. — 10. Incorrect

EXERCISE 3 CHOOSING THE BEST WORD

Decide which vocabulary word or related form best expresses the meaning of the italicized word or phrase in the sentence. On the answer line, write the letter of the correct choice.

1. Many people *interpreted* Mr. Switzler's interview with the press as a statement of his intent to run for election. — 1. b
   a. equivocated b. construed c. confounded d. adduced

2. Lou's boss reprimanded her for her *obvious* disregard of established procedure. 2. a
a. patent b. cryptic c. confounded d. perspicacious

3. Russell tends to *avoid making an explicit statement* until he knows all the options. 3. d
a. adduce b. confound c. construe d. equivocate

4. Writers often use a *seemingly contradictory statement that may be true* to attract attention and create emphasis. 4. a
a. paradox b. conundrum c. perspicacity d. rudiment

5. The rookie pitcher *bewildered* the majority of batters with his fast ball. 5. c
a. construed b. equivocated c. confounded d. adduced

6. In her doctoral thesis, Margo proved that social behavior in young chimpanzees is *in the earliest stages of development*. 6. b
a. cryptic b. rudimentary c. paradoxical d. confounding

7. Having expected a long, detailed explanation, we were surprised and confused by his *ambiguous* one-word reply. 7. d
a. perspicacious b. rudimentary c. patent d. cryptic

8. Only a few investors had the *acuteness of perception* to foresee the growth potential of the stock. 8. a
a. perspicacity b. conundrum c. paradox d. rudiment

9. "Let me *bring forward for consideration* several other economic factors you should be aware of," said the bank president. 9. c
a. construe b. confound c. adduce d. equivocate

10. For Aleta deciding which of two jobs would be more challenging seemed at first to be a *problem without a satisfactory solution*. 10. a
a. conundrum b. rudiment c. equivocation d. paradox

EXERCISE 4 USING DIFFERENT FORMS OF WORDS

Decide which form of the vocabulary word in parentheses best completes the sentence. The form given may be correct. Write your answer on the answer line.

1. "Can increased appetite be ______ as a side effect of the medication?" the Davidsons asked the veterinarian. *(construe)* 1. **construed**

2. That crossword puzzle completely ______ Joseph. *(confound)* 2. **confounded**

3. Miss Rickenbacker replied ______ to all of our questions. *(cryptic)* 3. **cryptically**

4. How hereditary characteristics are transmitted remained a ______ until the discovery of DNA. *(conundrum)* 4. **conundrum**

5. Because the candidate did not want to offend anyone during the election, he answered the questions ______. *(equivocal)* 5. **equivocally**

6. "The clues are so varied and so ______," muttered the detective, "that some of the evidence must have been contrived." *(paradox)* 6. **paradoxical**

7. Having been confused by the ______ of second-year algebra, Matt decided to take review math. *(rudimentary)* 7. **rudiments**

8. The television commentator enjoyed a reputation as a ______ and dedicated journalist. *(perspicacity)* 8. **perspicacious**

9. "The question of a change in the tax rate will be ______ at the next city council meeting," said the mayor to the citizens' group. *(adduce)* 9. **adduced**

10. Ira has a difficult time being friendly to someone who is ______ insincere. *(patent)* 10. **patently**

NAME ______________________ DATE __________

READING COMPREHENSION

Each numbered sentence in the following passage contains an italicized vocabulary word or related form. After you read the passage, you will complete an exercise.

THE MYSTERY OF THE NAZCA PLAIN

In the early 1930s, pilots flying above the Nazca plain in Peru saw giant lines crisscrossing the desert. Many formed rectangles and had a surprising similarity to a landing field. Some formed wedges measuring more than 2,500 feet. Outlines of animals—spider, monkey, condor, and lizard—also emerged. One, a stylized heron, had a neck 900 feet long.

(1) Since then, the meaning of the plain has ***confounded*** researchers. It is believed that the "Nazca Lines" were produced between 1000 B.C. and A.D. 1000, but little else is known. (2) Perhaps the most puzzling ***conundrum*** is how the ancient peoples who built them could have needed or wanted them. (3) These massive figures and patterns can only be ***construed*** from at least 1,000 feet in the air. (4) Although the figures and shapes are ***patently*** obvious from a high-flying plane, from the ground they look only like small mounds of stones placed deliberately, but with no special pattern. (5) It is surely a ***paradox*** that the earth-bound ancient peoples who labored to build them almost certainly could not see their work. (6) They would have needed astonishing ***perspicacity*** even to have imagined what the figures looked like.

Several theories have been put forward to explain their presence. Some have claimed that they were indeed an ancient landing field. (7) Yet even if we presume that the people who built them controlled ***rudimentary*** aviation techniques, a problem remains. The desert floor at Nazca is soft earth and would not support a landing aircraft. Indeed, it is doubtful that the Nazca Lines are related to any mode of transportation. They surely are not roads; many of the lines begin and end in mid-desert. They are also not irrigation canals since they do not lead to sources of water.

Maria Reiche, a mathematician who has spent her life studying and protecting the Nazca Lines, has suggested that they may be a gigantic astronomical calendar or observatory. (8) Indeed, the well-known mathematical sophistication of ancient American cultures ***adduces*** this interpretation. However, Gerald Hawkins tested this theory by taking a sample of the lines and calculating how many coincided with major astronomical events. The vast amount of data processed by computer unfortunately yielded only chance relationships to astronomy. (9) The function of the lines and figures remained as ***cryptic*** as ever.

Others have maintained that the lines and figures were used for religious purposes. Toni Morrison, an explorer who researched customs of the Andes mountain people, discovered a tradition of shrines linked by straight lines and pathways. Worshipers moved from one shrine to another, praying at each one. The small piles of stones found at Nazca might have been shrines, and Morrison suggested that the animals and symbols served as special enclosures.

Peru boasts some other landscape figures that seem to have more obvious explanations. A human figure of almost 400 feet decorates the side of the Solitary Mountain. A candelabrum is carved into another mountain. Finally, Sierra Pintada, "the painted mountain," is covered with giant pictures of spirals, circles, warriors, and a condor. Researchers speculate that these figures, clearly visible from the ground, served as traveling guideposts. (10) But when asked for an explanation of the Nazca plain, they may be tempted to ***equivocate.*** For whether they were used for transportation, irrigation, astronomy, religion, travel, or some yet unknown purpose, the Nazca Lines remain an unsolved mystery.

READING COMPREHENSION EXERCISE

Each of the following statements corresponds to a numbered sentence in the passage. Each statement contains a blank and is followed by four answer choices. Decide which choice fits best in the blank. The word or phrase that you choose must express roughly the same meaning as the italicized word in the passage. Write the letter of your choice on the answer line.

1. Since then, the meaning of the plain has ____ researchers. — 1. d
   a. troubled b. haunted c. amazed d. bewildered

2. Perhaps the most puzzling ____ is how the ancient peoples who built them could have needed or wanted them. — 2. b
   a. solution b. problem c. happening d. research

3. These massive figures and patterns can only be ____ from at least 1,000 feet in the air. — 3. c
   a. seen b. noticed c. interpreted d. symbolized

4. Although the figures and shapes are ____ obvious from a high-flying plane, from the ground they look only like small mounds of stones placed deliberately, but with no special pattern. — 4. d
   a. relatively b. often c. similarly d. plainly

5. It is surely a(n) ____ that the earth-bound ancient peoples who labored to build them almost certainly could not see their work. — 5. a
   a. contradiction b. certainty c. amazement d. fiction

6. They would have needed astonishing ____ even to imagine what the figures looked like. — 6. a
   a. understanding b. imagination c. technology d. momentum

7. Yet even if we presume that the people who built them controlled ____ aviation techniques, a problem remains. — 7. c
   a. advanced b. surprising c. basic d. prehistoric

8. Indeed, the well-known mathematical sophistication of ancient American cultures ____ this interpretation. — 8. b
   a. helps disprove b. helps prove c. helps complicate d. helps ease

9. The function of the lines and figures remained as ____ as ever. — 9. c
   a. open c. secret
   b. useful d. known

10. But when asked for an explanation of the Nazca plain, they may be tempted to ____. — 10. c
    a. answer b. remain silent c. hedge d. lie

WRITING ASSIGNMENT

Suppose that you are the author of an advice-to-teenagers column in your school newspaper. For this week's column, you have selected a letter that presents an especially difficult problem. Write a response to the letter, offering several alternatives for dealing with the situation. In your column use at least five of the vocabulary words from this lesson and underline each one.

LESSON 24 SIZE AND AMOUNT

24

Despite the array of descriptive words in our language for mass, volume, dimension, proportion, and capacity, people tend to use a few words over and over again. *Great, huge, tiny,* and *slight* are so general that they usually fail to provide us with a visual image of actual size. Physical size and quantity are important characteristics; the words in this lesson will help you to describe these characteristics with more precision.

WORD LIST

commodious
finite
gamut
incalculable
iota
lofty
magnitude
minuscule
picayune
vestige

DEFINITIONS

After you have studied the definitions and example for each vocabulary word, write the word on the line to the right.

1. **commodious** (kə-mō'dē-əs) *adjective* Spacious; roomy. (From the Latin *com-*, meaning "with," and *modus*, meaning "measure") 1. ____________

Related Words **commodiously** *adverb;* **commodiousness** *noun*
Example Although smaller cars are less expensive, cars that are bigger and more *commodious* may be worth the added expense for a large family that likes to travel comfortably.

2. **finite** (fī'nīt') *adjective* **a.** Limited; having boundaries. **b.** Existing for a limited time only. (From the Latin word *finis,* meaning "limit" or "boundary") 2. ____________

Example We have only a *finite* list of choices to consider in making the decision.

3. **gamut** (găm'ət) *noun* **a.** The complete range or extent of something. **b.** The entire series of recognized musical notes. (From the Medieval Latin phrase *gamma ut,* the lowest notes in the ancient and medieval musical scales) 3. ____________

Example In one day the price of the stock ran the *gamut* from its yearly high to its yearly low.

4. **incalculable** (ĭn-kăl'kyə-lə-bəl) *adjective* **a.** Not capable of being conceived of or determined. **b.** Being beyond calculation; very great. **c.** Unpredictable; uncertain. 4. ____________

Related Word **incalculably** *adverb*
Example The influence of environment on character development is *incalculable.*

5. **iota** (ī-ō′tə) *noun* An extremely small amount; bit. (From the Greek word *iota,* the ninth and smallest letter of the Greek alphabet) 5. ____________

Example The teacher would not budge one *iota* when the student asked for a short extension of time for his project.

6. **lofty** (lôf′tē, lŏf′tē) *adjective* **a.** Of great height; towering. **b.** Elevated in character; noble. **c.** Affecting grandness; pompous. **d.** Arrogant; haughty. (From the Old Norse word *lopt,* meaning "upstairs room") 6. ____________

Related Words **loftily** *adverb;* **loftiness** *noun*
Example Sir Edmund Hillary and Tenzing Norgay were the first known human beings to stand on the *lofty* summit of Mount Everest, the world's highest mountain.

7. **magnitude** (măg′nĭ-to͞od′, măg′nĭ-tyo͞od′) *noun* **a.** Greatness in size or extent. **b.** Greatness of rank or position. **c.** Greatness in significance or influence. (From the Latin word *magnus,* meaning "great") 7. ____________

Example Shakespeare is known not only for the excellence of his literary works but also for their sheer *magnitude.*

8. **minuscule** (mĭn′ə-skyo͞ol′) *adjective* Very small; tiny. (From the Latin word *minus,* meaning "less") 8. ____________

MEMORY CUE: *Minuscule* begins with *minus.*

Example A *minuscule* amount of phosphorus is added to a silicon chip to produce the microchip conductors that run many computers and calculators.

9. **picayune** (pĭk′ə-yo͞on′) *adjective* **a.** Of little value or importance. **b.** Petty; mean. (From the French word *picaillon,* meaning "small coin") 9. ____________

Example The workers wanted their new contract to address overall improvements in working conditions rather than *picayune* issues.

10. **vestige** (vĕs′tĭj) *noun* A visible trace, evidence, or sign of something that has once existed but exists or appears no more. (From the Latin word *vestigium,* meaning "footprint") 10. ____________

Related Word **vestigial** *adjective*
Example Archaeologists dig into the earth to find *vestiges* of ancient civilizations.

NAME ______________________________ DATE ______________

EXERCISE 1 WRITING CORRECT WORDS

On the answer line, write the word from the vocabulary list that fits each definition.

1. The complete range or extent of something — 1. gamut
2. A visible trace of something that once existed but exists no more — 2. vestige
3. Of little value or importance; petty — 3. picayune
4. Spacious; roomy — 4. commodious
5. An extremely small amount; bit — 5. iota
6. Greatness in size or extent; greatness of rank or position — 6. magnitude
7. Of great height; elevated in character; affecting grandness — 7. lofty
8. Limited; having boundaries; existing for a limited time only — 8. finite
9. Very small; tiny — 9. minuscule
10. Not capable of being conceived of or determined; being beyond calculation — 10. incalculable

EXERCISE 2 USING WORDS CORRECTLY

Decide whether the italicized vocabulary word has been used correctly in the sentence. On the answer line, write *Correct* for correct use and *Incorrect* for incorrect use.

1. *Minuscule* circuit boards have made possible the development of calculators that are as thin as credit cards. — 1. Correct
2. Having found no boundaries to the universe, scientists can only speculate that it is *finite.* — 2. Incorrect
3. *Mom's Guide to Home Cooking* contains a *gamut* of recipes from soup to nuts. — 3. Correct
4. Derek's *lofty* stature as well as his talent made him one of the youngest basketball players ever to sign with a professional team. — 4. Correct
5. The committee was nearly overwhelmed by the *magnitude* of its task. — 5. Correct
6. Some people take *incalculable* risks, while others prefer to play safe. — 6. Correct
7. *Commodious* entertainers such as Bill Cosby and Tim Allen have kept audiences laughing for years. — 7. Incorrect
8. Because of the *picayune* contributions of an anonymous philanthropist, the hospital was able to build its much-needed new wing. — 8. Incorrect
9. The police had to release the suspect because they did not have an *iota* of evidence to implicate him in the crime. — 9. Correct
10. Clark was looking for a three-piece suit with a jacket, slacks, and contrasting *vestige.* — 10. Incorrect

EXERCISE 3 CHOOSING THE BEST WORD

Decide which vocabulary word or related form best completes the sentence, and write the letter of your choice on the answer line.

1. In the labor dispute, each side claimed that the other was interested only in ______ details. — 1. d

   a. commodious **b.** finite **c.** vestigial **d.** picayune

2. The principal's stern expression betrayed not a(n) _____ of sympathy for the two truants. 2. c
a. gamut b. magnitude c. iota d. loftiness

3. Interior designers sometimes use a mirrored wall to make a small room appear more _____. 3. c
a. incalculable b. picayune c. commodious d. minuscule

4. Rosalind Franklin was a British scientist whose photographs of the molecular structure of DNA proved to be a scientific breakthrough of great _____. 4. a
a. magnitude b. gamut c. vestige d. commodiousness

5. Woodrow Wilson's _____ hopes for the League of Nations were never fully realized because his own country would not join. 5. c
a. minuscule b. picayune c. lofty d. commodious

6. Although much research has been done, the overall results of the "greenhouse effect" on world climate remain _____. 6. d
a. commodious b. finite c. lofty d. incalculable

7. Even _____ amounts of plant food can be of benefit to indoor plants. 7. a
a. minuscule b. finite c. vestigial d. incalculable

8. Personal-computer dealers offer a(n) _____ of software programs from children's games to sophisticated spreadsheets. 8. a
a. gamut b. vestige c. iota d. loftiness

9. Our _____ minds cannot comprehend the immensity of a black hole in space. 9. b
a. picayune b. finite c. minuscule d. commodious

10. A good bloodhound can follow even the merest _____ of a scent. 10. c
a. gamut b. loftiness c. vestige d. magnitude

EXERCISE 4 USING DIFFERENT FORMS OF WORDS

Decide which form of the vocabulary word in parentheses best completes the sentence. The form given may be correct. Write your answer on the answer line.

1. The constitutional system of checks and balances ensures that the three branches of government have _____ powers. *(finite)* 1. finite

2. Leslie was proud to have responsibility of such _____. *(magnitude)* 2. magnitude

3. During the Great Depression, many families learned to use every _____ of their meager resources. *(iota)* 3. iota

4. Many people like the feeling of _____ that cathedral ceilings give to a room. *(commodious)* 4. commodiousness

5. Doctors can glean important genetic information from a _____ sample of tissue. *(minuscule)* 5. minuscule

6. Pat sometimes resents the seemingly _____ comments that her editor makes about her manuscripts. *(picayune)* 6. picayune

7. Marion responded _____ to the suggestion that she had been embarrassed. *(lofty)* 7. loftily

8. Some critics of the two party system feel that it does not adequately represent the full _____ of political views. *(gamut)* 8. gamut

9. While some people applaud the educational benefits of computers, others view the machines as having an _____ negative effect on students' basic skills. *(incalculable)* 9. incalculably

10. Humans, unlike most mammals, have only a _____ tail. *(vestige)* 10. vestigial

NAME ______________________ DATE __________

READING COMPREHENSION

Each numbered sentence in the following passage contains an italicized vocabulary word or related form. After you read the passage, you will complete an exercise.

THE ATOM: NATURE'S BUILDING BLOCK

Early theories about the composition of matter were a mixture of mythology, speculation, and philosophy. Lacking factual information, the ancient Greeks sought to understand the underlying nature of things so that they could logically explain how and why creation, change, and destruction occurred. The ancient Greek notion of the atom is remarkably one of the most permanent of all the conceptions of early science.

(1) The first person to propose the idea that matter is made up of ***minuscule*** particles invisible to the human eye was the Greek philosopher Leucippus. His student Democritus further refined this theory, calling the particles *atomos,* the Greek word meaning "indivisible." (2) Although things appear to change, said Democritus, all that really happens is that an ***incalculable*** number of atoms join together for a time, only to fall apart again. The variety in nature reflects the variety of ways in which atoms combine.

(3) The ***magnitude*** of the theories or Leucippus and Democritus was largely ignored for many centuries. (4) Lacking one ***iota*** of observable evidence of atoms, even Renaissance scientists discounted them in favor of Aristotle's conception of the composition of matter. (5) They dismissed atoms as ***picayune*** in comparison with the traditional four elements—fire, water, air, and earth—that could actually be observed.

(6) More than a ***vestige*** of the work of Leucippus and Democritus survived into the eighteenth and nineteenth centuries, however, when chemical research led to the study of the way elements combine to form compounds. Such scientists as John Dalton still viewed the atom as a hard, indestructible ball. Dalton, in his work with the properties of gases, postulated that all atoms of an element are identical, that atoms of different elements have different properties, and that the redistribution or matter in chemical reactions neither destroys nor creates atoms.

The structure of the atom was unknown until the discovery of one of its component parts, the electron, in 1897. Additional evidence about the structure and components came about after the discoveries of x-rays and radioactivity. Although the atom can now be seen under the high magnification of the electron microscope, it cannot be examined in detail. Much about its structure can be inferred only through mathematical formulas and experimental evidence.

Today we know that an atom consists of particles called protons, neutrons, and electrons. Protons and neutrons are clustered tightly in the nucleus, a tiny central area within the atom. The remainder of the atom is mostly empty space. (7) Within this relatively ***commodious*** area surrounding the nucleus, electrons arranged in theoretical "shells," or layers, revolve at incredible speeds.

The most important aspect of electrons is their property of allowing atoms to interact and form molecules. (8) Although each "shell" of an atom contains a ***finite*** number of electrons, those electrons in the outermost shells can be shared, lost, or gained. When the electrons of two or more atoms interact, various molecules are created. For example, if two atoms of hydrogen combine with one atom of oxygen, a water molecule is formed.

Every neutron or electron in matter is the same as every other neutron or electron. Similarly, all protons are the same. What makes an atom of one element different from the atom of another is the number of protons. (9) Atoms run the ***gamut*** from the 1-proton hydrogen atom to the complex 103-proton lawrencium atom.

With the aid of modern technology, scientists are continually making new discoveries about the atom. In 1964, for example, protons and neutrons were found to be composed of even smaller subatomic particles called "quarks." Each generation of researchers finds that the atom is more complex and dynamic than previously thought. (10) Yet despite the seemingly ***lofty*** attitude of contemporary science, Leucippus and Democritus were not far off in imagining the atom as the building block of matter.

READING COMPREHENSION EXERCISE

Each of the following statements corresponds to a numbered sentence in the passage. Each statement contains a blank and is followed by four answer choices. Decide which choice fits best in the blank. The word or phrase that you choose must express roughly the same meaning as the italicized word in the passage. Write the letter of your choice on the answer line.

1. Leucippus proposed the idea that matter is made up of _____ particles. 1. a
   a. extremely small b. rather loose c. complex d. mixed

2. Democritus believed that a(n) _____ number of atoms join together, only to fall apart again. 2. c
   a. given c. incapable of being determined
   b. reduced d. incapable of being observed

3. The _____ of the early theories was ignored for many centuries. 3. b
   a. unusual quality b. significance c. elimination d. recklessness

4. Because they lacked even one _____ observable evidence, Renaissance scientists discounted atoms. 4. b
   a. type of b. bit of c. recollection of d. opportunity for

5. They dismissed atoms as _____ in comparison with the four elements. 5. d
   a. too expensive c. being too experimental
   b. uninteresting d. having little value

6. More than a(n) _____ of the work of Leucippus and Democritus survived into the eighteenth and nineteenth centuries. 6. a
   a. trace b. memory c. summary d. appraisal

7. Electrons arranged in "shells" revolve at incredible speeds within the relatively _____ area surrounding the nucleus. 7. c
   a. limited b. narrow c. spacious d. shapeless

8. Each "shell" of an atom contains a(n) _____ number of electrons. 8. b
   a. random b. limited c. material d. economical

9. The _____ of protons in atoms of different elements is from 1 to 103. 9. a
   a. range b. size c. weight d. sequence

10. Despite the seemingly _____ attitude of contemporary science, Leucippus and Democritus were not far off in imagining the atom as the building block of matter. 10. d
    a. retiring b. universal c. restrained d. haughty

WRITING ASSIGNMENT

Suppose that you are an architect who has submitted a controversial plan for a new city hall, courthouse, or other public building. Although the city council supports your plan, many residents of your community object to the style of the building. Write a persuasive speech that you will deliver at an open hearing. In the speech describe the physical characteristics of the building and explain how it will serve the functions for which it was designed. Use at least five of the words from this lesson in your speech and underline each word that you use.

The **Test** for Lessons 22, 23, and 24 is on page T30.

NAME ______________________ DATE __________

READING SKILLS

THE PREFIXES *COUNTER-, CONTRA-,* AND *ANTI-*

When added to roots, the prefixes *counter-, contra-,* and *anti-* form words with different meanings. All three prefixes usually have the meaning of "against" or "opposite," as the table shows. The procedure following the table explains how to determine the meaning of an unfamiliar word that begins with one of the prefixes.

Word	Sentence	Word Definition
counterbalance	Her high test score *counterbalanced* the low scores on quizzes.	balanced against
contraindicate	The patient's allergy to penicillin *contraindicated* its use in his treatment.	indicated against the advisability of
antigravity	Astronauts must adapt themselves to *antigravity.*	opposite of gravity; effect of canceling a gravitational field

PROCEDURE

1. *Substitute the prefix and root definitions for the prefix and root.*
2. *Think of a possible definition of the entire word.*
3. *Use the context to help you develop the possible definition.*
4. *Check your definition of the word in a dictionary.*

EXERCISE USING THE PREFIXES *COUNTER-, CONTRA-,* AND *ANTI-*

Each sentence in this exercise contains a word beginning with one of the three prefixes in this lesson. When appropriate, the root word and its meaning are given in parentheses after the sentence. *Step 1:* Taking the context into consideration, write your own definition of the word. *Step 2:* Write the dictionary definition of the word. *Step 3:* Write a sentence of your own in which you use the word correctly.

1. The attorney presented a *counterproposal,* which the other attorney wisely accepted on behalf of her client.

   Your Definition **A proposal offered to replace one by an opponent**

   Dictionary Definition **A proposal offered to nullify or substitute for a previous one**

   Sentence **Numerous proposals and counterproposals were made at the conference.**

2. The police searched the smugglers' ship for *contraband.* (Latin root word: *bannus,* "proclamation")

   Your Definition **Goods that are against the law**

   Dictionary Definition **Goods prohibited by law or treaty from being imported or exported**

   Sentence **The customs officials discovered that the suitcases were filled with contraband.**

3. The Canadian Prime Minister met his *counterpart,* the Prime Minister of Australia.

Your Definition **Someone who holds a similar position**

Dictionary Definition **One that has the same functions and characteristics as another**

Sentence **The sales manager found that he shared many problems with his counterpart in another firm.**

4. The writer *antagonized* government officials with his critical attacks on their policies. (Greek root word: *agon,* "contest")

Your Definition **Provoked the angry feelings of**

Dictionary Definition **To incur the dislike of**

Sentence **The pitcher deliberately antagonized the nervous batter.**

5. Architecture, in *contradistinction* to poetry, is a highly public art.

Your Definition **Distinction based on opposition to something else**

Dictionary Definition **Distinction by contrasting or opposing qualities**

Sentence **She spoke of our industrial society in contradistinction to the rural society of the 1800s.**

6. The workers were confused when the manager *countermanded* her previous order. (Latin root word: *mandare,* "to command")

Your Definition **Went against**

Dictionary Definition **To cancel or reverse a command or order**

Sentence **The order to attack was countermanded by the order to retreat.**

7. The residents of one province had a traditional *antipathy* toward those of other provinces. (Greek root word: *pathos,* "feeling")

Your Definition **Feeling of opposition**

Dictionary Definition **A strong feeling of aversion, repugnance, or opposition**

Sentence **At first he felt only antipathy toward his victorious opponent.**

8. It is often *counterproductive* to work when you are tired.

Your Definition **Not productive**

Dictionary Definition **Tending to hinder rather than serve one's purpose**

Sentence **It is counterproductive to lose one's temper in an argument.**

9. The park ranger knew that she could not *contravene* the rules for anyone. (Latin root word: *venire,* "to come")

Your Definition **Go against**

Dictionary Definition **To act or be counter to; violate**

Sentence **The border incident contravened the peace treaty between the two nations.**

10. The senator's election defeat was a miserable *anticlimax* to a dazzling career.

Your Definition **Disappointing end**

Dictionary Definition **A decline viewed in disappointing contrast with a previous rise**

Sentence **After all the excitement and preparation, the party itself was an anticlimax.**

NAME ______________________ DATE __________

EXERCISE 1 WRITING CORRECT WORDS

On the answer line, write the word from the vocabulary list that fits each definition.

1. Capture and charm; enthrall; hypnotize — 1. **mesmerize**
2. Extremely loud — 2. **stentorian**
3. A rigid military disciplinarian; a person who demands absolute adherence to rules — 3. **martinet**
4. Having great stature or enormous strength; of enormous scope or power — 4. **titanic**
5. Exceedingly harsh; of or designating a law or code of extreme severity — 5. **draconian**
6. An outline that appears dark against a light background; a drawing consisting of the outline of something filled in with a solid color — 6. **silhouette**
7. A place or situation of noisy uproar and confusion — 7. **bedlam**
8. Weakly and excessively tearful; sentimental — 8. **maudlin**
9. A prejudiced belief in the superiority of one's group; militant and boastful devotion to and glorification of one's country or cause — 9. **chauvinism**
10. Of or requiring unusual size, power, or difficulty; of or resembling Hercules — 10. **herculean**

EXERCISE 2 USING WORDS CORRECTLY

Decide whether the italicized vocabulary word has been used correctly in the sentence. On the answer line, write *Correct* for correct use and *Incorrect* for incorrect use.

1. Coach Jennings used *draconian* workouts to get his team into shape. — 1. **Correct**
2. Having never been away from home before, the child experienced moments of *chauvinism* during her first few days at camp. — 2. **Incorrect**
3. This morning I awoke to the sound of a *martinet* chirping near my window. — 3. **Incorrect**
4. The Great Wall of China was a *titanic* construction project. — 4. **Correct**
5. Many drivers become *herculean* during rush-hour traffic jams. — 5. **Incorrect**
6. *Maudlin* speeches about the "good old days" often bore young audiences. — 6. **Correct**
7. Alfred Hitchcock's *silhouette* was always used to introduce his television show. — 7. **Correct**
8. Because of her careful attention to details, Lucille found a job as a court *stentorian.* — 8. **Incorrect**
9. Bobby was *mesmerized* by the magician's tricks. — 9. **Correct**
10. You'll find the *bedlam* in the medicine cabinet just behind the toothpaste. — 10. **Incorrect**

EXERCISE 3 CHOOSING THE BEST WORD

Decide which vocabulary word or related form best expresses the meaning of the italicized word or phrase in the sentence. On the answer line, write the letter of the correct choice.

1. As she watched the demonstrators, the reporter thought that she had rarely seen such *noise and confusion.* — 1. **a**
   a. bedlam **b.** mesmerism **c.** chauvinism **d.** martinets

2. With *excessively tearful* eloquence, Mr. Fowler announced his resignation. 2. a
a. maudlin **b.** mesmerizing **c.** titanic **d.** stentorian

3. The *colossal* rock formations of Carlsbad Caverns attract millions of tourists each year. 3. b
a. silhouetted **b.** titanic **c.** chauvinistic **d.** mesmerizing

4. A disgruntled worker accused the company of female *prejudiced belief in the superiority of one's group* in its hiring practices. 4. d
a. mesmerism **b.** bedlam **c.** titan **d.** chauvinism

5. Over the din of traffic, we heard the *extremely loud* cry, "Extra! Read all about it!" 5. c
a. herculean **b.** draconian **c.** stentorian **d.** titanic

6. The exquisite voice of Jenny Lind had an *enthralling* effect on an audience. 6. c
a. maudlin **b.** herculean **c.** mesmerizing **d.** draconian

7. With *unusually powerful* effort, Jill managed to lift the enormous box. 7. b
a. stentorian **b.** herculean **c.** draconian **d.** chauvinistic

8. Ichabod Crane, the superstitious schoolmaster in "The Legend of Sleepy Hollow," used *rigorous* methods of discipline. 8. a
a. draconian **b.** titanic **c.** herculean **d.** stentorian

9. The photograph of the jagged tree branches *outlined* against the amber sky was beautifully composed. 9. d
a. mesmerized **b.** titanic **c.** maudlin **d.** silhouetted

10. Fagin, one of the characters in *Oliver Twist*, was not the *person who exacts harsh discipline* that everyone in the novel expected him to be. 10. b
a. stentorian **b.** martinet **c.** chauvinist **d.** silhouette

EXERCISE 4 USING DIFFERENT FORMS OF WORDS

Decide which form of the vocabulary word in parentheses best completes the sentence. The form given may be correct. Write your answer on the answer line.

1. The _____ junior class believes it is the best class in the history of Paint Branch High School. *(chauvinism)* 1. chauvinistic

2. Organizing the spring flower show requires _____ energy. *(herculean)* 2. herculean

3. Sue was _____ by the young lead dancer's performance in the ballet *Romeo and Juliet*. *(mesmerize)* 3. mesmerized

4. The candidates debated whether _____ penalties are effective in reducing crime. *(draconian)* 4. draconian

5. Edward's weightlifting coach is a _____ who demands strict adherence to training rules. *(martinet)* 5. martinet

6. The Fords are considered _____ of American industry. *(titanic)* 6. titans

7. "Be _____ when you say your lines, Janice, or the audience will never hear you," said the drama teacher. *(stentorian)* 7. stentorian

8. The artist Edouart was considered the most remarkable creator of freehand _____ in the eighteenth century. *(silhouette)* 8. silhouettes

9. The enormous number of boats at the centennial celebration of the Statue of Liberty created _____ in the harbor. *(bedlam)* 9. bedlam

10. Many people object to _____ interpretations of the poetry of Emily Dickinson. *(maudlin)* 10. maudlin

NAME ______________________ DATE __________

READING COMPREHENSION

Each numbered sentence in the following passage contains an italicized vocabulary word or related form. After you read the passage, you will complete an exercise.

THE "UNSINKABLE" TITANIC

In the early morning hours of April 15, 1912, the English ocean liner *Titanic* sank, in what was considered one of the greatest disasters in maritime history. The pride of the British passenger service, the *Titanic* was on its maiden voyage, from Southampton to New York, when it struck an iceberg off the coast of Newfoundland.

(1) The name of the ocean liner was apt; eleven stories high and four city blocks long, the ***titanic*** ship, weighing 46,328 tons, was the largest vessel then afloat. It was also the most lavishly appointed, containing art treasures, elevators, a Turkish bath, and a swimming pool.

Furthermore, the *Titanic* had been designed with every shipbuilding advance in mind. Its most arresting feature was a double-bottomed hull that was divided into sixteen watertight compartments. Four of the compartments could be flooded without endangering the liner's buoyancy. (2) It is little wonder that the ship's owners and builders, the White Star line, ***chauvinistically*** regarded the *Titanic* as the safest vessel ever built. Believing that the ship's gargantuan size and technological complexity provided security, the owners included a mere twenty lifeboats, which had the capacity to rescue only half of the ocean liner's 2,200 passengers.

The commanding officer of the *Titanic* was Edward Smith, a prudent, experienced officer who captained all the White Star ships on their maiden voyages. (3) Although something of a ***martinet*** with his crew as a rule, Smith was slated for retirement after his crowning trip aboard the *Titanic* and may have relaxed his standards somewhat. He also was forced to respond to pressure exerted by J. Bruce Ismay, the managing director of White Star, who was eager to see how fast the ship could actually go. Therefore, even though Smith received many warnings of icebergs ahead, he decided to follow the prevailing practice of relying on sharp-eyed sailors who acted as lookouts rather than reducing speed to meet the conditions.

On the night of April 14, 1912, the sea was unusually calm and the weather uncommonly clear and cold. (4) After a lookout's ***stentorian*** voice warned of an iceberg directly in the path of the ship, the men at the helm tried to reverse engines. Their efforts were vain: the upper-deck passengers felt a slight tremor, while below both crew members and passengers were awakened by an enormous crash. (5) ***Bedlam*** broke out in steerage class as all the watertight compartments flooded from a three-hundred-foot gash in the *Titanic's* starboard side.

(6) Organizing the few lifeboats required ***herculean*** effort on the part of the ship's officers. Believing that lifeboat drills were not necessary in an unsinkable vessel, the captain had done nothing to plan rescue procedures. People on the lower decks were panic-stricken, while those above, not entirely aware of the gravity of the situation, assembled casually and unhurriedly. (7) ***Draconian*** measures were used to restrict lifeboat passengers to women and children only, yet some lifeboats were lowered to the water partially filled. (8) The ship's orchestra played Dixieland jazz as separated family members said their farewells bravely, without becoming ***maudlin.***

(9) Soon the 687 passengers in lifeboats watched as if ***mesmerized*** while the *Titanic* tilted upward. (10) With 150 feet of its stern ***silhouetted*** against the sky, the great ship remained motionless for several minutes until it plunged into the Atlantic. Two and a half hours after it had collided with the iceberg, the *Titanic* disappeared in the motionless sea, a warning against human trust in size and technology.

READING COMPREHENSION EXERCISE

Each of the following statements corresponds to a numbered sentence in the passage. Each statement contains a blank and is followed by four answer choices. Decide which choice fits best in the blank. The word or phrase that you choose must express roughly the same meaning as the italicized word in the passage. Write the letter of your choice on the answer line.

1. The ____ ship was the largest vessel then afloat. 1. c
   a. peculiar b. inferior c. enormous d. powerful

2. The ship's owners ____ regarded the *Titanic* as the safest vessel ever built. 2. a
   a. with prejudiced superiority c. without justification
   b. with official interest d. innocently

3. Captain Smith was usually a(n) ____ with his crew. 3. c
   a. popular figure c. strict disciplinarian
   b. able communicator d. disdainful supervisor

4. A lookout's ____ voice warned of an iceberg directly in the path of the ship. 4. b
   a. echoing b. extremely loud c. monotone d. timid

5. ____ occurred in steerage as the watertight compartments flooded. 5. d
   a. Fights c. Choked screaming
   b. Intrigue d. Noisy confusion

6. Organizing the few lifeboats required ____ effort on the part of the ship's officers. 6. a
   a. immense b. little c. solemnly devoted d. purposeful

7. ____ measures were used to limit lifeboat passengers to women and children only. 7. b
   a. Impartial c. Benevolent
   b. Exceedingly rigorous d. Somewhat exasperating

8. Families made their farewells bravely, without becoming ____. 8. b
   a. terrified c. listless
   b. excessively tearful d. incoherent

9. The passengers in lifeboats watched as if ____ while the *Titanic* tilted upward. 9. d
   a. paralyzed b. frightened c. sleepwalking d. hypnotized

10. Its stern ____ against the sky, the great ship remained motionless for several minutes. 10. a
    a. outlined b. sparkling c. delicate d. ghastly

PRACTICE WITH ANALOGIES

See pages 32, 66, and 86 for some strategies to use with analogies.

Directions On the answer line, write the vocabulary word or a form of it that completes each analogy.

1. INDISTINCT : SEE :: ____ : predict *(Lesson 23)* 1. confound
2. MALADROIT : SKILL :: ____ : commitment *(Lesson 23)* 2. equivocate
3. EMBRYONIC : MATURITY :: ____ : finality *(Lesson 23)* 3. rudimentary
4. TITANIC : LARGE :: ____ : small *(Lesson 24)* 4. minuscule
5. ZEALOT : CAUSE :: ____ : nation *(Lesson 25)* 5. chauvinist
6. FEATURE : FACE :: ____ : outline *(Lesson 25)* 6. silhouette

The **Bonus activity** for Lessons 21–25 is on page T32.

LESSON 26 TIME

26

Time is an essential and ever-present part of our lives. Not only does it govern our bodies, as in the rhythm of the heart and the electrical impulses to and from the brain, but it also provides a continuity and a pattern to our activities. On the one hand, time is represented by the continuum of history and tradition. On the other, it is symbolized by the pulse beat, the stopwatch, or the school bell. Time is a great healer, a great teacher, and a great leveler. It may fly, slip away, or simply stand still. Time is a commodity that we can beat, kill, save, spend, waste, or lose. The words in this lesson will help you to express the many dimensions of time.

WORD LIST

concomitant
eon
extant
hiatus
inure
irrevocable
millennium
perpetuity
pristine
transience

DEFINITIONS

After you have studied the definitions and example for each vocabulary word, write the word on the line to the right.

1. **concomitant** (kən-kŏm′ĭ-tənt) *adjective* Existing or occurring at the same time; accompanying; attendant. *noun* An accompanying state, circumstance, or thing. (From the Latin *com-*, meaning "together," and *comes*, meaning "companion") 1. ______

Related Words **concomitance** *noun;* **concomitantly** *adverb*
Example In ancient Greece the *concomitant* results of cultivating olives as food were the uses of olive oil as a body cleanser, a medication, and a lubricant for moving heavy objects.

2. **eon** (ē′ŏn′, ē′ən) *noun* **a.** An indefinitely long period of time; an age; an eternity. **b.** The longest division of geologic time, containing two or more eras, or one billion years. (From the Latin word *aeon*, meaning "age") 2. ______

Example Other than fossils we have no record of the obscure *eons* of prehistory.

3. **extant** (ĕk′stənt, ĕk′-stănt′) *adjective* Still in existence; not destroyed, lost, or extinct. (From the Latin *ex-*, meaning "out," and *stare*, meaning "to stand") 3. ______

Example Several species of birds, such as the dodo and the archaeopteryx, are no longer *extant*.

4. **hiatus** (hī-ā′təs) *noun* A gap or interruption in space, time, or continuity; break. (From the Latin word *hiare*, meaning "to gape") 4. ______

USAGE NOTE: Compare with *extent*, which means "the range, magnitude, or distance over which a thing extends."

Example During the *hiatus* between semesters, Martin will serve a month-long internship with a magazine publisher.

5\. **inure** (ĭn-yo͝or′) *trans. verb* To make used to something undesirable, especially by prolonged subjection; accustom; harden. (From the Middle English phrase *in ure,* meaning "customary")

5\. ____________

USAGE NOTE: *Enure* is a variant form of *inure.* Its meaning is the same.

Related Word **inured** *adjective*
Example Two years in the Peace Corps have *inured* Elsa to being away from her family.

6\. **irrevocable** (ĭ-rĕv′ə-kə-bəl) *adjective* Incapable of being changed, undone, or retracted; irreversible.

6\. ____________

Related Words **irrevocability** *noun;* **irrevocably** *adverb*
Example The first surnames represented the *irrevocable* past of a primitive clan or the personal traits or habits of family ancestors.

7\. **millennium** (mə-lĕn′ē-əm) *noun* **a.** A span of one thousand years. **b.** A hoped-for period of great joy, prosperity, and justice. (From the Latin words *mille,* meaning "thousand," and *annus,* meaning "year")

7\. ____________

USAGE NOTE: Either *millenniums* or *millennia* is correct as the plural of *millennium.*

Example By the fifth *millennium* B.C., the Chinese had mastered the relatively difficult science of raising rice.

8\. **perpetuity** (pûr′pĭ-to͞o′ĭ-tē, pûr′pĭ-tyo͞o′ĭ-tē) *noun* The quality, state, or condition of being everlasting; time without end; eternity. (From the Latin word *perpetuus,* meaning "continuous")

8\. ____________

USAGE NOTE: The adjective *perpetual,* a related word, means "lasting for eternity."

Related Word **perpetual** *adjective*
Example The flame that burns in *perpetuity* at the grave of John F. Kennedy symbolizes hope even in times of conflict and distress.

9\. **pristine** (prĭs′tēn′, prĭ-stēn′) *adjective* **a.** Of, pertaining to, or typical of the earliest time or condition; primitive; original. **b.** Remaining in a pure state; uncorrupted: *the pristine beauty of the wilderness.* (From the Latin word *pristinus,* meaning "belonging to earlier times" or "ancient")

9\. ____________

Related Word **pristinely** *adverb*
Example The first people to reach the peak of Mount Everest were taken aback by its *pristine* beauty.

10\. **transience** (trăn′shəns, trăn′zhəns) *noun* The state or quality of passing into and out of existence; impermanence. (From the Latin *trans-,* meaning "over," and *ire,* meaning "to go")

10\. ____________

Related Words **transient** *adjective;* **transiently** *adverb*
Example The *transience* of the pale blossoms adds to their delicate charm.

NAME ______________________ DATE ____________

EXERCISE 1 MATCHING WORDS AND DEFINITIONS

Match the definition in Column B with the word in Column A. Write the letter of the correct definition on the answer line.

Column A

1. perpetuity
2. irrevocable
3. eon
4. inure
5. transience
6. extant
7. millennium
8. concomitant
9. hiatus
10. pristine

Column B

a. existing or occurring at the same time; an accompanying state, condition, or thing

b. still in existence; not destroyed, lost, or extinct

c. of, pertaining to, or typical of the earliest time or condition; primitive; remaining in a pure state

d. incapable of being changed, undone, or retracted; irreversible

e. a gap or interruption in space, time, or continuity

f. to make used to something undesirable, especially by prolonged subjection; accustom

g. the quality, state, or condition of being everlasting; time without end; eternity

h. the state or quality of passing into and out of existence; impermanence

i. a span of one thousand years; a hoped-for period of great joy, prosperity, and justice

j. an indefinitely long period of time; the longest division of geologic time, containing two or more eras

1. g
2. d
3. j
4. f
5. h
6. b
7. i
8. a
9. e
10. c

EXERCISE 2 USING WORDS CORRECTLY

Each of the following statements contains an italicized vocabulary word or related form. Decide whether the sentence is true or false, and write *True* or *False* on the answer line.

1. A species that no longer exists is said to be *extant.* 1. **False**
2. A *concomitant* might have served in several military or naval campaigns. 2. **False**
3. An extended farewell is called a *millennium.* 3. **False**
4. Music and dance have a *pristine* appeal. 4. **True**
5. An *eon* is shorter than a century. 5. **False**
6. Workers who travel the country picking seasonal crops are called *transience.* 6. **False**
7. A *hiatus* between the acts of a play is called an intermission. 7. **True**
8. Some people who live beneath the flight paths of airplanes never become *inured* to the noise level. 8. **True**
9. Few artists can expect that their fame will endure in *perpetuity.* 9. **True**
10. An *irrevocable* decision is one that can be changed at whim. 10. **False**

EXERCISE 3 IDENTIFYING SYNONYMS AND ANTONYMS

Decide which word or phrase has the meaning that is the same as (a synonym) or opposite to (an antonym) that of the capitalized vocabulary word. Write the letter of your choice on the answer line.

1. EXTANT (synonym): — 1. c
   a. believable b. contradictory c. existing d. supreme
2. TRANSIENCE (antonym): — 2. b
   a. novice b. permanence c. repute d. civility
3. IRREVOCABLE (synonym): — 3. a
   a. unalterable b. authentic c. merciless d. novel
4. EON (antonym): — 4. a
   a. moment b. multitude c. allotment d. juncture
5. MILLENNIUM (synonym): — 5. b
   a. eternity b. future period c. present time d. past period
6. PERPETUITY (antonym): — 6. c
   a. validity b. negligence c. momentariness d. vigilance
7. CONCOMITANT (synonym): — 7. b
   a. intense b. simultaneous c. lavish d. explicit
8. PRISTINE (antonym): — 8. a
   a. sullied b. petty c. indifferent d. frivolous
9. HIATUS (synonym): — 9. d
   a. pliancy b. plausibility c. distortion d. gap
10. INURE (antonym): — 10. c
    a. habituate b. victimize c. wean d. rally

EXERCISE 4 USING DIFFERENT FORMS OF WORDS

Decide which form of the vocabulary word in parentheses best completes the sentence. The form given may be correct. Write your answer on the answer line.

1. The love letters of the Duke of Windsor and Wallis Simpson were once believed to have been burned, but in recent years many have been found to be _____. *(extant)* — 1. extant
2. The _____ of an umpire's decision makes it useless for players to argue over it. *(irrevocable)* — 2. irrevocability
3. The alabaster pitcher is thought to be many _____ old. *(millennium)* — 3. millenniums
4. Diane was relieved when her bout of boredom and listlessness proved to be only _____. *(transience)* — 4. transient
5. Jessica quickly became _____ to the pungent odor of the stable. *(inure)* — 5. inured
6. Blood pressure and heart rate tend to vary _____. *(concomitant)* — 6. concomitantly
7. Jason particularly enjoys the first ski run of the morning on _____ glistening snow. *(pristine)* — 7. pristinely
8. Alissa was uncomfortable with the _____ in the conversation and filled it with babble. *(hiatus)* — 8. hiatus
9. It felt as if _____ had passed before the phone finally rang. *(eon)* — 9. eons
10. The property by the lake had been bequeathed to the Dollers in _____. *(perpetuity)* — 10. perpetuity

NAME ________________________ DATE ____________

READING COMPREHENSION

Each numbered sentence in the following passage contains an italicized vocabulary word or related form. After you read the passage, you will complete an exercise.

THE LA BREA TAR PITS: DEATHTRAP OF THE AGES

(1) ***Eons*** ago the region of southern California known as Los Angeles was geographically much the same as it is today— broad, grassy plains rimmed by mountains. (2) During the ***millennia*** of the Ice Age, or Pleistocene epoch, the climate was less influenced by the ocean than it is today. Temperatures were probably warmer, and seasons of moderate rainfall alternated with summer and autumn droughts. Tar pools, which dotted the low spots of the plain, were often the only source of water for the animals of the area during dry periods. Animals that remained on the shores to drink were safe; those that ventured into the pools however, were trapped in the sticky tar. (3) Preserved for ***perpetuity,*** hundreds of thousands of prehistoric animal bones unearthed from the tar pits constitute the largest and most varied fossil assemblage ever taken from one location.

The existence of bones in the tar pits had been known for generations. (4) Native American and Spanish explorers, ***inured*** to protruding animal skeletons, used the sticky asphalt to waterproof baskets, canoes, and adobe houses. In the 1870s, Major Hancock, owner of Rancho La Brea, began selling the tar for fuel and as a roofing and paving material. His diggers uncovered so many bones that they were faced with a serious disposal problem. It was not until 1901, however, that the curiosity of scientists was aroused. In that year William Orcutt, a petroleum geologist investigating the possibility that the pits might contain oil, uncovered what he recognized as prehistoric skeletons.

(5) After a ***hiatus*** of five years, paleontologists began to excavate the rich deposits. The tar pits yielded numerous bones of a wide variety of animals in excellent states of preservation. (6) Since 1906 millions of bones from giant prehistoric bears, mammoth elephants, mastodons, saber-toothed tigers, ground sloths, and other animals no longer ***extant*** have been dug from layers of oil and tar.

(7) Scientists have been able to reconstruct the more or less orderly sequence of events that must have occurred at the ***pristine*** pools. They theorize that herbivores, or plant-eating animals, traveled long distances to drink from the water that accumulated on top of the tar. (8) In their haste to drink, they made the ***irrevocable*** step that mired them in the tar. As they struggled to escape, they sank deeper, attracting the attention of the carnivores, or meat-eating animals. The herbivores made an easy kill for the carnivores, yet the carnivores, too, became trapped. (9) ***Concomitantly,*** hawks, eagles, and vultures watching the struggles competed for any remaining flesh of the animals. When several birds attacked one body, the beating of wings and the fights that ensued would cause one or more of them to lose their balance and fall into the tar. Blowflies laid eggs in the carrion, and beetles fed on it. Insects, too, fell into the tar or were buried with the carcasses as they sank.

Because many of the bones are deeply weathered or show signs of being gnawed after the carnivores finished, scientists believe that the bones must have lain at the surface for weeks or months, perhaps in such large, tangled piles that they could not sink rapidly. These piles attracted still more mammals and served as perches for small birds whose remains have also been found in the tar.

Today the area of the La Brea tar pits is a park and natural history landmark where tourists can view the reconstructed models of prehistoric animals. (10) Just off busy Wilshire Boulevard, the La Brea tar pits continue to preserve and yield the richest record of the ***transient*** forces of nature ever found.

READING COMPREHENSION EXERCISE

Each of the following statements corresponds to a numbered sentence in the passage. Each statement contains a blank and is followed by four answer choices. Decide which choice fits best in the blank. The word or phrase that you choose must express roughly the same meaning as the italicized word in the passage. Write the letter of your choice on the answer line.

1. _____ ago the region of southern California known as Los Angeles was geographically much the same as it is today. 1. ___a___
 a. Ages b. A short time c. A while d. Some time

2. The climate was less influenced by the ocean during the _____ of the Ice Age. 2. ___c___
 a. brief period c. thousands of years
 b. several years d. single generation

3. Hundreds of thousands of prehistoric animal bones unearthed from the tar pits have been preserved for _____. 3. ___d___
 a. antiquity b. brief moments c. several days d. eternity

4. Native Americans and Spanish explorers, who used the sticky asphalt, were _____ protruding animal skeletons. 4. ___c___
 a. inconvenienced by c. accustomed to
 b. superstitious about d. horrified by

5. Paleontologists began to excavate the deposits after a(n) _____ of five years. 5. ___b___
 a. study period b. interruption c. recovery d. banishment

6. Dug from layers of oil and tar, many bones are from animals no longer _____. 6. ___a___
 a. in existence b. common c. popular d. domesticated

7. Scientists have been able to reconstruct the sequence of events that must have occurred at the _____ pools. 7. ___d___
 a. sticky b. unsafe c. separate d. ancient

8. In their haste to drink, the herbivores made the _____ step that mired them in tar. 8. ___b___
 a. one b. irreversible c. inevitable d. dangerous

9. _____, hawks, eagles, and vultures competed for the flesh of the animals. 9. ___a___
 a. At the same time c. Hundreds of years later
 b. At an earlier time d. Unbelievably

10. The La Brea tar pits continue to preserve and yield the richest record of the _____ forces of nature ever found. 10. ___d___
 a. astonishing b. kindly c. ideal d. impermanent

WRITING ASSIGNMENT

Ever since H. G. Wells created the time machine in 1895, it has been a popular science-fiction device. Suppose that you have the use of a time machine for just one day. Using at least five of the words from this lesson, write a brief essay in which you explain which historical or future time period you would visit and why. Underline each of the vocabulary words that you use.

LESSON 27 EMOTIONS

27

How much feeling can be expressed in public? Is crying a sign of strength or weakness? Is it healthier to express or suppress emotion? Is depression actually anger turned inward? The way in which you answer these questions depends to a large extent on cultural and family influences. While some people are encouraged to show emotion, others are taught to intellectualize their feelings. As Jack London said, "emotion is the hardest thing in the world to put . . . into words." This lesson, nonetheless, will help you to express the complex range of sentiments that you experience and encounter.

WORD LIST

deplore
disconsolate
distraught
halcyon
lachrymose
mercurial
revel
tirade
trauma
vex

DEFINITIONS

After you have studied the definitions and example for each vocabulary word, write the word on the line to the right.

1. **deplore** (dĭ-plôr') *trans. verb* **a.** To feel or express strong disapproval of. **b.** To feel or express sorrow over; lament. **c.** To feel or express regret about. (From the Latin *de-*, an intensive prefix, and *plorare*, meaning "to wail")

   Related Word **deplorable** *adjective*
   Example Father *deplored* the dilapidated condition of Cal's relatively new car.

1. ____________________

2. **disconsolate** (dĭs-kŏn'sə-lĭt) *adjective* **a.** Beyond comfort; hopelessly sad. **b.** Cheerless; causing gloom. (From the Latin *dis-*, meaning "not," and *consolari*, meaning "to console")

   Related Word **disconsolately** *adverb*
   Example The child remained *disconsolate* for a week after her puppy ran away from home.

2. ____________________

3. **distraught** (dĭ-strôt') *adjective* **a.** Agitated with anxiety; worried. **b.** Crazed or mad. (From the Middle English *distracten*, meaning "to distract")

   Example Kameko was *distraught* over the loss of her address book.

3. ____________________

4. **halcyon** (hăl'sē-ən) *adjective* **a.** Calm and peaceful; tranquil. **b.** Prosperous; golden. *noun* A fabled bird with the power to calm the wind and waves. (From the Greek word *alkuōn*, the name of a mythical bird)

   Example We always look back on those *halcyon* days of summer whenever we get together.

4. ____________________

5. **lachrymose** (lăk′rə-mōs′) *adjective* **a.** Weeping or inclined to weep; tearful. **b.** Causing or tending to cause tears; sorrowful. (From the Latin word *lacrima,* meaning "tear") 5. ____________

Related Word **lachrymosely** *adverb*
Example My favorite character from *Alice's Adventures in Wonderland* is the *lachrymose* Mock Turtle.

6. **mercurial** (mər-kyŏŏr′ē-əl) *adjective* **a.** Being quick and changeable in character; fickle. **b.** Having the characteristics of eloquence, shrewdness, and swiftness attributed to the god Mercury. (From the Latin word *Mercurius,* the god Mercury) 6. ____________

Related Word **mercurially** *adverb*
Example Glenn's *mercurial* moods made a poor impression on colleagues, who never knew what to expect.

7. **revel** (rĕv′əl) *intrans. verb* **a.** To take great pleasure or delight in. **b.** To engage in uproarious festivities; make merry. (From the Latin word *rebellare,* meaning "to rebel") 7. ____________

Related Word **revelry** *noun*
Example Hoshi *reveled* in the knowledge that she had gotten a bargain on the silk dress.

8. **tirade** (tī′rād′, tī-rād′) *noun* A long angry or violent speech, usually denouncing or criticizing someone or something; diatribe. (From the Old Italian word *tirare,* meaning "to draw fire") 8. ____________

Example Nate's *tirade* on keeping their shared room clean had little effect on his younger brother.

9. **trauma** (trô′mə, trou′mə) *noun* **a.** An emotional shock that has a profound and lasting effect on the mind and functioning of an individual. **b.** A wound, especially one produced by sudden physical injury. 9. ____________

Related Words **traumatic** *adjective;* **traumatize** *verb*
Example For three months after the *trauma* of her accident, Lisa resisted driving or even riding in a car.

10. **vex** (vĕks) *trans. verb* **a.** To irritate or annoy; bother. **b.** To baffle; puzzle. 10. ____________

Related Words **vexation** *noun;* **vexatious** *adjective*
Example The sound of trucks going by *vexed* Kevin, especially when he was trying to sleep.

NAME ______________________ DATE ____________

EXERCISE 1 WRITING CORRECT WORDS

On the answer line, write the word from the vocabulary list that fits each definition.

1. Weeping or inclined to weep; tearful — 1. lachrymose
2. An emotional shock that has a profound and lasting effect on the mind and functioning of an individual; a wound, especially one produced by sudden physical injury — 2. trauma
3. Beyond comfort or hopelessly sad; cheerless or causing gloom — 3. disconsolate
4. Calm and peaceful; prosperous — 4. halcyon
5. A long angry or violent speech, usually denouncing or criticizing someone or something; diatribe — 5. tirade
6. To feel or express strong disapproval of; feel or express sorrow over; feel or express regret about — 6. deplore
7. To irritate or annoy; bother; baffle — 7. vex
8. Agitated with anxiety; crazed or mad — 8. distraught
9. To take great pleasure or delight in; engage in uproarious festivities — 9. revel
10. Being quick and changeable in character; fickle — 10. mercurial

EXERCISE 2 USING WORDS CORRECTLY

Each of the following statements contains an italicized vocabulary word. Decide whether the sentence is true or false, and write *True* or *False* on the answer line.

1. A *halcyon* period is characterized by turbulence and controversy. — 1. False
2. Pet peeves are minor things that *vex* people. — 2. True
3. To soap opera devotees, the stories are often tempestuous and *lachrymose.* — 3. True
4. Recovery from a psychological *trauma* occurs quickly and easily. — 4. False
5. A softball team might feel *disconsolate* about four consecutive losses. — 5. True
6. *Mercurial* people may be regarded as temperamental. — 6. True
7. A *tirade* is a particularly inspiring graduation speech. — 7. False
8. Most people *deplore* accurate timepieces. — 8. False
9. The parents of a lost toddler might become *distraught.* — 9. True
10. A large dog would probably *revel* in the freedom of a spacious yard. — 10. True

EXERCISE 3 CHOOSING THE BEST WORD

Decide which vocabulary word or related form best completes the sentence, and write the letter of your choice on the answer line.

1. To ancient sailors, _____ days were fourteen consecutive days of calm seas and beautiful weather. — 1. b

   a. mercurial **b.** halcyon **c.** lachrymose **d.** disconsolate

2. Mother delivered a short _____ on the dangers of leaving the house without carefully extinguishing the fire in the fireplace. 2. d
a. halcyon b. revelry c. trauma d. tirade

3. Long after the _____ of being pushed off the high diving board, Kelly refused to swim in deep water. 3. b
a. tirade b. trauma c. revelry d. vexation

4. The once-beautiful Victorian house was in _____ condition. 4. a
a. deplorable b. mercurial c. vexatious d. lachrymose

5. Chase, attempting his first steps, _____ in all the attention he got from his family. 5. c
a. deplored b. vexed c. reveled d. traumatized

6. The members of the museum's board were _____ about the resignation of the innovative director so close to the opening of a new show. 6. d
a. deplorable b. halcyon c. mercurial d. distraught

7. Marco was _____ when he could not think of an appropriate synonym. 7. c
a. mercurial b. lachrymose c. vexed d. traumatized

8. The witty, _____ nature of Mercutio serves as a contrast to his friend Romeo's personality. 8. b
a. disconsolate b. mercurial c. distraught d. traumatic

9. In Lewis Carroll's poem, the _____ Walrus holds his handkerchief "before his streaming eyes" as he talks to the Carpenter. 9. d
a. traumatic b. halcyon c. mercurial d. lachrymose

10. The _____ landscape of the English moors was a perfect backdrop for the romantic tale. 10. a
a. disconsolate b. vexatious c. distraught d. traumatic

EXERCISE 4 USING DIFFERENT FORMS OF WORDS

Decide which form of the vocabulary word in parentheses best completes the sentence. The form given may be correct. Write your answer on the answer line.

1. Mr. Jennings stared _____ at the empty garage from which his car had been stolen. *(disconsolate)* 1. **disconsolately**

2. Grandmother looks back nostalgically on the _____ years of her childhood on the farm. *(halcyon)* 2. **halcyon**

3. On the first day of kindergarten, many parents and children find leave-taking _____. *(trauma)* 3. **traumatic**

4. "Yes . . . No . . . Maybe," Liza responded _____. *(mercurial)* 4. **mercurially**

5. Leroy's _____ was clear as both the phone and the doorbell rang. *(vex)* 5. **vexation**

6. The complete schedule for the _____ of Harborfest is in today's paper. *(revel)* 6. **revelry**

7. The mere mention of computer technology is enough to send Uncle Charlie into a _____. *(tirade)* 7. **tirade**

8. The review of the new play called attention to the _____ manners of the audience. *(deplore)* 8. **deplorable**

9. Kate apologized _____ for accidentally breaking the vase. *(lachrymose)* 9. **lachrymosely**

10. Angie was _____ about making her deadline. *(distraught)* 10. **distraught**

NAME ______________________ DATE __________

READING COMPREHENSION

Each numbered sentence in the following passage contains an italicized vocabulary word or related form. After you read the passage, you will complete an exercise.

THE BRONTË SISTERS

The Brontë sisters—Charlotte, Emily, and Anne—share a unique position in literary history. Their brief lives were a continual struggle against poor health and defeated aspirations, yet their close bonds of temperament, imagination, and experience enabled them to influence strongly the direction of the modern English novel.

Charlotte, born in 1816, Emily, born in 1818, and Anne, born in 1820, were three of the six children of Patrick Brontë, an Anglican clergyman, and Maria Branwell Brontë. (1) Always unsociable, Mr. Brontë grew more eccentric and more easily ***vexed*** by the demands of his children after his wife died in 1821. Life at the parsonage was increasingly lonely and restrictive. (2) Left to their own devices, the sisters ***reveled*** in the stark beauty of the open stretches of the Yorkshire moors. (3) Charlotte, Emily, and Anne, precocious and imaginative, created their own ***halcyon*** times by reading, writing, and dramatizing stories.

In 1824 Charlotte, Emily, and their two older sisters were sent to boarding school. (4) Although they appreciated the value of a formal education, the ***deplorable*** conditions and the harsh environment of the school made all the Brontës homesick. (5) Charlotte and Emily, ***traumatized*** by the deaths of their older sisters from tuberculosis, returned home. (6) Several other attempts at boarding school left them equally ***lachrymose.*** (7) ***Distraught*** over the enforced absence from their beloved moors, each had to be withdrawn from school because of illness.

The only jobs available to women during the early nineteenth century were in teaching and the Brontë sisters took a succession of positions as governesses in order to contribute to family funds. None of these positions were suitable, however. Homesick and socially humiliated in their subservient roles, Charlotte, Emily, and Anne returned home once again.

Although writing had always been a relief from despair, none of the sisters had thought of writing for a living. In 1845, however, Charlotte accidentally found a manuscript of Emily's poems and persuaded Emily to share with her sisters a joint volume of twenty-one poems each. The Brontës chose masculine pseudonyms that matched their initials so as to keep secret their identity as women. Published in 1846 at the authors' expense, *Poems*, by Currer, Ellis, and Acton Bell, sold only two copies. Fortunately, the failure of the book did not deter the sisters from further publishing attempts.

Anne published *Agnes Grey* in 1847 and *The Tenant of Wildfell Hall* in 1848. (8) Both books contained what amounted to ***tirades*** against the injustices faced by women. Neither brought Anne any significant acknowledgment.

Emily, too, had a novel published in 1847. Unlike Anne's two novels, *Wuthering Heights* caused a sensation in Victorian England. Emily broke new ground in fiction by using flashbacks and two narrative points of view. The novel was unparalleled in her time in its primitive emotional power and intricate dramatic form. Even today *Wuthering Heights* is viewed as the crowning triumph of the Brontës.

Charlotte's first novel, *The Professor,* was turned down in 1847, but she was soon hard at work on *Jane Eyre,* published later that year. (9) As if to demonstrate the ***mercurial*** tastes of the reading public, the book was an immediate success and won praise for its courageous realism and depth of feeling.

(10) After the death of Emily in 1848 and Anne in 1849, both from tuberculosis, Charlotte Brontë was ***disconsolate.*** Trying to cope with her own ill health and depression, she threw herself into her writing, producing *Shirley* in 1849 and *Vilette* in 1853. Although neither book was as popular as *Jane Eyre,* both reflect her preoccupation with a central theme: the needs of a woman for independence, on the one hand, and love, on the other.

Charlotte found happiness for a few months in 1854 when she married her father's assistant. She died of complications from her pregnancy in 1855.

All three of the Brontë sisters managed to some degree to transform their lonely, circumscribed lives into memorable fiction. Each was an innovator in her own right, bringing into fiction an awareness of the writer's emotional consciousness. In the imaginative power and frankness of their novels, Anne, Emily, and Charlotte Brontë made a serious impact on the nineteenth-century novel and foreshadowed the direction of twentieth-century literature.

READING COMPREHENSION EXERCISE

Each of the following statements corresponds to a numbered sentence in the passage. Each statement contains a blank and is followed by four answer choices. Decide which choice fits best in the blank. The word or phrase that you choose must express roughly the same meaning as the italicized word in the passage. Write the letter of your choice on the answer line.

1. Mr. Brontë was easily _____ by his children's demands. 1. a
   a. irritated b. taken advantage of c. delighted d. fascinated

2. The sisters _____ the open stretches of the Yorkshire moors. 2. d
   a. painted c. were depressed by
   b. wrote about d. took great pleasure in

3. The sisters created their own _____ moments. 3. d
   a. entertaining b. significant c. enduring d. tranquil

4. The _____ conditions of the school made them homesick and miserable. 4. c
   a. agreeable b. improvised c. lamentable d. praiseworthy

5. The sisters were _____ by the deaths of their older sisters. 5. b
   a. unaffected b. emotionally shocked c. confused d. made lonely

6. They were equally _____ during several other attempts at boarding school. 6. a
   a. tearful b. scholarly c. disgusted d. casual

7. All three were _____ about the enforced absence from their moors. 7. c
   a. relieved b. delighted c. disturbed d. stoic

8. Both books were _____ injustices faced by women. 8. d
   a. thoughtful appraisals of c. mild apologies for
   b. support for d. angry criticisms of

9. The book seemed to demonstrate the _____ tastes of the public. 9. a
   a. changeable b. absurd c. disdainful d. wise

10. Charlotte Brontë was _____ after the deaths of Anne and Emily. 10. b
    a. somewhat lonely b. hopelessly sad c. troubled d. angry

WRITING ASSIGNMENT

Suppose that you are an editor for a company that publishes photography books. You are working on a volume of portraits of children. Write an introduction to the book in which you provide some background about the emotional reactions captured by the photographer. You might discuss how different children appear to express the same emotion or how the interplay of mixed emotions affects facial features. Use at least five of the vocabulary words from this lesson and underline each one.

VOCABULARY ENRICHMENT

Halcyon comes originally from the Greek word *alkuōn*, the name of a mythical bird. The ancient Greeks believed that the bird had the power to calm the wind and the waves during the winter solstice, when it nested on the sea.

Activity Using a dictionary and other reference works as needed, find out all that you can about each of the following birds. Write several sentences about each. Include the language from which the word comes and one legend or literary work in which the bird appears.

1. albatross 2. phoenix 3. raven 4. roc

The **Test** for Lessons 25, 26, and 27 is on page T33.

NAME ______________________ DATE __________

READING SKILLS

THE PREFIXES *CIRCUM-* AND *PERI-*

The prefixes *circum-* and *peri-* add the meaning of "around" to a root or root word, as the following table shows.

Prefix	Root Word	Word	Word Definition
circum-	*scribere,* "to write"	circumscribe	to draw a line around
peri-	*meter,* "measure"	perimeter	the measurement around

To determine the meaning of words beginning with *circum-* or *peri-,* use the following procedure. Remember that the more prefixes and roots you know, the more often you will be able to analyze unfamiliar words.

PROCEDURE

1. *Substitute the prefix and root definitions for the prefix and root.*
2. *Think of a possible definition of the entire word.*
3. *Use the context to help you develop the possible definition.*
4. *Check your definition of the word in a dictionary.*

EXERCISE USING THE PREFIXES *CIRCUM-* AND *PERI-*

Each sentence in this exercise contains an italicized word beginning with *circum-* or *peri-*. The root word and its meaning are given in parentheses after the sentence. *Step 1:* Taking the context into consideration, write your own definition of the word. *Step 2:* Write the dictionary definition of the word. Choose the definition that fits the way in which the word is used in the sentence. *Step 3:* Write a sentence of your own in which you use the word correctly.

1. Magellan was the first mariner to *circumnavigate* the world. (Latin root word: *navigare,* "to sail")

   Your Definition Sail around

   Dictionary Definition To sail completely around

   Sentence It took an entire day for the schooner to circumnavigate the island.

2. Good dental hygiene helps to prevent periodontal disease. (Latin root word: *dentis,* "of a tooth")

   Your Definition Around the teeth

   Dictionary Definition Of the tissue surrounding and supporting the teeth

   Sentence Dr. Torres specializes in periodontal dentistry.

3. The manager was famous for *circumventing* normal office procedure. (Latin root word: *venire*, "to come")

Your Definition **Coming around in order to avoid**

Dictionary Definition **To avoid by or as if by passing around**

Sentence **Joanne is a master at circumventing red tape.**

4. The examination of a driver may include a test of *peripheral* vision. (Greek root word: *pherein*, "to carry")

Your Definition **All around**

Dictionary Definition **Pertaining to the outermost areas of**

Sentence **The surveyor measured the entire property, including the peripheral areas.**

5. While the case was being tried, both lawyers were *circumspect* in discussing it with others. (Latin root word: *specere*, "to look")

Your Definition **Cautious**

Dictionary Definition **Heedful of circumstances or consequences; prudent**

Sentence **Stanley told himself that he must be circumspect during his job interview.**

6. The medical students were taught about the protective function of the *pericardial* sac. (Greek root word: *kardia*, "heart")

Your Definition **Around the heart**

Dictionary Definition **Pertaining to the membranous sac enclosing the heart**

Sentence **The patient was relieved to learn that the treatment had cured her pericardial infection.**

7. The embassy spokesperson used so many *circumlocutions* that it was hard to tell what had actually happened. (Latin root word: *loqui*, "to speak")

Your Definition **Words that speak around a topic**

Dictionary Definition **Roundabout expressions**

Sentence **A speaker who has not prepared a talk adequately may resort to confusing circumlocutions.**

8. Street musicians are *peripatetic* workers. (Greek root word: *patein*, "to walk")

Your Definition **Involving walking around**

Dictionary Definition **Of or relating to walking**

Sentence **The two old friends had a peripatetic conversation while they went sightseeing in Montreal.**

9. Derived from French, the word *fête* is sometimes printed with a *circumflex*. (Latin root word: *flectere*, "to bend")

Your Definition **An accent mark of some kind**

Dictionary Definition **A mark used over a vowel in certain languages or in phonetic keys**

Sentence **The expression *bête noire*, "something one particularly dislikes," contains a circumflex.**

10. The astronomer spoke of the *perigee* of a three-year-old satellite. (Greek root word: *ge*, "earth")

Your Definition **Traveling around Earth; orbit**

Dictionary Definition **The point nearest Earth in the orbit of the moon or a satellite**

Sentence **Jason made a chart of the perigees of all American satellites still in operation.**

LESSON 28 WORDS AND PHRASES FROM FRENCH 28

In 1066 the triumph of William of Normandy at the Battle of Hastings signaled the beginning of several centuries of Norman French domination over England. Although the French influence on language and culture was initially experienced by the upper classes only, it was not long before an influx of French words was incorporated into the general vocabulary. Ecclesiastical terms, such as *chaplain, procession, incense,* and *relic,* and words connected with the nobility, such as *tower, castle, palace, manor,* and *baron,* are only a few examples of French contributions.

The borrowing of French words and expressions continues even today. We have become accustomed to using French in connection with food, fashion, the arts, manners, history, and diplomacy. This lesson will familiarize you with some of the French words and phrases that have added color and sophistication to English.

WORD LIST

coup d'état
élan
entrée
esprit de corps
laissez faire
nouveau riche
par excellence
potpourri
savoir-faire
tête-à-tête

DEFINITIONS

After you have studied the definitions and example for each vocabulary word, write the word on the line to the right.

1. **coup d'état** (ko͞o′ dā-tä′) *noun* A sudden overthrow or alteration of an existing government by a small group. (From the French words *coup,* meaning "stroke," *de,* meaning "of," and *état,* meaning "state") 1. ______________

   Example In a *coup d'état,* the general and his officers forced the leader to abdicate.

2. **élan** (ā-län′) *noun* a. Enthusiastic vigor and liveliness; zest. **b.** Style; flair. (From the French word *élan,* meaning "rush") 2. ______________

   Example Nicholas played several stringed instruments with *élan.*

3. **entrée** (ŏn′trā, ŏn-trā′) *noun* **a.** The liberty to enter; admittance. **b.** The main course of a meal. (From the French word *entrer,* meaning "to enter") 3. ______________

   Example Only members of the club have *entrée* to its facilities.

4. **esprit de corps** (ĕ-sprē′ də kôr′) *noun* A common feeling of devotion to a cause among the members of a group; team spirit; comradeship. (From the French words *esprit,* meaning "spirit," *de,* meaning "of," and *corps,* meaning "body") 4. ______________

   Example Some athletes demonstrate their *esprit de corps* by their willingness to sacrifice their individual needs for the needs of the team.

5. **laissez faire** (lĕs′ā fâr′) *noun* **a.** An economic doctrine that opposes governmental regulation of commerce beyond the minimum necessary for a free-enterprise system to operate according to its own economic laws. **b.** Noninterference in the affairs of others. (From the French phrase *laisser faire,* meaning "to let [people] do [as they choose]") 5. ______

USAGE NOTE: An alternate spelling is *laisser faire.*

Example Principles of *laissez faire* were popularized by the Physiocrats, French economists of the eighteenth century who sought to free industry and agriculture from mercantilist controls.

6. **nouveau riche** (no͞o′ vō rēsh′) *noun* A person who has recently become rich, especially one who flaunts his or her wealth. *adjective* Referring to the actions of such a person. (From the French words *nouveau,* meaning "new," and *riche,* meaning "rich") 6. ______

Example Scott proved that he is *nouveau riche* by purchasing an excessive number of expensive but useless items.

7. **par excellence** (pär ĕk-sə-läns′) *adjective* Superior; outstanding; of the highest degree. *adverb* Outstandingly. (From the French words *par,* meaning "by," and *excellence,* meaning "excellence") 7. ______

Example Alicia is a reader *par excellence;* her bedroom contains hundreds of books, and her most prized possession is her library card.

8. **potpourri** (pō′po͝o-rē′) *noun* **a.** A combination of diverse elements; medley. **b.** A mixture of dried flower petals and spices kept in a jar and used to scent the air. (From the French translation of the Spanish phrase *olla podrida,* meaning "vegetable and meat stew") 8. ______

Example Dana cooked a hearty main dish that was a *potpourri* of leftovers.

9. **savoir-faire** (săv′wär-fâr′) *noun* The ability to say and do the appropriate thing in any situation; tact. (From the French words *savoir,* meaning "to know," and *faire,* meaning "to do") 9. ______

Example With her usual *savoir-faire,* Andrea averted an awkward moment by letting her host do all the talking.

10. **tête-á-tête** (tāt′ə-tāt′) *noun* A private conversation between two people. *adverb* Together without the intrusion of a third person; in intimate privacy. (From the French words *tête,* meaning "head," and *à,* meaning "to") 10. ______

Example In our luncheon *tête-à-tête,* Ellen confidentially told me of her plans to look for another job.

NAME ______________________ DATE ____________

EXERCISE 1 WRITING CORRECT WORDS

On the answer line, write the word from the vocabulary list that fits each definition.

1. An economic doctrine opposing governmental regulation of commerce beyond the minimum necessary for a free-enterprise system to operate; noninterference in the affairs of others — 1. **laissez faire**
2. A private conversation between two people; together without the intrusion of a third person — 2. **tête-à-tête**
3. A sudden overthrow or alteration of an existing government by a small group — 3. **coup d'état**
4. A person who has recently become rich, especially one who flaunts his or her wealth — 4. **nouveau riche**
5. A combination of diverse elements; medley — 5. **potpourri**
6. The liberty to enter; admittance; main course of a meal — 6. **entrée**
7. The ability to say and do the appropriate thing in any situation; tact — 7. **savoir-faire**
8. Enthusiastic vigor and liveliness; style; flair — 8. **élan**
9. Superior; outstanding; of the highest degree — 9. **par excellence**
10. A common feeling of devotion to a cause among the members of a group; team spirit — 10. **esprit de corps**

EXERCISE 2 USING WORDS CORRECTLY

Decide whether the italicized vocabulary word has been used correctly in the sentence. On the answer line, write *Correct* for correct use and *Incorrect* for incorrect use.

1. Napoleon Bonaparte seized power in France in a *coup d'état* in 1799. — 1. **Correct**
2. To overcome her *élan* on the long bus trip, Jane knitted an afghan. — 2. **Incorrect**
3. Dad's recipe was a *tête-à-tête* of noodles and tomato sauce. — 3. **Incorrect**
4. At the dinner party, Nancy had the *savoir-faire* to eat her peas with her knife. — 4. **Incorrect**
5. Only the hiking party's *esprit de corps* kept its members from panicking when forced to spend the night in a cave in bear country. — 5. **Correct**
6. The town council's policy of *laissez faire* meant that it provided neither trash pickup nor street cleaning. — 6. **Correct**
7. A skier *par excellence,* Jean-Claude Killy did much to popularize the sport. — 7. **Correct**
8. The lobster appetizer was too *nouveau riche* for all but the heartiest appetites. — 8. **Incorrect**
9. The band played a *potpourri* of popular tunes from the forties. — 9. **Correct**
10. "Once my great American novel is written," Mark boasted, "it will be my *entrée* into literary circles." — 10. **Correct**

EXERCISE 3 CHOOSING THE BEST DEFINITION

For each italicized vocabulary word in the following sentences, write the letter of the best definition on the answer line.

1. Gordan performed the difficult concerto with *élan.* — 1. **a**
   a. zest **b.** excitement **c.** strength **d.** practiced technique

2. A tasty vegetarian *entrée* is acorn squash stuffed with cheese. 2. c
a. salad b. meal c. main dish d. favorite food

3. In the Fitzgerald novel, Jay Gatsby represents the pretentiousness of the *nouveau riche.* 3. c
a. old families c. newly wealthy
b. newly famous d. conspicuous consumers

4. Sue made sachets from a *potpourri* of dried violets and roses. 4. b
a. container b. mixture c. small amount d. large amount

5. In a violent *coup d'état,* the military ousted the tyrannical ruler. 5. d
a. battle b. strike c. act of terrorism d. change of government

6. The strong *esprit de corps* of the chorus added to the group's reputation. 6. c
a. discipline b. group rule c. group spirit d. energy

7. Miss Betty Thoughtless, the main character of an eighteenth-century novel, is so lacking in *savoir-faire* that she is constantly embarrassed. 7. a
a. tact b. coordination c. knowledge d. trust

8. After a brief *tête-à-tête* with the teacher, Sarita decided that she would rewrite her composition after all. 8. b
a. confrontation c. correspondence
b. private conversation d. stroll

9. Antitrust laws support *laissez faire.* 9. d
a. governmental intervention c. anarchy
b. equal opportunity d. governmental nonintervention

10. Leonardo da Vinci was a Renaissance man *par excellence:* painter, sculptor, architect, musician, engineer, and scientist. 10. a
a. of the highest degree c. to emulate
b. without restraint d. with great fame

EXERCISE 4 CHOOSING THE BEST WORD

Decide which vocabulary word best completes the sentence, and write the letter of your choice on the answer line.

1. "How was the _____ of Adolf Hitler similar to the way in which Benito Mussolini came into power?" asked Mr. Kwame. 1. b
a. élan b. coup d'état c. tête-à-tête d. potpourri

2. The _____ may carry acquisitiveness to a tasteless extreme. 2. d
a. savoir-faire b. esprit de corps c. laissez faire d. nouveau riche

3. A rather odd _____ popular in sixteenth-century France was roasted whale tongue served with orange sauce. 3. b
a. potpourri b. entrée c. coup d'état d. par excellence

4. A collage is a(n) _____ of materials and textures. 4. a
a. potpourri b. tête-à-tête c. esprit de corps d. laissez faire

5. Mariel dresses with a certain _____. 5. c
a. nouveau riche b. entrée c. élan d. esprit de corps

6. Emily Post wrote her book of etiquette for those desiring to display _____. 6. b
a. laissez faire b. savoir-faire c. entrée d. esprit de corps

7. Mrs. Batesly interrupted her _____ with Mr. Scott to introduce the new arrivals. 7. c
a. laissez faire b. savoir-faire c. tête-à-tête d. élan

8. Our climbing club has a wonderful _____. 8. a
a. esprit de corps b. coup d'état c. par excellence d. potpourri

9. Trying to affect an attitude of _____, Michael told his sister that he would study when she had finished playing her stereo. 9. c
   a. nouveau riche b. esprit de corps c. laissez faire d. par excellence

10. The school variety show will feature singers, dancers, musicians, and comics _____; we have many talented students performing. 10. d
   a. élan b. nouveau riche c. potpourri d. par excellence

READING COMPREHENSION

Each numbered sentence in the following passage contains an italicized vocabulary word. After you read the passage, you will complete an exercise.

BENJAMIN FRANKLIN: STATESMAN AND DIPLOMAT

Some people associate the name Benjamin Franklin with *Poor Richard's Almanack* and other contributions in printing and journalism. Others think of this famous American as a scientist and inventor. Still others remember him in connection with the Declaration of Independence and the United States Constitution. (1) Possessing an astonishing ***potpourri*** of talents, Benjamin Franklin was all of these: inventor, philosopher, publisher, and scientist. Furthermore, as a statesman and diplomat, Franklin stood in the front ranks of those who built the United States.

In 1748, at the age of forty-two, Benjamin Franklin retired to live comfortably on the income of his printing business. (2) Rather than pursuing the leisure of the ***nouveau riche,*** however, Franklin used the opportunity to become involved in community affairs.

In 1757 the Pennsylvania legislature sent Franklin to London to speak for the colony in a tax dispute. He remained in Great Britain for most of the next fifteen years as an unofficial ambassador and the spokesman for the American point of view.

Benjamin Franklin wanted America to remain in the British Empire but only if the rights of the colonists were recognized and protected. (3) A firm believer in ***laissez faire*** and the benefits of free trade, he pledged his entire fortune to pay for the tea destroyed during the Boston Tea Party of 1773 if the British government would repeal the unjust tax on tea. When government officials ignored his proposal, he realized that his usefulness in Great Britain had ended.

Franklin arrived in Philadelphia two weeks after the Revolutionary War had begun. Chosen to serve in the Second Continental Congress, he submitted a plan that laid the groundwork for the Articles of Confederation. The Congress, realizing that an alliance with France might mean the difference between victory and defeat, sent Franklin on a diplomatic mission to France.

In France Benjamin Franklin combined skillful diplomacy with astute public relations. Although inclined to the colonists' cause, the French government was uneasy about signing an aid agreement that could involve the country in a war with Great Britain. (4) Franklin worked behind the scenes to send war supplies across the Atlantic and to establish an ***esprit de corps*** with influential French officials. (5) Through tact, patience, and courtesy, he arranged ***tête-à-têtes*** with the French foreign affairs minister. Without Franklin's efforts and the aid agreement, signed on February 6, 1778, the colonies probably would not have won their independence.

(6) Benjamin Franklin's ***entrée*** into French society was a personal triumph. (7) The nobility and the common people alike were charmed by his ***élan,*** his simple dress and manners, and his witty sayings. (8) With characteristic ***savoir-faire,*** he inspired people from all levels of society to keep loans and gifts of money flowing to the colonies.

For ten years Franklin worked in France as a diplomat. He helped draft the Treaty of Paris, ending the Revolutionary War, and managed to satisfy the conflicting demands of France, Great Britain, and Spain, all of which had interests in America. (9) He also sparked the political imagination of the French, who later staged their own ***coup d'état*** against the French monarchy.

At home and abroad, Franklin was admired as commonsensical, observant, witty, sharp-tongued, and loyal. His qualities are those that have come to be regarded as characteristically American. (10) Benjamin Franklin, statesman and diplomat ***par excellence,*** who helped bring about the United States of America, has remained a well-loved figure in a long line of national heroes.

READING COMPREHENSION EXERCISE

Each of the following statements corresponds to a numbered sentence in the passage. Each statement contains a blank and is followed by four answer choices. Decide which choice fits best in the blank. The word or phrase that you choose must express roughly the same meaning as the italicized word in the passage. Write the letter of your choice on the answer line.

1. Benjamin Franklin possessed am astonishing ____ of talents.
   a. encyclopedia **b.** number **c.** combination **d.** package

   1. c

2. Franklin became involved in community affairs rather than pursuing the leisure of the ____.
   a. newly wealthy **b.** privileged class **c.** invalid **d.** old guard

   2. a

3. Franklin was a firm believer in ____ and the benefits of free trade.
   a. civic participation **c.** commercial regulation
   b. equal compensation **d.** governmental noninterference

   3. d

4. Franklin worked behind the scenes to establish a ____ with influential French officials.
   a. common devotion to a cause **c.** contract
   b. good personal relationship **d.** basis of negotiation

   4. a

5. He arranged ____ with the French foreign affairs minister.
   a. trade alliances **c.** private conversations
   b. recompense **d.** secret negotiations

   5. c

6. Franklin's ____ French society was a personal triumph.
   a. remoteness from **c.** spontaneity with
   b. entrance into **d.** surrender to

   6. b

7. The nobility and the common people alike were charmed by his ____.
   a. intellect **b.** background **c.** friendliness **d.** zest

   7. d

8. With characteristic ____ he inspired everyone to keep loans and gifts of money flowing to the colonies.
   a. jokes **b.** plans **c.** tact **d.** sympathy

   8. c

9. He also sparked the political imagination of the French, who later carried out their own ____ of the French monarchy.
   a. sudden overthrow **b.** torture **c.** reform **d.** analysis

   9. a

10. This statesman and diplomat ____ has remained a prominent figure in a long line of national heroes.
    a. of the lowest level **c.** with many equals
    b. of the highest degree **d.** without peer

    10. b

PRACTICE WITH ANALOGIES

Directions On the answer line, write the vocabulary word or a form of it that completes each analogy.

See pages 32, 66, and 86 for some strategies to use with analogies.

1. INTERMISSION : PERFORMANCE :: ____ : activity *(Lesson 26)* — 1. **hiatus**
2. INVINCIBLE : SUBDUED :: ____ : changed *(Lesson 26)* — 2. **irrevocable**
3. ETERNAL : END :: ____ : stop *(Lesson 26)* — 3. **perpetual**
4. EULOGY : PRAISE :: ____ : criticism *(Lesson 27)* — 4. **tirade**
5. VOLATILE : TEMPER :: ____ : mood *(Lesson 27)* — 5. **mercurial**
6. SEA : MUTINY :: land : ____ *(Lesson 28)* — 6. **coup d'état**

LESSON 29 ART

29

Great artists often show us the world in a new way. In fact, their visions of reality may be so different from what we expect that they are at first rejected. For example, in 1863 a group of French painters held an exhibition of works that captured the momentary effects of sunlight on objects. People were critical of this new interpretation of nature and laughingly called the painters "Impressionists." Today Impressionism is considered one of the most important movements in the history of art, and the once-rejected paintings are now highly valued. The words in this lesson will help you to understand the creative world of the artist.

WORD LIST

abstract
aesthetic
avant-garde
eclectic
grotesque
hackneyed
perspective
representational
surrealistic
verisimilitude

DEFINITIONS

After you have studied the definitions and example for each vocabulary word, write the word on the line to the right.

1. **abstract** (ăb-străkt', ăb'străkt') *adjective* **a.** Concerned with designs or shapes that do not represent any recognizable person or thing. **b.** Considered apart from concrete existence. **c.** Theoretical rather than practical: *an abstract approach to the problem.* (From the Latin *ab-*, meaning "away," and *trahere,* meaning "to draw") 1. ______

Related Word **abstraction** *noun*
Example The invention of photography freed art from the public's demands for imitation and encouraged artists to experiment with *abstract* techniques.

2. **aesthetic** (ĕs-thĕt'ĭk) *adjective* **a.** Of or pertaining to the sense of the beautiful. **b.** Having a love of beauty. **c.** Artistic: *an aesthetic success.* **d.** Of or pertaining to the criticism of taste. (From the Greek word *aisthenasthai,* meaning "to feel" or "to perceive") 2. ______

USAGE NOTE: An alternate spelling is *esthetic.*

Related Words **aesthete** *noun;* **aesthetically** *adverb;* **aestheticism** *noun*
Example As a young child, Mary Cassatt developed her *aesthetic* sensibilities by visiting museums throughout Europe.

3. **avant-garde** (ä'vänt-gärd') *noun* A group, as of writers and artists, who are the leaders in inventing unconventional styles and new techniques in a given field. *adjective* Of or exhibiting new or advanced ideas, as in the arts; ultramodern. (From the French word *avant-garde,* meaning "vanguard") 3. ______

Example In 1910 the Russian artist Vasili Kandinsky was in the *avant-garde* of painters who adopted a lyrical expressionistic style.

4. **eclectic** (ĭ-klĕk'tĭk) *adjective* **a.** Choosing what appears to be the best from diverse sources, systems, or styles. **b.** Consisting of elements taken from diverse sources. (From the Greek *ek-*, meaning "out," and *legein*, meaning "to choose") 4. ____________

Related Words **eclectically** *adverb;* **eclecticism** *noun*
Example The art museum's *eclectic* collection included works from many periods and traditions.

5. **grotesque** (grō-tĕsk') *adjective* **a.** Characterized by ludicrous or incongruous distortion: *a grotesque face, part man and part rat.* **b.** Extravagant; outlandish; bizarre: *grotesque costumes.* (From the Italian word *grottesco*, meaning "of a grotto [cave]") 5. ____________

Related Words **grotesquely** *adverb;* **grotesqueness** *noun*
Example The paintings of Hieronymus Bosch, a fifteenth-century Flemish artist, abound in *grotesque* creatures and scenes.

6. **hackneyed** (hăk'nēd) *adjective* Lacking in freshness because of overuse; trite. 6. ____________

Example The artist's paintings of sad-eyed children were imitated so often that the subject matter was soon *hackneyed.*

7. **perspective** (pər-spĕk'tĭv) *noun* **a.** The technique of representing objects on a flat surface so that they have a three-dimensional quality. **b.** A view or vista. **c.** Point of view; one's manner of viewing things. **d.** A mental view of the relationships of the aspects of a subject to each other and to a whole: *a narrow perspective of the situation.* (From the Latin *per-*, an intensive prefix, and *specere*, meaning "to look") 7. ____________

Example *Perspective* provides an optical illusion of depth.

8. **representational** (rĕp'rĭ-zĕn-tā'shə-nəl) *adjective* Of or pertaining to realistic graphic portrayal in art; lifelike. (From the Latin *re-*, meaning "again," and *praesentare*, meaning "to present") 8. ____________

Related Words **represent** *verb;* **representation** *noun*
Example Ancient Greek and Roman paintings were *representational,* concerned with the natural portrayal of the human form.

9. **surrealistic** (sə-rē'ə-lĭs'tĭk) *adjective* **a.** Of or pertaining to the twentieth-century literary and artistic movement that attempts to express the workings of the subconscious by fantastic imagery and incongruous juxtaposition of subject matter. **b.** Characterized by unusual and unexpected arrangements and distortions of images. **c.** Having an oddly dreamlike or unreal quality. (From the French *sur-*, meaning "beyond," and *réalisme*, meaning "realism") 9. ____________

Related Words **surrealism** *noun;* **surrealist** *noun*
Example *Surrealistic* writers and painters upheld the ideal of spontaneity uninhibited by reason or technique.

10. **verisimilitude** (vĕr'ə-sĭ-mĭl'ĭ-to͞od', vĕr'ə-sĭ-mĭl'ĭ-tyo͞od') *noun* The quality of appearing to be true or real; likelihood. (From the Latin words *verus*, meaning "true," and *similis*, meaning "similar") 10. ____________

Example The main styles of twentieth-century painting have abandoned *verisimilitude.*

NAME ______________________ DATE ____________

EXERCISE 1 WRITING CORRECT WORDS

On the answer line, write the word from the vocabulary list that fits each definition.

1. Lacking in freshness because of overuse; trite — 1. hackneyed
2. The quality of appearing to be true or real; likelihood — 2. verisimilitude
3. Of or pertaining to the sense of the beautiful; having a love of beauty; artistic — 3. aesthetic
4. Of or pertaining to realistic graphic portrayal in art — 4. representational
5. A group, as of writers and artists, who are the leaders in inventing unconventional styles and new techniques in a given field — 5. avant-garde
6. Of or pertaining to the twentieth-century literary and artistic movement that attempts to express the workings of the subconscious by fantastic imagery and incongruous juxtaposition of subject matter — 6. surrealistic
7. Concern with designs or shapes that do not represent any recognizable person or thing; considered apart from concrete existence — 7. abstract
8. Choosing what appears to be the best from diverse sources, systems, or styles — 8. eclectic
9. The technique of presenting objects on a flat surface so that they have a three-dimensional quality; view or vista — 9. perspective
10. Characterized by ludicrous or incongruous distortion; extravagant; outlandish; bizarre — 10. grotesque

EXERCISE 2 USING WORDS CORRECTLY

Each of the following questions contains an italicized vocabulary word. Choose the correct answer to the question, and write *Yes* or *No* on the answer line.

1. Does the use of natural colors enhance the *verisimilitude* of a painting? — 1. Yes
2. Would a *surrealistic* work of art emphasize intuition, dreams, fantasies, and subjective experiences? — 2. Yes
3. Would a *grotesque* sculpture have natural proportions and realistic detail? — 3. No
4. Is a *hackneyed* comparison unique? — 4. No
5. Might it be impossible to identify objects in an *abstract* work of art? — 5. Yes
6. Would the pieces of furniture in an *eclectic* assortment all come from the same period? — 6. No
7. Do *avant-garde* artists base their techniques on the combined efforts of artists of the past? — 7. No
8. Does *representational* art have recognizable figures and objects? — 8. Yes
9. Do most people think that blooming flowers have an *aesthetic* value? — 9. Yes
10. Would the lack of *perspective* in a drawing make a scene look flat and unrealistic? — 10. Yes

EXERCISE 3 CHOOSING THE BEST WORD

Decide which vocabulary word or related form best expresses the meaning of the italicized word or phrase in the sentence. On the answer line, write the letter of the correct choice.

1. In creating *the appearance of depth,* artists show less detail as objects recede in the distance. 1. b
   a. representation b. perspective c. abstraction d. grotesqueness
2. Gertrude Stein was a member of the literary *leaders in inventing unconventional styles* who believed that words should be used for their associations rather than for their literal meaning. 2. d
   a. eclecticism b. representations c. surrealism d. avant-garde
3. During the Byzantine period, an emphasis on *realistic* art and historical accuracy gave way to greater stylization and symbolism. 3. a
   a. representational b. hackneyed c. eclectic d. aesthetic
4. Although many nineteenth-century realist painters chose sentimental subject matter, they concentrated on portraying their subjects with *accuracy.* 4. b
   a. abstraction b. verisimilitude c. perspective d. surrealism
5. Twentieth-century art is *from diverse sources* and international. 5. c
   a. hackneyed b. avant-garde c. eclectic d. surrealistic
6. Salvador Dali, the most famous of the *distorted-image* painters, depicted familiar objects in illogical settings. 6. b
   a. aesthetic b. surrealistic c. representational d. hackneyed
7. Many *concerned with designs or shapes that do not represent any recognizable thing* artists confine themselves to simple two-dimensional geometric forms. 7. d
   a. avant-garde b. grotesque c. aesthetic d. abstract
8. Similes such as "white as snow" and "pretty as a picture" are *overused* expressions that detract from the overall effect of a description. 8. a
   a. hackneyed b. grotesque c. aesthetic d. surrealistic
9. The winning painting was a decorative though *ludicrously distorted* rendition of a jungle scene filled with animal-like people. 9. c
   a. avant-garde b. representational c. grotesque d. abstract
10. Changes in *artistic* standards are illustrated by the poor initial receptions given to many artists who later were considered masters. 10. b
    a. abstract b. aesthetic c. hackneyed d. eclectic

EXERCISE 4 USING DIFFERENT FORMS OF WORDS

Decide which form of the vocabulary word in parentheses best completes the sentence. The form given may be correct. Write your answer on the answer line.

1. Such _____ as truth, bravery, and love are generally considered difficult to define. *(abstract)* 1. abstractions
2. T. S. Eliot's daring innovations in poetry place him among the _____ twentieth-century writers. *(avant-garde)* 2. avant-garde
3. Guilt and anger obscured Luke's _____, making him unable to evaluate the situation objectively. *(perspective)* 3. perspective
4. With smog _____ concealing the late-afternoon sun, the city looked like a scene from a science-fiction movie. *(surrealistic)* 4. surrealistically

5. The soft pink, gray, and mauve tones of the restaurant are _____ pleasing. *(aesthetic)* 5. **aesthetically**

6. The _____ of the concert program kept the audience entertained. *(eclectic)* 6. **eclecticism**

7. The dialogue in the short story was too stilted and antiquated for _____. *(verisimilitude)* 7. **verisimilitude**

8. The _____ of the painted masks frightened several children. *(grotesque)* 8. **grotesqueness**

9. "The use of arches is classic, not _____," said the architect. *(hackneyed)* 9. **hackneyed**

10. Pablo Picasso's *Guernica* is the artist's _____ of moral outrage against the bombing of a city during the Spanish Civil War. *(representational)* 10. **representation**

READING COMPREHENSION

Each numbered sentence in the following passage contains an italicized vocabulary word. After you read the passage, you will complete an exercise.

THE BEGINNINGS OF MODERN ART

When a painting of a black square on a white background wins critical and popular acclaim, many people cannot understand why. (1) Those used to appreciating ***representational*** works may experience frustration when viewing art that seems to deny the values of ordinary beauty and significance that are more easily apparent in traditional paintings. (2) Indeed, the ***aesthetic*** standards of modern art can be difficult to understand.

(3) Artists in the early 1900s grew tired of the centuries of art that had sought to capture with ***verisimilitude*** every detail of an object, person, or scene. (4) They felt that this approach had become ***hackneyed.*** Instead, painters and sculptors began to charge form and color with purely personal meaning. (5) Such French artists as Henri Matisse, Georges Rouault, and Georges Braque abandoned ***perspective*** for flat, two-dimensional space and used color without regard for its previously descriptive function. These painters, who were discredited with the cognomen of Fauvists, or "wild beasts," openly disregarded traditional forms of reality.

(6) Pablo Picasso, though not a Fauvist, was a member of the artistic ***avant-garde.*** (7) His imagination stimulated by the whole range of art history, he developed an ***eclectic*** style that was the basis of many new trends. *Guernica,* his famous mural of war, is an example of the expression of personal reaction in art with no attempt to imitate reality. Through symbolism rather than through graphically violent scenes, he shows the reality of unbearable pain. (8) ***Grotesque*** faces and forms reveal his horrified reaction to brutality. As the war haunts the artist, so, too, does the mural haunt the viewer.

(9) Even more shocking to the public eye than Picasso's fragments and sharp edges are the dream images created by the ***surrealistic*** artist Salvador Dali. He transforms the subconscious world of the mind into the disturbing images of nightmares. Through distortions of space and grotesque juxtapositions of objects and ideas, Dali creates intriguing effects and arouses in observers a number of responses on several levels of thought and feeling.

(10) Because of the ***abstract*** character of modern art, the Fauvists, Picasso, and Dali, as well as the artists who have followed them, have been called barbarous, eccentric, and infantile. What has mattered to these painters is not an imitation of nature but an expression of feelings and reactions through a choice of line and color. Breaking with the traditions of the past, the modern artist seeks to stimulate the imagination. The revolutionary approaches and techniques of today may eventually be the classical traditions of tomorrow.

READING COMPREHENSION EXERCISE

Each of the following statements corresponds to a numbered sentence in the passage. Each statement contains a blank and is followed by four answer choices. Decide which choice fits best in the blank. The word or phrase that you choose must express roughly the same meaning as the italicized word in the passage. Write the letter of your choice on the answer line.

1. Those accustomed to appreciating _____ works may experience frustration when viewing modern art. 1. ____d____
   a. controversial b. experimental c. unusual d. lifelike

2. The _____ standards of modern works can be difficult to understand. 2. ____c____
   a. high b. declining c. artistic d. commercial

3. Artists grew tired of art that captured details with _____. 3. ____a____
   a. realism b. excitement c. drudgery d. astonishment

4. They felt that this approach had become _____. 4. ____b____
   a. popular b. overused c. superfluous d. overpowering

5. French artists abandoned _____ for flat, two-dimensional space. 5. ____d____
   a. complex organization
   b. perfect foregrounds
   c. impressionistic tendencies
   d. the appearance of three-dimensional space

6. Pablo Picasso was a member of the artistic _____. 6. ____c____
   a. elite
   b. clique
   c. group of those who invented new styles
   d. group of critics

7. Picasso developed a(n) _____ style. 7. ____b____
   a. consisting solely of imaginary elements
   b. consisting of elements from diverse sources
   c. pleasing
   d. uncompromising

8. _____ faces and forms reveal his horrified reaction to brutality. 8. ____d____
   a. Attractive b. Insignificant c. Flowing d. Distorted

9. The dream images created by the _____ Dali shocked the public. 9. ____a____
   a. expressing the workings of the subconscious
   b. expressing combined standards of the ages
   c. supreme
   d. mediocre

10. Modern art is essentially _____. 10. ____c____
    a. unusual
    b. controversial
    c. concerned with designs that do not represent reality
    d. concerned with re-creating exactly what is seen

WRITING ASSIGNMENT

Your school has decided on a beautification program, and you have been chosen as a member of the panel that will select art works to decorate the hallways and classrooms. Write a brief paragraph in which you explain how the panel will make its choices. In your report use at least five of the vocabulary words from this lesson and underline each one.

VOCABULARY ENRICHMENT

At one time *grotesque* was narrowly applied to wall paintings found in ruins excavated by the Romans. These creations combined monstrous human and animal forms with elaborate designs. In the seventeenth century, people began to use the word *grotesque* in a more generalized way to mean "bizarre" or "incongruous."

Activity Other English words have derivations related to the monstrous. Look up the following words in a dictionary and write their etymologies and definitions. Then use each word in a sentence.

1. chimera 2. Fury 3. gargoyle 4. harpy 5. Siren

LESSON 30 HUMOR

30

A sense of humor, the ability to perceive, enjoy, or express what is amusing or incongruous, has long been part of our cultural heritage. Although comic styles and subject matter differ according to time and place, humor continues to celebrate our capacity to endure. Whether we laugh at slapstick, jokes, plays on words, or witticisms, we find humor in the unexpected, the extreme, and the foolish. The words in this lesson will help you to express the broad range of amusement that both entertains and gives insight into the human condition.

WORD LIST

buffoon
farce
irony
jocular
lampoon
levity
parody
raillery
regale
satirical

DEFINITIONS

After you have studied the definitions and example for each vocabulary word, write the word on the line to the right.

1. **buffoon** (bə-fo͞on′) *noun* **a.** A clown; jester. **b.** A person given to making undignified or rude jokes. (From the Old Italian word *buffare,* meaning "to puff")

   Related Word **buffoonery** *noun*
   Example With his sad face, once-elegant hat, and large, floppy shoes, the circus *buffoon* made the audience laugh.

1. ______________

2. **farce** (färs) *noun* **a.** A comic play in which exaggerations and improbabilities of plot and characterization are used for humorous effect. **b.** Humor typical of a farce. **c.** A ludicrous and empty show; absurd pretense; mockery: *The trial was a mere farce.* (From the Latin word *farcire,* meaning "to stuff")

   Related Words **farcical** *adjective;* **farcically** *adverb*
   Example Visual humor and plot twists were typical of Charlie Chaplin's movie *farces.*

2. ______________
See *satirical.*

3. **irony** (ī′rə-nē) *noun* **a.** The use of words to convey the opposite of their literal meaning; an expression or utterance marked by a deliberate contrast between the apparent and the intended meanings. **b.** Incongruity between what might be expected and what actually occurs. (From the Greek word *eironeia,* meaning "feigned ignorance")

   Related Words **ironic** *adjective;* **ironically** *adverb*
   Example Ambrose Bierce uses *irony* when he defines a bore as "a person who talks when you wish him to listen."

3. ______________
USAGE NOTE: *Dramatic irony* is created when the audience knows more than the characters do about what is going to happen.

4. **jocular** (jŏk′yə-lər) *adjective* **a.** Given to or characterized by joking; fun-loving. **b.** Meant in jest; facetious. (From the Latin word *jocularis,* meaning "droll")

   Related Words **jocularity** *noun;* **jocularly** *adverb*
   Example At the close of an uncommonly successful selling season, the usually serious Mr. Kistner was in a *jocular* mood.

4. ______________

5. **lampoon** (lăm-po͞on′) *noun* **a.** A broad comic piece that uses ridicule to attack a person, group, or institution. **b.** A light, good-natured criticism. *trans. verb* To ridicule or criticize in a lampoon.

Example Will Rogers's *lampoons* of the government are both accurate and humorous.

5. ______________

See *satirical.*

6. **levity** (lĕv′ĭ-tē) *noun* A light manner or attitude, especially when inappropriate; frivolity; flippancy. (From the Latin word *levis,* meaning "light")

Example Because a relaxation of discipline might prove unsettling, *levity* among staff members is discouraged.

6. ______________

USAGE NOTE: An antonym of *levity* is *gravity,* "solemnity or dignity of manner," from the Latin *gravis,* "heavy."

7. **parody** (păr′ə-dē) *noun* **a.** A comic imitation of a person, literary work, or style that exaggerates the characteristics of the original to make it seem ridiculous. **b.** A performance so bad as to be equivalent to intentional mockery: *The trial was a parody of justice.* *trans. verb* To make a parody of.

Example *Parody* is to literature what caricature and cartoon are to art.

7. ______________

See *satirical.*

8. **raillery** (rā′lə-rē) *noun* Good-natured teasing; banter. (From the Old French word *railler,* meaning "to attack with abusive language")

Example Always too sensitive for her own good, Paula was hurt by the *raillery* of her friends.

8. ______________

USAGE NOTE: Compare with the verb *rail,* "to attack in bitter or harsh language."

9. **regale** (rĭ-gāl′) *trans. verb* **a.** To delight or entertain; give pleasure to. **b.** To entertain lavishly with food and drink; provide a feast for. (From the Old French *re-,* an intensive prefix, and *gale,* meaning "pleasure")

Related Word **regalement** *noun*
Example The talk-show host *regaled* both his guests and the audience with Hollywood gossip.

9. ______________

10. **satirical** (sə-tĭr′ĭ-kəl) *adjective* Of, relating to, or characterized by a sarcastic, mocking, or witty attack on human vice or folly, sometimes with the intent to bring about improvement. (From the Latin word *satura,* meaning "a mixture" or "a poem treating various subjects")

Related Words **satire** *noun;* **satirically** *adverb;* **satirist** *noun;* **satirize** *verb*
Example *Don Quixote,* a *satirical* novel by Cervantes, ridicules the exaggerated notion of chivalry prevalent during the sixteenth century.

10. ______________

USAGE NOTE: A theatrical *farce* is lighthearted comedy; *parody, satire,* and *lampoon* all ridicule something or someone. A parody uses imitation and exaggeration, a satire uses witty criticism (with the aim of improvement), and a lampoon uses caustic wit.

NAME ______________________ DATE __________

EXERCISE 1 WRITING CORRECT WORDS

On the answer line, write the word from the vocabulary list that fits each definition.

1. A light manner or attitude, especially when inappropriate; frivolity — 1. levity
2. Good-natured teasing; banter — 2. raillery
3. A clown; jester; person given to making undignified or rude jokes — 3. buffoon
4. Given to or characterized by joking; fun-loving; meant in jest — 4. jocular
5. Of, relating to, or characterized by a sarcastic, mocking, or witty attack on human vice or folly, sometimes with the intent to bring about improvement — 5. satirical
6. The use of words to convey the opposite of their literal meaning; incongruity between what might be expected and what actually occurs — 6. irony
7. To delight or entertain; entertain lavishly with food and drink — 7. regale
8. A comic play in which exaggerations and improbabilities of plot and characterization are used for humorous effect; a ludicrous and empty show — 8. farce
9. A comic imitation of a person, literary work, or style that exaggerates the characteristics of the original to make it seem ridiculous; a performance so bad as to be equivalent to intentional mockery — 9. parody
10. A broad comic piece that uses ridicule to attack a person, group, or institution; a light, good-natured criticism — 10. lampoon

EXERCISE 2 USING WORDS CORRECTLY

Each of the following statements contains an italicized vocabulary word. Decide whether the sentence is true or false, and write *True* or *False* on the answer line.

1. A *jocular* person tends to be gloomy or dejected. — 1. False
2. If you *regale* someone, you bore that person with trivial details. — 2. False
3. A *lampoon* is a comic assault on a person or group. — 3. True
4. *Farce* is serious drama with a humorous moral. — 4. False
3. *Levity* is a lack of proper seriousness for the occasion. — 5. True
6. Someone who wants attention might choose to act like a *buffoon.* — 6. True
7. A *parody* of a person's style of speaking ridicules his or her mannerisms. — 7. True
8. *Raillery* is serious, constructive criticism. — 8. False
9. An example of *irony* might be awarding a prize to the slowest runner in a race. — 9. True
10. *Satirical* comments tend to be good-natured. — 10. False

EXERCISE 3 CHOOSING THE BEST WORD

Decide which vocabulary word or related form best expresses the meaning of the italicized word or phrase in the sentence. On the answer line, write the letter of the correct choice.

1. The French playwright Molière was a master of the *play containing exaggerated and absurd comic situations.* — 1. b

   a. lampoon **b.** farce **c.** buffoon **d.** parody

2. Lewis Carroll's "Father William," a *humorous imitation* of a poem by Robert Southey, has become famous on its own. 2. d
a. lampoon **b.** farce **c.** raillery **d.** parody

3. When he tripped over an electric cord on his way across the stage to receive his diploma, Eric felt like a *clown.* 3. c
a. levity **b.** farce **c.** buffoon **d.** satirist

4. Solana offered several inadequate excuses that were clearly *meant in jest.* 4. c
a. satirical **b.** ironic **c.** jocular **d.** farcical

5. English literature of the seventeenth and eighteenth centuries contains *humorous attacks on people* that would be considered libelous today. 5. a
a. lampoons **b.** buffoons **c.** farces **d.** regalements

6. Once liftoff had been completed, the astronauts engaged in some *light banter* with mission control in Houston. 6. b
a. irony **b.** raillery **c.** farce **d.** parody

7. In Chaucer's *Canterbury Tales,* the pilgrims *entertain* one another with stories while on their way to a famous shrine. 7. d
a. satirize **b.** parody **c.** lampoon **d.** regale

8. The bride's parents were dismayed by the *frivolity* of the guests during the ceremony. 8. b
a. raillery **b.** levity **c.** regalement **d.** farce

9. Mark Antony resorts to *the use of words to convey the opposite of their literal meaning* when he calls Julius Caesar's assassins "honorable men." 9. c
a. levity **b.** farce **c.** irony **d.** jocularity

10. Voltaire was imprisoned for his *sarcastically attacking* essays on the vices of the French king's regent. 10. b
a. farcical **b.** satirical **c.** jocular **d.** ironic

EXERCISE 4 USING DIFFERENT FORMS OF WORDS

Decide which form of the vocabulary word in parentheses best completes the sentence. The form given may be correct. Write your answer on the answer line.

1. *The Dunciad* was Alexander Pope's _____ of epic poems like the *Iliad. (parody)* 1. parody
2. Molière's _____ were directed against those who preyed on innocent people. *(satirical)* 2. satires
3. The atmosphere in the classroom before the final exam was one of _____. *(levity)* 3. levity
4. Rachel discovered that young campers respond well to criticism when it is delivered _____. *(jocular)* 4. jocularly
5. Several publications are devoted solely to _____ contemporary ideas and situations. *(lampoon)* 5. lampooning
6. Oedipus curses the murderer of King Laius, not realizing that—_____—he is cursing himself. *(irony)* 6. ironically
7. The children howled with laughter at each clown's _____ antics. *(farce)* 7. farcical
8. Susan's informal _____ of her friends with funny stories eventually led to a career as a comic. *(regale)* 8. regalement
9. As Wendell became more self-confident, he stopped hiding his shyness in _____. *(buffoon)* 9. buffoonery
10. *Romeo and Juliet* opens with a bit of humorous _____ between two minor characters. *(raillery)* 10. raillery

NAME ______________________ DATE ________

READING COMPREHENSION

Each numbered sentence in the following passage contains an italicized vocabulary word or related form. After you read the passage, you will complete an exercise.

JESTERS AND FOOLS

Comedy, dealing as it does with the lighter aspects of human existence, has long been a source of entertainment regardless of time period or culture. In fact, professional comedians, called fools or jesters, were employed by the wealthy and powerful from ancient Egyptian times through the Renaissance. With a repertoire that included everything from coarse practical jokes to more intellectual witticisms, the jesters continued to be a fashionable source of entertainment. (1) Dressed in a hood crowned by donkey's ears, a patchwork suit, and long, pointy shoes decorated with bells, the jester of Renaissance times was often called upon to turn the seriousness of life at court into a spontaneous ***farce.***

Centuries earlier, in ancient Greece, some jesters were permanently employed by nobles, although most were free-lance entertainers who congregated in public places waiting for invitations. (2) They earned tips and a meal in return for ***parodying*** dancers and making impertinent comparisons and personal remarks directed against the guests. (3) If their mimicry and ***raillery*** were appreciated, they were richly rewarded; if host or guests took offense, the jester was beaten.

Some wealthy and powerful Romans collected insane or deformed slaves whose antics caused amusement. (4) These jesters, or fools, were kept as much for good luck as for ***regalement.*** (5) The Romans believed that deformity could avert the evil eye and that the jester, with his abusive ***buffoonery,*** would absorb ill luck from those he abused.

It was during the Middle Ages that the jester actually got his name. As a court minstrel, he sang of *gestes,* or heroic deeds. (6) With the decline of minstrelsy, the word *geste* changed in meaning, and the *gestour* developed into the ***jocular*** clown, a relater of witty stories. In Italy, in particular, the role of court jester evolved into a highly skilled profession. (7) Often, the court fool was a man of taste and imagination, talented in music and poetry as well as in ***satirizing*** the rich and powerful.

During the fifteenth and sixteenth centuries, jesters played significant roles in the social life of most European countries. Their business was to provide their masters with diversion from the responsibilities of state affairs. (8) There was also a belief that nourishment taken amidst mirth and jollity produces a light and healthy blood; therefore, the jester was expected to excite dinner guests to laughter through the use of sarcasm and ***irony.*** (9) He was given license to ***lampoon*** the pretensions and self-deceptions of society.

During the sixteenth century, licenses were issued to court jesters, and their collections of jests, practical jokes, comic sermons, and anecdotes were much in fashion. Court jesters continued to make their living by cleverly steering a precarious course between wit and horseplay, flattery and insult. Many gained an enduring reputation for humor and won the affections of their masters. Toward the end of the century, however, their popularity waned. (10) Serious statesmen began to object to their influence, and some fools were banished for their ***levity*** and impudent wit. Once printing was widespread enough to provide entertainment and freedom of speech, the unique services of the jesters and fools were no longer needed.

READING COMPREHENSION EXERCISE

Each of the following statements corresponds to a numbered sentence in the passage. Each statement contains a blank and is followed by four answer choices. Decide which choice fits best in the blank. The word or phrase that you choose must express roughly the same meaning as the italicized word in the passage. Write the letter of your choice on the answer line.

1. The jester was called upon to turn life at court into a(n) _____.
   a. melodrama **c.** exciting challenge
   b. benefit **d.** absurd pretense

1. ____d____

2. Ancient jesters earned tips and a meal in return for _____ dancers. 2. a
a. imitating b. performing as c. applauding d. accompanying

3. They were richly rewarded if their mimicry and _____ were appreciated. 3. b
a. cynicism b. banter c. criticism d. innuendos

4. These jesters were kept as much for good luck as for _____. 4. a
a. entertainment b. advice c. wisdom d. prestige

5. The Romans believed that the jester, with his abusive _____, would absorb ill luck from those he abused. 5. c
a. nastiness b. curses c. joking d. rivals

6. The *gestour* developed into the _____ clown. 6. d
a. insignificant b. sad-eyed c. appealing d. fun-loving

7. The court fool often was talented in music and poetry as well as in _____ the rich and powerful. 7. b
a. complimenting b. mocking c. representing d. disturbing

8. The jester was expected to excite dinner guests to laughter through sarcasm and _____. 8. a
a. reversal of expectations
b. realization of expectations
c. discomfort
d. hysteria

9. He was given license to _____ the pretensions and self-deceptions of society. 9. c
a. explain
b. encourage
c. criticize good-naturedly
d. provoke incessantly

10. Some jesters were banished for their _____ and impudent wit. 10. b
a. honesty
b. inappropriate humor
c. incorrect information
d. disdain

PRACTICE WITH ANALOGIES

See pages 32, 66, and 86 for some strategies to use with analogies.

Directions On the answer line, write the letter of the phrase that best completes the analogy.

1. AESTHETICS : BEAUTY :: (A) ethics : etiquette (B) logistics : truth (C) linguistics : speech (D) theology : morals (E) rhetoric : reasoning 1. C

2. BUFFOON : FARCICAL :: (A) laggard : attentive (B) politician : concise (C) expert : proficient (D) scholar : snobbish (E) stickler : flexible 2. C

3. LAMPOON : SATIRE :: (A) setting : novel (B) fable : moral (C) plot : character (D) limerick : poem (E) picture : collage 3. D

4. PARODY : IMITATION :: (A) caricture : potrait (B) skit : play (C) film : theater (D) chapter : novel (E) lyric : song 4. A

5. STAID : LEVITY :: (A) harmonious : perfection (B) shy : beauty (C) prominent : recognition (D) admirable : esteem (E) lethargic : vitality 5. E

6. JESTER : JOCULAR :: (A) artist : surrealistic (B) hack : trite (C) expert : eclectic (D) sculptor : abstract (E) designer : grotesque 6. B

The **Bonus activity** for Lessons 26–30 is on page T35.
The **Test** for Lessons 28, 29, and 30 is on page T36.

NAME ______________________________ DATE ____________

READING SKILLS

THE PREFIXES *EXTRA-, SUPER-,* AND *ULTRA-*

When added to roots, the prefixes *extra-, super-,* and *ultra-* form words with different meanings. All three prefixes have the meaning of "beyond," "above," or "exceeding(ly)," as the table demonstrates.

Word	Sentence	Word Definition
extraordinary	The gymnast had an *extraordinary* sense of balance.	beyond the ordinary
superscript	Footnote numbers often appear as *superscripts.*	a character that is above a line of type or writing
ultramodern	*Ultramodern* furniture does not appeal to everyone.	exceedingly modern

You can determine the meaning of unfamiliar words that begin with *extra-, super-,* or *ultra-* by adding the prefix meaning to the meaning of the root or root word. Remember that context clues may also help you to arrive at a possible definition. Be sure to verify the meaning by looking the word up in a dictionary.

EXERCISE **USING THE PREFIXES *EXTRA-, SUPER-,* AND *ULTRA-***

Each sentence in this exercise contains an italicized word beginning with one of the three prefixes. When appropriate, the root word and its meaning are given in parentheses after the sentence. *Step 1:* Taking the context into consideration, write your own definition of the word. *Step 2:* Write the dictionary definition of the word. Choose the definition that fits the way in which the word is used in the sentence. *Step 3:* Write a sentence of your own in which you use the word correctly.

1. The information was obtained by *extralegal* means.

   Your Definition Beyond the legal

   Dictionary Definition Not governed or permitted by law

   Sentence The extralegal nature of the sales campaign was reported to the proper authorities.

2. Except for Earth, the planets in our solar system are *superlunary.* (Latin root word: *luna,* "the moon")

   Your Definition Beyond the moon

   Dictionary Definition Situated beyond the moon

   Sentence The science-fiction novel had a superlunary setting.

3. Some *ultrasonic* devices are used to relieve chronic pain.

   Your Definition Beyond what is normally heard

   Dictionary Definition Pertaining to acoustic frequencies above the range audible to the human ear

   Sentence The dog responded to the ultrasonic whistle.

4. That some people have *extrasensory* perception seems to be borne out by scientific studies.

Your Definition **Beyond what is normally preceived by the senses**

Dictionary Definition **Beyond the normal range or bounds of the senses**

Sentence **Dreams that foretell actual events exemplify extrasensory messages.**

5. Great Uncle Fred jokingly refers to himself as *superannuated* (Latin root word: *annus,* "year")

Your Definition **Beyond the average in years; old**

Dictionary Definition **Retired because of advanced age**

Sentence **This superannuated Pierce Arrow is a prized antique auto.**

6. Opposing the concept of a strong central government, the candidate described herself as *ultraconservative.*

Your Definition **Exceedingly conservative**

Dictionary Definition **Conservative to an extreme, particularly in political beliefs**

Sentence **It is impossible to know how many conservatives may correctly be termed ultraconservative.**

7. Jennifer's many friends say that she is *extroverted.* (Latin root word: *vertere,* "to turn")

Your Definition **Turned beyond or outward to others**

Dictionary Definition **Interested in others as opposed to the self**

Sentence **One pitfall of being extroverted is the tendency to spread oneself too thin.**

8. To make the poster, a pale green overlay was *superimposed* on the black lettering. (Latin root word: *impositus,* "placed upon")

Your Definition **Placed on top of**

Dictionary Definition **To lay or place over something**

Sentence **He had a surface friendliness that seemed to be superimposed on a basic hostility.**

9. The painting of the sea was notable for its *ultramarine* hue. (Latin root word: *mare,* "sea")

Your Definition **Exceedingly blue**

Dictionary Definition **Having a deep-blue purplish color**

Sentence **Ultramarine pigment was once made from the gemstone called lapis lazuli.**

10. My great-grandfather was once a *supernumerary* in an opera that starred the famous tenor Enrico Caruso. (Latin root word: *numerus,* "number")

Your Definition **Someone in addition to the regular cast members**

Dictionary Definition **A performer without a speaking part, as in a crowd scene**

Sentence **Shelly has been a supernumerary in productions of the Barnswallows.**

CONTENTS

USING BONUS ACTIVITIES AND TESTS

For your convenience, the lesson **Tests** and **Bonus** activities that accompany *Vocabulary for Achievement,* Sixth Course, are available as reproducible masters in this section. Answers are printed in color on the front side of each reproducible master for ease in locating. In addition, two **Verbal Aptitude Tests** provide students with practice in preparing for college-entrance examinations. The two reproducible student answer sheets contain the answers for these tests on their front sides.

This section also contains recordkeeping charts, that may be reproduced for each of your classes. These will help you to keep track of student progress on **lesson exercises, Bonus** activities, **Tests, skill features,** and the **Verbal Aptitude Tests.**

TESTS

There are ten multiple-choice tests, each covering three consecutive lessons. This format ensures that students can demonstrate proficiency with a wider set of vocabulary words than is found in a single lesson.

Test formats resemble those of the lesson exercises. Each test is divided into two parts of fifteen items each, allowing for the testing of all words in the three lessons. Part A focuses on recognizing and recalling definitions, while Part B emphasizes placing words within context or discriminating among a choice of antonyms.

BONUSES

Seven Bonus activities, each covering four or five consecutive lessons, offer students further opportunities for reinforcement and enrichment. These activities consist of crossword puzzles, word searches, sentence completions, scrambled words, and other word-game formats. Depending on classroom needs, use these activities as added practice, as reviews of already-mastered words, or as extra-credit assignments.

VERBAL APTITUDE TESTS

Each of the four-page tests reinforces material taught in the skill features and helps prepare students for taking college-entrance examinations. Each test covers antonyms, sentence completions, word analogies, and reading comprehension.

In order to conform to the customary fall and early-spring scheduling of college-entrance testing, Test 1 appears after Lesson 10; Test 2 appears after Lesson 20.

Many of the words from this grade level are used in the Verbal Aptitude Tests; these words are marked for your reference with a colored asterisk on the **Complete Word List** on page xv in the Teacher's Edition.

SIXTH COURSE

Student Record

Class Period ____	Lesson 1 Exercises	Lesson 2 Exercises	Lesson 3 Exercises	Test: Lessons 1, 2, 3	Skill Lesson	Lesson 4 Exercises	Bonus: Lessons 1–4	Lesson 5 Exercises	Lesson 6 Exercises	Test: Lessons 4, 5, 6	Skill Lesson	Lesson 7 Exercises	Lesson 8 Exercises	Bonus: Lessons 5–8	Lesson 9 Exercises	Test: Lessons 7, 8, 9	Skill Lesson	Lesson 10 Exercises	Verbal Aptitude Test 1	Lesson 11 Exercises	Lesson 12 Exercises	Bonus: Lessons 9–12	Test: Lessons 10, 11, 12	Skill Lesson	Lesson 13 Exercises	Lesson 14 Exercises	Lesson 15 Exercises	Test: Lessons 13, 14, 15	Skill Lesson
1.																													
2.																													
3.																													
4.																													
5.																													
6.																													
7.																													
8.																													
9.																													
10.																													
11.																													
12.																													
13.																													
14.																													
15.																													
16.																													
17.																													
18.																													
19.																													
20.																													
21.																													
22.																													
23.																													
24.																													
25.																													
26.																													
27.																													
28.																													
29.																													
30.																													
31.																													
32.																													
33.																													
34.																													
35.																													

	Lesson 16 Exercises	Bonus: Lessons 13–16	Lesson 17 Exercises	Lesson 18 Exercises	Test: Lessons 16, 17, 18	Skill Lesson	Lesson 19 Exercises	Lesson 20 Exercises	Bonus: Lessons 17–20	Verbal Aptitude Test 2	Lesson 21 Exercises	Test: Lessons 19, 20, 21	Skill Lesson	Lesson 22 Exercises	Lesson 23 Exercises	Lesson 24 Exercises	Test: Lessons 22, 23, 24	Skill Lesson	Lesson 25 Exercises	Bonus: Lessons 21–25	Lesson 26 Exercises	Lesson 27 Exercises	Test: Lessons 25, 26, 27	Skill Lesson	Lesson 28 Exercises	Lesson 29 Exercises	Lesson 30 Exercises	Bonus: Lessons 26–30	Test: Lessons 28, 29, 30	Skill Lesson
1.																														
2.																														
3.																														
4.																														
5.																														
6.																														
7.																														
8.																														
9.																														
10.																														
11.																														
12.																														
13.																														
14.																														
15.																														
16.																														
17.																														
18.																														
19.																														
20.																														
21.																														
22.																														
23.																														
24.																														
25.																														
26.																														
27.																														
28.																														
29.																														
30.																														
31.																														
32.																														
33.																														
34.																														
35.																														

NAME ______________________________ DATE ____________

TEST LESSONS 1, 2, AND 3

(pages 1–18)

PART A MATCHING WORDS AND DEFINITIONS

Match the definition in Column B with the word in Column A. Write the letter of the correct definition on the answer line.

Column A

1. undulate
2. paradigm
3. nefarious
4. syntax
5. philology
6. belie
7. serpentine
8. meander
9. stratagem
10. perfidious
11. probity
12. retrogress
13. emanate
14. collusion
15. scrupulous

Column B

a. to originate; emit

b. to follow a winding and turning course; wander without fixed direction

c. to revert to an earlier, inferior, or less complex condition

d. serpentlike in form or movement; subtly sly and tempting

e. to move with a wavelike motion; ripple

f. to misrepresent; contradict

g. extremely wicked or infamous

h. treacherous; disloyal

i. complete integrity; uprightness

j. having principles; conscientious

k. a clever scheme for attaining a goal

l. a list of all the inflectional endings of a word; an especially clear or typical example or model

m. the chronological study of language development; the study of language as used in literature

n. the manner in which words are combined to form clauses, phrases, and sentences

o. a secret agreement between two or more people for a deceitful purpose; conspiracy

1. e
2. l
3. g
4. n
5. m
6. f
7. d
8. b
9. k
10. h
11. i
12. c
13. a
14. o
15. j

PART B CHOOSING THE BEST WORD

On the answer line, write the letter of the word that best completes the sentence.

16. Despite his convincing _____ and appealing manner, the congressman's voting record may prevent his re-election. — 16. a

a. rhetoric **b.** orthography **c.** collusion **d.** philology

17. The German words *Schule, Freund,* and *Haus* are _____ of the English words *school, friend,* and *house.* — 17. d

a. paradigms **b.** inflections **c.** phonologies **d.** cognates

NAME ______________________________ DATE ____________

TEST LESSONS 1, 2, AND 3

(pages 1–18)

PART A MATCHING WORDS AND DEFINITIONS

Match the definition in Column B with the word in Column A. Write the letter of the correct definition on the answer line.

Column A

1. undulate
2. paradigm
3. nefarious
4. syntax
5. philology
6. belie
7. serpentine
8. meander
9. stratagem
10. perfidious
11. probity
12. retrogress
13. emanate
14. collusion
15. scrupulous

Column B

a. to originate; emit

b. to follow a winding and turning course; wander without fixed direction

c. to revert to an earlier, inferior, or less complex condition

d. serpentlike in form or movement; subtly sly and tempting

e. to move with a wavelike motion; ripple

f. to misrepresent; contradict

g. extremely wicked or infamous

h. treacherous; disloyal

i. complete integrity; uprightness

j. having principles; conscientious

k. a clever scheme for attaining a goal

l. a list of all the inflectional endings of a word; an especially clear or typical example or model

m. the chronological study of language development; the study of language as used in literature

n. the manner in which words are combined to form clauses, phrases, and sentences

o. a secret agreement between two or more people for a deceitful purpose; conspiracy

1. ____________
2. ____________
3. ____________
4. ____________
5. ____________
6. ____________
7. ____________
8. ____________
9. ____________
10. ____________
11. ____________
12. ____________
13. ____________
14. ____________
15. ____________

PART B CHOOSING THE BEST WORD

On the answer line, write the letter of the word that best completes the sentence.

16. Despite his convincing _____ and appealing manner, the congressman's voting record may prevent his re-election.
    a. rhetoric **b.** orthography **c.** collusion **d.** philology

16. ____________

17. The German words *Schule, Freund,* and *Haus* are _____ of the English words *school, friend,* and *house.*
    a. paradigms **b.** inflections **c.** phonologies **d.** cognates

17. ____________

NAME ____________ DATE ____________

TEST LESSONS 1, 2, AND 3

PART B CHOOSING THE BEST WORD (CONTINUED)

18. A week of _____ cold rain demoralized the campers. 18. c
    a. serpentine b. nefarious c. unremitting d. spurious

19. Nylon and other synthetic fibers are _____ of petroleum. 19. d
    a. diminutives b. cognates c. paradigms d. derivatives

20. _____ during hot summer weather, even the laziest horse seems reinvigorated with the arrival of fall. 20. b
    a. Serpentine b. Torpid c. Scrupulous d. Diminutive

21. The study of _____ helps to explain why the spelling of certain words is so different from their pronunciation. 21. a
    a. phonology b. undulations c. syntax d. rhetoric

22. In establishing their priorities, the staff determined that an advertising campaign should _____ new product development. 22. c
    a. collude b. dissemble c. supersede d. emanate

23. Through the _____ activities of the Underground Railroad, many slaves escaped to freedom during the Civil War. 23. d
    a. transitory b. nefarious c. diminutive d. clandestine

24. Lasting only one month, William Henry Harrison's presidency was the most _____ in the history of the United States. 24. b
    a. unremitting b. transitory c. scrupulous d. clandestine

25. Grandmother, though _____ in stature, was considered a giant in the clothing industry. 25. c
    a. scrupulous b. nefarious c. diminutive d. serpentine

26. Lucia tends to be shy and _____ among strangers. 26. a
    a. inhibited b. transitory c. unremitting d. spurious

27. Tired of _____ self-control, the children clamored impatiently. 27. d
    a. colluding b. retrogressing c. undulating d. dissembling

28. The invention of the printing press helped to standardize English _____. 28. b
    a. emanations b. orthography c. probity d. rhetoric

29. The allegedly valuable painting was nothing more than a _____ copy of an old master. 29. a
    a. spurious b. scrupulous c. perfidious d. transitory

30. Dwight attempted to eliminate the sarcastic _____ that dominated all of his responses to Theo's questions. 30. c
    a. paradigm b. collusion c. inflection d. stratagem

NAME ______________________________ DATE __________

TEST LESSONS 1, 2, AND 3

PART B CHOOSING THE BEST WORD (CONTINUED)

18. A week of _____ cold rain demoralized the campers. 18. __________
    a. serpentine b. nefarious c. unremitting d. spurious

19. Nylon and other synthetic fibers are _____ of petroleum. 19. __________
    a. diminutives b. cognates c. paradigms d. derivatives

20. _____ during hot summer weather, even the laziest horse seems reinvigorated with the arrival of fall. 20. __________
    a. Serpentine b. Torpid c. Scrupulous d. Diminutive

21. The study of _____ helps to explain why the spelling of certain words is so different from their pronunciation. 21. __________
    a. phonology b. undulations c. syntax d. rhetoric

22. In establishing their priorities, the staff determined that an advertising campaign should _____ new product development. 22. __________
    a. collude b. dissemble c. supersede d. emanate

23. Through the _____ activities of the Underground Railroad, many slaves escaped to freedom during the Civil War. 23. __________
    a. transitory b. nefarious c. diminutive d. clandestine

24. Lasting only one month, William Henry Harrison's presidency was the most _____ in the history of the United States. 24. __________
    a. unremitting b. transitory c. scrupulous d. clandestine

25. Grandmother, though _____ in stature, was considered a giant in the clothing industry. 25. __________
    a. scrupulous b. nefarious c. diminutive d. serpentine

26. Lucia tends to be shy and _____ among strangers. 26. __________
    a. inhibited b. transitory c. unremitting d. spurious

27. Tired of _____ self-control, the children clamored impatiently. 27. __________
    a. colluding b. retrogressing c. undulating d. dissembling

28. The invention of the printing press helped to standardize English _____. 28. __________
    a. emanations b. orthography c. probity d. rhetoric

29. The allegedly valuable painting was nothing more than a _____ copy of an old master. 29. __________
    a. spurious b. scrupulous c. perfidious d. transitory

30. Dwight attempted to eliminate the sarcastic _____ that dominated all of his responses to Theo's questions. 30. __________
    a. paradigm b. collusion c. inflection d. stratagem

NAME ______________________________ DATE ____________

BONUS LESSONS 1–4

(pages 1–18, 21–26)

Use the clues to complete the crossword puzzle.

			[1] C		[2] C	O	N	[3] S	P	I	R	A	C	Y		
[4] S	M	A	L	L				Y								
			A					N								
		[5] I	N	H	I	B	I	T								
			D					A								
[6] W	A	V	E	S		[7] E		X								
			S			V										
[8] R	H	E	T	O	R	I	C									
			I			L										
			N									[9] F				
		[10] B	E	R	[11] S	E	R	K				A		[12] C		
					E					[13] S		L		O		
			[14] P	E	R	F	I	D	I	O	U	S		G		
		[15] S			P					U		E		N		
		L		[16] M	E	C	C	A		N			[17] S	A	G	A
		O			N					D				T		
		G			T		[18] P	E	R	S	I	S	[19] T	E	N	T
		A			I								R			
[20] W	I	N	D	I	N	G			[21] R	E	S	P	E	C	T	
					E								K			

Across

2. Synonym for *collusion*
4. *Diminutive* indicates _____ size.
5. To restrain or hold back
6. *Undulate* means "to move in _____."
8. The art of using language effectively
10. Destructively violent
14. Antonym for loyal
16. A place regarded as the center of activity or interest
17. A prose narrative
18. Synonym for *unremitting*
20. *Meander* refers to a(n) _____ course.
21. To *kowtow* is to show _____.

Down

1. Concealed or kept secret
3. The arrangement of words to form phrases, clauses, and sentences
7. Synonym for *nefarious*
9. *Spurious* comes from a Latin word meaning "_____."
11. Resembling a snake or eel in movement
12. Related by being derived or borrowed from the same word or root
13. *Phonology* refers to the _____ of language.
15. Synonym for *shibboleth*
19. To make a difficult journey

NAME ______________________ DATE ____________

BONUS LESSONS 1–4

(pages 1–18, 21–26)

Use the clues to complete the crossword puzzle.

Across

2. Synonym for *collusion*
4. *Diminutive* indicates _____ size.
5. To restrain or hold back
6. *Undulate* means "to move in _____."
8. The art of using language effectively
10. Destructively violent
14. Antonym for loyal
16. A place regarded as the center of activity or interest
17. A prose narrative
18. Synonym for *unremitting*
20. *Meander* refers to a(n) _____ course.
21. To *kowtow* is to show _____.

Down

1. Concealed or kept secret
3. The arrangement of words to form phrases, clauses, and sentences
7. Synonym for *nefarious*
9. *Spurious* comes from a Latin word meaning "_____."
11. Resembling a snake or eel in movement
12. Related by being derived or borrowed from the same word or root
13. *Phonology* refers to the _____ of language.
15. Synonym for *shibboleth*
19. To make a difficult journey

NAME ______________________ DATE ____________

TEST LESSONS 4, 5, AND 6

(pages 21–28)

PART A CHOOSING THE BEST DEFINITION

On the answer line, write the letter of the best definition of the italicized word.

1. Even in medieval Europe, alchemy was an *arcane* pursuit. 1. ___b___
   a. sophisticated b. esoteric c. ancient d. engrossing

2. Modern historians have retraced Marco Polo's *trek* over the silk route. 2. ___b___
   a. procession b. long journey c. exploration d. barter

3. The graduating class sang the school song *in unison.* 3. ___a___
   a. simultaneously b. tearfully c. grimly d. expressively

4. "Fifty-four forty or fight!" was the *shibboleth* of supporters of the American occupation of the Oregon Territory. 4. ___c___
   a. threat b. proverb c. slogan d. demand

5. The *synergy* of the lymphatic system and the bloodstream is an important mechanism in the body's ability to fight disease. 5. ___a___
   a. combined action b. construction c. energy d. strength

6. The language of music *transcends* cultural barriers. 6. ___d___
   a. breaks down b. enhances c. replaces d. goes beyond

7. *Roughing It* is the amusing *saga* of Mark Twain's western travels. 7. ___a___
   a. story b. operetta c. rendition d. biography

8. The British celebrated the *jubilee* of Queen Victoria's coronation. 8. ___b___
   a. holiday b. anniversary c. solemn occasion d. honor

9. Although the pottery shop started out as an *adjunct* of the craft school, it soon became the most busy part of the entire operation. 9. ___b___
   a. special feature c. technological advance
   b. attachment d. obsolete feature

10. The *juggernaut* of imperialism contributed to Britain's colonial expansion in the eighteenth century. 10. ___d___
    a. adoption c. popular notion
    b. cessation d. overwhelming force

11. The reporter's subtle questions *educed* many previously unknown facts. 11. ___c___
    a. outlined b. reproduced c. brought out d. withheld

12. Wolfgang Mozart's talent *manifested* itself when he was very young. 12. ___d___
    a. emphasized b. translated c. benefited d. revealed

13. The airline owners engaged in *covert* negotiations. 13. ___a___
    a. secret b. public c. minimal d. intensive

14. The developer situated the houses so that many are *contiguous.* 14. ___c___
    a. parallel b. unsteady c. touching d. inadequate

15. The moonstone is admired for its *translucent* surface. 15. ___b___
    a. allowing no reflection of light c. shiny
    b. allowing the partial spread of light d. cloudy

NAME ______________________________ DATE ____________

TEST LESSONS 4, 5, AND 6

(pages 21–28)

PART A CHOOSING THE BEST DEFINITION

On the answer line, write the letter of the best definition of the italicized word.

1. Even in medieval Europe, alchemy was an *arcane* pursuit. 1. ____________
   a. sophisticated b. esoteric c. ancient d. engrossing

2. Modern historians have retraced Marco Polo's *trek* over the silk route. 2. ____________
   a. procession b. long journey c. exploration d. barter

3. The graduating class sang the school song *in unison.* 3. ____________
   a. simultaneously b. tearfully c. grimly d. expressively

4. "Fifty-four forty or fight!" was the *shibboleth* of supporters of the American occupation of the Oregon Territory. 4. ____________
   a. threat b. proverb c. slogan d. demand

5. The *synergy* of the lymphatic system and the bloodstream is an important mechanism in the body's ability to fight disease. 5. ____________
   a. combined action b. construction c. energy d. strength

6. The language of music *transcends* cultural barriers. 6. ____________
   a. breaks down b. enhances c. replaces d. goes beyond

7. *Roughing It* is the amusing *saga* of Mark Twain's western travels. 7. ____________
   a. story b. operetta c. rendition d. biography

8. The British celebrated the *jubilee* of Queen Victoria's coronation. 8. ____________
   a. holiday b. anniversary c. solemn occasion d. honor

9. Although the pottery shop started out as an *adjunct* of the craft school, it soon became the most busy part of the entire operation. 9. ____________
   a. special feature c. technological advance
   b. attachment d. obsolete feature

10. The *juggernaut* of imperialism contributed to Britain's colonial expansion in the eighteenth century. 10. ____________
    a. adoption c. popular notion
    b. cessation d. overwhelming force

11. The reporter's subtle questions *educed* many previously unknown facts. 11. ____________
    a. outlined b. reproduced c. brought out d. withheld

12. Wolfgang Mozart's talent *manifested* itself when he was very young. 12. ____________
    a. emphasized b. translated c. benefited d. revealed

13. The airline owners engaged in *covert* negotiations. 13. ____________
    a. secret b. public c. minimal d. intensive

14. The developer situated the houses so that many are *contiguous.* 14. ____________
    a. parallel b. unsteady c. touching d. inadequate

15. The moonstone is admired for its *translucent* surface. 15. ____________
    a. allowing no reflection of light c. shiny
    b. allowing the partial spread of light d. cloudy

NAME ______________________ DATE __________

TEST LESSONS 4, 5, AND 6

PART B CHOOSING THE BEST WORD

On the answer line, write the letter of the word that best expresses the meaning of the italicized word or phrase.

16. By *blending* copper and titanium, scientists produced a new alloy. 16. c
    a. fathoming b. adumbrating c. amalgamating d. diffusing

17. Erika still feels that her job responsibilities are *vague*. 17. d
    a. limpid b. impervious c. peripheral d. nebulous

18. Several players *showed submission* to Coach Murphy, hoping to improve their chances of making the football team. 18. a
    a. kowtowed b. diffused c. adumbrated d. diverged

19. It is difficult for many students to *get to the bottom of and understand* quantum mechanics. 19. b
    a. amalgamate b. fathom c. manifest d. transcend

20. The fires that left many homeless were the *destructively violent* work of the same individual. 20. a
    a. berserk b. nebulous c. impervious d. contiguous

21. Francisco's new jacket was *incapable of being penetrated by* water. 21. c
    a. nebulous to b. limpid to c. impervious to d. diffuse to

22. A Canadian shopping and recreational complex has become a *place regarded as the center of interest* for both shoppers and vacationers. 22. d
    a. shibboleth b. maelstrom c. parity d. mecca

23. Although Clara came from humble beginnings, she became a *person of great wealth and prominence* who headed a manufacturing conglomerate. 23. d
    a. juggernaut b. adjunct c. adumbration d. nabob

24. Sam *departed from* family tradition, becoming a jazz trombonist. 24. a
    a. diverged from b. kowtowed to c. diffused d. transcended

25. The doctor *gave a sketchy outline of* the new medical procedure. 25. b
    a. amalgamated b. adumbrated c. fathomed d. manifested

26. Ryan tritely called Jane's eyes "*transparently clear* pools of beauty." 26. c
    a. fathomable b. nebulous c. limpid d. arcane

27. *Pertaining to the outermost region of a precise boundary* vision is important in many sports, such as racquetball. 27. d
    a. Contiguous b. Adjunct c. Impervious d. Peripheral

28. The proposal created a *situation resembling a turbulent whirlpool.* 28. c
    a. shibboleth b. mecca c. maelstrom d. juggernaut

29. Mayor La Guardia *poured out* a sense of well-being wherever he went. 29. a
    a. diffused b. adumbrated c. amalgamated d. educed

30. The state's high schools were organized into divisions to achieve a degree of *equality* in athletic competition. 30. b
    a. periphery b. parity c. synergy d. unison

NAME ________________________________ DATE ____________

TEST LESSONS 4, 5, AND 6

PART B CHOOSING THE BEST WORD

On the answer line, write the letter of the word that best expresses the meaning of the italicized word or phrase.

16. By *blending* copper and titanium, scientists produced a new alloy. 16. ________
a. fathoming b. adumbrating c. amalgamating d. diffusing

17. Erika still feels that her job responsibilities are *vague*. 17. ________
a. limpid b. impervious c. peripheral d. nebulous

18. Several players *showed submission* to Coach Murphy, hoping to improve their chances of making the football team. 18. ________
a. kowtowed b. diffused c. adumbrated d. diverged

19. It is difficult for many students to *get to the bottom of and understand* quantum mechanics. 19. ________
a. amalgamate b. fathom c. manifest d. transcend

20. The fires that left many homeless were the *destructively violent* work of the same individual. 20. ________
a. berserk b. nebulous c. impervious d. contiguous

21. Francisco's new jacket was *incapable of being penetrated by* water. 21. ________
a. nebulous to b. limpid to c. impervious to d. diffuse to

22. A Canadian shopping and recreational complex has become a *place regarded as the center of interest* for both shoppers and vacationers. 22. ________
a. shibboleth b. maelstrom c. parity d. mecca

23. Although Clara came from humble beginnings, she became a *person of great wealth and prominence* who headed a manufacturing conglomerate. 23. ________
a. juggernaut b. adjunct c. adumbration d. nabob

24. Sam *departed from* family tradition, becoming a jazz trombonist. 24. ________
a. diverged from b. kowtowed to c. diffused d. transcended

25. The doctor *gave a sketchy outline of* the new medical procedure. 25. ________
a. amalgamated b. adumbrated c. fathomed d. manifested

26. Ryan tritely called Jane's eyes "*transparently clear* pools of beauty." 26. ________
a. fathomable b. nebulous c. limpid d. arcane

27. *Pertaining to the outermost region of a precise boundary* vision is important in many sports, such as racquetball. 27. ________
a. Contiguous b. Adjunct c. Impervious d. Peripheral

28. The proposal created a *situation resembling a turbulent whirlpool.* 28. ________
a. shibboleth b. mecca c. maelstrom d. juggernaut

29. Mayor La Guardia *poured out* a sense of well-being wherever he went. 29. ________
a. diffused b. adumbrated c. amalgamated d. educed

30. The state's high schools were organized into divisions to achieve a degree of *equality* in athletic competition. 30. ________
a. periphery b. parity c. synergy d. unison

NAME ______________________________ DATE __________

BONUS LESSONS 5–8

(pages 27–38, 41–53)

Use the following clues to identify the words, and write the words on the lines to the right. Then circle each word in the word-search box below. The words may overlap and may read in any direction.

1. Synonym for *amalgamate* (7 letters) — 1. combine
2. Antonym for *open* or *unconcealed* (6 letters) — 2. covert
3. *Verifiable* statements can be proved ____. (4 letters) — 3. true
4. *Inception* refers to the ____ of something. (9 letters) — 4. beginning
5. From a Greek word meaning "working together" (7 letters) — 5. synergy
6. Self-evident (9 letters) — 6. axiomatic
7. To provide food, services, or entertainment (5 letters) — 7. cater
8. Synonym for *capacious* (5 letters) — 8. roomy
9. Sharing a boundary or edge (10 letters) — 9. contiguous
10. A *rebuttal* presents ____ evidence. (8 letters) — 10. opposing
11. *Arcane* comes from a Latin word meaning "____." (6 letters) — 11. secret
12. Synonym for *hypothetical* (11 letters) — 12. theoretical
13. To *presuppose* is to assume in ____. (7 letters) — 13. advance
14. To get to the bottom of and understand (6 letters) — 14. fathom
15. From the Latin words meaning "one" and "sound" (6 letters) — 15. unison

T H E O R E T I C A L C A P T I O U S
H A E A F A T H O M C A T P I R E P T
E V D T N U D N R S Y N E R G Y U A G
T R E V O C O P P O S I N G R E A E P
O S R I A P I S E U N T H E L N F D E
S U G O E N A L O A O O H G I I E U R
Y O Y N B E C U C L S P L N M B S C C
N L C A U R G E E W I M G I R M T E E
E U O L L I T S P R N A A N P O I O Z
R B N I T E R C E S U M T N I C O U D
U E T N U S E P T C N A E I D N P M I
N N O Z O I T E R O E H T G M I E S Y
I C A T E R L R E C I P I E N T R F O
S D R C I T A M O I X A P B A F V S E

Challenge

Locate and circle the five additional vocabulary words in the word-search box.

captious
educe
nebulous
periphery
recipient

NAME ______________________________ DATE ____________

BONUS LESSONS 5–8

(pages 27–38, 41–53)

Use the following clues to identify the words, and write the words on the lines to the right. Then circle each word in the word-search box below. The words may overlap and may read in any direction.

1. Synonym for *amalgamate* (7 letters) 1. ____________
2. Antonym for *open* or *unconcealed* (6 letters) 2. ____________
3. *Verifiable* statements can be proved _____. (4 letters) 3. ____________
4. *Inception* refers to the _____ of something. (9 letters) 4. ____________
5. From a Greek word meaning "working together" (7 letters) 5. ____________
6. Self-evident (9 letters) 6. ____________
7. To provide food, services, or entertainment (5 letters) 7. ____________
8. Synonym for *capacious* (5 letters) 8. ____________
9. Sharing a boundary or edge (10 letters) 9. ____________
10. A *rebuttal* presents _____ evidence. (8 letters) 10. ____________
11. *Arcane* comes from a Latin word meaning "_____." (6 letters) 11. ____________
12. Synonym for *hypothetical* (11 letters) 12. ____________
13. To *presuppose* is to assume in _____. (7 letters) 13. ____________
14. To get to the bottom of and understand (6 letters) 14. ____________
15. From the Latin words meaning "one" and "sound" (6 letters) 15. ____________

T H E O R E T I C A L C A P T I O U S

H A E A F A T H O M C A T P I R E P T

E V D T N U D N R S Y N E R G Y U A G

T R E V O C O P P O S I N G R E A E P

O S R I A P I S E U N T H E L N F D E

S U G O E N A L O A O O H G I I E U R

Y O Y N B E C U C L S P L N M B S C C

N L C A U R G E E W I M G I R M T E E

E U O L L I T S P R N A A N P O I O Z

R B N I T E R C E S U M T N I C O U D

U E T N U S E P T C N A E I D N P M I

N N O Z O I T E R O E H T G M I E S Y

I C A T E R L R E C I P I E N T R F O

S D R C I T A M O I X A P B A F V S E

Challenge

Locate and circle the five additional vocabulary words in the word-search box.

NAME ________________________ DATE ____________

TEST LESSONS 7, 8, AND 9

(pages 41–58)

PART A COMPLETING THE DEFINITION

On the answer line, write the letter of the word or phrase that correctly competes each sentence.

1. An *axiomatic* proposition is _____. 1. c
   a. misleading b. debatable c. self-evident d. technical

2. Someone who is a *paragon* of good taste is _____. 2. a
   a. a model of excellence c. historically significant
   b. a disgraceful example d. one who acts superior

3. A *receptacle* is also called a(n) _____. 3. d
   a. ensemble b. equation c. principle d. container

4. Air is *ubiquitous* on Earth because it is _____. 4. d
   a. necessary for life b. polluted c. invisible d. everywhere

5. A *hypothetical* situation is _____. 5. c
   a. perilous b. humorous c. theoretical d. irreconcilable

6. A *captious* film critic is likely to _____. 6. b
   a. be literate c. have poor eyesight
   b. find fault d. frighten easily

7. *Aberrant* test scores _____. 7. b
   a. attract attention c. are extremely high
   b. deviate from the norm d. need further analysis

8. A *synthesis* of proteins is the _____ of proteins. 8. a
   a. combination b. digestion c. breakdown d. neutralization

9. *Mundane* tasks are _____ activities. 9. b
   a. healthy b. ordinary c. challenging d. competitive

10. A *capacious* auditorium is _____. 10. d
    a. empty b. contemporary c. efficient d. roomy

11. *Verifiable* information _____. 11. a
    a. can be confirmed c. is useless
    b. has unreliable sources d. depends on variable factors

12. A *precept* is regarded as a(n) _____. 12. a
    a. guiding principle c. complex theory
    b. accurate fact d. curious notion

13. *Empirical* information is obtained from _____. 13. b
    a. calculation b. observation c. an authority d. details

14. In one's experience an *anomaly* is a(n) _____. 14. c
    a. common occurrence c. unusual event
    b. frightening event d. predictable pattern

15. An *unwonted* procedure is _____. 15. d
    a. unpopular c. inadvisable
    b. inexcusable d. not customary

NAME ______________________ DATE __________

TEST LESSONS 7, 8, AND 9

(pages 41–58)

PART A COMPLETING THE DEFINITION

On the answer line, write the letter of the word or phrase that correctly competes each sentence.

1. An *axiomatic* proposition is _____. 1. __________
   a. misleading b. debatable c. self-evident d. technical
2. Someone who is a *paragon* of good taste is _____. 2. __________
   a. a model of excellence c. historically significant
   b. a disgraceful example d. one who acts superior
3. A *receptacle* is also called a(n) _____. 3. __________
   a. ensemble b. equation c. principle d. container
4. Air is *ubiquitous* on Earth because it is _____. 4. __________
   a. necessary for life b. polluted c. invisible d. everywhere
5. A *hypothetical* situation is _____. 5. __________
   a. perilous b. humorous c. theoretical d. irreconcilable
6. A *captious* film critic is likely to _____. 6. __________
   a. be literate c. have poor eyesight
   b. find fault d. frighten easily
7. *Aberrant* test scores _____. 7. __________
   a. attract attention c. are extremely high
   b. deviate from the norm d. need further analysis
8. A *synthesis* of proteins is the _____ of proteins. 8. __________
   a. combination b. digestion c. breakdown d. neutralization
9. *Mundane* tasks are _____ activities. 9. __________
   a. healthy b. ordinary c. challenging d. competitive
10. A *capacious* auditorium is _____. 10. __________
    a. empty b. contemporary c. efficient d. roomy
11. *Verifiable* information _____. 11. __________
    a. can be confirmed c. is useless
    b. has unreliable sources d. depends on variable factors
12. A *precept* is regarded as a(n) _____. 12. __________
    a. guiding principle c. complex theory
    b. accurate fact d. curious notion
13. *Empirical* information is obtained from _____. 13. __________
    a. calculation b. observation c. an authority d. details
14. In one's experience an *anomaly* is a(n) _____. 14. __________
    a. common occurrence c. unusual event
    b. frightening event d. predictable pattern
15. An *unwonted* procedure is _____. 15. __________
    a. unpopular c. inadvisable
    b. inexcusable d. not customary

NAME ______________________ DATE __________

T8

TEST LESSONS 7, 8, AND 9

PART B CHOOSING THE BEST WORD

On the answer line, write the letter of the word that best expresses the meaning of the italicized word or phrase.

16. The use of tomato sauce is *peculiar* to southern Italian cooking. 16. d
    a. perceptible b. ubiquitous c. definitive d. endemic

17. The window displays *fascinate* both children and adults. 17. b
    a. cater to b. captivate c. rationalize d. repudiate

18. Legal rights for children is a twentieth-century *notion.* 18. a
    a. concept b. precept c. rebuttal d. paragon

19. Heavy industry is *inappropriate* with the ecology of the wilderness. 19. b
    a. outlandish b. incongruous c. aberrant d. endemic

20. Relatives *rejected the validity of* the will that named the deceased's fifteen parakeets as heirs. 20. a
    a. repudiated b. presupposed c. rationalized d. synthesized

21. Downtown boutiques *provide for* a different type of clientele. 21. c
    a. captivate b. rebut c. cater to d. verify

22. Ms. Harris believes that her biography of Max Beerbohm will be the *authoritative* work on the English satirist. 22. a
    a. definitive b. incongruous c. ubiquitous d. captious

23. Silvio's tuneless humming is one of his many *unconventional practices.* 23. d
    a. precepts b. axioms c. presuppositions d. eccentricities

24. Thelma was the proud *receiver* of the mayor's award for bravery. 24. a
    a. recipient b. rebuttal c. inception d. receptacle

25. Even minor tremors are *discernible* with modern seismological equipment. 25. c
    a. empirical b. incongruous c. perceptible d. mundane

26. Our current space program had its *beginning* in Robert Goddard's work with rockets. 26. a
    a. inception b. synthesis c. rebuttal d. hypothesis

27. A balanced budget *requires as a necessary condition* the continued growth of the economy. 27. a
    a. presupposes b. rationalizes c. caters to d. repudiates

28. Harvey *devised a self-satisfying but false reason* that eating one slice of the cake would not break his diet. 28. b
    a. verified b. rationalized c. repudiated d. hypothesized

29. The senator offered a convincing *statement of opposing evidence* of allegations that she was allied with special-interest groups. 29. c
    a. rationalization b. repudiation c. rebuttal d. anomaly

30. Allen collects antique, *bizarre* advertisements for home remedies. 30. d
    a. aberrant b. axiomatic c. ubiquitous d. outlandish

NAME ______________________ DATE ____________

TEST LESSONS 7, 8, AND 9

PART B CHOOSING THE BEST WORD

On the answer line, write the letter of the word that best expresses the meaning of the italicized word or phrase.

16. The use of tomato sauce is *peculiar* to southern Italian cooking. 16. ________
a. perceptible **b.** ubiquitous **c.** definitive **d.** endemic

17. The window displays *fascinate* both children and adults. 17. ________
a. cater to **b.** captivate **c.** rationalize **d.** repudiate

18. Legal rights for children is a twentieth-century *notion.* 18. ________
a. concept **b.** precept **c.** rebuttal **d.** paragon

19. Heavy industry is *inappropriate* with the ecology of the wilderness. 19. ________
a. outlandish **b.** incongruous **c.** aberrant **d.** endemic

20. Relatives *rejected the validity of* the will that named the deceased's fifteen parakeets as heirs. 20. ________
a. repudiated **b.** presupposed **c.** rationalized **d.** synthesized

21. Downtown boutiques *provide for* a different type of clientele. 21. ________
a. captivate **b.** rebut **c.** cater to **d.** verify

22. Ms. Harris believes that her biography of Max Beerbohm will be the *authoritative* work on the English satirist. 22. ________
a. definitive **b.** incongruous **c.** ubiquitous **d.** captious

23. Silvio's tuneless humming is one of his many *unconventional practices.* 23. ________
a. precepts **b.** axioms **c.** presuppositions **d.** eccentricities

24. Thelma was the proud *receiver* of the mayor's award for bravery. 24. ________
a. recipient **b.** rebuttal **c.** inception **d.** receptacle

25. Even minor tremors are *discernible* with modern seismological equipment. 25. ________
a. empirical **b.** incongruous **c.** perceptible **d.** mundane

26. Our current space program had its *beginning* in Robert Goddard's work with rockets. 26. ________
a. inception **b.** synthesis **c.** rebuttal **d.** hypothesis

27. A balanced budget *requires as a necessary condition* the continued growth of the economy. 27. ________
a. presupposes **b.** rationalizes **c.** caters to **d.** repudiates

28. Harvey *devised a self-satisfying but false reason* that eating one slice of the cake would not break his diet. 28. ________
a. verified **b.** rationalized **c.** repudiated **d.** hypothesized

29. The senator offered a convincing *statement of opposing evidence* of allegations that she was allied with special-interest groups. 29. ________
a. rationalization **b.** repudiation **c.** rebuttal **d.** anomaly

30. Allen collects antique, *bizarre* advertisements for home remedies. 30. ________
a. aberrant **b.** axiomatic **c.** ubiquitous **d.** outlandish

VERBAL APTITUDE TEST I

For each question in this section, choose the best answer and blacken the corresponding space on the answer sheet.

PART A ANTONYMS

Each question below consists of a word in capital letters, followed by five lettered words or phrases. Choose the word or phrase that is most nearly opposite in meaning to the word in capital letters. Since some of the questions require you to distinguish fine shades of meaning, consider all the choices before deciding which is best.

EXAMPLE:

GOOD: (A) sour (B) bad (C) red (D) hot (E) ugly

Ⓐ ●  

1. DIMINUTIVE: (A) enormous (B) accelerated (C) odious (D) tedious (E) incandescent
2. AMELIORATE: (A) recoup (B) disseminate (C) reprehend (D) mediate (E) retrogress
3. ABERRANT: (A) sumptuous (B) salient (C) transcendent (D) customary (E) exceptional
4. OBFUSCATE: (A) elucidate (B) cleanse (C) obliterate (D) liberate (E) adumbrate
5. BELIE: (A) gull (B) agitate (C) confute (D) mistrust (E) confirm
6. INDISCERNIBLE: (A) discriminating (B) credible (C) vigilant (D) perceptible (E) ulterior
7. MOROSE: (A) fulfilled (B) amenable (C) exuberant (D) reclusive (E) venal
8. MENDICANT: (A) paragon (B) neophyte (C) ingenue (D) pariah (E) nabob
9. EFFULGENT: (A) deadly (B) obscure (C) poignant (D) fragrant (E) axiomatic
10. DENUNCIATION: (A) panegyric (B) paradigm (C) exigency (D) harangue (E) exemption

PART B SENTENCE COMPLETIONS

Each sentence below has one or two blanks, each blank indicating that something has been omitted. Below the sentence are five lettered words or sets of words. Choose the word or set of words that best fits the meaning of the sentence as a whole.

EXAMPLE:

Although its publicity has been - - - - , the film itself is intelligent, well-acted, handsomely produced, and altogether - - - - .

(A) tasteless .. respectable
(B) extensive .. moderate
(C) sophisticated .. amateur
(D) risqué .. crude (E) perfect .. spectacular

11. Without - - - - , our speech would convey meaning less efficiently and would tend to sound - - - - .
    (A) syllogism .. erratic
    (B) pomposity .. exaggerated
    (C) irony .. bizarre
    (D) inflection .. monotonous
    (E) enunciation .. bombastic
12. The discovery of Mayor Queeg's embezzlement makes him a prime candidate for - - - - .
    (A) adulation (B) censure
    (C) re-election (D) euphemism
    (E) interment

13. While bears are - - - - and burning stored fat, many other woodland animals are - - - - and searching for food throughout the winter.
(A) vigorous .. lethargic
(B) hibernating .. torpid
(C) dormant .. active
(D) sluggish .. benumbed
(E) foraging .. fasting

14. Life insurance companies may refuse to pay the - - - - of a policy if - - - - information has been provided by the policyholder.
(A) principal .. nefarious
(B) annuity .. corroborating
(C) survivors .. licit
(D) premiums .. embellished
(E) beneficiaries .. fraudulent

15. If the actions of consumers and producers in the competitive marketplace are not in harmony, the market price will spontaneously adjust to bring the actions of the two groups into - - - - .
(A) probity (B) disparity
(C) juxtaposition (D) estrangement
(E) equilibrium

16. Steel manufacturers played a vital role in the postwar economic - - - - of the United States, but they have recently found themselves - - - - by foreign competition, a situation creating a crisis in the industry.
(A) resurgence .. besieged
(B) inflation .. vivified
(C) synergy .. buoyed
(D) shortages .. stimulated
(E) debility .. depredated

17. In 1824 the Supreme Court decided in *Gibbons v. Ogden* that a New York law granting - - - -rights for the operation of a ferryboat was unconstitutional because it interfered with interstate commerce, a(n) - - - - of the federal government.
(A) exclusive .. prerogative
(B) arcane .. province (C) obvious .. right
(D) unlimited .. obligation
(E) efficacious .. enterprise

18. This new Thomas Wolfe biography seems definitive, and because the author was the first person to be given free access to all Wolfe's papers, it - - - - all its predecessors.
(A) revokes (B) precludes
(C) supersedes (D) dissipates (E) repels

19. In 1946 the United States had a monopoly on available atomic weapons and was, according to official policy, seeking the - - - - , or at least the - - - - , of further nuclear production.
(A) rationalization .. diffusion
(B) abolition .. amplification
(C) cessation .. curtailment
(D) annihilation .. allocation
(E) stockpiling .. accumulation

20. The putative respect for nature that a given society professes can be - - - - by the actions of some of its citizens, such as exfoliation and other - - - - practices.
(A) reinforced .. baneful
(B) elicited .. heinous
(C) refuted .. regenerative
(D) contradicted .. deleterious
(E) evoked .. ecological

PART C ANALOGIES

Each question below consists of a related pair of words or phrases, followed by five lettered pairs of words or phrases. Select the lettered pair that best expresses a relationship similar to that expressed in the original pair.

EXAMPLE:

YAWN : BOREDOM :: (A) dream : sleep
(B) anger : madness (C) smile : amusement
(D) face : expression (E) impatience : rebellion

21. MAELSTROM : EDDY :: (A) schism : union
(B) flight : departure (C) derelict : rebel
(D) tsunami : isobar
(E) leviathan : juggernaut

22. SCHOONER : SAIL :: (A) axle : car
(B) kerosene : wick
(C) mezzanine : theater
(D) receiver : transmitter
(E) computer : memory

23. ARCHITECTURE : BAROQUE ::
(A) spasm : nerve (B) taxidermy : wildlife
(C) novel : grotesque
(D) corpulence : hormone
(E) muscle : pectoral

24. LITIGATE : ADJUDICATE ::
(A) rejuvenate : enervate
(B) testify : witness
(C) initiate : charge
(D) pollinate : burgeon
(E) dictate : govern

25. CHIDE : CASTIGATE ::
(A) tease : torment
(B) dilate : constrict
(C) injure : succor
(D) captivate : preoccupy
(E) indulge : cater

26. EQUANIMITY : UNABASHED ::
(A) nuance : candid
(B) melancholia : dispirited
(C) circumvention : elusive
(D) resilience : blithe
(E) cadaver : nascent

27. LOATH : AVID :: (A) eccentric : incongruous
(B) larcenous : felonious
(C) precursory : consequential
(D) abject : craven (E) chatty : voluble

28. KOWTOW : FLAUNT :: (A) pine : yearn
(B) emend : gloss (C) swagger : putter
(D) grovel : toady (E) rue : exult

29. CRISIS : DÉNOUEMENT ::
(A) jubilee : anniversary
(B) détente : amnesty
(C) matriculation : graduation
(D) crescendo : staccato
(E) undulation : vacillation

30. TROPE : METAPHOR ::
(A) primate : chimpanzee
(B) species : genus (C) Earth : planet
(D) autocracy : tyranny (E) corpus : body

PART D READING COMPREHENSION

Each passage below is followed by questions based on its content. Answer all questions following a passage on the basis of what is stated or implied in that passage.

Business enterprises in the United States (and in capitalist countries in general) are divided into three categories on the basis of legal organization: sole proprietorships, partnerships, and corporations.

The sole proprietorship is owned by one individual, who makes all the business decisions and receives the profits (or losses) that the business earns. A partnership is owned by two or more partners, who make all the business decisions and share in the profits and losses of the business. The major advantages of these forms of business organizations are their relative simplicity (the proprietorship is simpler than the partnership) and the fact that, under existing tax law, their profits are taxed only once. They have two major disadvantages: (1) the owners are personally liable for the debts of the business, and (2) the ability to raise capital is limited, dependent on the owners' ability to borrow against personal assets.

The third form of business organization, the corporation, is a business enterprise owned by a number of stockholders and having the legal status of a fictional individual and authorization to act as a single person. A board of directors, elected by the stockholders, appoints a professional management team to run the corporation. The advantages of the corporation are (1) its owners (the stockholders) are not personally liable for the debts of the corporation (limited liability), (2) its management team can be changed if necessary, and (3) it has more options for raising capital (through the sale of bonds and additional stock) than does a partnership or proprietorship. A major disadvantage of this form of organization is that its income is taxed twice if corporate earnings are distributed to stockholders as dividends. . . .

31. The title that best expresses the ideas of the passage is
(A) How to Organize a Business
(B) A Business Stratagem
(C) Corporate Organization
(D) Parity in Business
(E) Basic Organizational Structures in Business

32. The author states all of the following except
(A) a corporation has the legal status of a hypothetical individual.
(B) the different categories of business enterprises are based on legal organization.
(C) one advantage of a partnership is its simplicity.
(D) sole proprietorships account for the majority of American businesses.
(E) a corporation can raise capital through the sale of bonds.

33. The author implies that businesses will avoid having earnings taxed twice if they
(A) incorporate.
(B) amalgamate.
(C) form a proprietorship or partnership.
(D) appoint a professional management team.
(E) raise capital through the sale of stock.

The former Soviet state tried to increase agricultural production in three main ways: by using new agricultural land on the cold or dry fringes, by improving methods and crops so new and old land would yield more, and by mechanizing and organizing the agricultural system as a whole. Under the Soviet agricultural system of collective and state farms, labor, land, and capital equipment were effectively controlled by the state. None of these three methods had fully succeeded by the late seventies; food production was just beginning to keep pace with urbanization and industrialization. Most of northern Russia was severely limited in its agricultural potential. *Permafrost,* ground permanently frozen a few inches or feet beneath the surface, is found in much of northern Siberia. It not only presented serious building and drainage problems but essentially ruled out deep-rooted plants. Some crops could be grown in the surface soil during its brief period of thaw. A few root crops were grown by the Soviets in the tundra where none grew before. Some drought-resistant crops were also grown in the arid areas farther south. Irrigation and other improvements extended cultivated areas substantially, especially in the southern part of Soviet Central Asia.

But this is poor land for the most part. To invest in it simply made the crop expensive. Cabbages were grown in northern Siberia but probably at two or three times the cost of growing them in France or in the Ukraine. They were planted in Siberia because the cost of shipping them from the Ukraine was even higher. Transport bottlenecks and total demand for food also made it desirable for every part of the then U.S.S.R. to produce as much food as possible locally. Scarce resources were used intensively here, but economically the quality of the resources did not justify intensive use. It was done because there was no preferable alternative. Apart from this, where new cultivation had been extended into semiarid areas without irrigation, or where original forest and grass cover had been removed by plowing marginal land, future trouble seemed probable. Dust bowls in this area worse than those in America were a possibility. Over seventy million acres of virgin land, mainly in Kazakstan in Central Asia and southwestern Siberia, and in central Siberia, had been newly cultivated after 1954. Yields were low and crops precarious, but the Russian planners said they would be content with two good crop years out of five in these areas. They argued that even a small food production from these previously unused lands was better than none or than the low return produced earlier from grazing some of the area. . . .

Soviet agriculture was increasingly mechanized. Wheat and other grain lands, especially the irrigated ones, were worked more intensively—with human, animal, and machine labor—than most wheat lands in North America. Although they increased, wheat yields in Russia remained relatively low by comparison with most other wheat-growing countries.

34. The author states that in areas where there is permafrost,

I irrigation brought more land under cultivation.
II the ground is permanently frozen a few inches or feet beneath the surface.
III many deep-rooted plants could not grow.
IV it was difficult to erect buildings.
V the long summer thaw permits extensive plant growth in the surface soil.

(A) I, II, and IV (B) II, IV and V
(C) III and V (D) II, III, and IV
(E) I and II

35. The author implies that

(A) Soviet food production was rapidly catching up to that of North America.
(B) Soviet resources were used effectively.
(C) Soviet efforts to improve production were inhibited by poor natural resources.
(D) state control of labor, land, and equipment was effective in dramatically increasing food production.
(E) collective and state farms left many workers unemployed.

36. The passage indicates that the author experienced a feeling of

(A) anger that deep-rooted plants could not be grown in northern Siberia.
(B) pride in the success that Soviet labor had achieved.
(C) confusion over why a variety of methods did not improve production.
(D) skepticism that much of the Soviet land would ever have been productive.
(E) sadness over the plight of the Soviet farmer.

37. Which of these words could be used to describe any of the three methods that the Soviets tried in order to increase agricultural production?

I cultivation II urbanization
III industrialization IV irrigation
V mechanization

(A) I, II, III, IV, and V (B) I, II, and III
(C) III, IV, and V (D) I, III, and V
(E) I, IV, and V

If you finish before time is called, check your work on this test.

VERBAL APTITUDE TEST 1

Answer Sheet

Use a No. 2 pencil for completing this answer sheet. Make sure that your marks are dark and completely fill the space. Erase any errors or stray marks. If a test has fewer than 50 questions, leave the extra answer spaces blank.

No.					
1.	**A**	B	C	D	E
2.	A	B	C	D	**E**
3.	A	B	C	**D**	E
4.	**A**	B	C	D	E
5.	A	B	C	D	**E**
6.	A	B	C	**D**	E
7.	A	B	**C**	D	E
8.	A	B	C	D	**E**
9.	A	**B**	C	D	E
10.	**A**	B	C	D	E
11.	A	B	C	**D**	E
12.	A	**B**	C	D	E
13.	A	B	**C**	D	E
14.	A	B	C	D	**E**
15.	A	B	C	D	**E**
16.	**A**	B	C	D	E
17.	**A**	B	C	D	E
18.	A	B	**C**	D	E
19.	A	B	**C**	D	E
20.	A	B	C	**D**	E
21.	A	**B**	C	D	E
22.	A	B	C	D	**E**
23.	A	B	C	D	**E**
24.	A	B	C	**D**	E
25.	**A**	B	C	D	E

No.					
26.	A	**B**	C	D	E
27.	A	B	**C**	D	E
28.	A	B	C	D	**E**
29.	A	B	**C**	D	E
30.	**A**	B	C	D	E
31.	A	B	C	D	**E**
32.	A	B	C	**D**	E
33.	A	B	**C**	D	E
34.	A	B	C	**D**	E
35.	A	B	**C**	D	E
36.	A	B	C	**D**	E
37.	A	B	C	D	**E**
38.	A	B	C	D	E
39.	A	B	C	D	E
40.	A	B	C	D	E
41.	A	B	C	D	E
42.	A	B	C	D	E
43.	A	B	C	D	E
44.	A	B	C	D	E
45.	A	B	C	D	E
46.	A	B	C	D	E
47.	A	B	C	D	E
48.	A	B	C	D	E
49.	A	B	C	D	E
50.	A	B	C	D	E

VERBAL APTITUDE TEST 1

Answer Sheet

Use a No. 2 pencil for completing this answer sheet. Make sure that your marks are dark and completely fill the space. Erase any errors or stray marks. If a test has fewer than 50 questions, leave the extra answer spaces blank.

1.	(A)	(B)	(C)	(D)	(E)	26.	(A)	(B)	(C)	(D)	(E)
2.	(A)	(B)	(C)	(D)	(E)	27.	(A)	(B)	(C)	(D)	(E)
3.	(A)	(B)	(C)	(D)	(E)	28.	(A)	(B)	(C)	(D)	(E)
4.	(A)	(B)	(C)	(D)	(E)	29.	(A)	(B)	(C)	(D)	(E)
5.	(A)	(B)	(C)	(D)	(E)	30.	(A)	(B)	(C)	(D)	(E)
6.	(A)	(B)	(C)	(D)	(E)	31.	(A)	(B)	(C)	(D)	(E)
7.	(A)	(B)	(C)	(D)	(E)	32.	(A)	(B)	(C)	(D)	(E)
8.	(A)	(B)	(C)	(D)	(E)	33.	(A)	(B)	(C)	(D)	(E)
9.	(A)	(B)	(C)	(D)	(E)	34.	(A)	(B)	(C)	(D)	(E)
10.	(A)	(B)	(C)	(D)	(E)	35.	(A)	(B)	(C)	(D)	(E)
11.	(A)	(B)	(C)	(D)	(E)	36.	(A)	(B)	(C)	(D)	(E)
12.	(A)	(B)	(C)	(D)	(E)	37.	(A)	(B)	(C)	(D)	(E)
13.	(A)	(B)	(C)	(D)	(E)	38.	(A)	(B)	(C)	(D)	(E)
14.	(A)	(B)	(C)	(D)	(E)	39.	(A)	(B)	(C)	(D)	(E)
15.	(A)	(B)	(C)	(D)	(E)	40.	(A)	(B)	(C)	(D)	(E)
16.	(A)	(B)	(C)	(D)	(E)	41.	(A)	(B)	(C)	(D)	(E)
17.	(A)	(B)	(C)	(D)	(E)	42.	(A)	(B)	(C)	(D)	(E)
18.	(A)	(B)	(C)	(D)	(E)	43.	(A)	(B)	(C)	(D)	(E)
19.	(A)	(B)	(C)	(D)	(E)	44.	(A)	(B)	(C)	(D)	(E)
20.	(A)	(B)	(C)	(D)	(E)	45.	(A)	(B)	(C)	(D)	(E)
21.	(A)	(B)	(C)	(D)	(E)	46.	(A)	(B)	(C)	(D)	(E)
22.	(A)	(B)	(C)	(D)	(E)	47.	(A)	(B)	(C)	(D)	(E)
23.	(A)	(B)	(C)	(D)	(E)	48.	(A)	(B)	(C)	(D)	(E)
24.	(A)	(B)	(C)	(D)	(E)	49.	(A)	(B)	(C)	(D)	(E)
25.	(A)	(B)	(C)	(D)	(E)	50.	(A)	(B)	(C)	(D)	(E)

NAME ______________________________ DATE ____________

BONUS LESSONS 9–12

(pages 53–58, 61–78)

Use the clues to complete the crossword puzzle.

	1 H		2 D						3 C										
	E		E		4 N			5 W	O	R	L	D							
6 P	A	R	A	G	O	N			R										
	L		T		X				P										
	T		H		7 I	N	I	Q	U	I	T	Y							
	H				O				S						8 C		9 M		
					U				C			10 W			O		E		
11 R	12 E	D	R	E	S	S		13 B	L	A	M	E			R		R		
	Q								E			14 A	T	Y	P	I	C	A	L
	U											K			U		Y		
	A		15 U				16 E			17 P					L				
	18 N	O	B	L	E		N			L					E				
	I		I				D			19 A	B	S	C	O	N	D			
	M		Q				E			G					T				
	I		U				M			U									
	T		I			20 W	I	T	H	E	R								
	Y		T				C												
			O																
			U																
			S																

Across

5. *Mundane* comes from a Latin word meaning "_____."
6. A peerless example
7. Wickedness
11. To rectify
13. To *vindicate* is to clear of _____.
14. Synonym for *aberrant*
18. A *magnanimous* person is _____ of mind and heart.
19. To leave quickly in order to hide
20. Synonym for *atrophy*

Down

1. *Salubrious* effects are favorable to _____.
2. A *moribund* animal is near _____.
3. A blood or lymph cell
4. Antonym for *beneficial*
8. Obese
9. Synonym for *clemency*
10. *Pusillanimous* comes from a Latin word meaning "_____."
12. The quality of being even-tempered
15. Omnipresent
16. Peculiar to a particular locality
17. *Pestilent* comes from a Latin word meaning "_____."

NAME ______________________ DATE ____________

BONUS LESSONS 9–12

(pages 53–58, 61–78)

Use the clues to complete the crossword puzzle.

Across

5. *Mundane* comes from a Latin word meaning "______."
6. A peerless example
7. Wickedness
11. To rectify
13. To *vindicate* is to clear of ______.
14. Synonym for *aberrant*
18. A *magnanimous* person is ______ of mind and heart.
19. To leave quickly in order to hide
20. Synonym for *atrophy*

Down

1. *Salubrious* effects are favorable to ______.
2. A *moribund* animal is near ______.
3. A blood or lymph cell
4. Antonym for *beneficial*
8. Obese
9. Synonym for *clemency*
10. *Pusillanimous* comes from a Latin word meaning "______."
12. The quality of being even-tempered
15. Omnipresent
16. Peculiar to a particular locality
17. *Pestilent* comes from a Latin word meaning "______."

NAME ______________________ DATE __________

TEST LESSONS 10, 11, AND 12

(pages 61–78)

PART A CHOOSING THE BEST DEFINITION

On the answer line, write the letter of the best definition of the italicized word.

1. The jury recommended *clemency* because the theft was a first offense. 1. b
   a. imprisonment b. leniency c. a small fine d. acquittal

2. Bathers at the hot springs attributed the water's *salubrious* effect to the gold dissolved in it. 2. b
   a. inexplicable b. favorable to health c. relaxing d. delicate

3. *Incorporate* the hot milk and cheese before beating in the eggs. 3. a
   a. blend indistinguishably b. measure c. heat d. liquefy

4. There is nothing *pusillanimous* about Seth except when it comes to heights. 4. a
   a. cowardly b. superficial c. foolhardy d. impulsive

5. Bubonic plague was the *scourge* of the Middle Ages. 5. c
   a. notable event c. cause of suffering
   b. main discovery d. negative aspect

6. Olivia could not forget Len's *reprehensible* attitude. 6. c
   a. prevalent b. escalating c. blameworthy d. dangerous

7. The yearly flu epidemic *prostrates* a large number of people. 7. d
   a. attacks b. unites c. animates d. weakens

8. Once a coup seemed imminent, the dictator *absconded* to a tiny island. 8. a
   a. left secretly to hide c. sent dissenters
   b. vacationed d. abdicated

9. The Graveses' usually luxurious garden was sabotaged by *noxious* insects. 9. c
   a. annoying b. persistent c. harmful d. innumerable

10. A high white *corpuscle* count may be a symptom of a serious illness. 10. b
    a. cholesterol b. cell c. tissue d. swollen gland

11. Many developing nations must deal with a *moribund* economy. 11. d
    a. unstable c. stagnant
    b. unequally distributed d. dying

12. The Singapura cat was so still that passers-by were convinced that it was an *inanimate,* decorative object. 12. c
    a. lonely b. valuable c. lifeless d. handmade

13. The *iniquity* and greed of some rulers have contributed to the decline of many great civilizations. 13. c
    a. laxness b. rashness c. wickedness d. intolerance

14. Silent and *contrite,* Zack stared at the floor. 14. c
    a. sullen b. thoughtful c. sorry d. embarrassed

15. The spoiled poodle became more *corpulent* as it grew older. 15. a
    a. obese b. demanding c. disobedient d. aloof

NAME ______________________ DATE ____________

TEST LESSONS 10, 11, AND 12

(pages 61–78)

PART A CHOOSING THE BEST DEFINITION

On the answer line, write the letter of the best definition of the italicized word.

1. The jury recommended *clemency* because the theft was a first offense. 1. ________
   a. imprisonment b. leniency c. a small fine d. acquittal

2. Bathers at the hot springs attributed the water's *salubrious* effect to the gold dissolved in it. 2. ________
   a. inexplicable b. favorable to health c. relaxing d. delicate

3. *Incorporate* the hot milk and cheese before beating in the eggs. 3. ________
   a. blend indistinguishably b. measure c. heat d. liquefy

4. There is nothing *pusillanimous* about Seth except when it comes to heights. 4. ________
   a. cowardly b. superficial c. foolhardy d. impulsive

5. Bubonic plague was the *scourge* of the Middle Ages. 5. ________
   a. notable event c. cause of suffering
   b. main discovery d. negative aspect

6. Olivia could not forget Len's *reprehensible* attitude. 6. ________
   a. prevalent b. escalating c. blameworthy d. dangerous

7. The yearly flu epidemic *prostrates* a large number of people. 7. ________
   a. attacks b. unites c. animates d. weakens

8. Once a coup seemed imminent, the dictator *absconded* to a tiny island. 8. ________
   a. left secretly to hide c. sent dissenters
   b. vacationed d. abdicated

9. The Graveses' usually luxurious garden was sabotaged by *noxious* insects. 9. ________
   a. annoying b. persistent c. harmful d. innumerable

10. A high white *corpuscle* count may be a symptom of a serious illness. 10. ________
    a. cholesterol b. cell c. tissue d. swollen gland

11. Many developing nations must deal with a *moribund* economy. 11. ________
    a. unstable c. stagnant
    b. unequally distributed d. dying

12. The Singapura cat was so still that passers-by were convinced that it was an *inanimate,* decorative object. 12. ________
    a. lonely b. valuable c. lifeless d. handmade

13. The *iniquity* and greed of some rulers have contributed to the decline of many great civilizations. 13. ________
    a. laxness b. rashness c. wickedness d. intolerance

14. Silent and *contrite,* Zack stared at the floor. 14. ________
    a. sullen b. thoughtful c. sorry d. embarrassed

15. The spoiled poodle became more *corpulent* as it grew older. 15. ________
    a. obese b. demanding c. disobedient d. aloof

NAME ______________________ DATE ____________

TEST LESSONS 10, 11, AND 12

PART B CHOOSING THE BEST WORD

On the answer line, write the letter of the word that best expresses the meaning of the italicized word or phrase.

16. Counterfeited goods *cheat* consumers out of billions of dollars. 16. a
    a. bilk **b.** vindicate **c.** debilitate **d.** impute

17. Public television stations are funded in part by *unselfish* contributions from viewers. 17. d
    a. incorporeal **c.** pusillanimous
    b. salubrious **d.** magnanimous

18. The umpire accepted the jeers of the crowd with *composure.* 18. b
    a. animus **b.** equanimity **c.** atrophy **d.** clemency

19. The discovery of the real culprit *cleared of blame* Gloria. 19. a
    a. vindicated **b.** incorporated **c.** imputed **d.** debilitated

20. When Jason is angry, his complexion becomes *very pale.* 20. c
    a. unscathed **b.** corpulent **c.** livid **d.** moribund

21. The *bitter hatred* between the Montagues and the Capulets serves as the obstacle to the love of Romeo and Juliet. 21. c
    a. corpus **b.** atrophy **c.** animus **d.** equanimity

22. A series of illnesses so *weakened* my uncle that he eventually became totally bedridden. 22. a
    a. debilitated **b.** redressed **c.** absconded **d.** imputed

23. Elena is attempting to overcome her *intangible* fears. 23. a
    a. incorporeal **b.** debilitating **c.** moribund **d.** unscathed

24. Diverging interests *caused the withering of* the boys' friendship. 24. a
    a. atrophied **b.** prostrated **c.** vindicated **d.** debilitated

25. Many people have the misconception that those who perform stunts in movies always walk away from these feats *unharmed.* 25. c
    a. livid **b.** contrite **c.** unscathed **d.** prostrate

26. Jeff repaired his neighbor's fence in *compensation* for the damage he had caused. 26. c
    a. vindication **b.** atrophy **c.** restitution **d.** equanimity

27. Ancient peoples *attributed* disasters to a host of nature deities. 27. d
    a. redressed **b.** absconded **c.** incorporated **d.** imputed

28. Louis Pasteur was the first to inoculate cattle against *tending to cause death* anthrax bacteria. 28. a
    a. pestilent **b.** magnanimous **c.** livid **d.** salubrious

29. The *collection of writings* of Ernest Hemingway was augmented by the discovery of several previously unpublished works. 29. b
    a. animus **b.** corpus **c.** clemency **d.** corpuscle

30. Consumers sought *amends for wrongdoing* from the car manufacturer. 30. a
    a. redress **b.** vindication **c.** imputation **d.** prostration

NAME ______________________ DATE __________

TEST LESSONS 10, 11, AND 12

PART B CHOOSING THE BEST WORD

On the answer line, write the letter of the word that best expresses the meaning of the italicized word or phrase.

16. Counterfeited goods *cheat* consumers out of billions of dollars. 16. __________
 a. bilk b. vindicate c. debilitate d. impute

17. Public television stations are funded in part by *unselfish* contributions from viewers. 17. __________
 a. incorporeal c. pusillanimous
 b. salubrious d. magnanimous

18. The umpire accepted the jeers of the crowd with *composure.* 18. __________
 a. animus b. equanimity c. atrophy d. clemency

19. The discovery of the real culprit *cleared of blame* Gloria. 19. __________
 a. vindicated b. incorporated c. imputed d. debilitated

20. When Jason is angry, his complexion becomes *very pale.* 20. __________
 a. unscathed b. corpulent c. livid d. moribund

21. The *bitter hatred* between the Montagues and the Capulets serves as the obstacle to the love of Romeo and Juliet. 21. __________
 a. corpus b. atrophy c. animus d. equanimity

22. A series of illnesses so *weakened* my uncle that he eventually became totally bedridden. 22. __________
 a. debilitated b. redressed c. absconded d. imputed

23. Elena is attempting to overcome her *intangible* fears. 23. __________
 a. incorporeal b. debilitating c. moribund d. unscathed

24. Diverging interests *caused the withering of* the boys' friendship. 24. __________
 a. atrophied b. prostrated c. vindicated d. debilitated

25. Many people have the misconception that those who perform stunts in movies always walk away from these feats *unharmed.* 25. __________
 a. livid b. contrite c. unscathed d. prostrate

26. Jeff repaired his neighbor's fence in *compensation* for the damage he had caused. 26. __________
 a. vindication b. atrophy c. restitution d. equanimity

27. Ancient peoples *attributed* disasters to a host of nature deities. 27. __________
 a. redressed b. absconded c. incorporated d. imputed

28. Louis Pasteur was the first to inoculate cattle against *tending to cause death* anthrax bacteria. 28. __________
 a. pestilent b. magnanimous c. livid d. salubrious

29. The *collection of writings* of Ernest Hemingway was augmented by the discovery of several previously unpublished works. 29. __________
 a. animus b. corpus c. clemency d. corpuscle

30. Consumers sought *amends for wrongdoing* from the car manufacturer. 30. __________
 a. redress b. vindication c. imputation d. prostration

NAME ______________________________ DATE ______________

TEST LESSONS 13, 14, AND 15

(pages 81–98)

PART A COMPLETING THE DEFINITION

On the answer line, write the letter of the word or phrase that correctly completes each sentence.

1. When you *append* one thing to another, you ____ it. 1. b
   a. compare b. attach c. contrast d. duplicate

2. The *sanctity* of the home refers to its ____. 2. a
   a. inviolability b. social value c. tranquility d. authority

3. A *laconic* individual tends to be ____. 3. d
   a. sluggish b. hospitable c. irritable d. terse

4. To *supplicate* for assistance is to ____ help. 4. c
   a. search for b. volunteer c. beg for d. deny offers of

5. When you receive *recompense* for a job, you receive ____. 5. a
   a. payment for services c. a bill
   b. an application d. gratitude

6. A *pious* worshipper is ____. 6. c
   a. hypocritical b. demonstrative c. devout d. intolerant

7. A *eulogy* is a(n) ____ someone. 7. a
   a. tribute to c. endorsement of
   b. critique of d. conjecture about

8. To *expatiate* on a subject is to ____ it. 8. d
   a. reject b. study about c. ignore d. elaborate on

9. A *perpendicular* line ____. 9. c
   a. is crooked c. intersects another at right angles
   b. is parallel to another d. is uneven

10. One who exhibits *sanctimony* displays ____. 10. b
    a. extravagance c. a disrespectful attitude
    b. pretended holiness d. opinionated views

11. To *exalt* someone's achievements is to ____ that person. 11. b
    a. amuse b. praise c. defer to d. prevail upon

12. A *garrulous* friend is ____. 12. c
    a. grateful c. excessively talkative
    b. prudent d. typically inconsiderate

13. A *suspension* of rules involves ____. 13. d
    a. punishing offenders c. automatic renewal
    b. reviewing their effectiveness d. temporary deferment

14. Those who *consecrate* their lives ____. 14. c
    a. abandon ideals c. dedicate themselves to worthy goals
    b. consider options d. show determination

15. Something that is *pending* is ____. 15. d
    a. harshly judged c. somewhat impaired
    b. periodically re-examined d. awaiting conclusion

NAME ______________________________ DATE ____________

TEST LESSONS 13, 14, AND 15

(pages 81–98)

PART A COMPLETING THE DEFINITION

On the answer line, write the letter of the word or phrase that correctly completes each sentence.

1. When you *append* one thing to another, you _____ it. 1. ____________
   a. compare b. attach c. contrast d. duplicate

2. The *sanctity* of the home refers to its _____. 2. ____________
   a. inviolability b. social value c. tranquility d. authority

3. A *laconic* individual tends to be _____. 3. ____________
   a. sluggish b. hospitable c. irritable d. terse

4. To *supplicate* for assistance is to _____ help. 4. ____________
   a. search for b. volunteer c. beg for d. deny offers of

5. When you receive *recompense* for a job, you receive _____. 5. ____________
   a. payment for services c. a bill
   b. an application d. gratitude

6. A *pious* worshipper is _____. 6. ____________
   a. hypocritical b. demonstrative c. devout d. intolerant

7. A *eulogy* is a(n) _____ someone. 7. ____________
   a. tribute to c. endorsement of
   b. critique of d. conjecture about

8. To *expatiate* on a subject is to _____ it. 8. ____________
   a. reject b. study about c. ignore d. elaborate on

9. A *perpendicular* line _____. 9. ____________
   a. is crooked c. intersects another at right angles
   b. is parallel to another d. is uneven

10. One who exhibits *sanctimony* displays _____. 10. ____________
    a. extravagance c. a disrespectful attitude
    b. pretended holiness d. opinionated views

11. To *exalt* someone's achievements is to _____ that person. 11. ____________
    a. amuse b. praise c. defer to d. prevail upon

12. A *garrulous* friend is _____. 12. ____________
    a. grateful c. excessively talkative
    b. prudent d. typically inconsiderate

13. A *suspension* of rules involves _____. 13. ____________
    a. punishing offenders c. automatic renewal
    b. reviewing their effectiveness d. temporary deferment

14. Those who *consecrate* their lives _____. 14. ____________
    a. abandon ideals c. dedicate themselves to worthy goals
    b. consider options d. show determination

15. Something that is *pending* is _____. 15. ____________
    a. harshly judged c. somewhat impaired
    b. periodically re-examined d. awaiting conclusion

NAME ______________________________ DATE ______________

TEST LESSONS 13, 14, AND 15

PART B IDENTIFYING ANTONYMS

On the answer line, write the letter of the word that has the meaning that is opposite to that of the capitalized word.

16. VENERATE: — 16. d
    a. confiscate **b.** eradicate **c.** oblige **d.** ridicule

17. GIST: — 17. a
    a. periphery **b.** inclination **c.** model **d.** amnesty

18. PREPONDERANCE: — 18. b
    a. preference **b.** dearth **c.** distinction **d.** lightness

19. EXHORT: — 19. c
    a. mandate **b.** afflict **c.** dissuade **d.** decree

20. LAUDABLE: — 20. a
    a. contemptible **b.** primary **c.** methodical **d.** austere

21. POLEMIC: — 21. d
    a. endowment **b.** exemption **c.** foresight **d.** corroboration

22. EXPENDABLE: — 22. b
    a. abject **b.** essential **c.** forbidding **d.** detrimental

23. SACRILEGIOUS: — 23. d
    a. obstinate **b.** affable **c.** irritable **d.** reverent

24. PEREMPTORY: — 24. a
    a. indulgent **b.** variable **c.** subordinate **d.** bold

25. DISPENSE: — 25. a
    a. retain **b.** entice **c.** abandon **d.** elude

26. DESECRATE: — 26. c
    a. summon **b.** magnify **c.** purify **d.** discern

27. EXPENDITURE: — 27. b
    a. invention **b.** income **c.** constancy **d.** origin

28. HISTRIONIC: — 28. d
    a. redolent **b.** delirious **c.** exempt **d.** natural

29 IMPEND: — 29. a
    a. conclude **b.** depend **c.** foil **d.** hazard

30. CREDO: — 30. c
    a. prank **b.** deprivation **c.** skepticism **d.** vanity

NAME ______________________________ DATE __________

TEST LESSONS 13, 14, AND 15

PART B IDENTIFYING ANTONYMS

On the answer line, write the letter of the word that has the meaning that is opposite to that of the capitalized word.

16. VENERATE: 16. ________
a. confiscate b. eradicate c. oblige d. ridicule

17. GIST: 17. ________
a. periphery b. inclination c. model d. amnesty

18. PREPONDERANCE: 18. ________
a. preference b. dearth c. distinction d. lightness

19. EXHORT: 19. ________
a. mandate b. afflict c. dissuade d. decree

20. LAUDABLE: 20. ________
a. contemptible b. primary c. methodical d. austere

21. POLEMIC: 21. ________
a. endowment b. exemption c. foresight d. corroboration

22. EXPENDABLE: 22. ________
a. abject b. essential c. forbidding d. detrimental

23. SACRILEGIOUS: 23. ________
a. obstinate b. affable c. irritable d. reverent

24. PEREMPTORY: 24. ________
a. indulgent b. variable c. subordinate d. bold

25. DISPENSE: 25. ________
a. retain b. entice c. abandon d. elude

26. DESECRATE: 26. ________
a. summon b. magnify c. purify d. discern

27. EXPENDITURE: 27. ________
a. invention b. income c. constancy d. origin

28. HISTRIONIC: 28. ________
a. redolent b. delirious c. exempt d. natural

29 IMPEND: 29. ________
a. conclude b. depend c. foil d. hazard

30. CREDO: 30. ________
a. prank b. deprivation c. skepticism d. vanity

NAME ______________________ DATE ____________

BONUS LESSONS 13–16

(pages 81–98, 101–106)

Use the clues to spell out the words on the answer blanks. Then identify the mystery person at the bottom of the page by writing the numbered letters on the lines with the corresponding numbers.

Clue	Answer	Numbered letters
1. *Sanctity* comes from a Latin word meaning "______."	1. H O L Y	Y = 11
2. A system of guiding principles	2. C R E D O	R = 6
3. A tribute	3. E U L O G Y	G = 2
4. Existing in name only	4. N O M I N A L	I = 7
5. A *laconic* person uses few ______.	5. W O R D S	W = 12
6. Excessively dramatic	6. H I S T R I O N I C	H = 4
7. A *laudable* act is worthy of ______.	7. P R A I S E	A = 1
8. Having unknown authorship	8. A N O N Y M O U S	M = 10
9. Fame	9. R E N O W N	E = 9
10. Irreverent toward something sacred	10. S A C R I L E G I O U S	C = 5
11. *Ignominy* involves humiliation or personal ______.	11. D I S H O N O R	S = 8
12. A *preponderance* of something is a(n) ______ in quantity, power, or importance.	12. S U P E R I O R I T Y	T = 3

A	G	A	T	H	A		C	H	R	I	S	T	I	E,
1	2	1	3	4	1		5	4	6	7	8	3	7	9

M	Y	S	T	E	R	Y		W	R	I	T	E	R
10	11	8	3	9	6	11		12	6	7	3	9	6

NAME ______________________________ DATE ____________

BONUS LESSONS 13–16

(pages 81–98, 101–106)

Use the clues to spell out the words on the answer blanks. Then identify the mystery person at the bottom of the page by writing the numbered letters on the lines with the corresponding numbers.

1. *Sanctity* comes from a Latin word meaning "______."
2. A system of guiding principles
3. A tribute
4. Existing in name only
5. A *laconic* person uses few ______.
6. Excessively dramatic
7. A *laudable* act is worthy of ______.
8. Having unknown authorship
9. Fame
10. Irreverent toward something sacred
11. *Ignominy* involves humiliation or personal ______.
12. A *preponderance* of something is a(n) ______ in quantity, power, or importance.

1. ___ ___ ___ ___ (4th letter: 11)
2. ___ ___ ___ ___ ___ (2nd letter: 6)
3. ___ ___ ___ ___ ___ ___ (5th letter: 2)
4. ___ ___ ___ ___ ___ ___ ___ (4th letter: 7)
5. ___ ___ ___ ___ ___ (1st letter: 12)
6. ___ ___ ___ ___ ___ ___ ___ ___ ___ ___ (1st letter: 4)
7. ___ ___ ___ ___ ___ ___ (3rd letter: 1)
8. ___ ___ ___ ___ ___ ___ ___ ___ ___ (6th letter: 10)
9. ___ ___ ___ ___ ___ ___ (2nd letter: 9)
10. ___ ___ ___ ___ ___ ___ ___ ___ ___ ___ ___ ___ (3rd letter: 5)
11. ___ ___ ___ ___ ___ ___ ___ ___ (3rd letter: 8)
12. ___ ___ ___ ___ ___ ___ ___ ___ ___ ___ ___ (10th letter: 3)

___ ___ ___ ___ ___ ___ ___ ___ ___ ___ ___ ___ ___ ___,
1 2 1 3 4 1 5 4 6 7 8 3 7 9

___ ___ ___ ___ ___ ___ ___ ___ ___ ___ ___ ___ ___
10 11 8 3 9 6 11 12 6 7 3 9 6

NAME ________________________________ DATE __________

TEST LESSONS 16, 17, AND 18

(pages 101–118)

PART A CHOOSING THE BEST DEFINITION

On the answer line, write the letter of the best definition of the italicized vocabulary word.

1. Although *homonyms,* the words *bear* and *bare* have very different etymologies. — 1. b
   a. words with the same letters
   b. words with similar sounds but different meanings
   c. words from the same root
   d. words with opposite meanings

2. This is a particularly *felicitous* time to travel abroad. — 2. d
   a. lucky b. difficult c. inexpensive d. well-chosen

3. The donkey remained *stoic* and immovable despite its owner's threats. — 3. a
   a. impassive b. stubborn c. defiant d. eager

4. The water near the shore looks *placid.* — 4. d
   a. inviting c. moderately warm
   b. temperate d. outwardly calm

5. The community garden is sponsored by an *anonymous* benefactor. — 5. c
   a. well-known c. unacknowledged
   b. reliable d. generous

6. The violinist's performance was devoid of *éclat.* — 6. c
   a. energy b. emotion c. brilliance d. personality

7. Few growers of house plants know the Latin *nomenclature* of their flora. — 7. a
   a. names b. relatives c. derivatives d. pronunciation

8. "Let's go watch those city slickers try to ride old Lightning," Slim said with a *sardonic* grin. — 8. d
   a. good-natured b. bitter c. amused d. mocking

9. Mr. Eriksen was *obdurate* in his requirements. — 9. a
   a. unyielding b. unfair c. teasing d. clever

10. Pursuing a career was once an *audacious* undertaking for a woman. — 10. c
    a. inadvisable b. reprehensible c. daring d. thoughtless

11. The *denomination* of many constellations comes from Greek myths. — 11. d
    a. description b. explanation c. grouping d. designation

12. Pit bull terriers are noted for their *truculence.* — 12. a
    a. fierceness b. obesity c. aloofness d. sensitivity

13. The prisoner's *contumacy* ensured that he would not be paroled. — 13. b
    a. humility b. rebelliousness c. sentence d. foolishness

14. In some cultures the *ignominy* of being banished is a major deterrent to crime. — 14. a
    a. humiliation b. unfairness c. inconvenience d. benefit

15. The cast performed Gilbert and Sullivan's *Mikado* with *ebullience.* — 15. b
    a. abandon b. exuberance c. devotion d. uncertainty

NAME ______________________________ DATE ____________

TEST LESSONS 16, 17, AND 18

(pages 101–118)

PART A CHOOSING THE BEST DEFINITION

On the answer line, write the letter of the best definition of the italicized vocabulary word.

1. Although *homonyms,* the words *bear* and *bare* have very different etymologies. 1. ____________
   a. words with the same letters
   b. words with similar sounds but different meanings
   c. words from the same root
   d. words with opposite meanings

2. This is a particularly *felicitous* time to travel abroad. 2. ____________
   a. lucky b. difficult c. inexpensive d. well-chosen

3. The donkey remained *stoic* and immovable despite its owner's threats. 3. ____________
   a. impassive b. stubborn c. defiant d. eager

4. The water near the shore looks *placid.* 4. ____________
   a. inviting c. moderately warm
   b. temperate d. outwardly calm

5. The community garden is sponsored by an *anonymous* benefactor. 5. ____________
   a. well-known c. unacknowledged
   b. reliable d. generous

6. The violinist's performance was devoid of *éclat.* 6. ____________
   a. energy b. emotion c. brilliance d. personality

7. Few growers of house plants know the Latin *nomenclature* of their flora. 7. ____________
   a. names b. relatives c. derivatives d. pronunciation

8. "Let's go watch those city slickers try to ride old Lightning," Slim said with a *sardonic* grin. 8. ____________
   a. good-natured b. bitter c. amused d. mocking

9. Mr. Eriksen was *obdurate* in his requirements. 9. ____________
   a. unyielding b. unfair c. teasing d. clever

10. Pursuing a career was once an *audacious* undertaking for a woman. 10. ____________
    a. inadvisable b. reprehensible c. daring d. thoughtless

11. The *denomination* of many constellations comes from Greek myths. 11. ____________
    a. description b. explanation c. grouping d. designation

12. Pit bull terriers are noted for their *truculence.* 12. ____________
    a. fierceness b. obesity c. aloofness d. sensitivity

13. The prisoner's *contumacy* ensured that he would not be paroled. 13. ____________
    a. humility b. rebelliousness c. sentence d. foolishness

14. In some cultures the *ignominy* of being banished is a major deterrent to crime. 14. ____________
    a. humiliation b. unfairness c. inconvenience d. benefit

15. The cast performed Gilbert and Sullivan's *Mikado* with *ebullience.* 15. ____________
    a. abandon b. exuberance c. devotion d. uncertainty

NAME ______________________________ DATE ____________

TEST LESSONS 16, 17, AND 18

PART B CHOOSING THE BEST WORD

On the answer line, write the letter of the word that best expresses the meaning of the italicized word or phrase.

16. Quentin Brooks, an avid genealogist, published a newsletter for those who shared his *surname.* — 16. c
a. metonymy b. misnomer c. cognomen d. renown

17. We tried to ignore the *insincerely earnest* salesperson. — 17. b
a. surly b. unctuous c. querulous d. irresolute

18. The *festive* atmosphere heightened as midnight approached. — 18. c
a. felicitous b. irascible c. convivial d. ebullient

19. Was Albert Schweitzer most *widely honored* as a physician, a philosopher, or a musician? — 19. d
a. nominal b. audacious c. indefatigable d. renowned

20. The term *polecat* is a *wrongly applied name* for the skunk because it is not a member of the cat family. — 20. a
a. misnomer b. metonymy c. nomenclature d. cognomen

21. Corinne is *vacillating* about what she wants to do with her life. — 21. d
a. surly b. convivial c. obdurate d. irresolute

22. Elizabeth II, the *existing in name only* ruler of Great Britain, has reigned since 1952. — 22. b
a. indefatigable b. nominal c. dour d. convivial

23. The *prone to outbursts of temper* orchestra leader exploded at least once each rehearsal. — 23. d
a. ebullient b. convivial c. irresolute d. irascible

24. Carson became *fawning* and apologetic with the police officer. — 24. a
a. obsequious b. querulous c. sardonic d. truculent

25. *Peevish* neighbors called to complain about the dog's incessant barking. — 25. a
a. Querulous b. Irascible c. Surly d. Dour

26. Referring to ranch workers as "hands" is an example of *a figure of speech in which an attribute of something designates the whole.* — 26. b
a. cognomen b. metonymy c. misnomer d. denomination

27. Lisette was rather *sullenly ill-tempered* with the nurses. — 27. a
a. surly b. sardonic c. convivial d. obsequious

28. Ralph Nader's *tireless* efforts have led to greater consumer awareness. — 28. c
a. audacious b. nominal c. indefatigable d. irresolute

29. A marathon runner must have the *quality of holding firmly to a purpose* to train in all kinds of weather. — 29. a
a. pertinacity b. indefatigability c. éclat d. contumacy

30. Wanda is a lonely person whose *glum* expression puts others off. — 30. b
a. convivial b. dour c. irresolute d. stoic

NAME ______________________ DATE __________

TEST LESSONS 16, 17, AND 18

PART B CHOOSING THE BEST WORD

On the answer line, write the letter of the word that best expresses the meaning of the italicized word or phrase.

16. Quentin Brooks, an avid genealogist, published a newsletter for those who shared his *surname.* 16. ________
   a. metonymy b. misnomer c. cognomen d. renown

17. We tried to ignore the *insincerely earnest* salesperson. 17. ________
   a. surly b. unctuous c. querulous d. irresolute

18. The *festive* atmosphere heightened as midnight approached. 18. ________
   a. felicitous b. irascible c. convivial d. ebullient

19. Was Albert Schweitzer most *widely honored* as a physician, a philosopher, or a musician? 19. ________
   a. nominal b. audacious c. indefatigable d. renowned

20. The term *polecat* is a *wrongly applied name* for the skunk because it is not a member of the cat family. 20. ________
   a. misnomer b. metonymy c. nomenclature d. cognomen

21. Corinne is *vacillating* about what she wants to do with her life. 21. ________
   a. surly b. convivial c. obdurate d. irresolute

22. Elizabeth II, the *existing in name only* ruler of Great Britain, has reigned since 1952. 22. ________
   a. indefatigable b. nominal c. dour d. convivial

23. The *prone to outbursts of temper* orchestra leader exploded at least once each rehearsal. 23. ________
   a. ebullient b. convivial c. irresolute d. irascible

24. Carson became *fawning* and apologetic with the police officer. 24. ________
   a. obsequious b. querulous c. sardonic d. truculent

25. *Peevish* neighbors called to complain about the dog's incessant barking. 25. ________
   a. Querulous b. Irascible c. Surly d. Dour

26. Referring to ranch workers as "hands" is an example of *a figure of speech in which an attribute of something designates the whole.* 26. ________
   a. cognomen b. metonymy c. misnomer d. denomination

27. Lisette was rather *sullenly ill-tempered* with the nurses. 27. ________
   a. surly b. sardonic c. convivial d. obsequious

28. Ralph Nader's *tireless* efforts have led to greater consumer awareness. 28. ________
   a. audacious b. nominal c. indefatigable d. irresolute

29. A marathon runner must have the *quality of holding firmly to a purpose* to train in all kinds of weather. 29. ________
   a. pertinacity b. indefatigability c. éclat d. contumacy

30. Wanda is a lonely person whose *glum* expression puts others off. 30. ________
   a. convivial b. dour c. irresolute d. stoic

NAME ______________________ DATE __________

BONUS LESSONS 17–20

(pages 107–118, 121–132)

Unscramble the letters of each italicized word, and write the word on the answer line to the right.

1. The *avvncliio* Zukroffs hosted another of their delightful parties. 1. convivial
2. Lise's *brtdaoue* approach to tasks prevents her from acknowledging more efficient methods. 2. obdurate
3. The dictator's *cdiet* forbade any citizen to leave the country. 3. edict
4. An excess of vitamins can have a(n) *seeiuodetrl* effect on one's health. 4. deleterious
5. The original courthouse was *zdrae* to make room for a modern judicial complex. 5. razed
6. Shakespeare made frequent use of the *lqyuoiosl* as a dramatic device. 6. soliloquy
7. In a(n) *rudo* mood, Mr. Hamlin barely muttered a greeting. 7. dour
8. Hillary was *oeltrsruei* about attending college in California. 8. irresolute
9. In a(n) *uouueqlsr* voice, the woman asked to see the manager. 9. querulous
10. The *eielblneuc* of the cheerleaders animated the crowd. 10. ebullience
11. The gymnast reached the *ncnlpiae* of her career when she won the national championship. 11. pinnacle
12. At this year's *luiulcoomq*, heart surgeons were exposed to new transplant techniques. 12. colloquium
13. Following the *nebitdenioc* the graduates will file out of the auditorium. 13. benediction
14. By carefully reading the computer instruction manual, you can *tobaive* many problems. 14. obviate
15. The editors sought a more *tefecfalu* way of producing an index. 15. effectual
16. His *lusyr* attitude and harsh judgments did not endear him to others. 16. surly
17. Beth remained *cisto* and ignored the discomfort of her burns. 17. stoic
18. The ballet was choreographed with *latéc*. 18. éclat
19. Yong Kim received the compliments of his guests with a(n) *daplic* smile. 19. placid
20. The editorial *tecindid* the redevelopment group for its failure to consider neighborhood interests. 20. indicted

NAME ____________________ DATE __________

BONUS LESSONS 17–20

(pages 107–118, 121–132)

Unscramble the letters of each italicized word, and write the word on the answer line to the right.

1. The *avvncliio* Zukroffs hosted another of their delightful parties. 1. __________
2. Lise's *brtdaoue* approach to tasks prevents her from acknowledging more efficient methods. 2. __________
3. The dictator's *cdiet* forbade any citizen to leave the country. 3. __________
4. An excess of vitamins can have a(n) *seeiuodetrl* effect on one's health. 4. __________
5. The original courthouse was *zdrae* to make room for a modern judicial complex. 5. __________
6. Shakespeare made frequent use of the *lqyuoiosl* as a dramatic device. 6. __________
7. In a(n) *rudo* mood, Mr. Hamlin barely muttered a greeting. 7. __________
8. Hillary was *oeltrsruei* about attending college in California. 8. __________
9. In a(n) *uouueqlsr* voice, the woman asked to see the manager. 9. __________
10. The *eielblneuc* of the cheerleaders animated the crowd. 10. __________
11. The gymnast reached the *ncnlpiae* of her career when she won the national championship. 11. __________
12. At this year's *luiulcoomq*, heart surgeons were exposed to new transplant techniques. 12. __________
13. Following the *nebitdenioc* the graduates will file out of the auditorium. 13. __________
14. By carefully reading the computer instruction manual, you can *tobaive* many problems. 14. __________
15. The editors sought a more *tefecfalu* way of producing an index. 15. __________
16. His *lusyr* attitude and harsh judgments did not endear him to others. 16. __________
17. Beth remained *cisto* and ignored the discomfort of her burns. 17. __________
18. The ballet was choreographed with *latéc.* 18. __________
19. Yong Kim received the compliments of his guests with a(n) *daplic* smile. 19. __________
20. The editorial *tecindid* the redevelopment group for its failure to consider neighborhood interests. 20. __________

VERBAL APTITUDE TEST 2

For each question in this section, choose the best answer and blacken the corresponding space on the answer sheet.

PART A ANTONYMS

Each question below consists of a word in capital letters, followed by five lettered words or phrases. Choose the word or phrase that is most nearly opposite in meaning to the word in capital letters. Since some of the questions require you to distinguish fine shades of meaning, consider all the choices before deciding which is best.

EXAMPLE:

GOOD: (A) sour (B) bad (C) red
(D) hot (E) ugly

   (D) (E)

1. EBULLIENCE: (A) nostalgia
(B) reluctance (C) despondency
(D) tranquility (E) repression

2. LANGUID: (A) solid (B) frigid
(C) introspective (D) energetic
(E) frivolous

3. SALUBRIOUS: (A) feckless (B) injurious
(C) tenuous (D) libelous
(E) controversial

4. TRUCULENT: (A) laconic (B) fawning
(C) brisk (D) aristocratic (E) conciliatory

5. ERRANT: (A) stationary (B) peerless
(C) coy (D) plebeian (E) mawkish

6. INNOCUOUS: (A) abominable (B) noxious
(C) culpable (D) fungible (E) crude

7. ERADICATE: (A) placate (B) dispense
(C) generate (D) espouse (E) splay

8. ESCHEW: (A) masticate (B) harass
(C) cajole (D) pursue (E) append

9. GALVANIZE: (A) squander (B) rend
(C) deteriorate (D) stupefy (E) vulcanize

10. INCHOATE: (A) mature (B) nominal
(C) explicit (D) healthy (E) vain

PART B SENTENCE COMPLETIONS

Each sentence below has one or two blanks, each blank indicating that something has been omitted. Below the sentence are five lettered words or sets of words. Choose the word or set of words that best fits the meaning of the sentence as a whole.

EXAMPLE:

Although its publicity has been - - - - , the film itself is intelligent, well-acted, handsomely produced, and altogether - - - - .
(A) tasteless .. respectable
(B) extensive .. moderate
(C) sophisticated .. amateur
(D) risqué .. crude (E) perfect .. spectacular

11. The litigants' acceptance of an out-of-court settlement - - - - the need for a long, costly courtroom battle.
(A) surmounted (B) denoted
(C) refracted (D) obviated (E) shirked

12. Some experts in the field of occupational disease now - - - - Goya's physical and mental illness to lead poisoning, which he contracted by working with certain pigments.
(A) ascribe (B) expostulate
(C) propose (D) indict (E) allude

13. Despite the recommendations of several financial advisers, the company's chief executive officer remained - - - - opposed to the proposed merger.
(A) irresolutely (B) perturbably
(C) futilely (D) adamantly (E) insatiably

14. The impending financial crises - - - - legislators to consider various - - - -, including tax increases and reductions in their own salaries.
(A) resolved .. rationales
(B) compelled .. expediencies
(C) deluded .. remuneration
(D) exhorted .. alternatives
(E) implored .. resolutions

15. Moira Steed's editor felt that her latest novel was too - - - - and proposed a number of changes to make it more - - - - .
(A) sentimental .. expressive
(B) effusive .. outré
(C) inventive .. formulaic
(D) abstruse .. intelligible
(E) redundant .. tautological

16. Although Judge King is known for her clemency toward first-time offenders, she is unsparing in her treatment of - - - - .
(A) recidivists (B) turncoats (C) atavists
(D) chauvinists (E) sociopaths

17. Unscrupulous - - - - might well seek to - - - - retirees with substantial assets.
(A) financiers .. enroll
(B) plutocrats .. declaim
(C) opportunists .. exploit
(D) malefactors .. implore
(E) prigs .. appraise

18. Whereas Mr. Cullen was hired to manage our payables files, he has become our - - - - , making himself indispensable in every facet of our operation.
(A) amanuensis (B) sophist (C) harlequin
(D) factotum (E) caviler

19. Because unguents can have a(n) - - - - effect on burns by promoting infection, doctors now agree that the simple application of cold water is often a(n) - - - - treatment.
(A) inconsequential .. erratic
(B) dissolute .. useless
(C) minuscule .. ideal
(D) salutary .. pragmatic
(E) pathogenic .. efficacious

20. What dweller of the - - - - regions of this country doesn't dream at least once each winter of escaping to sunny southern climes?
(A) meridional (B) surfeited
(C) hyperborean (D) bosky (E) fenny

PART C ANALOGIES

Each question below consists of a related pair of words or phrases, followed by five lettered pairs of words or phrases. Select the lettered pair that best expresses a relationship similar to that expressed in the original pair.

EXAMPLE:

YAWN : BOREDOM :: (A) dream : sleep
(B) anger : madness (C) smile : amusement
(D) face : expression (E) impatience : rebellion

21. RUMINATE : DELIBERATE ::
(A) impair : abolish (B) enunciate : define
(C) ingest : digest (D) revere : devote
(E) jettison : discard

22. PLACATE : PROVOKE ::
(A) disabuse : mistreat (B) assent : demur
(C) dispatch : dispose (D) emulate : mulct
(E) preen : vaunt

23. OBSTRUCTION : IMPEDE ::
(A) toxin : contaminate
(B) treatise : incite
(C) demagogue : subvert
(D) appraisal : redeem
(E) liaison : meander

24. DEMOGRAPHY : POPULATION ::
(A) taxonomy : classification
(B) hermeneutics : history
(C) entomology : meaning
(D) linguistics : Turkish
(E) paleontology : geology

25. ARBITRATION : RECONCILIATION ::
(A) computation: solution
(B) expedition : announcement
(C) innovation : stagnation
(D) expatriation : treason
(E) arbitrage : rehabilitation

26. STENTORIAN : AUDIBLE ::
(A) petulant : sassy
(B) dull : ponderous
(C) orotund : eloquent
(D) talkative : garrulous
(E) dappled : stippled

27. ARTICLE : CONTRACT ::
   (A) sonnet : poetry
   (B) numeration : integer
   (C) escarpment : contravention
   (D) curriculum : pedagogy
   (E) abridgment : condensation

28. AUDACITY : INTREPID ::
   (A) discordant : mnemonic
   (B) affinity : retroactive
   (C) sycophancy : truckling
   (D) rectitude : rigid
   (E) insouciance : haughty

29. SCROFULOUS : DEGENERATE ::
   (A) tumid : banal (B) saccharine : cloying
   (C) keen : listless (D) rubicund : inflamed
   (E) ersatz : genuine

30. INTERDICT : TABOO ::
   (A) scourge : levity
   (B) arouse : resignation
   (C) sequester : confinement
   (D) revel : mayhem
   (E) parry : conviction

PART D READING COMPREHENSION

Each passage below is followed by questions based on its content. Answer all questions following a passage on the basis of what is stated or implied in that passage.

The distinction between equity and common law is a historical one. Equity in the United States is that portion of remedial justice that was formerly administered in England by the court of chancery. English equity was a system of justice administered by a tribunal apart from the common-law courts. The common-law system of justice in England was deficient in that its procedural requirements were rigid and highly technical. These requirements confined the courts to redressing wrongs usually by just awarding money damages to an injured party.

In situations in which a common-law remedy either did not exist or was inadequate to redress the wrong, the king referred the matter to the Lord High Chancellor. Chancellors were high-ranking clergy of the church and advisers to the king. When a person came to a chancellor with an unusual situation for which there was no remedy at common law, the chancellor was given power by the king to grant relief. This practice became institutionalized to the point where the chancellor, presiding over a court of chancery, issued decrees on his own authority. The court of chancery, or equity court, came into being to provide a forum for granting relief in accordance with broad principles of right and justice in cases in which restrictive technicalities of the common-law system prevented it.

For centuries, common law and equity were administered in England by two separate sets of courts, each applying its own system of jurisprudence and following its own system of procedure. . . . Equity furnished a remedy only when the common-law procedure was deficient or the remedy at common law was inadequate. A case in equity involves questions of discretion or judgment, or possibly principles of justice and conscience rather than rigid legal rules. Much of traditional equity is based on an analysis of concepts such as adequacy, practicality, clean hands, estoppel, and hardship. The underlying concepts of law and equity have been retained in the United States, although the formalism that historically distinguished the two has largely disappeared.

31. The gist of the passage is best expressed by which of the following statements?
   (A) Common-law courts in England were debilitated by restrictive technicalities.
   (B) Equity and common law are necessarily administered by separate court systems.
   (C) Chancery or equity law arose to dispense justice for wrongs that could not be adequately remedied under common law.
   (D) The foundations of American jurisprudence were derived from England.
   (E) The feasibility of enforcement is one of the distinctions between common law and chancery law.

32. Which of the following is implied in the passage?
   (A) The court of chancery could decide procedural matters exclusively.
   (B) Legal concepts such as estoppel and clean hands are principles of discretion.
   (C) In the United States, equity and law have identical underlying principles.
   (D) Anti-monarchist parties in England were unlikely to be treated fairly in courts of chancery.
   (E) Matters of equity were less likely to be codified than matters of common law.

33. In the passage which of the following is not stated about the chancellor?
   (A) He established laws dealing with monetary matters.
   (B) He was authorized to decide on matters without remedy in courts of common law.
   (C) He was not constrained by the procedural requirements of common law.
   (D) He provided counsel to the sovereign.
   (E) He had the authority to issue edicts.

Semiotics distinguishes two aspects of language. The system of rules and conventions established by society is *langue;* the individual act of communication is *parole.* Because two speakers share the same knowledge of grammatical rules, for example, they can communicate through a virtually unlimited range of individual utterance. They take the rules for granted. If they do not—if they try to think about the rules while using them—their speech becomes difficult or impossible. All communication depends on some complex system that remains *assumed* between people. . . .

In discussing language, semioticians consider two axes of meaning: a *syntagmatic axis* and a *paradigmatic* (or *systemic*) *axis.* The syntagmatic axis refers to the way in which words, or other verbal or nonverbal units called *signifiers,* must be linked to be conventionally meaningful. The paradigmatic axis refers to the choice of words available to the speaker or writer given the context that has been set up. If we take the words "John hit the . . . ," we know by the syntagmatic organization of the language that the next word will most likely be either a noun like *ball* or an adjective preceding a noun, like *furry.* To say "John hit the abruptly ball" is to break a rule of the language, although the listener may still guess what you're talking about. The syntagmatic level of language involves the rules whereby words are joined together.

When we talk about the paradigmatic aspects of communication, we mean the number of possible words or signifiers that could be used in a given situation. That is, if I were to say "John hit the sphere," my choice of word *sphere* is meaningful because in English I could have used *ball,* which would indeed be the more common word. My choice of *sphere* is not just meaningful in itself, but in implicit comparison with all the words that could be used following "John hit the . . ."— such as *ball, policeman,* or *punching bag.* The paradigmatic level of language systems refers to the choices available to a communicator within the system of signifiers the medium uses.

An example based on the language system of a restaurant menu may clarify the two components. On the syntagmatic level, one eats an appetizer followed by a soup, an entree, and a dessert. On the paradigmatic level, one can choose between clam chowder and onion soup, between roast chicken and steak, between apple pie and chocolate pudding. One *can* break the rules of dining and eat one's chocolate pudding before clam chowder, or a restaurant could list steak under desserts, but these actions would respectively break the syntagmatic and paradigmatic grammar of our culture's system of eating. Yet only by studying the menu as a whole could a foreigner get some sense of what the eating "codes" of our country are.

34. Which of the following best states the main idea of the passage?

(A) Words and signifiers can make manifest a virtually infinite number of concepts.

(B) Language rules and acts of communication are separate, but interrelated, phenomena.

(C) Embedded within all communication systems is an implicit, bipartite structure.

(D) Semiotics is the study of paradigmatic and syntagmatic axes.

(E) Meaning is derived from the relationship of signifiers to paradigms.

35. Which of the following does the author imply in the passage?

I Individual utterances must emerge from a conventional speech system.

II Meaning requires a shared system of rules between the interlocutors in any act of communication.

III Food, like language, has two axes.

IV The syntagmatic organization of languages limits the choice of signifiers to be used in an individual act of communication.

V For *parole* to yield meaning, *langue* cannot be violated.

(A) I, II, and V (B) II, III, and V

(C) II, IV, and V (D) I, III, and IV

(E) I and IV

36. In addition to the example of the restaurant menu, which of the following could the author best use to illustrate paradigmatic and syntagmatic structures?

(A) The relationship of styles and colors to fashion

(B) The relationship of melodic phrases to the chords that compose them

(C) The uses of paradox in rhetoric

(D) The more concentrated means of expression in poetry contrasted with the more expansive expression of prose fiction

(E) The relationship of longitude and latitude to navigation

If you finish before time is called, check your work on this test.

VERBAL APTITUDE TEST 2

Answer Sheet

Use a No. 2 pencil for completing this answer sheet. Make sure that your marks are dark and completely fill the space. Erase any errors or stray marks. If a test has fewer than 50 questions, leave the extra answer spaces blank.

No.					
1.	A	B	**C**	D	E
2.	A	B	C	**D**	E
3.	A	**B**	C	D	E
4.	A	B	C	D	**E**
5.	**A**	B	C	D	E
6.	A	**B**	C	D	E
7.	A	B	**C**	D	E
8.	A	B	C	**D**	E
9.	A	B	C	**D**	E
10.	**A**	B	C	D	E
11.	A	B	C	**D**	E
12.	**A**	B	C	D	E
13.	A	B	C	**D**	E
14.	A	**B**	C	D	E
15.	A	B	C	**D**	E
16.	**A**	B	C	D	E
17.	A	B	**C**	D	E
18.	A	B	C	**D**	E
19.	A	B	C	D	**E**
20.	A	B	**C**	D	E
21.	A	B	C	D	**E**
22.	A	**B**	C	D	E
23.	**A**	B	C	D	E
24.	**A**	B	C	D	E
25.	**A**	B	C	D	E
26.	A	B	**C**	D	E
27.	A	B	C	**D**	E
28.	A	B	**C**	D	E
29.	A	**B**	C	D	E
30.	A	B	**C**	D	E
31.	A	B	**C**	D	E
32.	A	B	C	D	**E**
33.	**A**	B	C	D	E
34.	A	B	**C**	D	E
35.	A	B	**C**	D	E
36.	A	**B**	C	D	E
37.	A	B	C	D	E
38.	A	B	C	D	E
39.	A	B	C	D	E
40.	A	B	C	D	E
41.	A	B	C	D	E
42.	A	B	C	D	E
43.	A	B	C	D	E
44.	A	B	C	D	E
45.	A	B	C	D	E
46.	A	B	C	D	E
47.	A	B	C	D	E
48.	A	B	C	D	E
49.	A	B	C	D	E
50.	A	B	C	D	E

VERBAL APTITUDE TEST 2

Answer Sheet

Use a No. 2 pencil for completing this answer sheet. Make sure that your marks are dark and completely fill the space. Erase any errors or stray marks. If a test has fewer than 50 questions, leave the extra answer spaces blank.

1.	A	B	C	D	E	26.	A	B	C	D	E
2.	A	B	C	D	E	27.	A	B	C	D	E
3.	A	B	C	D	E	28.	A	B	C	D	E
4.	A	B	C	D	E	29.	A	B	C	D	E
5.	A	B	C	D	E	30.	A	B	C	D	E
6.	A	B	C	D	E	31.	A	B	C	D	E
7.	A	B	C	D	E	32.	A	B	C	D	E
8.	A	B	C	D	E	33.	A	B	C	D	E
9.	A	B	C	D	E	34.	A	B	C	D	E
10.	A	B	C	D	E	35.	A	B	C	D	E
11.	A	B	C	D	E	36.	A	B	C	D	E
12.	A	B	C	D	E	37.	A	B	C	D	E
13.	A	B	C	D	E	38.	A	B	C	D	E
14.	A	B	C	D	E	39.	A	B	C	D	E
15.	A	B	C	D	E	40.	A	B	C	D	E
16.	A	B	C	D	E	41.	A	B	C	D	E
17.	A	B	C	D	E	42.	A	B	C	D	E
18.	A	B	C	D	E	43.	A	B	C	D	E
19.	A	B	C	D	E	44.	A	B	C	D	E
20.	A	B	C	D	E	45.	A	B	C	D	E
21.	A	B	C	D	E	46.	A	B	C	D	E
22.	A	B	C	D	E	47.	A	B	C	D	E
23.	A	B	C	D	E	48.	A	B	C	D	E
24.	A	B	C	D	E	49.	A	B	C	D	E
25.	A	B	C	D	E	50.	A	B	C	D	E

NAME ______________________________ DATE ____________

TEST LESSONS 19, 20, AND 21

(pages 121–138)

PART A CHOOSING THE BEST DEFINITION

On the answer line, write the letter of the best definition of the italicized word.

1. Sumiko will participate in a *colloquium* on environmental issues. 1. b
   a. debate **b.** conference **c.** lecture **d.** film
2. *Stultified* by stage fright, Henri stammered his opening lines. 2. a
   a. crippled **b.** bewitched **c.** humiliated **d.** annoyed
3. Although the defendant had been previously arrested, she had never been *indicted* before. 3. a
   a. formally accused **c.** incarcerated
   b. acquitted **d.** convicted
4. Researchers must determine the *effectual* dosage of the new medication. 4. b
   a. minimal **b.** adequate **c.** harmful **d.** safe
5. A *surfeit* of imported ore sent copper prices plummeting. 5. c
   a. insufficiency **c.** excessive amount
   b. backlog **d.** new shipment
6. A well-educated young lady was once schooled in *elocution.* 6. d
   a. cooking **c.** correspondence
   b. etiquette **d.** public speaking
7. In 1973 a military junta *wrested* power from Chile's president. 7. d
   a. requested **b.** abused **c.** achieved **d.** usurped
8. By presidential *edict,* flags were flown at half mast. 8. b
   a. whim **b.** proclamation **c.** insistence **d.** veto
9. Announcers at classical music stations tend to use *grandiloquent* language. 9. b
   a. expressive **b.** lofty **c.** informal **d.** technical
10. Introverted people are more comfortable as observers than they are as *interlocutors.* 10. c
    a. attention seekers **c.** conversationalists
    b. travelers **d.** teachers
11. Even as a child, Marco was an *insatiable* reader. 11. b
    a. incapable of being hurried **c.** dedicated
    b. incapable of being satisfied **d.** proficient
12. With the invention of Braille, blind people *surmounted* many of the difficulties in reading and writing. 12. c
    a. increased **b.** identified **c.** overcame **d.** lessened
13. Mr. Ordonez's orchards are *replete* with fruit. 13. d
    a. lacking **b.** stacked **c.** never **d.** abounding
14. In a fairy tale, a king's *avarice* causes his daughter's destruction. 14. d
    a. insensitivity **b.** opulence **c.** pride **d.** greed
15. Many ancient tombs have been *despoiled* by grave robbers. 15. b
    a. ruined **b.** plundered **c.** vandalized **d.** occupied

NAME ______________________ DATE __________

TEST LESSONS 19, 20, AND 21

(pages 121–138)

PART A CHOOSING THE BEST DEFINITION

On the answer line, write the letter of the best definition of the italicized word.

1. Sumiko will participate in a *colloquium* on environmental issues. 1. ________
   a. debate b. conference c. lecture d. film

2. *Stultified* by stage fright, Henri stammered his opening lines. 2. ________
   a. crippled b. bewitched c. humiliated d. annoyed

3. Although the defendant had been previously arrested, she had never been *indicted* before. 3. ________
   a. formally accused c. incarcerated
   b. acquitted d. convicted

4. Researchers must determine the *effectual* dosage of the new medication. 4. ________
   a. minimal b. adequate c. harmful d. safe

5. A *surfeit* of imported ore sent copper prices plummeting. 5. ________
   a. insufficiency c. excessive amount
   b. backlog d. new shipment

6. A well-educated young lady was once schooled in *elocution.* 6. ________
   a. cooking c. correspondence
   b. etiquette d. public speaking

7. In 1973 a military junta *wrested* power from Chile's president. 7. ________
   a. requested b. abused c. achieved d. usurped

8. By presidential *edict,* flags were flown at half mast. 8. ________
   a. whim b. proclamation c. insistence d. veto

9. Announcers at classical music stations tend to use *grandiloquent* language. 9. ________
   a. expressive b. lofty c. informal d. technical

10. Introverted people are more comfortable as observers than they are as *interlocutors.* 10. ________
    a. attention seekers c. conversationalists
    b. travelers d. teachers

11. Even as a child, Marco was an *insatiable* reader. 11. ________
    a. incapable of being hurried c. dedicated
    b. incapable of being satisfied d. proficient

12. With the invention of Braille, blind people *surmounted* many of the difficulties in reading and writing. 12. ________
    a. increased b. identified c. overcame d. lessened

13. Mr. Ordonez's orchards are *replete* with fruit. 13. ________
    a. lacking b. stacked c. never d. abounding

14. In a fairy tale, a king's *avarice* causes his daughter's destruction. 14. ________
    a. insensitivity b. opulence c. pride d. greed

15. Many ancient tombs have been *despoiled* by grave robbers. 15. ________
    a. ruined b. plundered c. vandalized d. occupied

NAME ______________________________ DATE ____________

TEST LESSONS 19, 20, AND 21

PART B IDENTIFYING ANTONYMS

On the answer line, write the letter of the word or phrase that has the meaning that is opposite to that of the capitalized word.

16. LOQUACIOUS: — 16. a
    a. silent **b.** inhospitable **c.** frugal **d.** pretentious

17. RAZE: — 17. d
    a. descend **b.** debase **c.** discard **d.** construct

18. PARSIMONY: — 18. d
    a. restraint **b.** greed **c.** empathy **d.** generosity

19. BENEDICTION: — 19. a
    a. curse **b.** restitution **c.** repeal **d.** annihilation

20. SOLILOQUY: — 20. b
    a. charade **b.** dialogue **c.** parody **d.** diversion

21. DELETERIOUS: — 21. c
    a. unused **b.** rational **c.** beneficial **d.** exceptional

22. TUMULT: — 22. a
    a. serenity **b.** commotion **c.** resignation **d.** cowardice

23. PINNACLE: — 23. c
    a. difficulty **b.** juncture **c.** depths **d.** summit

24. INTERDICT: — 24. d
    a. extradite **b.** exonerate **c.** insist **d.** sanction

25. VOLUMINOUS: — 25. b
    a. subdued **b.** skimpy **c.** facile **d.** eloquent

26. MYRIAD: — 26. b
    a. plenitude **b.** paucity **c.** nobility **d.** diversity

27. PRODIGAL: — 27. d
    a. wasteful **b.** unrepentant **c.** submissive **d.** stingy

28. JETTISON: — 28. b
    a. renounce **b.** retain **c.** redress **d.** reduce

29. INUNDATE: — 29. d
    a. express **b.** revoke **c.** withhold **d.** drain

30. OBVIATE: — 30. a
    a. allow **b.** enliven **c.** alleviate **d.** illuminate

NAME ______________________ DATE __________

TEST LESSONS 19, 20, AND 21

PART B IDENTIFYING ANTONYMS

On the answer line, write the letter of the word or phrase that has the meaning that is opposite to that of the capitalized word.

16. LOQUACIOUS: 16. __________
    a. silent **b.** inhospitable **c.** frugal **d.** pretentious

17. RAZE: 17. __________
    a. descend **b.** debase **c.** discard **d.** construct

18. PARSIMONY: 18. __________
    a. restraint **b.** greed **c.** empathy **d.** generosity

19. BENEDICTION: 19. __________
    a. curse **b.** restitution **c.** repeal **d.** annihilation

20. SOLILOQUY: 20. __________
    a. charade **b.** dialogue **c.** parody **d.** diversion

21. DELETERIOUS: 21. __________
    a. unused **b.** rational **c.** beneficial **d.** exceptional

22. TUMULT: 22. __________
    a. serenity **b.** commotion **c.** resignation **d.** cowardice

23. PINNACLE: 23. __________
    a. difficulty **b.** juncture **c.** depths **d.** summit

24. INTERDICT: 24. __________
    a. extradite **b.** exonerate **c.** insist **d.** sanction

25. VOLUMINOUS: 25. __________
    a. subdued **b.** skimpy **c.** facile **d.** eloquent

26. MYRIAD: 26. __________
    a. plenitude **b.** paucity **c.** nobility **d.** diversity

27. PRODIGAL: 27. __________
    a. wasteful **b.** unrepentant **c.** submissive **d.** stingy

28. JETTISON: 28. __________
    a. renounce **b.** retain **c.** redress **d.** reduce

29. INUNDATE: 29. __________
    a. express **b.** revoke **c.** withhold **d.** drain

30. OBVIATE: 30. __________
    a. allow **b.** enliven **c.** alleviate **d.** illuminate

NAME ________________________________ DATE ____________

TEST LESSONS 22, 23, AND 24

(pages 141–158)

PART A MATCHING WORDS AND DEFINITIONS

Match the definition in Column B with the word in Column A. Write the letter of the correct definition on the answer line.

Column A	Column B	
1. vestige	a. to use amiguous and misleading language intentionally	1. g
2. extenuation	b. of little value or importance	2. c
3. patent	c. a partial justification or excuse	3. d
4. picayune	d. obvious; plain	4. b
5. paradox	e. to cite as a means of proof in an argument	5. i
6. retentive	f. an indication of something momentous about to happen; omen	6. l
7. construe	g. a visible trace of something that no longer exists	7. n
8. retinue	h. having boundaries; limited	8. m
9. adduce	i. a seemingly contradictory statement that may nonetheless be true	9. e
10. finite	j. capable of being defended; logical	10. h
11. gamut	k. the complete range or extent of something	11. k
12. portent	l. having the ability to remember or store	12. f
13. confound	m. the attendants accompanying a high-ranking person	13. o
14. tenable	n. to place a certain meaning on; interpret	14. j
15. equivocate	o. to cause someone to become confused; bewilder	15. a

PART B CHOOSING THE BEST WORD

On the answer line, write the letter of the word that best completes the sentence.

16. Peterson's _____ as university president was marked by numerous conflicts between the students and the administration. 16. d

a. extenuation b. gamut c. conundrum d. tenure

17. For several weeks following surgery, the patient maintained only a _____ hold on life. 17. a

a. tenuous b. cryptic c. rudimentary d. minuscule

NAME ______________________________ DATE ____________

TEST LESSONS 22, 23, AND 24

(pages 141–158)

PART A MATCHING WORDS AND DEFINITIONS

Match the definition in Column B with the word in Column A. Write the letter of the correct definition on the answer line.

Column A	Column B	
1. vestige	a. to use amiguous and misleading language intentionally	1. ________
2. extenuation	b. of little value or importance	2. ________
3. patent	c. a partial justification or excuse	3. ________
4. picayune	d. obvious; plain	4. ________
5. paradox	e. to cite as a means of proof in an argument	5. ________
6. retentive	f. an indication of something momentous about to happen; omen	6. ________
7. construe	g. a visible trace of something that no longer exists	7. ________
8. retinue	h. having boundaries; limited	8. ________
9. adduce	i. a seemingly contradictory statement that may nonetheless be true	9. ________
10. finite	j. capable of being defended; logical	10. ________
11. gamut	k. the complete range or extent of something	11. ________
12. portent	l. having the ability to remember or store	12. ________
13. confound	m. the attendants accompanying a high-ranking person	13. ________
14. tenable	n. to place a certain meaning on; interpret	14. ________
15. equivocate	o. to cause someone to become confused; bewilder	15. ________

PART B CHOOSING THE BEST WORD

On the answer line, write the letter of the word that best completes the sentence.

16. Peterson's _____ as university president was marked by numerous conflicts between the students and the administration. 16. ________
a. extenuation b. gamut c. conundrum d. tenure

17. For several weeks following surgery, the patient maintained only a _____ hold on life. 17. ________
a. tenuous b. cryptic c. rudimentary d. minuscule

NAME ______________________________ DATE ____________

TEST LESSONS 22, 23, AND 24

PART B CHOOSING THE BEST WORD (CONTINTUED)

18. Raoul's _____ grasp of the English language permitted him to order from a menu and to engage in simple conversations. 18. c
   a. pretentious b. finite c. rudimentary d. lofty

19. The _____ of the eruption of Vesuvius was equal to that of many kilotons of TNT. 19. c
   a. loftiness b. conundrum c. magnitude d. paradox

20. In the first scene of the play, a peasant woman utters a _____ warning before disappearing. 20. d
   a. minuscule b. retentive c. tenacious d. cryptic

21. The child held onto her toy with a _____ grip. 21. a
   a. tenacious b. commodious c. picayune d. pretentious

22. Eliminating hunger and disease from the world is a _____ goal that we still have not fulfilled. 22. a
   a. lofty b. cryptic c. minuscule d. tenuous

23. There was not a(n) _____ of humility in Miss Marvel's claim to being the strongest woman in the world. 23. b
   a. sustenance b. iota c. paradox d. conundrum

24. The portions served at the fashionable restaurant were so _____ that Harold and Aline were still hungry when they left. 24. c
   a. lofty b. picayune c. minuscule d. rudimentary

25. Denise hoped for a more _____ bedroom when her family moved into their new house. 25. d
   a. tenacious b. retentive c. finite d. commodious

26. After working with members of the club for only a day, Brandon's _____ about the group's interaction amazed everyone. 26. b
   a. sustenance b. perspicacity c. vestige d. tenuousness

27. The legendary Sphinx was supposed to have required travelers to respond to a _____ that was all but impossible to answer. 27. a
   a. conundrum b. gamut c. paradox d. extenuation

28. During the famine, many people did not receive enough _____ to prevent starvation. 28. d
   a. equivocation b. rudiment c. iota d. sustenance

29. The worth of the Hope diamond is _____. 29. c
   a. tenable b. lofty c. incalculable d. picayune

30. The _____ decor of the new shop attracted much attention. 30. b
   a. equivocal b. pretentious c. tenacious d. cryptic

NAME ______________________ DATE __________

TEST LESSONS 22, 23, AND 24

PART B CHOOSING THE BEST WORD (CONTINTUED)

18. Raoul's _____ grasp of the English language permitted him to order from a menu and to engage in simple conversations. 18. __________
 a. pretentious b. finite c. rudimentary d. lofty

19. The _____ of the eruption of Vesuvius was equal to that of many kilotons of TNT. 19. __________
 a. loftiness b. conundrum c. magnitude d. paradox

20. In the first scene of the play, a peasant woman utters a _____ warning before disappearing. 20. __________
 a. minuscule b. retentive c. tenacious d. cryptic

21. The child held onto her toy with a _____ grip. 21. __________
 a. tenacious b. commodious c. picayune d. pretentious

22. Eliminating hunger and disease from the world is a _____ goal that we still have not fulfilled. 22. __________
 a. lofty b. cryptic c. minuscule d. tenuous

23. There was not a(n) _____ of humility in Miss Marvel's claim to being the strongest woman in the world. 23. __________
 a. sustenance b. iota c. paradox d. conundrum

24. The portions served at the fashionable restaurant were so _____ that Harold and Aline were still hungry when they left. 24. __________
 a. lofty b. picayune c. minuscule d. rudimentary

25. Denise hoped for a more _____ bedroom when her family moved into their new house. 25. __________
 a. tenacious b. retentive c. finite d. commodious

26. After working with members of the club for only a day, Brandon's _____ about the group's interaction amazed everyone. 26. __________
 a. sustenance b. perspicacity c. vestige d. tenuousness

27. The legendary Sphinx was supposed to have required travelers to respond to a _____ that was all but impossible to answer. 27. __________
 a. conundrum b. gamut c. paradox d. extenuation

28. During the famine, many people did not receive enough _____ to prevent starvation. 28. __________
 a. equivocation b. rudiment c. iota d. sustenance

29. The worth of the Hope diamond is _____. 29. __________
 a. tenable b. lofty c. incalculable d. picayune

30. The _____ decor of the new shop attracted much attention. 30. __________
 a. equivocal b. pretentious c. tenacious d. cryptic

NAME ______________________ DATE __________

BONUS LESSONS 21–25

(pages 133–138, 141–158, 161–166)

Use the clues to complete the crossword puzzle.

		1 S		2 V						3 P									
		O		E						A			4 G						
		L		5 S	U	R	6 F	E	I	T			R		7 A				
		U		T			L			E			E		V				
		T		I			I			N			A		A				
		I		G			M		8 S	T	E	N	T	O	R	I	A	N	
		9 O	M	E	N		S								I				
10 F		N				11 M	Y	R	12 I	A	D				C				
I									O					13 B	E	D	L	A	M
N							14 T	I	T	A	N	I	C						
15 I	N	U	N	D	A	T	E		A										
T							N										16 H		
E							A								17 B		E		
							18 C	R	Y	P	T	I	C		A		R		
							I								S		C		
							19 O	S	T	E	N	T	A	T	I	O	U	S	
							U								C		L		
							S										E		
																	A		
																	N		

Across

5. Antonym for *scarcity*
8. Extremely loud
9. Synonym for *portent*
11. Innumerable
13. The word _____ derives from the name of an English insane asylum.
14. Huge
15. To overwhelm as if with a flood
18. Enigmatic
19. Synonym for *pretentious*

Down

1. A *conundrum* is a problem with no satisfactory _____.
2. _____ comes from a Latin word meaning "footprint."
3. Obvious or plain
4. *Magnitude* comes from a Latin word meaning "_____."
6. Synonym for *tenuous*
7. Antonym for *generosity*
10. Having boundaries
12. An extremely small amount
14. Holding firmly
16. Requiring unusual power or size
17. *Rudimentary* skills are _____.

NAME ______________________ DATE ____________

BONUS LESSONS 21–25

(pages 133–138, 141–158, 161–166)

Use the clues to complete the crossword puzzle.

Across

5. Antonym for *scarcity*
8. Extremely loud
9. Synonym for *portent*
11. Innumerable
13. The word _____ derives from the name of an English insane asylum.
14. Huge
15. To overwhelm as if with a flood
18. Enigmatic
19. Synonym for *pretentious*

Down

1. A *conundrum* is a problem with no satisfactory _____.
2. _____ comes from a Latin word meaning "footprint."
3. Obvious or plain
4. *Magnitude* comes from a Latin word meaning "_____."
6. Synonym for *tenuous*
7. Antonym for *generosity*
10. Having boundaries
12. An extremely small amount
14. Holding firmly
16. Requiring unusual power or size
17. *Rudimentary* skills are _____.

NAME ______________________ DATE ____________

TEST LESSONS 25, 26, AND 27

(pages 161–178)

PART A COMPLETING THE DEFINITION

On the answer line, write the letter of the word or phrase that correctly completes each sentence.

1. A *draconian* ruler is ____. 1. a
   a. cruel b. beloved c. aged d. inflexible
2. A person may be accused of *chauvinism* if he or she is ____. 2. d
   a. temperamental c. dishonest
   b. reserved d. fanatically patriotic
3. Someone who delivers a *tirade* gives a(n) ____. 3. a
   a. angry speech c. court order
   b. list of demands d. commendation
4. A *halcyon* scene is ____. 4. d
   a. somber b. ancient c. noisy d. tranquil
5. A *disconsolate* person is ____. 5. b
   a. radiant c. friendly
   b. beyond comfort d. often stubborn
6. One who acts like a *martinet* is ____. 6. b
   a. inaccessible c. sympathetic
   b. a rigid disciplinarian d. a talented entertainer
7. An *irrevocable* decree is ____. 7. c
   a. controversial b. unproductive c. irreversible d. unjust
8. A *millennium* refers to a ____. 8. b
   a. poor attitude c. long distance
   b. thousand-year period d. discovery
9. A *titanic* building is ____. 9. b
   a. well designed b. huge c. unstable d. historical
10. An *eon* of time is ____. 10. d
    a. immeasurably small c. one thousand years
    b. equal to a decade d. indefinitely long
11. A person whose tastes are *mercurial* tends to be ____. 11. d
    a. unbending b. liberal c. superficial d. changeable
12. A *maudlin* play is ____. 12. a
    a. sentimental b. uninteresting c. plotless d. old-fashioned
13. A fund that has *perpetuity* ____. 13. a
    a. lasts forever c. is taxable
    b. is strictly regulated d. has many claimants
14. A *distraught* person feels ____. 14. d
    a. tired b. rebellious c. gallant d. anxious
15. *Transience* refers to ____. 15. b
    a. criticism b. impermanence c. accord d. imbalance

NAME ______________________ DATE __________

TEST LESSONS 25, 26, AND 27

(pages 161–178)

PART A COMPLETING THE DEFINITION

On the answer line, write the letter of the word or phrase that correctly completes each sentence.

1. A *draconian* ruler is ____. 1. ________
   a. cruel b. beloved c. aged d. inflexible

2. A person may be accused of *chauvinism* if he or she is ____. 2. ________
   a. temperamental c. dishonest
   b. reserved d. fanatically patriotic

3. Someone who delivers a *tirade* gives a(n) ____. 3. ________
   a. angry speech c. court order
   b. list of demands d. commendation

4. A *halcyon* scene is ____. 4. ________
   a. somber b. ancient c. noisy d. tranquil

5. A *disconsolate* person is ____. 5. ________
   a. radiant c. friendly
   b. beyond comfort d. often stubborn

6. One who acts like a *martinet* is ____. 6. ________
   a. inaccessible c. sympathetic
   b. a rigid disciplinarian d. a talented entertainer

7. An *irrevocable* decree is ____. 7. ________
   a. controversial b. unproductive c. irreversible d. unjust

8. A *millennium* refers to a ____. 8. ________
   a. poor attitude c. long distance
   b. thousand-year period d. discovery

9. A *titanic* building is ____. 9. ________
   a. well designed b. huge c. unstable d. historical

10. An *eon* of time is ____. 10. ________
    a. immeasurably small c. one thousand years
    b. equal to a decade d. indefinitely long

11. A person whose tastes are *mercurial* tends to be ____. 11. ________
    a. unbending b. liberal c. superficial d. changeable

12. A *maudlin* play is ____. 12. ________
    a. sentimental b. uninteresting c. plotless d. old-fashioned

13. A fund that has *perpetuity* ____. 13. ________
    a. lasts forever c. is taxable
    b. is strictly regulated d. has many claimants

14. A *distraught* person feels ____. 14. ________
    a. tired b. rebellious c. gallant d. anxious

15. *Transience* refers to ____. 15. ________
    a. criticism b. impermanence c. accord d. imbalance

NAME ______________________________ DATE ____________

TEST LESSONS 25, 26, AND 27

PART B CHOOSING THE BEST WORD

On the answer line, write the letter of the word that best expresses the meaning of the italicized word or phrase.

16. A *situation of noisy confusion* resulted from the announcement that World War II had ended. 16. d
    a. Transience b. Hiatus c. Trauma d. Bedlam

17. Two of the *still in existence* Gutenberg Bibles are preserved in the Yale University library. 17. a
    a. extant b. concomitant c. stentorian d. pristine

18. To prevent yourself from becoming *tearful* while chopping onions, hold a piece of bread in your mouth. 18. b
    a. pristine b. lachrymose c. disconsolate d. vexed

19. Geraldine has mastered cutting freehand *outlines of human profiles.* 19. d
    a. martinets b. eons c. revels d. silhouettes

20. The editorial *expressed strong disapproval of* the council's decision. 20. a
    a. deplored b. inured c. reveled in d. mesmerized

21. Overseeing the fund-raising activities was an *unusually difficult* task. 21. c
    a. lachrymose b. maudlin c. herculean d. draconian

22. After an *interruption in time* of five years, the diva returned triumphantly to the operatic stage. 22. d
    a. trauma b. millennium c. silhouette d. hiatus

23. Snake charmers use rhythmic sound to *hypnotize* their reptiles. 23. c
    a. traumatize b. vex c. mesmerize d. inure

24. The Tates *took great delight in* the antics of their grandchildren. 24. a
    a. reveled in c. deplored
    b. were vexed by d. were inured to

25. Ann hopes to earn *simultaneous* degrees in linguistics and math. 25. d
    a. irrevocable b. transient c. stentorian d. concomitant

26. Emergency room doctors must be experts in treating *wounds caused by sudden physical injury.* 26. b
    a. revelry b. trauma c. chauvinism d. bedlam

27. The *extremely loud* voices kept us awake most of the night. 27. c
    a. herculean b. traumatic c. stentorian d. mercurial

28. Mr. Post becomes *irritated* when anything interferes with his schedule. 28. b
    a. distraught b. vexed c. disconsolate d. inured

29. The ecosystem of Antarctica has been characterized as the last *uncorrupted* environment on Earth. 29. d
    a. extant b. titanic c. halcyon d. pristine

30. Years of deprivation *hardened* the peasants to their lack of amenities. 30. a
    a. inured b. mesmerized c. vexed d. traumatized

NAME ______________________ DATE __________

TEST LESSONS 25, 26, AND 27

PART B CHOOSING THE BEST WORD

On the answer line, write the letter of the word that best expresses the meaning of the italicized word or phrase.

16. A *situation of noisy confusion* resulted from the announcement that World War II had ended. 16. __________
 a. Transience b. Hiatus c. Trauma d. Bedlam

17. Two of the *still in existence* Gutenberg Bibles are preserved in the Yale University library. 17. __________
 a. extant b. concomitant c. stentorian d. pristine

18. To prevent yourself from becoming *tearful* while chopping onions, hold a piece of bread in your mouth. 18. __________
 a. pristine b. lachrymose c. disconsolate d. vexed

19. Geraldine has mastered cutting freehand *outlines of human profiles.* 19. __________
 a. martinets b. eons c. revels d. silhouettes

20. The editorial *expressed strong disapproval of* the council's decision. 20. __________
 a. deplored b. inured c. reveled in d. mesmerized

21. Overseeing the fund-raising activities was an *unusually difficult* task. 21. __________
 a. lachrymose b. maudlin c. herculean d. draconian

22. After an *interruption in time* of five years, the diva returned triumphantly to the operatic stage. 22. __________
 a. trauma b. millennium c. silhouette d. hiatus

23. Snake charmers use rhythmic sound to *hypnotize* their reptiles. 23. __________
 a. traumatize b. vex c. mesmerize d. inure

24. The Tates *took great delight in* the antics of their grandchildren. 24. __________
 a. reveled in c. deplored
 b. were vexed by d. were inured to

25. Ann hopes to earn *simultaneous* degrees in linguistics and math. 25. __________
 a. irrevocable b. transient c. stentorian d. concomitant

26. Emergency room doctors must be experts in treating *wounds caused by sudden physical injury.* 26. __________
 a. revelry b. trauma c. chauvinism d. bedlam

27. The *extremely loud* voices kept us awake most of the night. 27. __________
 a. herculean b. traumatic c. stentorian d. mercurial

28. Mr. Post becomes *irritated* when anything interferes with his schedule. 28. __________
 a. distraught b. vexed c. disconsolate d. inured

29. The ecosystem of Antarctica has been characterized as the last *uncorrupted* environment on Earth. 29. __________
 a. extant b. titanic c. halcyon d. pristine

30. Years of deprivation *hardened* the peasants to their lack of amenities. 30. __________
 a. inured b. mesmerized c. vexed d. traumatized

NAME ______________________ DATE __________

BONUS LESSONS 26–30

(pages 167–178, 181–198)

Choose a vocabulary word from the box to complete each of the following sentences. You may need to change the form of some of the words to fit correctly in the sentence. Use each word only once, and write your answer on the answer line to the right.

abstract	élan	halcyon	nouveau riche	revel
aesthetic	entrée	hiatus	par excellence	surrealistic
buffoon	eon	irony	perpetuity	transience
deplore	farce	jocular	potpourri	trauma
eclectic	grotesque	levity	pristine	vex

1. During the _____ between workshops, Philip interviewed a visiting professor. 1. **hiatus**
2. Having lived in a small apartment, the family _____ in the spaciousness of their new house. 2. **reveled**
3. Donald, once a skater _____, is now an extraordinary skating choreographer. 3. **par excellence**
4. The gothic novel was peopled with numerous _____ characters. 4. **grotesque**
5. Alex's _____ mood probably means that he passed his driving test. 5. **jocular**
6. Many parents mourn the _____ of their offsprings' childhoods. 6. **transience**
7. Mother was _____ by the disappearance of the fruit salad that she had prepared just hours before. 7. **vexed**
8. Although April had never tried crawfish, she thoroughly enjoyed the well-prepared _____. 8. **entrée**
9. The different styles of furniture in Jan's apartment reflect her _____ tastes. 9. **eclectic**
10. "Jason acts like a(n) _____ simply to get our attention," said Grace. 10. **buffoon**
11. The author left his correspondence and unpublished work to the university library in _____. 11. **perpetuity**
12. Shakespeare's *Taming of the Shrew* is considered a(n) _____ because of its incongruities, coarse wit, and horseplay. 12. **farce**
13. Critics _____ the modern rendition of the classical tragedy that opened last night. 13. **deplored**
14. Our foreign language club banquet offered a(n) _____ of foods from different countries. 14. **potpourri**
15. The stories of Franz Kafka contain the subconscious imagery of _____ art. 15. **surrealistic**

NAME ______________________ DATE __________

BONUS LESSONS 26–30

(pages 167–178, 181–198)

Choose a vocabulary word from the box to complete each of the following sentences. You may need to change the form of some of the words to fit correctly in the sentence. Use each word only once, and write your answer on the answer line to the right.

abstract	élan	halcyon	nouveau riche	revel
aesthetic	entrée	hiatus	par excellence	surrealistic
buffoon	eon	irony	perpetuity	transience
deplore	farce	jocular	potpourri	trauma
eclectic	grotesque	levity	pristine	vex

1. During the _____ between workshops, Philip interviewed a visiting professor. 1. __________
2. Having lived in a small apartment, the family _____ in the spaciousness of their new house. 2. __________
3. Donald, once a skater _____, is now an extraordinary skating choreographer. 3. __________
4. The gothic novel was peopled with numerous _____ characters. 4. __________
5. Alex's _____ mood probably means that he passed his driving test. 5. __________
6. Many parents mourn the _____ of their offsprings' childhoods. 6. __________
7. Mother was _____ by the disappearance of the fruit salad that she had prepared just hours before. 7. __________
8. Although April had never tried crawfish, she thoroughly enjoyed the well-prepared _____. 8. __________
9. The different styles of furniture in Jan's apartment reflect her _____ tastes. 9. __________
10. "Jason acts like a(n) _____ simply to get our attention," said Grace. 10. __________
11. The author left his correspondence and unpublished work to the university library in _____. 11. __________
12. Shakespeare's *Taming of the Shrew* is considered a(n) _____ because of its incongruities, coarse wit, and horseplay. 12. __________
13. Critics _____ the modern rendition of the classical tragedy that opened last night. 13. __________
14. Our foreign language club banquet offered a(n) _____ of foods from different countries. 14. __________
15. The stories of Franz Kafka contain the subconscious imagery of _____ art. 15. __________

NAME ______________________________ DATE ____________

TEST LESSONS 28, 29, AND 30

(pages 181–198)

PART A COMPLETING THE DEFINITION

On the answer line, write the letter of the word or phrase that correctly completes each sentence.

1. In a *coup d'état* a government is ____. 1. c
   a. unified **b.** accommodated **c.** overthrown **d.** manipulated

2. Artists use *perspective* to create ____. 2. b
   a. a pyramid effect **c.** rich colors
   b. a three-dimensional quality **d.** realism

3. *Satirical* comments are ____. 3. a
   a. mockingly critical **c.** trite
   b. restrained **d.** exaggerated

4. One who is *nouveau riche* tends to ____. 4. b
   a. lose possessions **c.** share ideas
   b. flaunt new wealth **d.** avoid debt

5. Writers use *irony* to ____. 5. a
   a. reverse expectations **c.** foreshadow events
   b. extend symbolism **d.** create realism

6. A *tête-à-tête* is a ____. 6. d
   a. festive occasion **c.** small party
   b. challenging problem **d.** private conversation

7. A *farce* is characterized by its ____. 7. d
   a. serious plot **c.** sad events
   b. lack of characters **d.** improbabilities

8. *Eclectic* tastes are ____. 8. a
   a. diverse **b.** flamboyant **c.** conservative **d.** practical

9. A *buffoon* is also known as a(n) ____. 9. a
   a. clown **b.** athlete **c.** introvert **d.** authority figure

10. *Surrealistic* art has ____. 10. a
    a. fantastic imagery **c.** classical influences
    b. geometrical forms **d.** mirror images

11. To *parody* is to ____. 11. b
    a. request endearingly **c.** praise repeatedly
    b. imitate comically **d.** attack knowingly

12. *Aesthetic* sensibilities refer to ____. 12. c
    a. love of nature **c.** love of beauty
    b. deep commitment **d.** scientific theories

13. *Raillery* is ____. 13. b
    a. enthusiasm **b.** banter **c.** anxiety **d.** approval

NAME ______________________ DATE ____________

TEST LESSONS 28, 29, AND 30

(pages 181–198)

PART A COMPLETING THE DEFINITION

On the answer line, write the letter of the word or phrase that correctly completes each sentence.

1. In a *coup d'état* a government is ____. 1. ________
   a. unified **b.** accommodated **c.** overthrown **d.** manipulated

2. Artists use *perspective* to create ____. 2. ________
   a. a pyramid effect **c.** rich colors
   b. a three-dimensional quality **d.** realism

3. *Satirical* comments are ____. 3. ________
   a. mockingly critical **c.** trite
   b. restrained **d.** exaggerated

4. One who is *nouveau riche* tends to ____. 4. ________
   a. lose possessions **c.** share ideas
   b. flaunt new wealth **d.** avoid debt

5. Writers use *irony* to ____. 5. ________
   a. reverse expectations **c.** foreshadow events
   b. extend symbolism **d.** create realism

6. A *tête-à-tête* is a ____. 6. ________
   a. festive occasion **c.** small party
   b. challenging problem **d.** private conversation

7. A *farce* is characterized by its ____. 7. ________
   a. serious plot **c.** sad events
   b. lack of characters **d.** improbabilities

8. *Eclectic* tastes are ____. 8. ________
   a. diverse **b.** flamboyant **c.** conservative **d.** practical

9. A *buffoon* is also known as a(n) ____. 9. ________
   a. clown **b.** athlete **c.** introvert **d.** authority figure

10. *Surrealistic* art has ____. 10. ________
    a. fantastic imagery **c.** classical influences
    b. geometrical forms **d.** mirror images

11. To *parody* is to ____. 11. ________
    a. request endearingly **c.** praise repeatedly
    b. imitate comically **d.** attack knowingly

12. *Aesthetic* sensibilities refer to ____. 12. ________
    a. love of nature **c.** love of beauty
    b. deep commitment **d.** scientific theories

13. *Raillery* is ____. 13. ________
    a. enthusiasm **b.** banter **c.** anxiety **d.** approval

NAME ______________________ DATE __________

TEST LESSONS 28, 29, AND 30

14. An *entrée* to a good job gives one _____ it. 14. d
   a. skills for
   b. information about
   c. confidence for
   d. admittance to

15. A *potpourri* of tastes would be a(n) _____ of flavors. 15. a
   a. medley b. dissemination c. analogy d. contrast

PART B IDENTIFYING ANTONYMS

On the answer line, write the letter of the word or phrase that has the meaning that is opposite to that of the capitalized word.

16. SAVOIR-FAIRE: 16. b
   a. perservance b. tactlessness c. silliness d. ignorance
17. GROTESQUE: 17. c
   a. formal b. pleasurable c. harmonious d. elegant
18. LEVITY: 18. d
   a. depravity b. futility c. industry d. solemnity
19. REGALE: 19. c
   a. demote b. unfetter c. bore d. calm
20. HACKNEYED: 20. c
   a. liberated b. mundane c. original d. superior
21. ABSTRACT: 21. b
   a. obstructive b. concrete c. casual d. restrictive
22. ESPRIT DE CORPS: 22. a
   a. individuality b. peace c. cooperation d. interior
23. VERISIMILITUDE: 23. d
   a. innuendo b. veracity c. opposite d. implausibility
24. ÉLAN: 24. c
   a. freedom b. brevity c. lethargy d. pretense
25. PAR EXCELLENCE: 25. d
   a. unintentional b. brilliant c. trivial d. inferior
26. LAISSEZ FAIRE: 26. a
   a. interference b. impropriety c. energy d. distraction
27. AVANT-GARDE: 27. b
   a. unprepared b. old-fashioned c. unassertive d. deceptive
28. LAMPOON: 28. a
   a. flatter b. subvert c. increase d. submit
29. JOCULAR: 29. c
   a. circular b. repressed c. grave d. unhealthy
30. REPRESENTATIONAL: 30. a
   a. imaginary b. dutiful c. probable d. prophetic

NAME ______________________ DATE __________

TEST LESSONS 28, 29, AND 30

14. An *entrée* to a good job gives one _____ it. 14. __________
   a. skills for
   b. information about
   c. confidence for
   d. admittance to

15. A *potpourri* of tastes would be a(n) _____ of flavors. 15. __________
   a. medley b. dissemination c. analogy d. contrast

PART B IDENTIFYING ANTONYMS

On the answer line, write the letter of the word or phrase that has the meaning that is opposite to that of the capitalized word.

16. SAVOIR-FAIRE: 16. __________
   a. perservance b. tactlessness c. silliness d. ignorance

17. GROTESQUE: 17. __________
   a. formal b. pleasurable c. harmonious d. elegant

18. LEVITY: 18. __________
   a. depravity b. futility c. industry d. solemnity

19. REGALE: 19. __________
   a. demote b. unfetter c. bore d. calm

20. HACKNEYED: 20. __________
   a. liberated b. mundane c. original d. superior

21. ABSTRACT: 21. __________
   a. obstructive b. concrete c. casual d. restrictive

22. ESPRIT DE CORPS: 22. __________
   a. individuality b. peace c. cooperation d. interior

23. VERISIMILITUDE: 23. __________
   a. innuendo b. veracity c. opposite d. implausibility

24. ÉLAN: 24. __________
   a. freedom b. brevity c. lethargy d. pretense

25. PAR EXCELLENCE: 25. __________
   a. unintentional b. brilliant c. trivial d. inferior

26. LAISSEZ FAIRE: 26. __________
   a. interference b. impropriety c. energy d. distraction

27. AVANT-GARDE: 27. __________
   a. unprepared b. old-fashioned c. unassertive d. deceptive

28. LAMPOON: 28. __________
   a. flatter b. subvert c. increase d. submit

29. JOCULAR: 29. __________
   a. circular b. repressed c. grave d. unhealthy

30. REPRESENTATIONAL: 30. __________
   a. imaginary b. dutiful c. probable d. prophetic